Deep Trade Agreements

Deep Trade Agreements
Anchoring Global Value Chains in Latin America and the Caribbean

Nadia Rocha
Michele Ruta

Editors

WORLD BANK GROUP

Contents

Figures

Maps

Tables

Foreword

The Latin America and Caribbean region has untapped potential for its trade and global value chains (GVCs) to grow in the wake of the COVID-19 pandemic. Trade is roughly one-third of the region's gross domestic product (GDP), compared with half for Europe and Central Asia and East Asia and Pacific, and this share has not grown since 2000. Latin America and the Caribbean's GVC performance also lags other regions across all sectors in both imported components for export production (backward participation) and components produced for export (forward participation). Geography, institutions, market size, and factor endowments explain much of the region's poor performance, but policy choices matter as well.

This report uses new data and evidence to illustrate how Latin American and Caribbean countries can deepen trade agreements to increase their participation in trade and GVCs. Starting in the 1990s, a growing number of countries worldwide signed deep trade agreements—preferential trade agreements that went beyond simple market access. Those agreements are now much deeper, covering a wide-ranging set of border and behind-the-border policy areas regulating investment, services trade, customs procedures, regulatory measures, intellectual property rights protection, and so on. Latin America and the Caribbean was no exception to this trend, with 74 new agreements signed in the past 20 years. But many agreements in the region lack depth or are poorly implemented.

If well designed, deep trade agreements can drive policy reforms and help the region overcome some of its disadvantageous fundamentals in several ways. First, trade facilitation can ease problems stemming from the countries' geographical remoteness. It is particularly important in Latin America and the Caribbean, where the time and cost of trading across borders are high. Second, regulatory cooperation can help the region's countries access larger markets. Nontariff measures have important public policy goals, but divergent regulations can segment the market and raise the fixed cost of entry for foreign firms. Third, opening the service economy can compensate for factor endowment scarcity. Commitments in preferential trade agreements should increasingly liberalize service sector policies and consider a broader range of service supply modes, particularly foreign investment and the movement of people. Fourth, regulating competition and state support to state-owned enterprises (SOEs) can improve the quality of economic institutions. SOEs play a large role in many Latin American and Caribbean countries, reducing market competition and having potentially large fiscal implications.

Deep trade agreements can also boost GVC integration in the region's countries as the global economy recovers from the COVID-19 pandemic. Trade policy tensions may be on the rise, as scarce demand tempts governments to use trade restrictions to redirect demand toward domestic production. And rising aversion to risks to health, security, and privacy might open the door to greater regulatory protectionism. Governments with limited fiscal space might weaken rules on competition or on SOEs as indirect support for the economy. In these uncertain times, policy commitments in deep trade agreements can create a more stable institutional environment for promoting the ability of Latin American and Caribbean countries to integrate into GVCs.

Carlos Felipe Jaramillo
Vice President, Latin American and Caribbean Region
The World Bank

Acknowledgments

This study has been produced by a team of experts coordinated by Nadia Rocha (senior economist, Trade and Regional Integration Unit) and Michele Ruta (lead economist, Trade and Regional Integration Unit). Contributors to the individual chapters include Ernani Checcucci, Mayra Alfaro de Morán, Gabriel Duque, Roberto Echandi, Alvaro Espitia, Ana Fernandes, Anabel González, Bernard Hoekman, Hiau Looi Kee, Woori Lee, Kevin Lefebvre, Gaston Nievas, Rodrigo Polanco, Nadia Rocha, Michele Ruta, Ben Shepherd, and Deborah Winkler.

The study is the outcome of a collaboration between the World Bank Group's Trade and Regional Integration Unit (ETIRI, part of the Equitable Growth, Finance and Institutions Practice Group) and the Latin America and the Caribbean Chief Economist Office (LCRCE). The team is grateful for the guidance and support provided by William Maloney (chief economist for Latin America and the Caribbean), Martin Rama (former chief economist for Latin America and the Caribbean), Elena Ianchovichina (lead economist, LCRCE), and Antonio Nucifora (practice manager, ETIRI).

The team would also like to thank the following colleagues inside and outside the World Bank Group who graciously gave their time to provide inputs at various stages of this project or acted as reviewers: Paulo Correa, Jaime de Melo, Donato De Rosa, Michael Ferrantino, Mary Hallward-Driemeier, Rafael Muñoz Moreno, and Ekaterina Vostroknutova.

The publication of the report was led by Patricia Katayama. Mary Fisk provided support during the process. The team is grateful to Bruce Ross-Larson and Communications Development Inc. (CDI), as well as to Mary Anderson, for their editorial services. The graphic concept, design, and layout of the cover were provided by Guillermo Varela and Bill Pragluski.

This work is a product of the regional studies program sponsored by the Latin America and the Caribbean Chief Economist's Office.

About the Editors and Contributors

Editors

Nadia Rocha is a senior economist in the World Bank's Macroeconomics, Trade and Investment Global Practice. Before joining the Bank in 2016, she worked in the Economic Research and Statistics division of the World Trade Organization (WTO). She was seconded to serve as a senior advisor on trade to the Colombian Ministry of Trade during 2015. Her work focuses on trade policy, regional integration, global value chains, and trade and gender. In recent years, Nadia has comanaged the World Bank's project on Deep Trade Agreements, which involved the coordination of experts from international organizations and academia to assess the content of deep integration agreements and the production of data and policy-relevant research on the evolution and impact of deep trade agreements. She has also been leading time-sensitive research on the links between COVID-19, trade, and global value chains and between COVID-19 and food prices, coordinating the data collection and monitoring of trade flows and policies on COVID-19 medical supplies and food. Nadia is a lead author of the World Bank-WTO report, *Women and Trade: The Role of Trade in Promoting Gender Equality*, and is one of the editors of two other recent volumes: *Handbook of Deep Trade Agreements* and *The Economics of Deep Trade Agreements*. She holds a doctorate in international economics from the Graduate Institute of Geneva, a master's degree in economics from Pompeu Fabra University of Barcelona, and a bachelor's degree in economics from Bocconi University in Milan.

Michele Ruta is lead economist in the World Bank's Macroeconomics, Trade and Investment Global Practice, where he oversees the work program on regional integration. He had previous appointments at the International Monetary Fund, the WTO, and the European University Institute. His research focuses on international and regional integration and has been extensively published in academic journals, including the *Journal of International Economics*, *Journal of Development Economics*, *Journal of the European Economic Association*, and *Journal of Public Economics*. His books and edited volumes include *Belt and Road Economics: Opportunities and Risks of*

Transport Corridors, Handbook of Deep Trade Agreements, and *The Economics of Deep Trade Agreements.* He holds a doctorate in economics from Columbia University and an undergraduate degree from the University of Rome La Sapienza.

CONTRIBUTORS

Ernani Checcucci, World Bank

Mayra Alfaro de Morán, World Bank

Gabriel Duque, Commercial Office of the Government of Colombia before the European Union, Brussels

Roberto Echandi, World Bank

Alvaro Espitia, World Bank

Ana Margarida Fernandes, World Bank

Anabel González, World Trade Organization

Bernard Hoekman, European University Institute, Florence

Hiau Looi Kee, World Bank

Woori Lee, World Bank

Kevin Levebvre, Center for Prospective Studies and International Information (CEPII), Paris

Gaston Nievas, World Bank

Rodrigo Polanco, World Trade Institute, Bern

Ben Shepherd, Developing Trade Consultants, New York

Deborah Winkler, World Bank

Abbreviations

AECID	Spanish Agency for International Development Cooperation
AEO	authorized economic operator (WTO TFA)
ALADI	Latin American Integration Association
AO	authorized operator
ASCM	Agreement on Subsidies and Countervailing Measures (WTO)
ASEAN	Association of Southeast Asian Nations
AVE	ad valorem tariff equivalent
AVPSA	Panamanian Food Safety Authority
BACI	Database for International Trade Analysis
BEC	Broad Economic Categories
CACM	Central American Common Market
CAFTA-DR	Dominican Republic-Central American Free Trade Agreement
CARICOM	Caribbean Community and Common Market
CEPII	Center for Prospective Studies and International Information
CETA	Comprehensive Economic and Trade Agreement (EU–Canada)
CPTPP	Comprehensive and Progressive Agreement for Trans-Pacific Partnership
CV	countervailing
DTA	deep trade agreement
EC-CARIFORUM	European Community-Caribbean Forum
EEA	European Economic Area
EFTA	European Free Trade Agreement
EU	European Union
FYDUCA	Central American Invoice and Single Declaration (Guatemala–Honduras)
GATS	General Agreement on Trade in Services
GBER	General Block Exemption Regulation
GDP	gross domestic product
GFSEC	Global Forum on Steel Excess Capacity

GTA	Global Trade Alert
GVC	global value chain
HHI	Herfindahl Hirschman Index
HS	Harmonized System
ICN	International Competition Network
IPR	intellectual property rights
LAIA	Latin American Integration Association
MERCOSUR	Southern Common Market
MFN	most-favored-nation
MIC	middle-income country
NGO	nongovernmental organization
NTM	nontariff measure
OECD	Organisation for Economic Co-operation and Development
PA	Pacific Alliance
PPML	Poisson pseudo maximum likelihood
PTA	preferential trade agreement
SIECA	Secretariat for Central American Economic Integration
SOE	state-owned enterprise
SPS	sanitary and phytosanitary
STRI	Services Trade Restrictiveness Index (OECD)
TAPED	Trade Agreements Provisions on Electronic-commerce and Data
TBT	technical barrier(s) to trade
TF	trade facilitation
TFA	Trade Facilitation Agreement (WTO)
TiSMoS	Trade in Services data by Mode of Supply
TiVA	Trade in Value Added
USMCA	United States–Mexico–Canada Agreement
VAT	value added tax
WTO	World Trade Organization

Overview

INTRODUCTION

International economic integration offers unexploited opportunities to Latin America and the Caribbean. This report studies how the region's countries can leverage trade agreements to promote their economies' participation in global value chains (GVCs). The gaps between potential and actual GVC integration follow from the region's economic fundamentals, such as geography, market size, institutions, and factor endowments. But policy choices matter as well. The report, based on new data and evidence, shows that trade agreements can drive policy reforms and help the region overcome some of its disadvantageous fundamentals.

The report makes specific policy recommendations to guide Latin American and Caribbean countries in leveraging trade agreements to pursue greater international integration and economic growth. Four main findings emerge from the analysis:

- Latin America and the Caribbean's poor international integration and limited participation in GVCs have contributed to its low economic growth over the past decade.
- Although the region's countries increasingly participate in preferential trade agreements (PTAs), there are gaps in the content of these agreements.[1]
- Deep trade agreements present an avenue to promote trade and boost GVC integration and upgrading, thus contributing to improved economic performance.
- Four areas of deep integration—trade facilitation, regulatory cooperation, services, and state support—are priorities to improve these countries' GVC participation and upgrading.

LATIN AMERICA AND THE CARIBBEAN'S POOR INTERNATIONAL INTEGRATION AND LIMITED PARTICIPATION IN GVCs HAVE CONTRIBUTED TO ITS LOW ECONOMIC GROWTH OVER THE PAST DECADE

After experiencing rapid economic growth in the first decade of the twenty-first century because of high commodity prices, Latin America and the Caribbean entered a phase of weak performance. Growth in exports, imports, and gross domestic product (GDP) per capita in 2000–18 was lower in Latin American and Caribbean countries than in comparator countries in the Europe and Central Asia and the East Asia and the Pacific regions (figure O.1). Globally, greater integration in international trade and GVCs were linked to increased GDP per capita and productivity (Constantinescu, Mattoo, and Ruta 2019; Dollar and Kraay 2004; Harrison and Rodríguez-Clare 2009). In Latin American and Caribbean countries, limited trade openness, low trade growth, and a scarcity of exporting firms contributed to their overall sluggish performance.

Latin American and Caribbean countries display limited trade openness and weak integration into GVCs on average. Their trade is roughly one-third of GDP on average, compared with half for Europe and Central Asia and East Asia and the Pacific, and that share has not grown since 2000. The region's GVC performance lags other regions across all sectors in both imported components to be embedded in production for export (backward participation) and in components produced for export (forward participation).

Although some of the region's countries (such as Costa Rica and Mexico) have broken that pattern and are more integrated into GVCs, most have low participation. The latest data show backward GVC participation at 16 percent of total exports on average across Latin American and Caribbean countries in 2015, compared with 20 percent in East Asia and the Pacific and 30 percent in Europe and Central Asia.[2] The region's forward participation is also low, at 19 percent of total exports on average, compared with 28 percent for Europe and Central Asia and 29 percent for East Asia and the Pacific. Although Latin America and the Caribbean's aggregate GVC participation is low, the region's firms that participate in GVCs perform better than firms that do not, revealing unexploited potential.[3]

The *World Development Report 2020* proposed a GVC taxonomy with four categories of participation: commodities, limited manufacturing, advanced manufacturing and services, and innovative activities (World Bank 2020). Latin American and Caribbean countries are mostly in commodity and limited manufacturing GVCs, except Mexico, which is in advanced manufacturing and services GVCs. (See chapter 1 for more about the GVC taxonomy, by country.) Countries in the region differ, but only three managed to upgrade to the limited manufacturing group over 1990–2015: Argentina, Costa Rica, and El Salvador.

Figure O.1   Trade and GDP growth, Latin America and the Caribbean and comparator regions, 2000–18

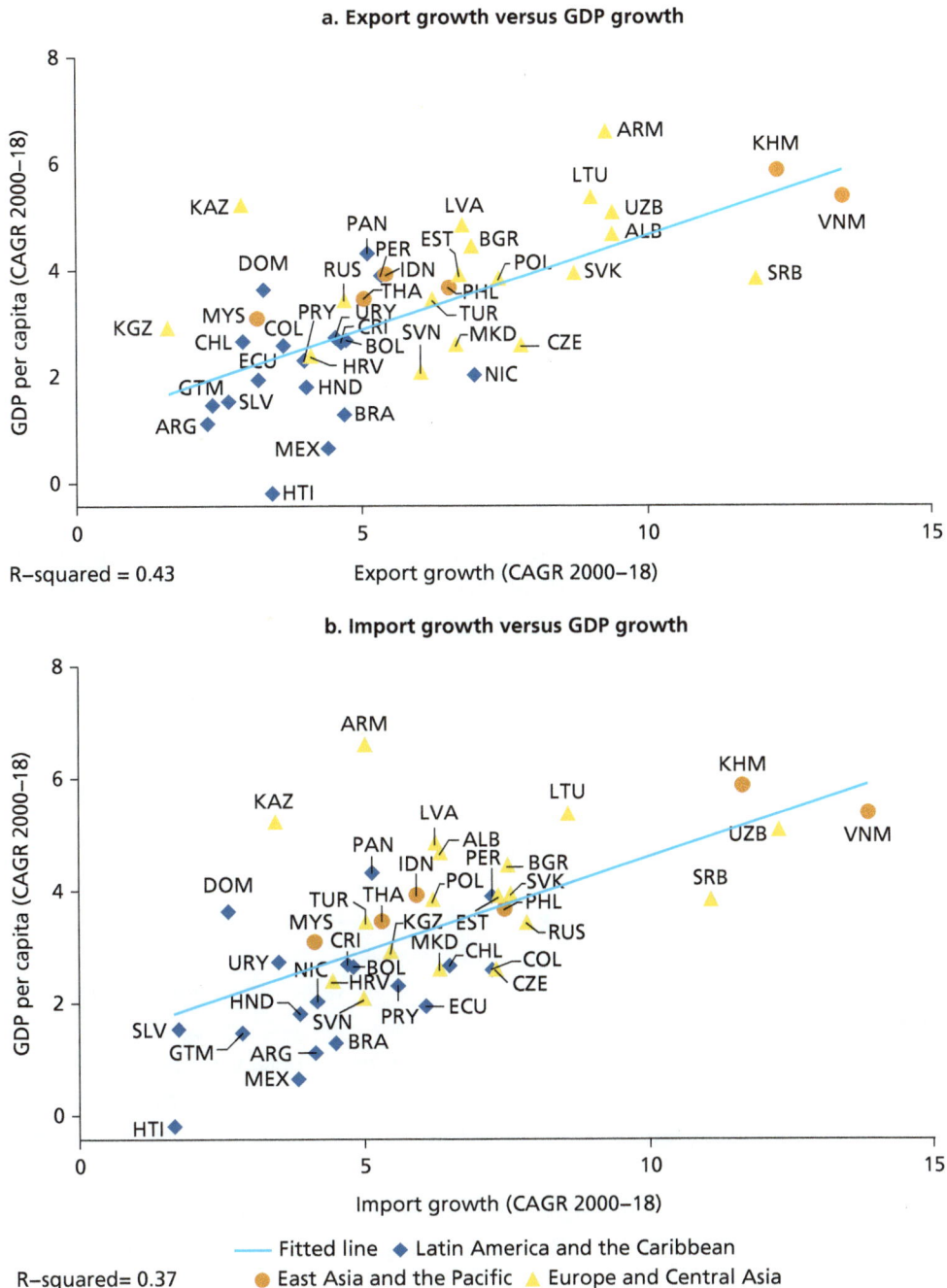

a. Export growth versus GDP growth

R–squared = 0.43

b. Import growth versus GDP growth

R–squared= 0.37

Legend: Fitted line · Latin America and the Caribbean · East Asia and the Pacific · Europe and Central Asia

Source: World Bank, based on World Development Indicators database.

Note: CAGR is compound annual growth rate. Export and import growth is based on 2010 constant trade values. The figure includes only countries that are part of the global value chain taxonomy (proposed in World Bank [2020] and further discussed in chapter 1) and were part of one of the World Bank operational lending categories in 2000. Countries are labeled by ISO alpha-3 code.

ALTHOUGH LATIN AMERICAN AND CARIBBEAN COUNTRIES INCREASINGLY PARTICIPATE IN PTAs, THE CONTENT AND DEPTH OF THESE AGREEMENTS ARE UNEVEN

Starting in the 1990s, a growing number of countries worldwide signed deep trade agreements (DTAs)—PTAs that went beyond simple market access (Mattoo, Rocha, and Ruta 2020). Modern-day trade agreements are increasingly deep, covering a wide-ranging set of border and behind-the-border policy areas regulating investment, services trade, customs procedures, regulatory measures, intellectual property rights protection, and so on. DTAs are PTAs that contain provisions to deepen economic integration between trading partners. If well designed, they allow countries to reduce cross-border spillover effects of national policies and provide an institutional mechanism to bolster reforms reducing trade costs and improving efficiency.

PTA participation has accelerated in Latin America and the Caribbean, but countries differ in the depth of the trade agreements they sign, as detailed in chapter 2. The region's countries are part of 82 PTAs—a third of all agreements notified to the World Trade Organization and in force by 2017. Many of those agreements are with partner countries outside the region. Chile, with 27 PTAs, is among the countries with the highest number in the region. Peru has 17; Mexico, 15; Colombia, 13; Argentina and Brazil, 4 each; and Ecuador and Bolivia, 3 each (map O.1). Latin America and the Caribbean presents a dichotomy in the depth of PTAs: members of the Pacific Alliance—Chile, Colombia, Mexico, and Peru—and several Caribbean countries tend to have deeper agreements, whereas Southern Common Market (MERCOSUR) countries have shallower ones.

PTAs have lowered the applied tariffs in the region. About 60 percent of Latin American and Caribbean countries have reduced trade-weighted average tariffs to less than 5 percent.[4] Beyond tariffs, the picture of PTAs is mixed. The coverage ratio of these countries' agreements—the share of possible provisions an agreement covers—is around 20 percent on average. That ratio is comparable to that of agreements signed by East Asia and Pacific and Europe and Central Asia countries.

But Latin American and Caribbean countries typically sign deeper agreements with extraregional partners and shallower agreements with intraregional partners (figure O.2). Their extraregional trade agreements also tend to have more substantive commitments, higher enforceability, and more transparency than intraregional agreements. The effectiveness of implementation is also questionable for many PTAs, especially intraregional ones.

PTAs in Latin America and the Caribbean are associated with stronger GVC links—a relationship more robust for PTA partners outside the region. PTA partner countries matter more as export destinations and sources of imported inputs than do nonpartners. And PTAs matter more when extraregional partners are included,

Map O.1   The number and depth of PTAs vary across Latin American and Caribbean countries, 2017

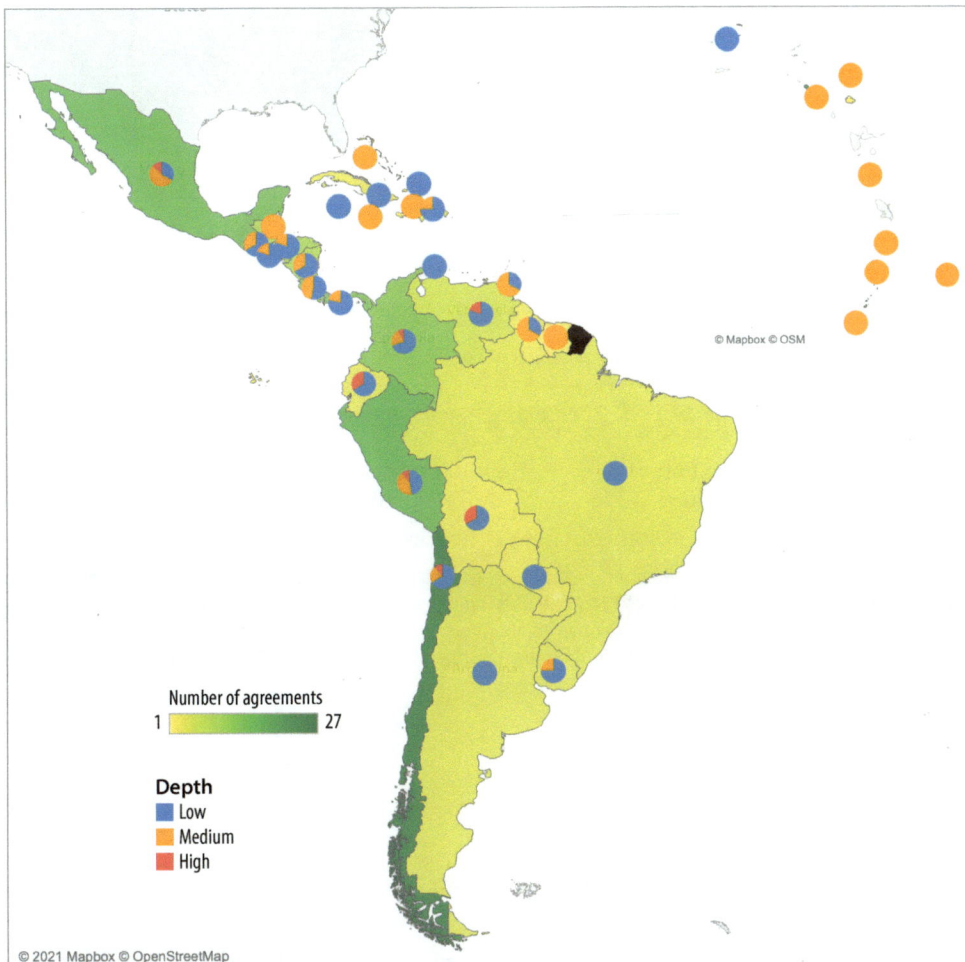

Number of agreements
1 — 27

Depth
■ Low
■ Medium
■ High

© 2021 Mapbox © OpenStreetMap

Source: Fontagné et al. 2021. © World Bank. Further permission required for reuse. No data are available for French Guiana.

consistent with the evidence (presented in chapter 2) that PTAs with extraregional countries are deeper than PTAs with intraregional countries.

Deeper trade agreements would promote GVC links since cooperation on border and behind-the-border policies is needed for GVCs to operate efficiently (Ruta 2017). First, new forms of negative cross-border policy spillovers can be created, given the international fragmentation of production. Second, governments might face credibility problems with behind-the-border measures in the context of GVCs. And third, heterogeneous regulations might create higher costs in the presence of cross-border production.

Figure O.2   Latin American and Caribbean countries typically sign deeper agreements with extraregional partners and shallower agreements with intraregional partners, selected years

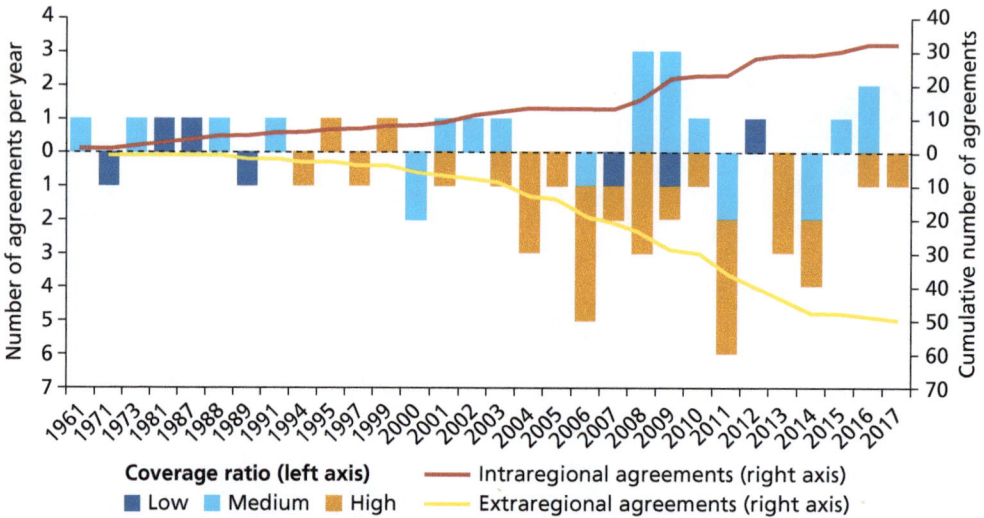

Source: World Bank Deep Trade Agreements database; Mattoo, Rocha, and Ruta 2020.

Note: The left axis indicates the number of preferential trade agreements (PTAs) signed in a single year; the right axis indicates the cumulative number of PTAs. The bars' color intensity indicates the coverage ratio—that is, the number of provisions in an agreement relative to the maximum number of possible provisions. The bars and red line above the rule at zero pertain to intraregional partners; bars and the yellow line below the rule are for extraregional partners.

DTAs PRESENT AN AVENUE FOR PROMOTING TRADE AND BOOSTING GVC INTEGRATION AND UPGRADING, THUS CONTRIBUTING TO IMPROVED ECONOMIC PERFORMANCE

DTAs can be a stepping-stone toward global integration. In the 1980s, Latin American and Caribbean countries saw trade agreements as an instrument to protect regional markets and a complement to import-substitution strategies. After the 1990s, "open regionalism" became prevalent, which emphasized trade agreements as promoting global integration rather than closing regional markets. The most recent literature on regional integration in Latin America and the Caribbean stresses the role of DTAs in the context of open regionalism (Bown et al. 2017). This report builds on that long-standing policy debate, using recent data on the content of trade agreements and providing new evidence that deepening trade agreements in areas beyond market access can support trade and GVC integration (Mattoo, Rocha, and Ruta 2020).

DTAs in Latin America and the Caribbean are associated with more GVC participation and with upgrading to more advanced GVC participation. Globally, deep provisions in trade agreements facilitate and promote GVCs, thus contributing to increased participation in them. GVC-related trade between countries after signing a deep trade agreement is 12 percent higher than it was before signing the agreement (Laget et al. 2018). The positive link between DTAs and GVC participation also appears in the Latin America and Caribbean region: the value of GVC-related trade in 2017 (proxied by trade in parts and components) was higher on average for the region's countries that had signed deeper agreements with their trading partners than for countries with shallower agreements (figure O.3). There is also evidence that deepening trade agreements are associated with GVC upgrading, though causation is more difficult to establish.

Figure O.3   GVC-related trade is higher for countries with deeper agreements

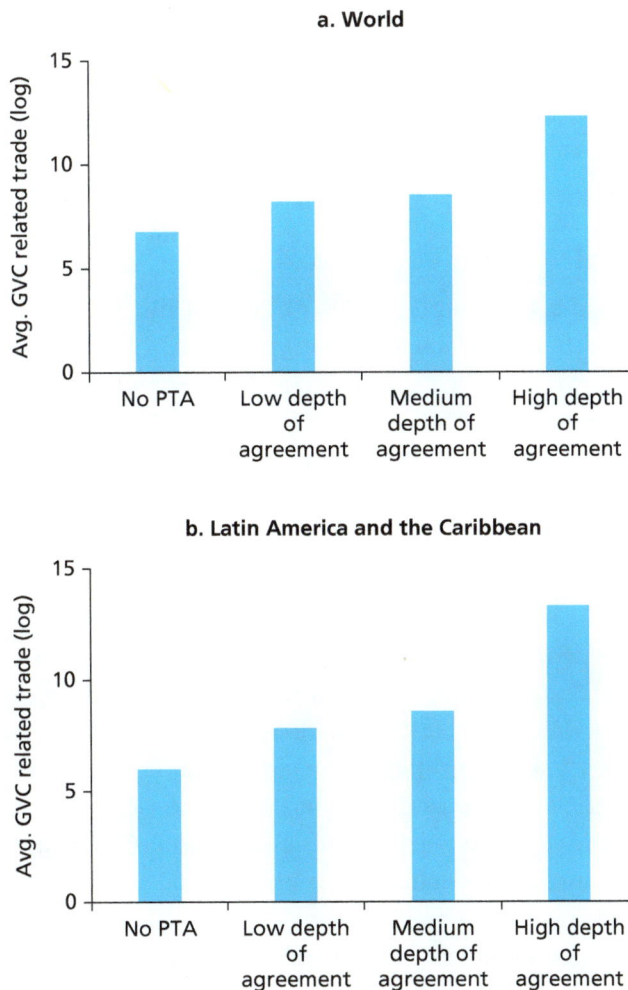

a. World

b. Latin America and the Caribbean

Source: Laget et al. 2018.

Note: Global value chain (GVC)-related trade is represented by 2017 trade in parts and components, defined as all nonfuel intermediates from the Broad Economic Categories (BEC) classification (codes 111, 121, 21, 22, 42, and 53) PTA = preferential trade agreement. Low depth = agreements with a number of provisions below or equal to 15. Medium depth = agreements with provisions between 16 and 29. High depth = agreements with 30 or more provisions.

Deepening existing trade agreements would deliver larger gains for Latin American and Caribbean countries than adding new agreements—a dilemma facing countries with limited negotiating resources. A static, general equilibrium analysis of the long-term effects of trade reforms shows that deepening existing PTAs signed by the region's countries would increase exports by 4.4 percent and GDP by 1.0 percent, on average (Fontagné et al. 2021). In the Pacific Alliance, Chile's GDP would surge by 3.2 percent, Colombia's by 1.0 percent, Mexico's by 2.1 percent, and Peru's by 1.8 percent. Signing new PTAs among Latin American and Caribbean countries that currently have none would also increase welfare gains, but by much less, with exports growing by 0.29 percent and GDP by 0.05 percent, on average.

FOUR AREAS OF DEEP INTEGRATION—TRADE FACILITATION, REGULATORY COOPERATION, SERVICES, AND STATE SUPPORT— ARE PRIORITIES TO IMPROVE LATIN AMERICAN AND CARIBBEAN COUNTRIES' GVC PARTICIPATION AND UPGRADING

GVC participation is determined by four fundamentals: geography, market size, factor endowments, and institutions (World Bank 2019). Latin American and Caribbean countries differ widely in fundamentals, but on average the region is disadvantaged compared with other regions by its relative far distance from major trading partners, smaller average domestic market size, lower capital and skilled labor endowments, and relatively inefficient institutions. DTAs can help overcome some of these disadvantages and shape the region's GVC participation.

Trade facilitation can ease problems stemming from remoteness of the region's countries

Trade facilitation is particularly important in Latin America and the Caribbean, where the time and cost of trading across borders are high. Border inefficiency and regulatory uncertainty are key barriers to boosting trade in low- and middle-income countries, even when tariffs are low. Completing the documents to import a standard container takes an average of 108 hours in the region's countries—on par with Sub-Saharan African countries and countries participating in commodity GVCs but more than three times as long as in Europe and Central Asia countries and almost seven times as long as in countries specializing in advanced manufacturing and services GVCs.[5] Trade facilitation can reduce tangible and intangible costs in the region by improving, simplifying, and harmonizing the procedures and controls governing the cross-border movement of goods.

DTAs can push trade facilitation reforms forward. Trade facilitation provisions in DTAs advance the free movement of goods between member countries by stipulating more advanced and sophisticated solutions than multilateral agreements contain. The DTA provisions promote coordination, collaboration, and information sharing between relevant agencies; harmonize processes and procedures that reduce transaction costs; and establish governance structures to pursue continuous improvement of border procedures as well as compliance and enforcement.

GVCs, in which goods cross borders multiple times, often magnify the impact of trade facilitation provisions. Because firms involved in GVCs rely on the timely and reliable delivery of foreign inputs, their export competitiveness is enhanced by more efficient import procedures. An econometric analysis using firm-level data from Peru shows that trade facilitation provisions boosted the export performance of GVC firms through efficiency enhancements at Peru's borders (Lee, Rocha, and Ruta 2021). Because many border improvements are nondiscriminatory, trade facilitation commitments in a DTA generate positive spillovers for GVC firms that import inputs from countries that are not partners to the DTA.

Commitments to trade facilitation require an effective governance structure to support implementation. Trade facilitation reforms entail major investments of time and resources over several years—a requirement that can challenge implementation, especially if the political environment is volatile. And PTA partners' different levels of development necessitate coordinated efforts to identify solutions suitable to national contexts. For Latin American and Caribbean countries to overcome these implementation challenges and reap the full benefits of trade facilitation, provisions must promote coordination among agencies and establish a clear governance structure, such as a trade facilitation committee.

Regulatory cooperation can help the region's countries exploit economies of scale

Nontariff measures (NTMs) raise trade costs in Latin American and Caribbean countries and reduce opportunities to exploit economies of scale. NTMs have important public policy goals, but divergent regulations can segment the market and raise the fixed cost of entry for foreign firms. In the region, 42 percent of imported products and 53 percent of import value are covered by NTMs (see chapter 4). The resulting high trade costs limit Latin American and Caribbean firms' ability to exploit economies of scale from regional markets. Countries in Europe, North America, and East Asia impose even more costly NTMs on their imports—particularly in the form of sanitary and phytosanitary (SPS) measures and technical barriers to trade (TBTs). The prevalence of SPS and TBT measures in those important destination markets for the region's countries can hamper their exporting firms' trade and growth prospects.

Although regulatory cooperation can reduce trade costs, the region's trade agreements have a mixed record of achieving it. SPS and TBT rules in trade agreements require members to increase transparency in NTMs, promote forms of regulatory cooperation such as harmonization or mutual recognition of standards, and improve enforcement of those commitments. Including SPS and TBT rules in DTAs reduces the potential negative impact of NTMs and lowers the trade costs resulting from regulatory divergence (Ederington and Ruta 2016). Trade agreements involving Latin American and Caribbean countries have increasingly included SPS and TBT rules, though implementation remains a challenge. Yet important differences persist. SPS provisions in the region's agreements tend to have more binding commitments than the TBT provisions have. The SPS provisions sometimes require mutual recognition or harmonization but are less stringent than the TBT provisions regarding transparency.

Regulatory cooperation in Latin American and Caribbean agreements boosts bilateral trade and GVC integration, particularly for small and medium enterprises. SPS provisions promote agricultural and food exports, whereas TBT provisions boost overall exports and imports of intermediate inputs. Firm-level evidence for Chile, Colombia, and Peru shows that the boost to exports from SPS and TBT provisions in DTAs is larger for small firms (Fernandes, Lefebvre, and Rocha 2021). That finding is consistent with the view that DTAs reduce the fixed entry costs of exporting created by NTMs, which are especially onerous for small exporters. And DTA rules promoting transparency in SPS and TBT measures foster small firms' exports by improving the predictability of foreign market conditions.

The implementation of SPS and TBT integration in the region's trade agreements is a concern, but recent experience shows the way to better outcomes. Extraregional PTAs involving Latin American and Caribbean countries have been more successfully implemented than intraregional PTAs, on average, but groups of more similar countries (such as the Pacific Alliance) have found innovative approaches for regulatory cooperation. Moreover, recent extraregional and intraregional agreements alike offer lessons: trade agreements can specify concrete, binding reform outcomes expected from measures for sectors or products and can establish institutional structures with clear mandates, work programs, and defined oversight powers and resources.

Opening the service economy can compensate for factor endowment scarcity constraining the region's countries

Although the service economy in Latin American and Caribbean countries is large, the region's trade in services is somewhat lower than in other regions and its integration into services GVCs is low.[6] Services account for 60 percent of economic activity in the region, and services trade accounts for 7.3 percent of GDP—less than in most other regions.[7]

In GVCs, services are increasingly important, both as inputs into production in other sectors (including manufacturing) and as sources of production. Latin America and the Caribbean tends to be an input supplier in services GVCs but has less backward integration. Compared with other regions in the world, Latin America and the Caribbean is less integrated into services GVCs, especially for intraregional trade. For instance, the East Asia and Pacific region has backward and forward links totaling 31 percent of gross intraregional exports, but the Latin American and Caribbean total is only 16 percent (Borin and Mancini 2019). And that share has stagnated since the early 2000s, indicating inactivity in regional services GVCs.

The content of the region's PTAs helps explain the scarcity of services trade, especially regionally, in its GVCs. Intraregional trade costs in Latin America and the Caribbean are higher than the region's trade costs with North America—an unusual condition. The region's PTAs with external partners tend to be more ambitious in content than those with regional partners, depending on the external partner. This configuration contributes to services trade patterns in Latin America and the Caribbean, aligning with evidence that deeper services PTAs increase services trade by 15–65 percent and lead to more service value added being sourced from PTA partners (Borchert and Di Ubaldo 2021). The analysis reveals, besides the role of commitments to open services trade and related enforcement mechanisms, that provisions related to investment and the movement of people boost the role of services in GVC trade.

Latin American and Caribbean countries can use DTAs to increasingly liberalize service sector policies—for instance, by setting a horizontal standstill on discriminatory measures and quantitative restrictions. They should also consider a broader range of services trade modes, particularly foreign investment and movement of people, which are associated with higher value added in services exports.[8] And PTAs can foster trade by including provisions to improve the transparency of measures that restrict trade in services and by strengthening data collection on services trade and policy.

Regulating state support and competition can improve the quality of economic institutions in the region's countries

Latin American and Caribbean countries use subsidies and state-owned enterprises (SOEs) intensively. Subsidies are often substantial, in the range of 4 percent of GDP in the region's countries that report these data (in contrast, for instance, to an average of 1.4 percent in European Union countries).[9] SOEs play a large role in many of the region's countries, potentially affecting market competition as well as having potentially large fiscal implications in cases of weak performance due to soft budget constraints. Latin America and the Caribbean ranks below other regions in its intensity of domestic competition on the World Economic Forum's composite measure (Schwab 2019).

DTAs can help overcome political economy constraints to policy reforms by providing an external anchor for frameworks of state support. Regulating or including provisions or commitments that regulate state support to enterprises in trade agreements can reduce national support policies' harm to market competition and reduce adverse cross-border spillover effects. Agreements could include commitments to (a) adopt a competitive neutrality framework in national legislation; (b) adopt a regulation on competition, subsidies, and SOEs; (c) require SOEs to operate on a commercial and nondiscriminatory basis; and (d) expand the mandate of competition authorities to govern subsidies and SOEs.

DTAs can also improve the quality of institutions by requiring higher policy transparency, promoting evidence-based assessment of policy impact, and creating frameworks for public-private partnerships. Trade agreements can enhance policy transparency on subsidies and SOEs, which is currently limited and so constrains the analysis of the economic effects of subsidies and SOEs on trade and on participation in regional and global value chains. Using trade agreements to improve the availability of data on state support and the analysis of its effects on value-chain-based investment incentives can also increase the appeal of trade agreements to the private sector and to communities with a stake in economic upgrading.

Trade agreements will be critical in the recovery from COVID-19

DTAs will be critical to boost GVC integration in Latin American and Caribbean countries as the global economy recovers from the COVID-19 pandemic while tensions in the multilateral trade system persist. The pandemic might reinforce old trade measures and stimulate new ones—many of a protectionist nature—that would limit Latin American and Caribbean countries' ability to integrate into GVCs. Unsynchronized recovery will create competition for scarce demand, tempting governments to use trade restrictions to redirect demand toward domestic production. And the appeal of tariffs as a source of government revenue might increase with worsening fiscal conditions and the need to use subsidies to help firms recover from the crisis. In addition, rising aversion to risks to health, security, and privacy might open the door to increased regulatory protectionism. Governments with limited fiscal space might be tempted to weaken rules on SOEs or on competition as an indirect support for the economy. In uncertain times, DTA policy commitments might create a more stable institutional environment for the smooth operation of GVCs, thus promoting DTA partners' ability to integrate into GVCs.

Today's tensions between large trading partners as well as the persistent fragility of the multilateral trade system increase the usefulness of DTAs for Latin American and Caribbean countries to promote domestic reforms at a critical moment. Tensions between the United States and China might prompt American production facilities to disperse their locations to other regions. And the COVID-19 pandemic could encourage further supply chain reshaping (Freund et al. 2021). These conditions offer the region's countries an opportunity to further integrate into GVCs. Given the fragilities in the multilateral trade system and the changing trade patterns, DTAs increasingly shape the rules of trade and can be a tool for Latin American and Caribbean countries to overcome structural disadvantages and attract opportunities for GVC participation.

NOTES

1. This report uses the term "preferential trade agreement" to refer to all types of reciprocal trade agreements, regional trade agreements, free trade agreements, and customs unions, both within and across regions.

2. GVC participation data are from the Trade in Value Added (TiVA) database of the Organisation for Economic Co-operation and Development.

3. These findings, and the underlying analysis, are presented in chapter 1.

4. Data on the region's trade-weighted average tariffs and PTA coverage ratios are taken from chapter 2.

5. The region's performance on several trade facilitation indicators is further discussed in chapter 3.

6. In addition to services, rules on investment in trade agreements are important to attract foreign direct investment that can remedy the scarcity of capital or technology. These issues will be analyzed in future work.

7. The data on services trade, by region, are from the World Development Indicators database.

8. The most common classification of services trade is that of the World Trade Organization treaty, the General Agreement on Trade in Services (GATS), which defines four modes of services trade: (1) cross-border supply, (2) consumption abroad, (3) commercial presence (including foreign direct investment), and (4) movement of natural persons (in which service delivery involves the travel of a service provider to the consumer's country).

9. Data on the share of subsidies in GDP or government budgets are from the International Monetary Fund's Government Finance Statistics database. See chapter 6 for a detailed discussion of state support through subsidies and state-owned enterprises.

REFERENCES

Borchert, I., and M. Di Ubaldo. 2021. "Deep Services Trade Agreements and Their Effect on Trade and Value Added." Policy Research Working Paper 9608, World Bank, Washington, DC.

Borin, A., and M. Mancini. 2019. "Measuring What Matters in Global Value Chains and Value Added Trade." Policy Research Working Paper 8804, World Bank, Washington, DC.

Bown, C. P., D. Lederman, S. Pienknagura, and R. Robertson. 2017. *Better Neighbors: Toward a Renewal of Economic Integration in Latin America*. World Bank Latin American and Caribbean Studies. Washington, DC: World Bank.

Constantinescu, C., A. Mattoo, and M. Ruta. 2019. "Does Vertical Specialisation Increase Productivity?" *The World Economy* 42 (8): 2385–402.

Dollar, D., and A. Kraay. 2004. "Trade, Growth, and Poverty." *Economic Journal* 114 (493): F22–F49.

Ederington, J., and M. Ruta. 2016. "Nontariff Measures and the World Trading System." In *Handbook of Commercial Policy*, Vol. 1, Part B, edited by K. Bagwell and R. W. Staiger, 211–77. Amsterdam: North-Holland.

Fernandes, A. M., K. Lefebvre, and N. Rocha. 2021. "Heterogeneous Impacts of SPS and TBT Regulations: Firm-Level Evidence from Deep Trade Agreements." Policy Research Working Paper 9700, World Bank, Washington, DC.

Fontagné, L., N. Rocha, M. Ruta, and G. Santoni. 2021. "A General Equilibrium Assessment of the Economic Impact of Deep Trade Agreements." Policy Research Working Paper 9630, World Bank, Washington, DC.

Freund, C., A. Mattoo, A. Mulabdic, and M. Ruta. 2021. "Natural Disasters and the Reshaping of Global Value Chains." Policy Research Working Paper 9719, World Bank, Washington, DC.

Harrison, A., and A. Rodríguez-Clare. 2009. "Trade, Foreign Investment, and Industrial Policy for Developing Countries." Working Paper 15261, National Bureau of Economic Research, Cambridge, MA.

Laget, E., A. Osnago, N. Rocha, and M. Ruta. 2018. "Deep Trade Agreements and Global Value Chains." Policy Research Working Paper 8491, World Bank, Washington, DC.

Lee, W., N. Rocha, and M. Ruta. 2021. "Trade Facilitation Provisions in Preferential Trade Agreements: Impact on Peru's Exporters." Policy Research Working Paper 9674, World Bank, Washington, DC.

Mattoo, A., N. Rocha, and M. Ruta, eds. 2020. *Handbook of Deep Trade Agreements*. Washington, DC: World Bank.

Ruta, Michele. 2017. "Preferential Trade Agreements and Global Value Chains: Theory, Evidence, and Open Questions." Policy Research Working Paper 8190, World Bank, Washington, DC.

Schwab, K., ed. 2019. *The Global Competitiveness Report 2019*. Geneva: World Economic Forum.

World Bank. 2019. *Trade Integration as a Pathway to Development?* Semiannual Report of the Latin America and Caribbean Region (October). Washington, DC: World Bank.

World Bank. 2020. *World Development Report 2020: Trading for Development in the Age of Global Value Chains*. Washington, DC: World Bank.

1 Trade and GVC Integration in Latin America and the Caribbean

Ana Fernandes, Gaston Nievas, and Deborah Winkler

KEY MESSAGES

- Trade in Latin America and the Caribbean is low in relation to the region's economic size, and the region is less open to trade than other regions at comparable levels of development.
- Latin American and Caribbean exports are concentrated in commodities and food, with some limited manufacturing and, for Mexico, advanced manufacturing and services.
- Both *backward participation* in global value chains (the use of imported inputs for production for export) and *forward participation* (the export of inputs used in production for the importing country's exports) are limited in Latin America and the Caribbean.
- Latin America and the Caribbean is disadvantaged by its geographical distance from global value chain (GVC) hubs, average domestic market size, and endowments of low-skilled labor and capital.
- These characteristics, along with Latin America and the Caribbean's sectoral specialization in commodities and food exports, explain the region's low average backward GVC participation and several Latin American and Caribbean countries' high forward GVC participation, though different patterns exist within the region.
- Deep trade agreements present an avenue to overcome geographical remoteness, expand effective market size, and increase access to imported services that could support GVC participation and upgrading in Latin America and the Caribbean. They can also improve domestic institutions, further strengthening GVC participation.

INTRODUCTION

In recent decades, the Latin America and Caribbean region made great advances in macroeconomic stability, per capita incomes, and institutional capacities. But it faces fundamental development challenges to avoid a "middle income trap," with insufficient economic diversification and competition and unimpressive productivity growth. Trade and global value chains are key to address these challenges, as the economies of East Asia and Eastern Europe clearly show.

The Latin America and Caribbean region's low integration into international trade and GVCs has coincided with a slowdown in economic growth, contrasting sharply with the real gross domestic product (GDP) growth in other emerging economies. Many factors have played a part, but one probable explanation for the region's low dynamism is the combination of its specialization in commodities and its limited participation in manufacturing GVCs. This contrasts with East Asia, Europe, and North America, which are more strongly integrated into advanced manufacturing, services, and innovative GVC activities (World Bank 2020b). Greater GVC participation is linked to gains in productivity, value added, and growth (Constantinescu, Mattoo, and Ruta 2019; Pahl and Timmer 2020; Stolzenburg, Taglioni, and Winkler 2019; World Bank 2020b).[1] And for firms, the productivity and employment gains from importing intermediate inputs magnify those from exporting only (Banh, Wingender, and Gueye 2020; Kasahara and Lapham 2013; Muûls and Pisu 2009; Wagner 2012; World Bank 2020b).

This chapter benchmarks trade and GVC integration in the Latin America and Caribbean region and countries against selected aspirational comparator regions and countries—zooming in on selected sectors. Latin America and the Caribbean is benchmarked against comparator countries in the East Asia and Pacific and Europe and Central Asia regions through aggregate and firm-level patterns.[2] The chapter includes only countries that are part of the GVC taxonomy (introduced below) and were eligible for World Bank lending in 2000. The countries considered for analysis based on aggregate data are Argentina, Bolivia, Brazil, Chile, Colombia, Costa Rica, the Dominican Republic, Ecuador, El Salvador, Guatemala, Haiti, Honduras, Jamaica, Mexico, Nicaragua, Panama, Paraguay, Peru, Trinidad and Tobago, Uruguay, and República Bolivariana de Venezuela. Analysis based on microdata considers only the subset of countries with customs data.

The chapter includes sectoral insights for mining and commodity-intensive manufacturing (petroleum, chemical, and nonmetallic minerals and metals); agribusiness (agriculture and food and beverages); and manufacturing (textiles and apparel, electrical and machinery, and transportation equipment). Where possible, the analysis also covers traditional services (wholesale trade and transportation) and modern services (telecommunications and financial and business activities).

TRADE INTEGRATION IN LATIN AMERICA AND THE CARIBBEAN

Trade has grown slowly, and openness remains low

Over the past two decades, growth in exports, imports, and GDP per capita in Latin American and Caribbean countries was generally lower than in comparator countries, though experiences varied.[3] One possible explanation for the sluggish growth could be the region's relatively low integration into international trade and GVCs (World Bank 2019) because trade growth is positively linked to increases in GDP per capita globally and in the selected sample of countries (Dollar and Kraay 2004; Harrison and Rodríguez-Clare 2009), as shown in figure 1.1.

Exports and imports enhance productivity and growth through several channels. In neoclassical trade theory, exports allow for specialization in a country's comparative advantage and thus boost growth. An export orientation also includes dynamic efficiency gains engineered by greater competition, increased economies of scale, better capacity utilization, faster dissemination of knowledge and technological progress, and improved allocation of scarce resources throughout the economy (Grossman and Helpman 1991; Helpman and Krugman 1985).

Similarly, in endogenous growth theory, imported inputs are crucial for growth because they are a channel for the diffusion of global technology (Aghion and Howitt 1998; Romer 1987, 1990). Gains in productivity also arise from the increased input variety ensuing from the use of imported intermediate inputs in the presence of imperfect substitution in production by domestic or imported intermediate inputs (Ethier 1982). Importing inputs and capital goods is also necessary for firms and countries to integrate and upgrade in value chains. Higher backward GVC participation—the use of imported inputs in production for export—helps firms and countries absorb valuable foreign technology and know-how. It also offers opportunities for countries to promote structural transformation (Taglioni and Winkler 2016).

Both exports and imports have a positive relationship with income growth, reflecting that gross exports in a GVC world embody many imported inputs used for export production. Export growth for the average Latin American and Caribbean country was 4.0 percent over 2000–18, but it reached 7.6 percent for East Asia and the Pacific and 7.0 percent for Europe and Central Asia. Among the Latin American and Caribbean countries, trade and income growth have been highest in the Dominican Republic, Panama, and Peru and lowest in Argentina, Brazil, and Mexico (probably because of a 2014 domestic economic recession in Brazil and a scale effect for Argentina and Mexico).

The Latin America and Caribbean region is much less open to trade than its comparator regions. Average exports of goods and services across these countries made up only 28 percent of the region's GDP in 2018, well below the more than 50 percent in East Asia and the Pacific and in Europe and Central Asia (figure 1.2, panel a).[4]

Figure 1.1 Latin American and Caribbean trade and GDP growth—below that of comparator regions, 2000–18

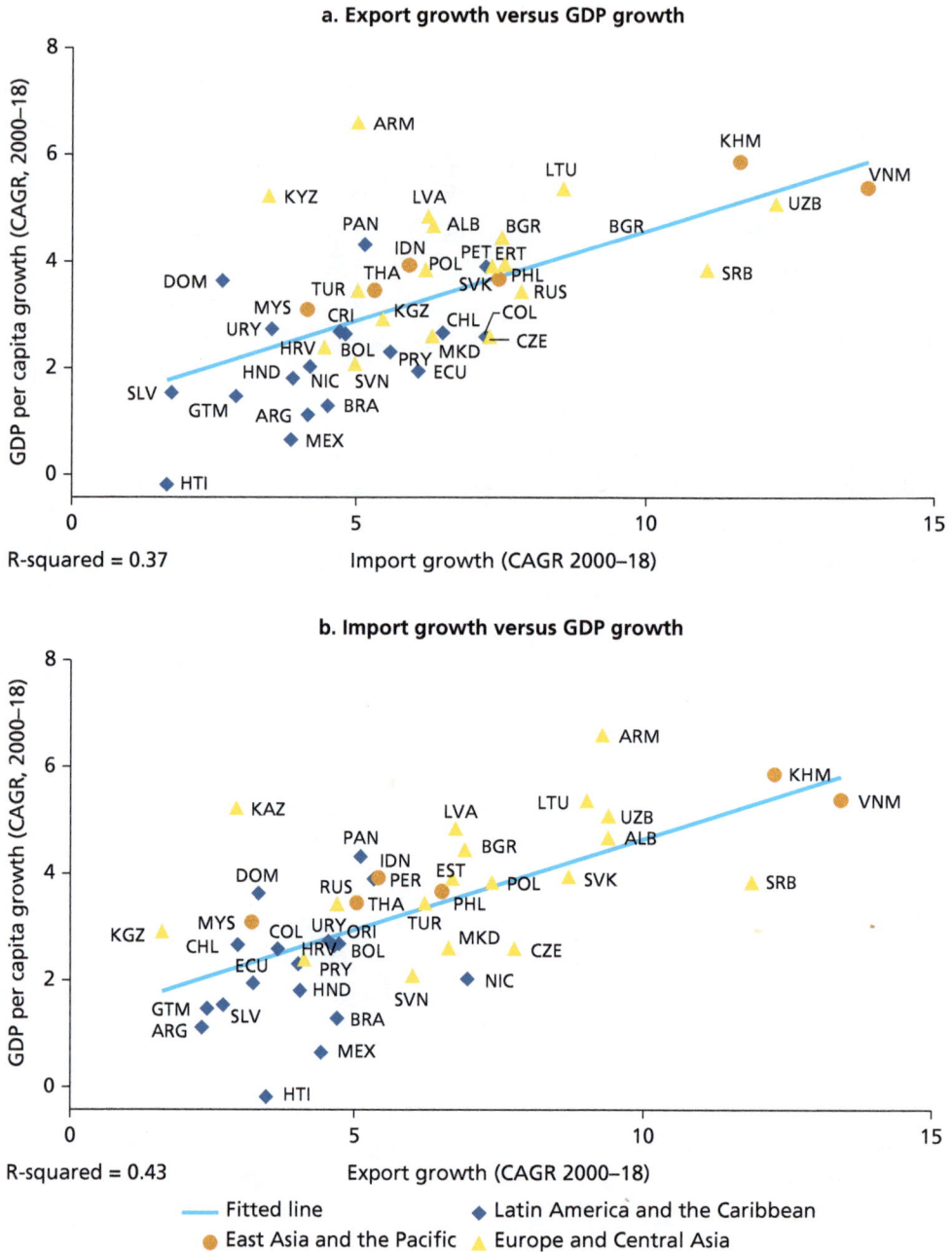

a. Export growth versus GDP growth

R-squared = 0.37

b. Import growth versus GDP growth

R-squared = 0.43

Fitted line   ◆ Latin America and the Caribbean
● East Asia and the Pacific   ▲ Europe and Central Asia

Source: World Bank, based on World Development Indicators database.

Note: CAGR is compound annual growth rate. Export and import growth are based on 2010 constant trade values. Figures include only countries that are part of the global value chain taxonomy (proposed in World Bank [2020b] and further discussed in this chapter) and were eligible for World Bank lending as of 2000. Countries are labeled by ISO alpha-3 code. GDP = gross domestic product.

Figure 1.2   Trade in goods and services as a percentage of GDP in Latin America and the Caribbean and comparator regions, 2018

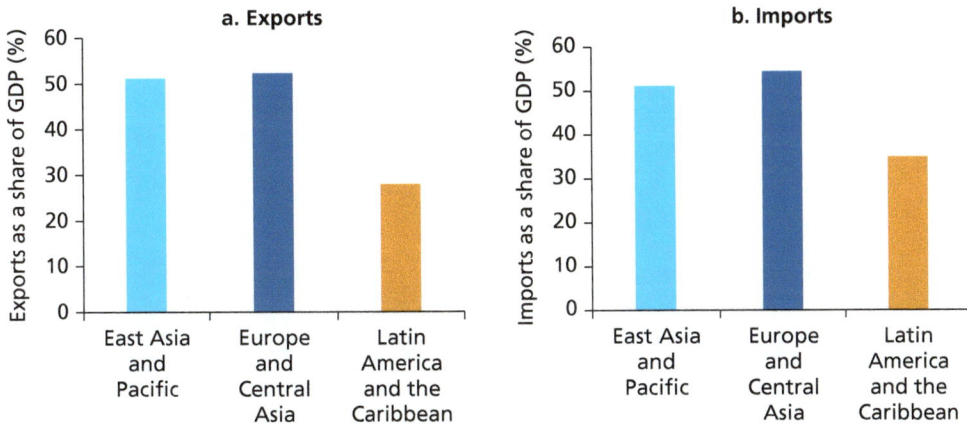

Source: World Bank, based on World Development Indicators database.

Note: The figures show simple averages across countries and include only countries that are part of the global value chain taxonomy (proposed in World Bank [2020b] and further discussed in this chapter) and were eligible for World Bank lending as of 2000. For the measures of import and export shares of gross domestic product (GDP) by country, see annex 1A, figure 1A.1.

On the import side, Latin America and the Caribbean's integration is slightly higher, with average imports of goods and services at 35 percent of GDP in 2018, compared with more than 50 percent in East Asia and the Pacific and in Europe and Central Asia (figure 1.2, panel b).

As such, the Latin America and Caribbean region's export and import shares of GDP have barely changed since 2000, when exports were 28 percent and imports 32 percent. Low trade openness may have prevented the region from experiencing higher economic growth.

Most Latin American and Caribbean countries exhibit low shares of both imports and exports in their GDP, with Mexico and a few other countries being exceptions. Export and import shares in GDP are especially low in Argentina, Brazil, and Colombia, at less than 10 percent for exports and less than 20 percent for imports (see annex 1A, figure 1A.1). For these large economies, trade openness can be expected to be lower owing to a larger domestic market. Mexico defies this rule, exhibiting much higher openness to trade—with both exports and imports amounting to about 40 percent of GDP—because of its strong integration with the United States. Honduras, Jamaica, Nicaragua, and Panama have the region's largest shares of exports (about 40 percent or more) and even higher shares of imports (48–60 percent) in their GDP. Costa Rica and Paraguay show a slightly lower integration than Mexico, but all three show a lower share of commodities in their export baskets than other Latin American and Caribbean countries.

Commodity-intensive countries in the comparator regions show similarly low integration (such as Indonesia in East Asia and Pacific or Kazakhstan and the Russian Federation in Europe and Central Asia), but other countries in these regions have ratios of imports and exports to GDP exceeding 60 percent (such as Bulgaria, the Czech Republic, Estonia, Lithuania, the Slovak Republic, and Slovenia)—and even reaching 100 percent in Vietnam.

The density of exporting firms is lower than in comparator regions, but those firms are larger

As countries develop and exports grow, their export expansion happens through both the number of exporters and increases in exporter size, while the microstructure of exports changes. Richer countries have more and larger exporters on average (Fernandes, Freund, and Pierola 2016). Given the ample evidence that exporting firms are more productive than nonexporting firms and that larger exporters are more productive than smaller ones, these patterns are consistent with improving allocative efficiency in export markets as countries develop, with more resources flowing to the largest and most productive firms. In addition, a higher density of exporters—number of exporters per capita—can lead to positive agglomeration economies, through sharing infrastructure and information and lowering transaction and transportation costs, thus reducing the sunk entry costs of exporting.

The largest exporting firms, which account for more than half of total exports in most emerging economies, transform sectoral patterns of exports and alter comparative advantage (Freund and Pierola 2015). In one study of export superstars—such as Intel in Costa Rica—the top five exporters in 32 low- and middle-income countries accounted for more than half the export growth and almost all the export diversification over a five-year period (Freund and Pierola 2015). Most of those large exporting firms were foreign owned. The extent to which host economies benefit from them is a subject of debate. The market power of such firms and their monopsony power in extractive sectors may be of concern (Autor et al. 2020). But the capital and technology spillovers they bring can boost long-run growth (Harrison and Rodríguez-Clare 2009) and have persistent benefits for living standards (Méndez-Chacón and Van Patten 2021).

Latin American and Caribbean countries do not suffer from a scarcity of exporting firms given their stage of development—especially not in its largest countries, Brazil and Mexico. A positive link between the number of exporters and country's GDP per capita is confirmed in a selected country sample (figure 1.3, panel a).[5]

In contrast, Latin American and Caribbean countries have larger exporting firms than expected given their stage of development when compared with European and Central Asian countries. The country sample confirms a positive association between level of development and average exports per firm, but for Latin American and Caribbean countries, average exports per firm tend to be larger than predicted by their stage of development, as seen for Brazil and Mexico, and to a lesser extent for Argentina, Chile, and even countries with lower incomes such as Bolivia, Ecuador, Nicaragua,

Figure 1.3 Export activity in relation to economic and demographic measures, in selected countries of Latin America and the Caribbean and comparator regions, annual averages

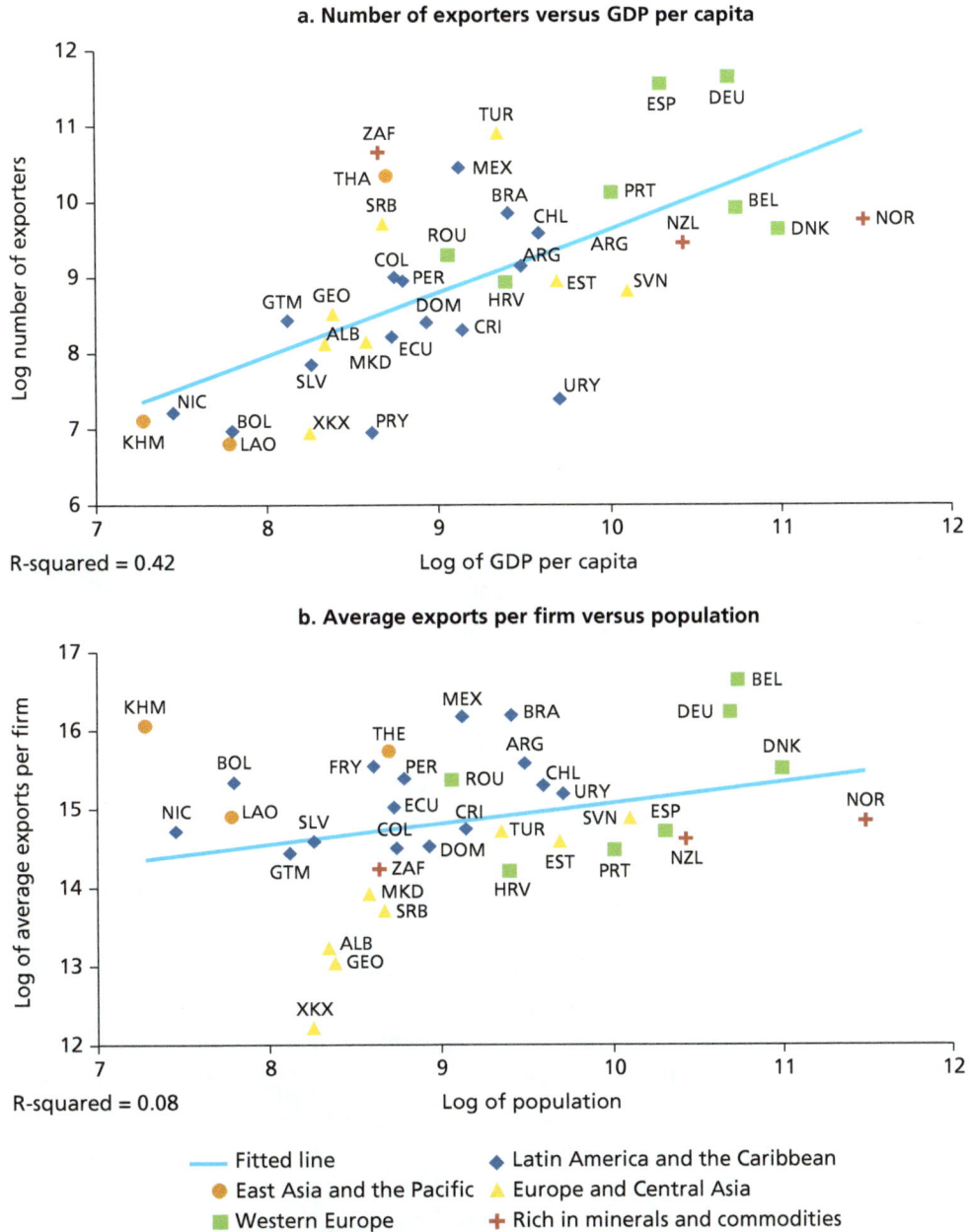

a. Number of exporters versus GDP per capita

R-squared = 0.42

b. Average exports per firm versus population

R-squared = 0.08

Legend:
— Fitted line
● East Asia and the Pacific
■ Western Europe
◆ Latin America and the Caribbean
▲ Europe and Central Asia
+ Rich in minerals and commodities

Source: Updates to the World Bank's Exporter Dynamics Database (described in Fernandes, Freund, and Pierola 2016) and data from the World Development Indicators database.

Note: The figure shows averages for available years in 2010–14 for Belgium, Bolivia, Brazil, Costa Rica, Denmark, Estonia, Germany, Guatemala, New Zealand, Nicaragua, Norway, Portugal, Romania, Slovenia, Spain, Thailand, and Turkey, and averages for available years in 2015–19 for Albania, Argentina, Cambodia, Chile, Colombia, Croatia, the Dominican Republic, Ecuador, Georgia, Lao PDR, Mexico, North Macedonia, Paraguay, Peru, Serbia, Slovenia, South Africa, and Uruguay. Countries are labeled by ISO alpha-3 code. GDP = gross domestic product.

Paraguay, and Peru (figure 1.3, panel b). This pattern may result from a specialization of many of these countries in exports of agricultural and commodity-related products.

The presence of export superstars that dominate exports and increase average exporter size is global (Freund and Pierola 2015), and export concentration in those superstars tends to increase as countries develop (Fernandes, Freund, and Pierola 2016). Latin American and Caribbean countries exhibit greater export concentration in the largest exporters (the top 1 percent) than other countries at the same level of development (see annex 1A, figure 1.A.2). Although a high degree of export concentration could be a sign of a highly distorted environment, an alternative interpretation is that this relationship indicates better resource reallocation as countries develop. The evidence here suggests that the allocation of resources in Latin America and the Caribbean does not suffer excessively from distortions as it allows resources to flow toward more efficient, larger exporters, resulting in more concentration at the top (Fernandes, Freund, and Pierola 2016).

But Latin American and Caribbean countries have a substantially lower number of exporters per capita than comparator countries in Europe (figure 1.4). The region's most populous countries—Argentina, Brazil, Colombia, and Mexico—have lower exporter densities despite their larger numbers of exporters overall. In contrast, exporter density in Costa Rica is the highest of the region's countries in the sample. Chile has both a relatively high exporter density and number of exporters given its medium population size.

The economy is concentrated in commodities and food exports

Reliance on only a few exports has negative consequences for growth (Lederman and Maloney 2007). Conversely, diversity in exports can reduce income volatility for countries with large populations living in poverty and reduce vulnerability to sharp declines in the terms of trade. Diversification also increases the potential for generating productivity spillovers: economic growth is positively affected by more diversified exports, including higher shares of manufactured products (Agosin 2007; Dodaro 1991).[6]

Food and commodities play large roles in Latin America and the Caribbean's goods exports, while manufactures matter substantially less. Commodities—including agricultural raw materials, fuel, and ores and metals—made up almost one-third of goods exports in the region in 2018, compared with 28 percent in Europe and Central Asia and 26 percent in East Asia and Pacific (figure 1.5, panel a). Food exports show even larger regional differences, making up 35 percent of Latin America and the Caribbean's exports of goods in 2018, compared with only 12 percent in East Asia and Pacific and Europe and Central Asia (figure 1.5, panel b). The region's share of manufactures in goods exports, at 31 percent, was well behind East Asia and Pacific's at 60 percent and Europe and Central Asia's at 56 percent (figure 1.5, panel c).

Despite these general trends, export specialization varies considerably across Latin American and Caribbean countries. Mexico and El Salvador exhibit the highest percentage of manufactures in their goods exports, each at about 80 percent in 2018,

Figure 1.4 Density of exporters in selected countries of Latin America and the Caribbean and comparator regions

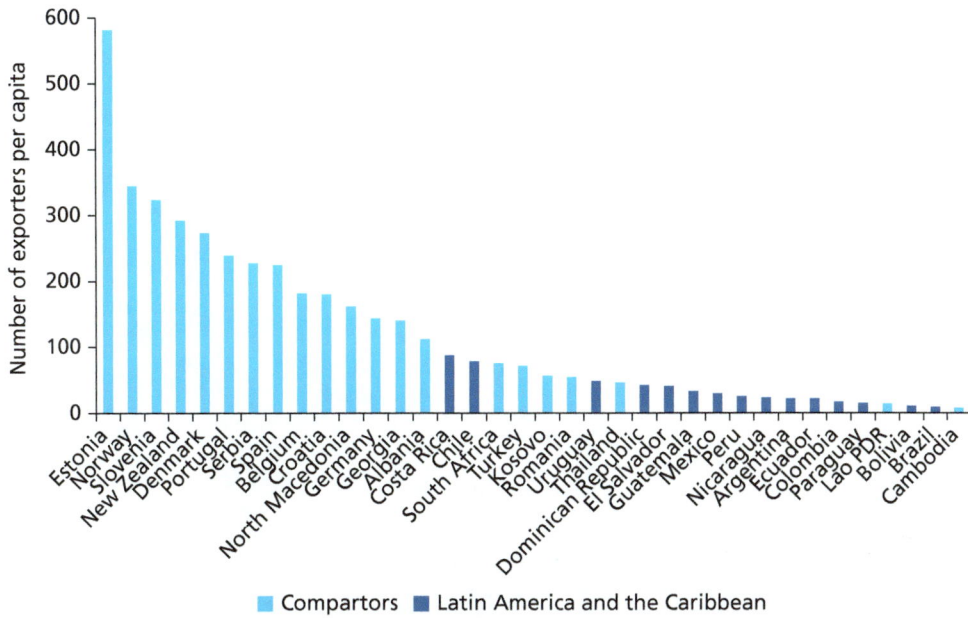

Source: Updates to the World Bank's Exporter Dynamics Database (described in Fernandes, Freund, and Pierola 2016).

Note: The figure shows averages for available years in 2010–14 for Belgium, Bolivia, Brazil, Costa Rica, Denmark, Estonia, Germany, Guatemala, New Zealand, Nicaragua, Norway, Portugal, Romania, Slovenia, Spain, Thailand, and Turkey, and averages for available years in 2015–19 for Albania, Argentina, Cambodia, Chile, Colombia, Croatia, the Dominican Republic, Ecuador, Georgia, Lao PDR, Mexico, North Macedonia, Paraguay, Peru, Serbia, Slovenia, South Africa, and Uruguay.

followed by Costa Rica and Nicaragua at about 50–60 percent, and Brazil at about 35 percent (figure 1.6, panel a). Commodities play a minor role in these countries, resulting in a highly diversified export basket (figure 1.6, panel b). But other countries in the region rely heavily on commodities, with shares in their goods exports exceeding 40 percent in Ecuador; 60 percent in Chile, Colombia, and Peru; and almost 80 percent in Bolivia (figure 1.6, panel a). These are also among the countries with the highest export product concentration (figure 1.6, panel b). Argentina, Paraguay, and Uruguay exhibit less reliance on both commodities and manufactures in their goods export baskets, suggesting a higher dependence on food exports (figure 1.6, panel a).

A closer look at the distribution of exports across more disaggregated sectors shows that the Latin America and Caribbean region specializes in food, agricultural, and mining exports. In 2018, those three sectors accounted on average for 55 percent of total goods exports in the region's countries, compared with 29 percent in East Asian and Pacific countries and 22 percent in European and Central Asian countries (figure 1.7).

Figure 1.5   Commodities, food, and manufactures as a share of goods exports in Latin America and the Caribbean and comparator regions, 2018

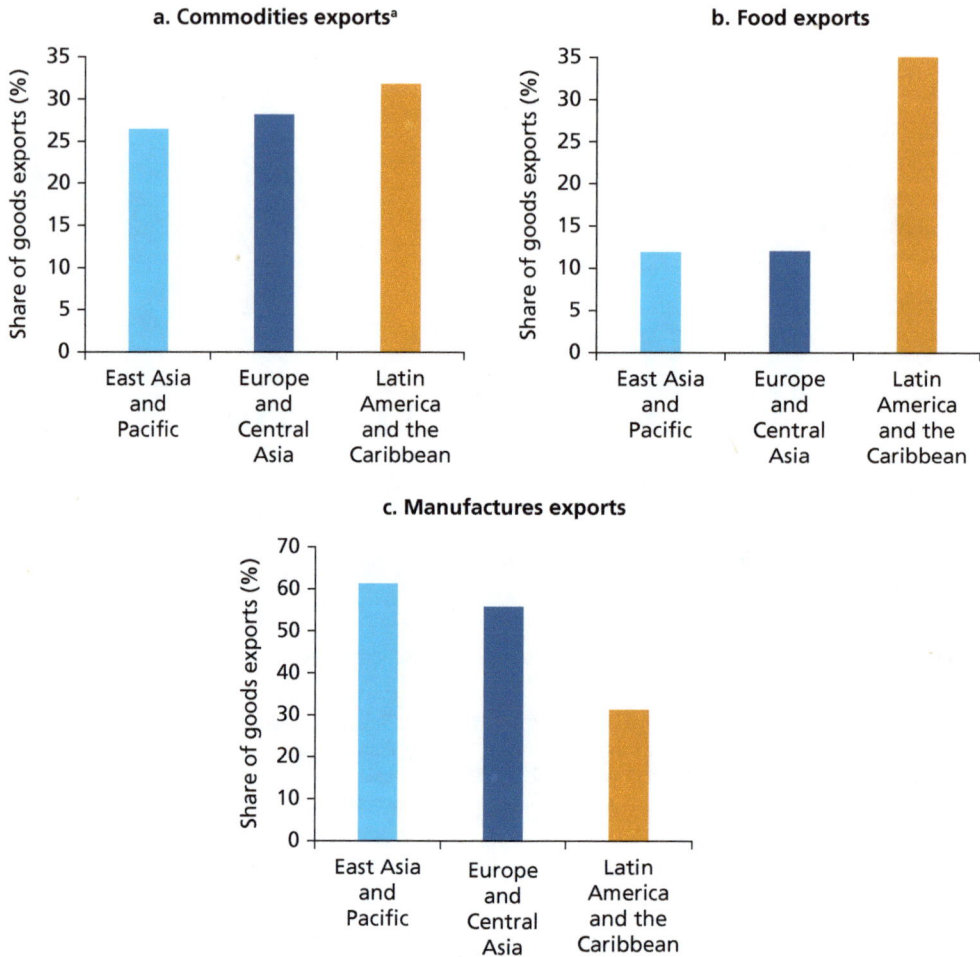

a. Commodities exports[a]

b. Food exports

c. Manufactures exports

Source: World Bank, based on the World Development Indicators database.

Note: The figures show simple averages across countries and include only countries that are part of the global value chain taxonomy (proposed in World Bank [2020b] and further discussed in this chapter) and were eligible for World Bank lending as of 2000.

a. Commodity exports are agricultural raw materials, fuel, and ores and metals.

The share of food and beverages in total exports averaged 22 percent across Latin American and Caribbean countries, followed by agriculture at 18 percent and mining and quarrying at 16 percent. Chemicals and mineral products; metal products; electrical and machinery; and textiles each represent around 9 percent of the region's goods exports on average, while transportation equipment makes up only 4 percent. By contrast, East Asia and Pacific and Europe and Central Asia both have a comparative advantage in electrical and machinery exports, while chemicals and mineral exports also matter most strongly for Europe and Central Asia.

Figure 1.6   Commodities versus manufactures as a share of goods exports and product concentration in selected countries, Latin America and the Caribbean and comparator regions, 2018

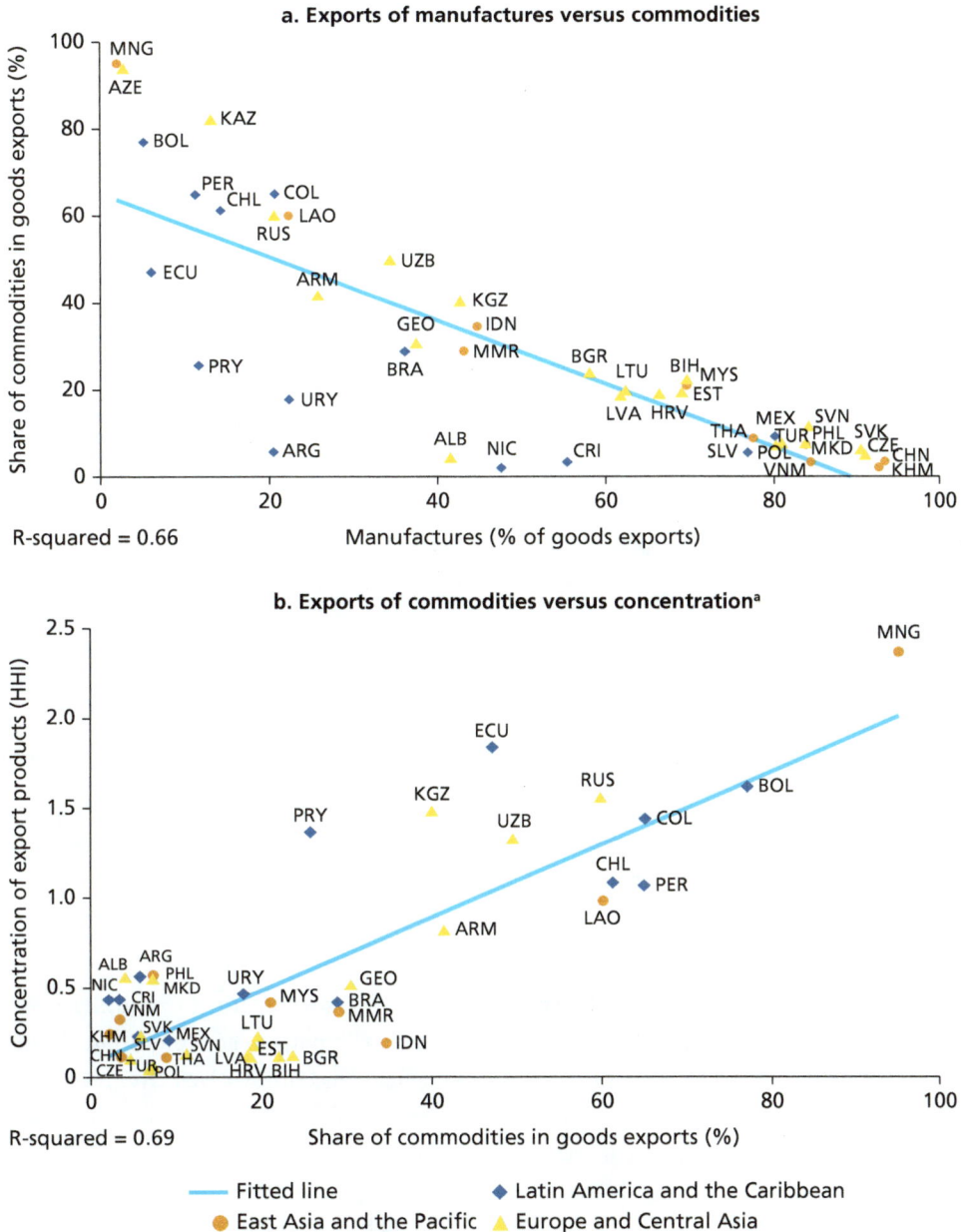

a. Exports of manufactures versus commodities

R-squared = 0.66

b. Exports of commodities versus concentration[a]

R-squared = 0.69

Fitted line   ◆ Latin America and the Caribbean
● East Asia and the Pacific   ▲ Europe and Central Asia

Source: World Bank, based on the World Development Indicators database.

Note: The figures include only countries that are part of the global value chain (GVC) taxonomy (proposed in World Bank [2020b] and further discussed in this chapter) and were eligible for World Bank lending as of 2000. Countries are labeled by ISO alpha-3 code. Total goods exports are made up of commodities, manufactures, and food exports. Commodity exports are agricultural raw materials, fuel, and ores and metals.

a. Panel b excludes Azerbaijan and Kazakhstan. HHI = Herfindahl Hirschman Index of product concentration, with higher indexes reflecting more concentration.

Figure 1.7   Shares of selected sectors in total goods exports, Latin America and the Caribbean and comparator regions, 2018

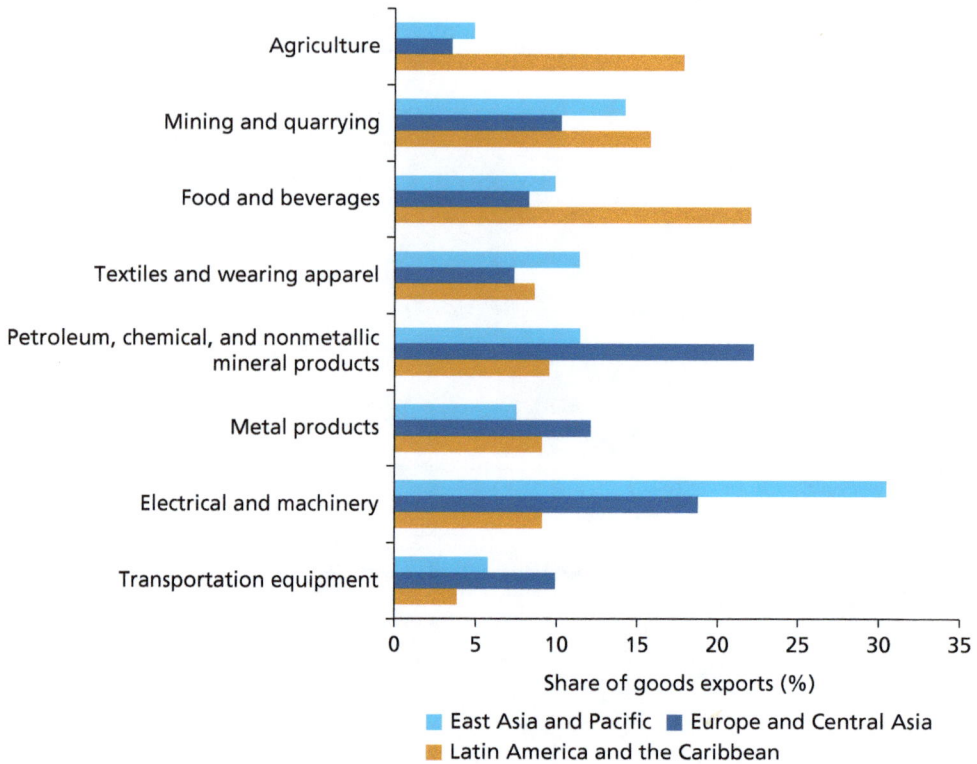

Source: World Bank, based on United Nations Comtrade database, using a Harmonized System 1992–Eora concordance to match Eora global supply chain database sectors.

Note: The figure shows mean average shares across countries and includes only countries that are part of the global value chain (GVC) taxonomy (proposed in World Bank [2020b] and further discussed in this chapter) and were eligible for World Bank lending as of 2000.

Countries specialize mainly in commodity or limited manufacturing GVCs

The *World Development Report 2020* proposed a GVC taxonomy for 146 countries over 1990–2015 that differentiated four types of GVC participation: commodities, limited manufacturing, advanced manufacturing and services, and innovative activities (World Bank 2020b). The classification is based on the extent of GVC participation, the goods and services exported, and measures of innovation.

Latin American and Caribbean countries participate mostly in commodities and limited manufacturing GVCs—except Mexico, which is in the advanced manufacturing and services category—thus contrasting sharply with East Asian and Pacific and European and Central Asian countries, which participate more in noncommodity GVCs (map 1.1). Only a few Latin American and Caribbean countries managed to upgrade to the limited manufacturing group over 1990–2015: Argentina, Costa Rica, and El Salvador (table 1.1).

Map 1.1   Classification of countries by GVC taxonomy, 2015

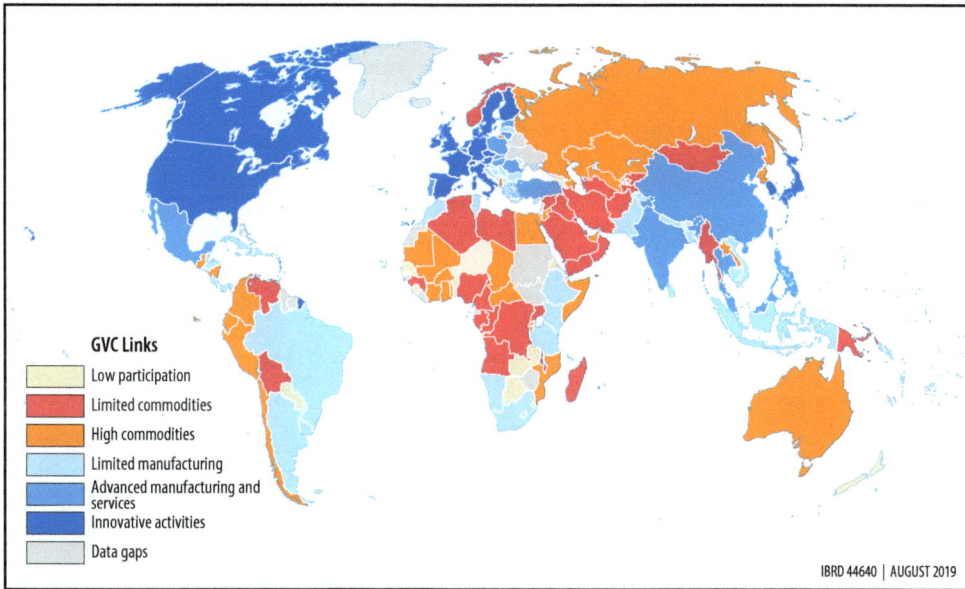

Source: Global value chain (GVC) taxonomy data from World Bank 2020b, 21–23.

Note: The GVC taxonomy developed by the *World Development Report 2020* (World Bank 2020b) differentiated four types of GVC participation: commodities, limited manufacturing, advanced manufacturing and services, and innovative activities. The classification is based on the extent of GVC participation, the goods and services exported, and measures of innovation.

Latin American and Caribbean countries vary in their GVC specialization, making them in some cases more like countries outside the region. Some of the region's countries that specialize in mining exports (such as Chile, Colombia, or Peru) could be likened to commodity exporters such as Australia. Other countries combine a larger agribusiness sector with apparel exports (including Guatemala, Nicaragua, and to a lesser extent, Haiti), which are more like Cambodia, Sri Lanka, and possibly Ethiopia. Argentina and Brazil participate in limited manufacturing GVCs and share some similarities with Indonesia and possibly South Africa. Costa Rica's type of GVC participation (in limited manufacturing) can be likened to that of many East Asian and Pacific or European and Central Asian countries, while Mexico's participation in advanced manufacturing and services GVCs resembles that of Poland or Thailand.

In line with the region's types of GVC specialization, its gross exports of goods and services are not very sophisticated. The average share of high-tech exports—products with high research and development intensity, such as aerospace, computers, pharmaceuticals, scientific instruments, and electrical machinery—is only 8 percent in the region, on par with the Europe and Central Asia average (about 9 percent) but substantially trailing the East Asia and Pacific average (26 percent), as shown in figure 1.8, panel a.

Table 1.1   Latin American and Caribbean countries by GVC taxonomy group, 1990 versus 2015

Country	Taxonomy 1990	Taxonomy 2015
Argentina	commodities	limited manufacturing
Bolivia	commodities	commodities
Brazil	limited manufacturing	limited manufacturing
Chile	commodities	commodities
Colombia	commodities	commodities
Costa Rica	commodities	limited manufacturing
Dominican Republic	limited manufacturing	limited manufacturing
Ecuador	commodities	commodities
El Salvador	commodities	limited manufacturing
Guatemala	commodities	commodities
Haiti	limited manufacturing	limited manufacturing
Honduras	limited manufacturing	limited manufacturing
Jamaica	commodities	commodities
Mexico	advanced manufacturing and services	advanced manufacturing and services
Nicaragua	commodities	commodities
Panama	limited manufacturing	limited manufacturing
Paraguay	commodities	commodities
Peru	commodities	commodities
Trinidad and Tobago	commodities	commodities
Uruguay	limited manufacturing	limited manufacturing
Venezuela, RB	commodities	commodities

Source: Global value chain (GVC) taxonomy data from World Bank 2020b.

Note: The GVC taxonomy developed by the *World Development Report 2020* (World Bank 2020b) differentiated four types of GVC participation: commodities, limited manufacturing, advanced manufacturing and services, and innovative activities. The classification is based on the extent of GVC participation, the goods and services exported, and measures of innovation. Shaded rows designate countries that upgraded their classifications between 1990 and 2015.

The low Latin America and Caribbean share is in line with the low average shares of high-tech exports in countries that specialize in commodity or limited manufacturing GVCs, while countries participating in advanced manufacturing and services GVCs or in innovative activities export larger shares of high-tech goods (figure 1.8, panel b).

Figure 1.8 Shares of high-tech goods and nontravel services in exports, by selected comparator regions and GVC group

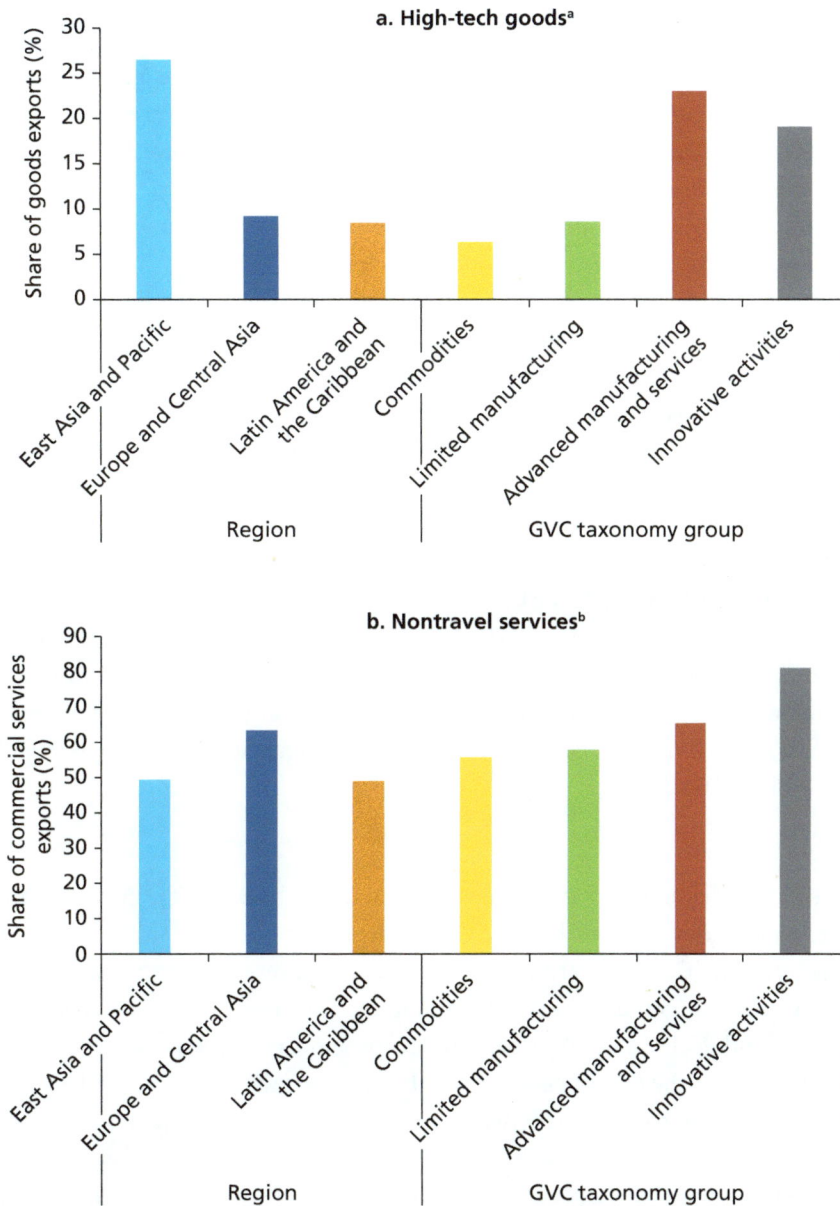

a. High-tech goods[a]

b. Nontravel services[b]

Source: World Bank, based on the World Development Indicators database and global value chain (GVC) taxonomy data from World Bank (2020b).

Note: Data are from 2018 and taxonomy classification from 2015. The figures include 146 countries that are part of the GVC taxonomy (proposed in World Bank [2020b] and further discussed in this chapter) and that were eligible for World Bank lending as of 2000.

a. High-technology exports are products with high research and development intensity, such as in aerospace, computers, pharmaceuticals, scientific instruments, and electrical machinery.

b. Commercial services (denominator) are total services exports minus government services not included elsewhere.

GVC INTEGRATION IN LATIN AMERICA AND THE CARIBBEAN

Backward and forward GVC integration is low

The sectors a country specializes in shape how it integrates into GVCs.[7] Countries specializing in advanced manufacturing and services have the greatest degree of backward GVC participation—the share of imported inputs used in production for export. Countries specializing in commodities have the lowest backward GVC participation. Countries in the limited manufacturing group have more than commodity-specializing countries, while countries in the innovation group have slightly less because they depend less on imported inputs.

Countries with abundant natural resources and agriculture have high forward GVC participation—the share of domestic value added that their bilateral trading partners reexport (rather than consuming it themselves)—typically using the commodities in processes that cross several further borders.[8] Countries in the limited manufacturing group have lower forward GVC participation: though they export commodities less than high commodity exporters, they export manufactured goods—such as garments— unlikely to be inputs for further production and export. Countries in the "advanced manufacturing and services" and "innovation" groups have the highest forward GVC participation (World Bank 2020b).

Both backward and forward GVC participation are linked to economic growth (Constantinescu, Mattoo, and Ruta 2019; Pahl and Timmer 2020; Stolzenburg, Taglioni, and Winkler 2019; World Bank 2020b). The gains are larger for less-developed countries (Pahl and Timmer 2020) and countries that break into limited manufacturing (World Bank 2020b).[9]

Regional comparisons

The Latin America and Caribbean region shows low backward GVC integration on average, which goes hand in hand with its specialization in commodity and limited manufacturing GVCs. Backward GVC participation represented, on average, 16 percent of total exports across the region's countries in 2015, whereas that share was 20 percent in East Asia and Pacific and 30 percent in Europe and Central Asia (figure 1.9, panel a). Latin America and the Caribbean's average backward GVC participation has remained unchanged over the past 15 years, whereas that of Europe and Central Asia increased and that of East Asia and Pacific declined.[10]

Average forward GVC participation in the region was only 19 percent of total exports in 2015, below the 28–29 percent in Europe and Central Asia and East Asia and Pacific (figure 1.9, panel b). The low Latin America and Caribbean average is unexpected, given the large number of countries specialized in commodity GVCs (see table 1.1). It suggests that other countries in the region have very low forward GVC participation, particularly those specialized in limited manufacturing GVCs, which export final rather than intermediate goods, contributing to the region's lower average participation.

Figure 1.9 Forward and backward GVC participation, by region and GVC taxonomy group, 2000 versus 2015

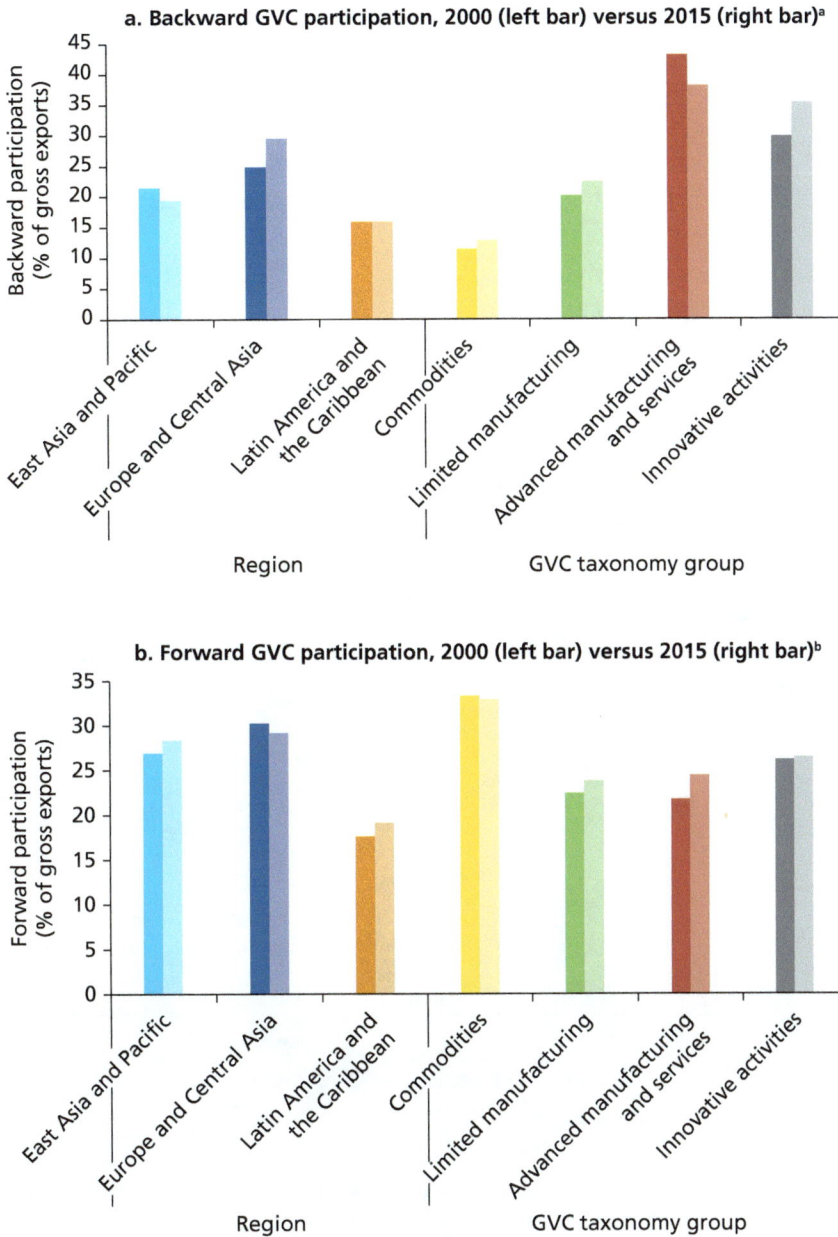

a. Backward GVC participation, 2000 (left bar) versus 2015 (right bar)[a]

b. Forward GVC participation, 2000 (left bar) versus 2015 (right bar)[b]

Source: World Bank, based on Eora global supply chain database (https://worldmrio.com/); Borin and Mancini 2019; World Development Indicators database; and global value chain (GVC) taxonomy data from World Bank 2020b.

Note: The figures show simple averages across countries and include 146 countries that are part of the GVC taxonomy (proposed in World Bank [2020b]) and that were eligible for World Bank lending as of 2000.

a. "Backward GVC participation" refers to the share of imported inputs in a sector's exports.

b. "Forward GVC participation" refers to the share of exports that are inputs for another country's production of exports.

Intraregional comparisons

A detailed look at GVC participation patterns in Latin American and Caribbean countries shows extremely low forward participation but high backward participation for the Dominican Republic, El Salvador, Honduras, Mexico, and Panama, driven by final apparel and transportation goods exports that rely heavily on imported inputs (figure 1.10). The sectors that rely heavily on imported inputs and contribute to such high backward participation are mostly textiles and apparel (in the Dominican Republic, El Salvador, Honduras, and Panama) and electrical and machinery and the transportation sector in Mexico (see annex 1A, figure 1A.4).

Because these sectors embody a large share of final goods exports, they contribute much less to forward GVC participation.[11] In contrast, Bolivia, Brazil, Colombia, Ecuador, Peru, and República Bolivariana de Venezuela exhibit low backward but high forward participation, driven by the large contribution of mining to exports.

Figure 1.10   Backward and forward GVC participation in Latin America and the Caribbean and comparator regions, by country, 2015

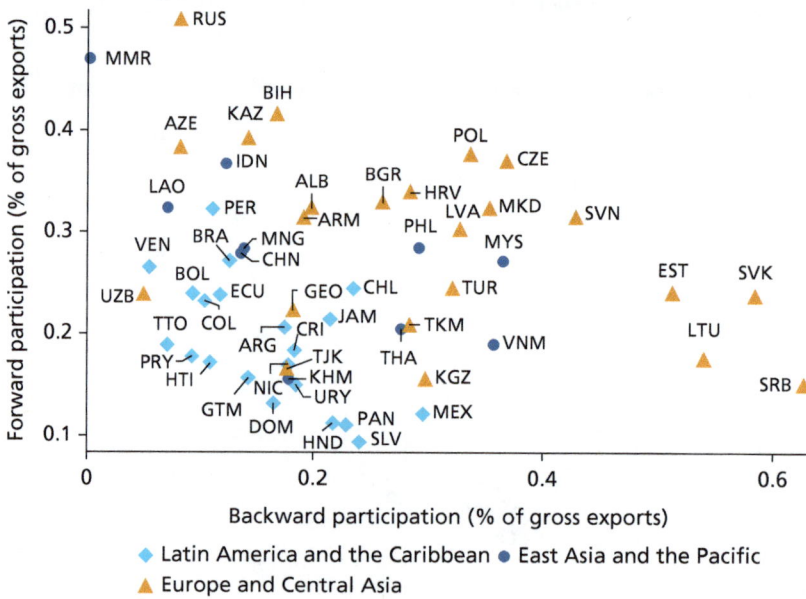

Source: World Bank, based on Eora global supply chain database (https://worldmrio.com/); Borin and Mancini 2019; World Development Indicators database; and global value chain (GVC) taxonomy data from World Bank 2020b.

Note: The figure shows an approximate distribution of backward and forward GVC participation across the four taxonomy groups: commodities, limited manufacturing, advanced manufacturing and services, and innovative activities. Backward GVC participation refers to the share of imported inputs in a sector's exports. Forward GVC participation refers to the share of exports that are inputs for another country's production of exports. The figure includes only countries that are part of the GVC taxonomy and were eligible for World Bank lending as of 2000. Countries are labeled by ISO alpha-3 code.

Argentina, Chile, Costa Rica, and Jamaica exhibit the most balanced GVC participation in the region. Chile and Jamaica are characterized by high backward and forward participation (figure 1.10). Although several sectors contribute to these countries' backward participation (particularly food in Jamaica), their high forward participation can be explained by mining in Chile and metals in Jamaica (see annex 1A, figure 1A.4). Costa Rica and Argentina exhibit medium backward participation—driven by electrical and machinery in the former and by petroleum, chemicals and nonmetallic minerals, and transportation in the latter—while their medium forward participation is driven by a combination of natural resources and manufacturing sectors.

The role of sectoral specialization

Across all sectors, backward GVC participation in Latin America and the Caribbean lags that of East Asia and Pacific and Europe and Central Asia, pointing to the region's specialization in more upstream tasks, such as textiles production as opposed to apparel, or in basic metals as opposed to processed metals. The share of imported inputs in a sector's exports is generally higher in nonfood manufacturing sectors than in agriculture, mining, or services across all regions (figure 1.11, panel a).

Forward GVC participation in Latin America and the Caribbean lags that of Europe and Central Asia and East Asia and Pacific across most sectors, indicating the region's specialization in final goods exports as opposed to intermediate input exports (figure 1.11, panel b). The exceptions are the agriculture, metals, and wholesale trade services sectors, where the Latin American and Caribbean countries are on par with East Asian and Pacific countries in forward GVC participation.

Some sectors in Latin America and the Caribbean saw increased forward and backward GVC participation after 2000: services, agriculture, and food and beverages. Forward GVC participation increased most in financial and business activities, telecommunications services, wholesale trade, and transportation services (see annex 1A, figure 1A.5). Most of these sectors also expanded their backward GVC participation, suggesting a greater reliance on imported inputs and a lower share of final services. Similarly, agriculture and food and beverages simultaneously increased their backward and forward GVC participation after 2000.

Backward GVC participation also expanded after 2000 in metals (by 3 percentage points); apparel; and petroleum, chemicals, and nonmetallic minerals, whereas forward GVC participation remained constant in these sectors. In contrast, transportation equipment saw lower backward and forward GVC participation, and electrical and machinery saw lower forward GVC participation.

In line with Latin America and the Caribbean's sector specialization, a decomposition of overall backward GVC participation by key sector suggests a larger role of food and beverages but a smaller role of electrical and machinery and apparel.

Figure 1.11   Backward and forward GVC participation in Latin America and the Caribbean and selected comparator regions, by sector, 2015

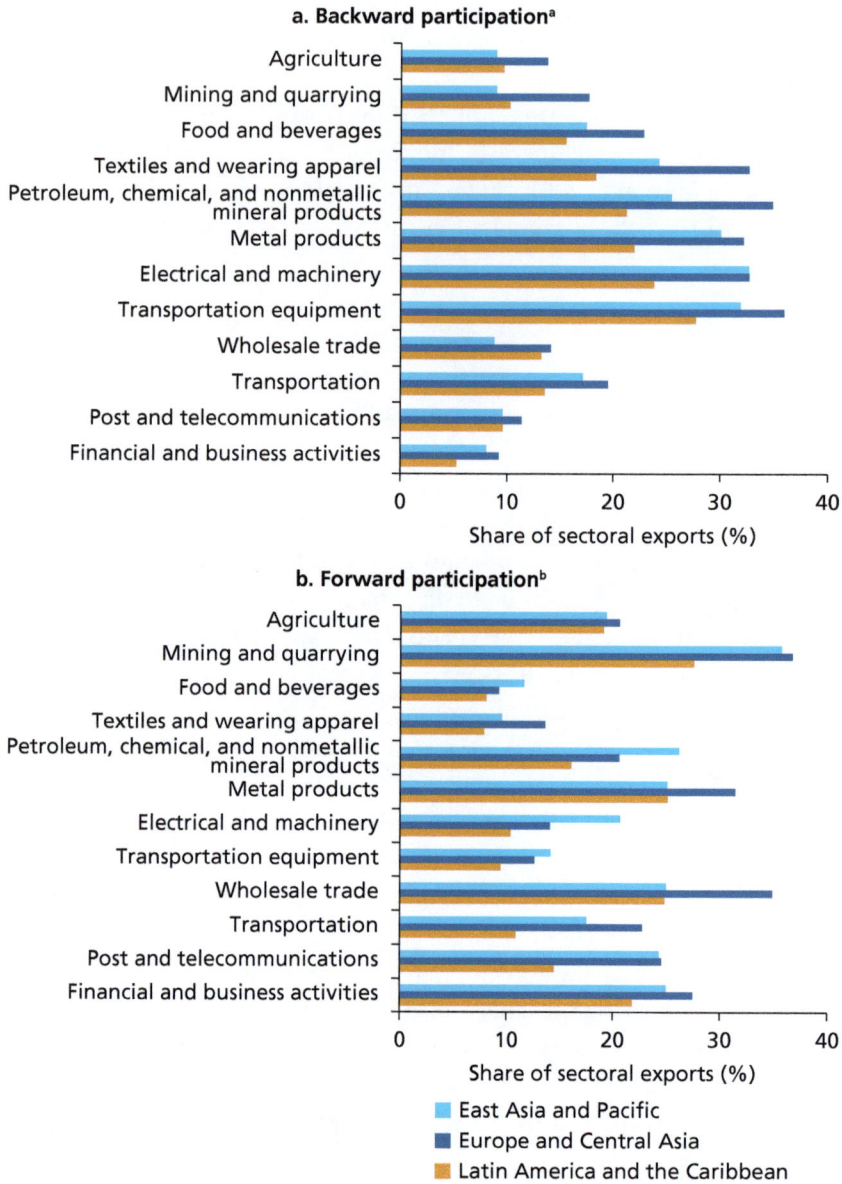

a. Backward participation[a]

Agriculture
Mining and quarrying
Food and beverages
Textiles and wearing apparel
Petroleum, chemical, and nonmetallic mineral products
Metal products
Electrical and machinery
Transportation equipment
Wholesale trade
Transportation
Post and telecommunications
Financial and business activities

Share of sectoral exports (%)

b. Forward participation[b]

Agriculture
Mining and quarrying
Food and beverages
Textiles and wearing apparel
Petroleum, chemical, and nonmetallic mineral products
Metal products
Electrical and machinery
Transportation equipment
Wholesale trade
Transportation
Post and telecommunications
Financial and business activities

Share of sectoral exports (%)

■ East Asia and Pacific
■ Europe and Central Asia
■ Latin America and the Caribbean

Source: World Bank, based on Eora global supply chain database (https://worldmrio.com/); Borin and Mancini 2019; World Development Indicators database; and global value chain (GVC) taxonomy data from World Bank 2020b.

Note: The figures show simple averages across countries and include only countries that are part of the GVC taxonomy and were eligible for World Bank lending as of 2000.

a. Backward GVC participation refers to the use of imported inputs in production for export.

b. Forward GVC participation refers to the export of inputs used in production for the importing country's exports.

Imported inputs used in the electrical and machinery sector represent only 2 percent of the region's total exports, compared with 4.1 percent in Europe and Central Asia and 6.6 percent in East Asia and Pacific (figure 1.12, panel a). Imported inputs used in apparel represent only 2.5 percent of Latin America and the Caribbean's total exports, below the roughly 3.5 percent in East Asia and Pacific and Europe and Central Asia. The contribution of imported inputs to metals is also smaller in Latin America and the Caribbean than in Europe and Central Asia, as are the contributions of imported inputs in other sectors. By contrast, the contribution of imported inputs to the food and beverages sector in total backward GVC participation is larger in Latin America and the Caribbean than in its comparator regions. Traditional wholesale and transportation services contribute the largest portion to backward GVC participation in Europe and Central Asia, followed by Latin America and the Caribbean and East Asia and Pacific.

As for forward GVC participation, domestic value added created in agriculture and mining that is reexported by Latin America and the Caribbean's bilateral trading partners contributes 1.6 percent and 3.3 percent, respectively, to the region's total exports, compared with 1.2 percent and 2.5 percent, respectively, in Europe and Central Asia (figure 1.12, panel b). These sectors' contribution is even higher in East Asia and Pacific. The lower contribution of manufacturing and services to forward GVC participation in Latin America and the Caribbean than in Europe and Central Asia reflects the former region's sectoral specialization in exports of commodities and in final goods and services.

GVC participation at the firm level is linked to better export performance

In practice, it is not countries or industries that trade but firms (World Bank 2020b). Customs datasets containing information on firms' export and import transactions can be used to construct measures of GVC participation parallel to those based on the country and industry information in global input-output tables.

A firm is defined as "GVC participating" if it is an exporter-importer—that is, it exports some products and imports intermediate inputs or capital goods. Such a firm is using foreign value added in its production destined for export. This definition is the micro analog of the definition of backward GVC participation at the country or at the country and industry level.[12] Exporter-only firms, in contrast, export some products but do not import inputs or capital goods.

The importance of GVC participating firms in the total number of exporters is highly variable across Latin American and Caribbean countries but is often lower than in Europe and Central Asia (figure 1.13, panel a). El Salvador, Paraguay, and Uruguay exhibit the largest shares of GVC participating firms (about 60 percent) whereas Chile, Ecuador, and Peru exhibit the lowest shares (just under 40 percent). European and Central Asian countries exhibit substantially higher shares.

Figure 1.12   Decomposition of sectoral contributions to backward and forward GVC participation in Latin America and the Caribbean and comparator regions, 2015

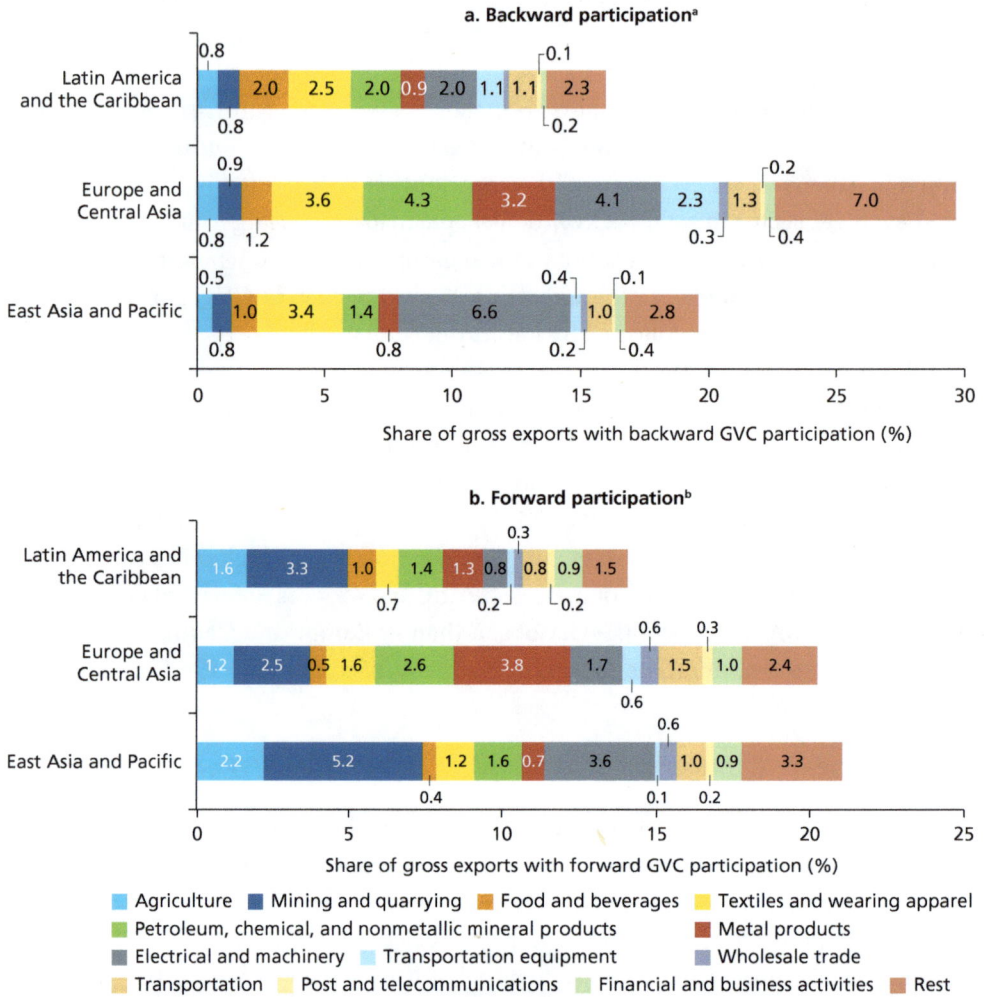

a. Backward participation[a]

b. Forward participation[b]

Agriculture — Mining and quarrying — Food and beverages — Textiles and wearing apparel — Petroleum, chemical, and nonmetallic mineral products — Metal products — Electrical and machinery — Transportation equipment — Wholesale trade — Transportation — Post and telecommunications — Financial and business activities — Rest

Source: World Bank, based on Eora global supply chain database (https://worldmrio.com/); Borin and Mancini 2019; World Development Indicators database; and global value chain (GVC) taxonomy data from World Bank 2020b.

Note: The figures include only countries that are part of the GVC taxonomy and were eligible for World Bank lending as of 2000. "Rest" refers to "rest of the sectors." For country-specific sectoral contributions, see annex 1A, figure 1A.4.

a. Backward GVC participation refers to the use of imported inputs in production for export.

b. Forward GVC participation refers to the export of inputs used in production for the importing country's exports.

Figure 1.13 Share of exporters and average size of GVC participating firms in selected Latin America and Caribbean and comparator countries

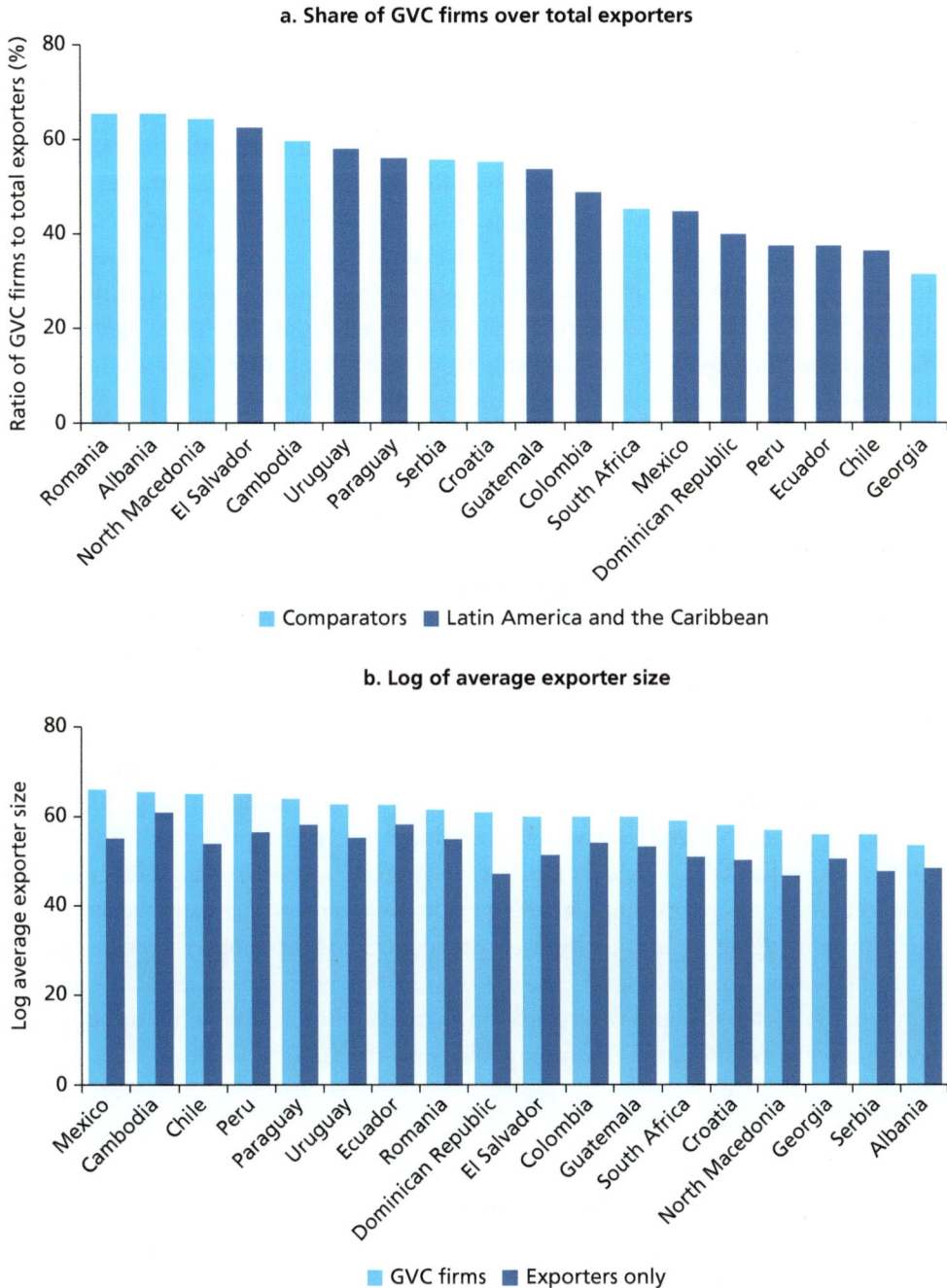

a. Share of GVC firms over total exporters

Comparators ■ Latin America and the Caribbean

b. Log of average exporter size

■ GVC firms ■ Exporters only

Source: Updates to World Bank's Exporter Dynamics Database (described in Fernandes, Freund, and Pierola 2016).

Note: A "GVC participating" firm is an exporter-importer—that is, it exports some products and imports intermediate inputs or capital goods. The figures show averages for available years in 2015–19, except for Guatemala and Romania, whose averages are for available years in 2010–14. GVC = global value chain.

GVC participating firms are substantially larger than exporter-only firms in Latin America and the Caribbean and elsewhere (figure 1.13, panel b). For example, in Peru, GVC participating firms have average annual exports almost six times as large as those of exporter-only firms.[13]

GVC participating firms are also more diversified in products and markets than exporter-only firms in both Latin American and Caribbean and comparator countries. But although GVC participating firms export more products and to more destinations than exporter-only firms in all regions, the differences are much smaller in Latin America and the Caribbean than in comparator countries (figure 1.14, panel a).

Ecuador is an outlier in market diversification, because its GVC participating firms export to close to four markets on average while its exporter-only firms serve six (figure 1.14, panel b). GVC participating firms are substantially more likely to survive in export markets than exporter-only firms in all Latin American and Caribbean countries (except Ecuador) as well as in comparator countries.

GVC links are robustly linked to better exporter performance in a two-way relationship. GVC firms are more productive, employ more workers, and have higher capital intensity than firms that only export or only import (World Bank 2020b). The advantages of GVC links for average exporter size, product and destination diversification, and survival in export markets for the sample of countries are confirmed in regressions finding that GVC participating firms enjoy premiums on these indicators. (The regressions control for comparative advantage differences, country business cycles, and global technological or demand shocks affecting sectors differentially.)[14]

The premium on exporter destination diversification is higher in Latin America and the Caribbean than in comparator countries elsewhere. But GVC participating firms also perform better as a result of importing inputs and capital goods.[15] Evidence for Peru shows that GVC participating firms relying on more-varied and higher-quality imported intermediates exhibit higher export levels and growth, greater market diversification, and higher export quality, even after controlling for unobserved firm heterogeneity (Pierola, Fernandes, and Farole 2018). Firm-level regressions for the sample show that exporter size and diversification increase when firms switch to becoming GVC participants (instead of continuing to be exporters only).

Patterns of GVC participation and links with trade performance

Four types of GVC participation in Latin America and the Caribbean can be categorized by the extent of backward relative to forward GVC participation: backward, balanced, forward, and low (table 1.2). Whereas both the "backward" and "balanced" groups have medium-to-high backward GVC participation, the "backward" group has low forward GVC participation, and the "balanced" group has medium-to-high forward GVC participation. The "forward" group shows high forward but low backward

Figure 1.14   Average number of products and destinations of GVC participating firms relative to exporter-only firms in selected Latin American and Caribbean and comparator countries

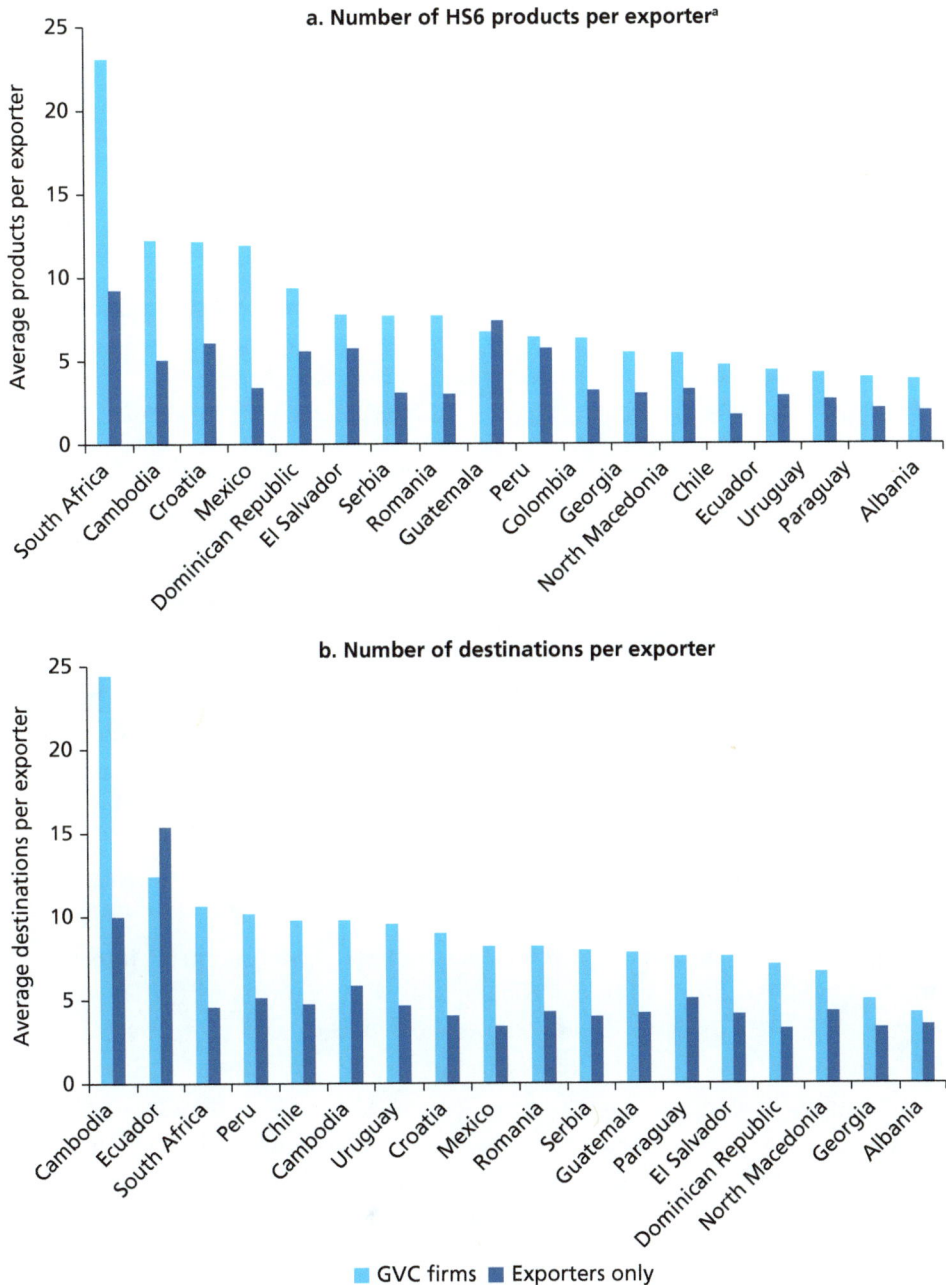

a. Number of HS6 products per exporter[a]

y-axis: Average products per exporter (0–25)

Countries (left to right): South Africa, Cambodia, Croatia, Mexico, Dominican Republic, El Salvador, Serbia, Romania, Guatemala, Peru, Colombia, Georgia, North Macedonia, Chile, Ecuador, Uruguay, Paraguay, Albania

b. Number of destinations per exporter

y-axis: Average destinations per exporter (0–25)

Countries (left to right): Cambodia, Ecuador, South Africa, Peru, Chile, Cambodia, Uruguay, Croatia, Mexico, Romania, Serbia, Guatemala, Paraguay, El Salvador, Dominican Republic, North Macedonia, Georgia, Albania

■ GVC firms   ■ Exporters only

Source: Updates to Exporter Dynamics Database (described in Fernandes, Freund, and Pierola 2016).

Note: The figures show averages for available years in 2015–19, except for Guatemala and Romania, whose averages are for available years in 2010–14.

a. Products are classified according to the international Harmonized System (HS). HS6 refers to HS classification at the six-digit code level. GVC = global value chain.

Table 1.2   Types of GVC participation in Latin America and the Caribbean

Type	Backward GVC participation	Forward GVC participation	Countries	GVC taxonomy groups
Backward	Medium to high	Low	Dominican Republic, El Salvador, Honduras, Mexico, and Panama	• Limited manufacturing • Advanced manufacturing and services
Balanced	Medium to high	Medium to high	Argentina, Brazil, Chile, Costa Rica, Jamaica, Nicaragua, and Uruguay	• Limited manufacturing • Commodities
Forward	Low	High	Bolivia, Colombia, Ecuador, Peru, and Venezuela, RB	• Commodities
Low	Low	Low	Guatemala, Haiti, Paraguay, and Trinidad and Tobago	• Mainly commodities

Source: World Bank, including global value chain (GVC) taxonomy data from World Bank 2020b.

Note: Backward GVC participation refers to the share of imported inputs in a sector's exports. Forward GVC participation refers to the share of exports that are inputs for another country's production of exports. The 21 countries in the study's Latin America and Caribbean study sample include those that are part of the GVC taxonomy and were eligible for World Bank lending as of 2000.

GVC participation, while the "low" group shows both low backward and low forward GVC participation.

Countries experiencing high trade growth can be found in all four GVC participation groups (see annex 1A, table 1A.1). Countries with stronger trade performance—that is, those with high trade openness, a large number of exporters, and larger exporters—tend to be classified within the backward or balanced groups. Higher backward GVC participation was associated with lower export declines during the early phases of the COVID-19 pandemic, whereas the link of exports with forward GVC participation varied over time (box 1.1).

Export diversification is high (concentration is low) in countries in the backward and balanced groups (except Nicaragua), while exports in the forward and low groups are less diversified. Similarly, export sophistication[16] and the share of high-tech goods in total goods exports are high for countries in the backward and balanced groups but low for countries in the forward and low groups (see annex 1A, table 1A.1). These findings suggest that higher shares of imported inputs in a country's exports are linked to more diversification and sophistication. But there is no clear-cut pattern for export survival, which seems to also depend strongly on other domestic factors.

Box 1.1   Export growth in relation to GVC participation during the COVID-19 pandemic

Forward GVC participation

Latin American and Caribbean countries with higher forward global value chain (GVC) participation saw lower export growth in the first quarter of 2020, possibly reflecting severe lockdown policies in response to COVID-19 in third countries that use inputs from the region. During the first quarter of 2020, average annualized export growth fell across most countries in the East Asia and Pacific, Europe and Central Asia, and Latin America and the Caribbean regions (figure B1.1.1, panel a). As indicated by the negative bivariate regression line, lockdowns and reduced production in third countries seem to have affected Latin American and Caribbean countries with higher forward GVC participation more strongly—notably Bolivia, Brazil, Colombia, Jamaica, Peru, and República Bolivariana de Venezuela. Export growth declined less in countries with low forward GVC participation, including the Dominican Republic, Honduras, Mexico, Panama, and to lesser extent, El Salvador.

But the relationship between forward GVC participation and export growth turned positive during the second quarter of 2020, reflecting falling demand from consumer markets for final goods exports (figure B1.1.1, panel b). Although the relationship between forward GVC participation and export growth became positive (as shown by the positive bivariate regression line), this was not driven by a trade recovery in countries with high forward GVC participation (figure B1.1.1, panels a and b). In fact, Bolivia, Colombia, Ecuador, Peru, and República Bolivariana de Venezuela continued to show large drops in export growth.

Countries that specialized in final goods exports with low forward GVC participation—including the Dominican Republic, El Salvador, Honduras, and Mexico—experienced even larger declines in export growth, which could reflect falling demand from important consumer markets. Brazil, Chile, and Jamaica fared better, possibly because of their more diversified export baskets.

Backward GVC participation

Latin American and Caribbean countries with higher backward GVC participation experienced higher export growth, though the most GVC-integrated countries suffered more as the pandemic progressed during the second quarter of 2020. A recent study shows that backward participation in GVCs increased exporting countries' vulnerability to foreign shocks during the COVID-19 pandemic, but it also reduced vulnerability to domestic shocks (Espitia et al. 2021).

The relationship between export growth and backward GVC participation across the region's countries was positive during both the earlier and later phase of the pandemic, as implied by the positive bivariate regression lines (figures B1.1.1, panels c and d). However, the dispersion was larger during the second quarter of 2020, with the most integrated countries—El Salvador, Honduras, and Mexico—showing export declines almost like those of countries with low backward GVC participation, including Bolivia, Colombia, and Haiti. This suggests that countries highly integrated into GVCs became more vulnerable to foreign shocks in the first half of 2020.

Continued

Box 1.1   Export growth in relation to GVC participation during the COVID-19 pandemic (*continued*)

Figure B1.1.1   Growth of exports to selected major markets in January–June 2020 in relation to forward and backward GVC participation of countries in Latin America and the Caribbean and comparator regions

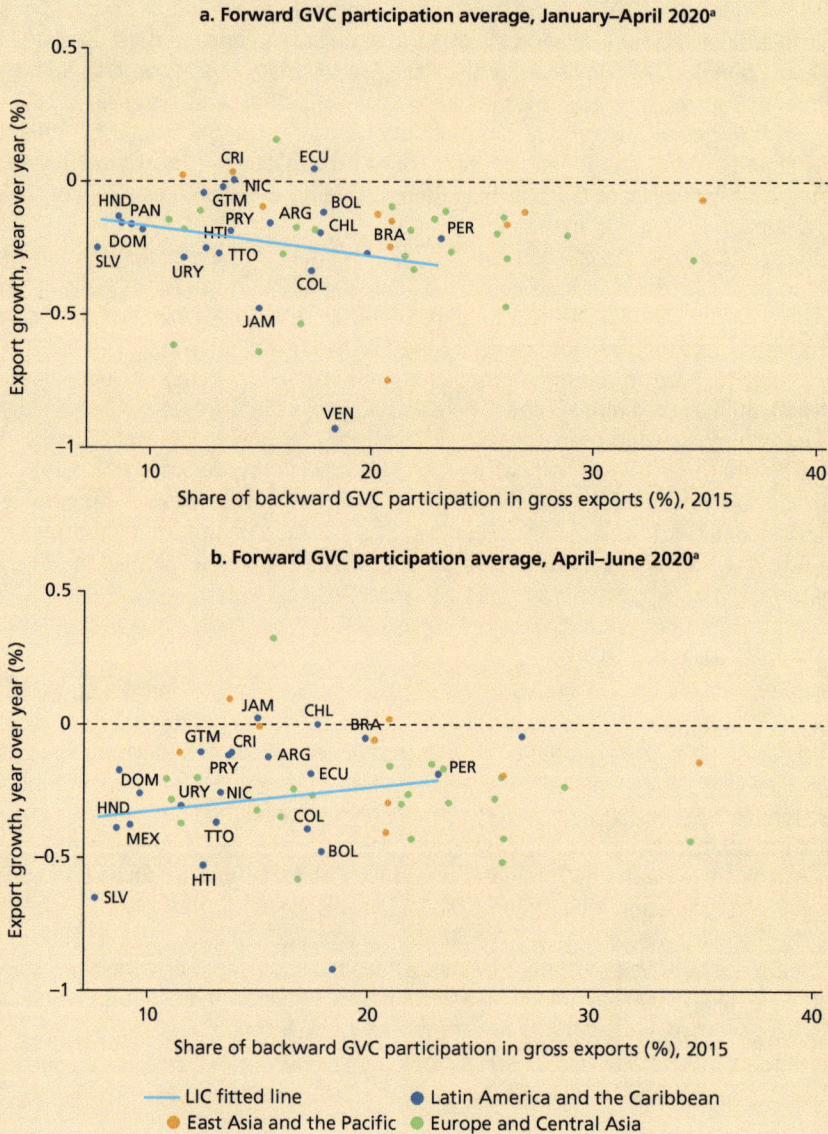

a. Forward GVC participation average, January–April 2020[a]

b. Forward GVC participation average, April–June 2020[a]

Continued

Figure B1.1.1 Growth of exports to selected major markets in January–June 2020 in relation to forward and backward GVC participation of countries in Latin America and the Caribbean and comparator regions *(continued)*

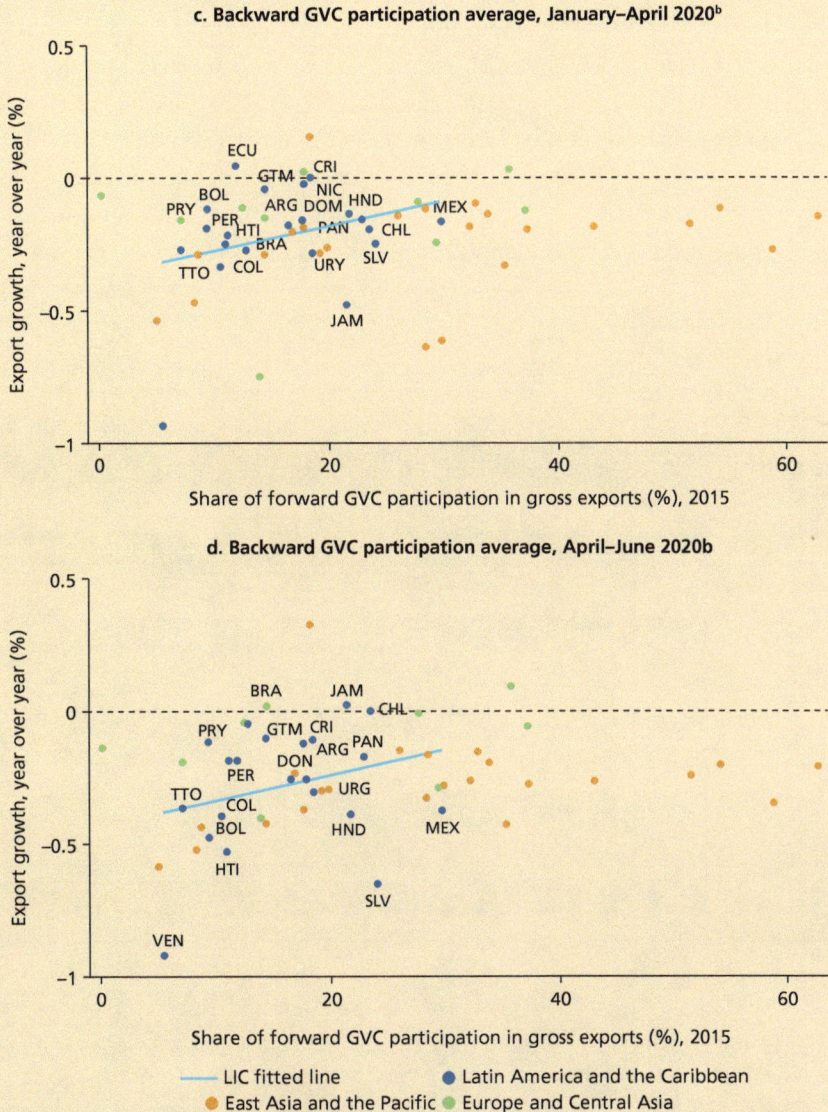

c. Backward GVC participation average, January–April 2020[b]

d. Backward GVC participation average, April–June 2020b

Source: World Bank computations, based on customs data for China, Eurostat data for the European Union (excluding Cyprus and the United Kingdom), Ministry of Finance data for Japan, and US International Trade Commission data for the United States (World Bank 2020a).

Note: Selected major markets are China, the European Union, Japan, and the United States. Export growth is measured as the average change, year over year, in the total exports of each country to those four destinations combined. The export growth data are from the specified three-month periods in 2020, whereas data on countries' forward or backward GVC participation are from 2015. The figure includes only countries that are part of the GVC taxonomy and were eligible for World Bank lending as of 2000. Countries are labeled by ISO alpha-3 code. GVC = global value chain.

a. Forward GVC participation refers to the share of exports that are inputs for another country's production of exports.

b. Backward GVC participation refers to the share of imported inputs in a sector's exports

THE MAIN SOURCE AND DESTINATION REGIONS FOR LATIN AMERICAN AND CARIBBEAN TRADE

Countries source a lower share of imported inputs from within the region

Intraregional imported inputs make up around two-thirds of such inputs in the Europe and Central Asia region and more than 60 percent in the East Asia and Pacific region, but only 14 percent in Latin America and the Caribbean, reflecting the absence of a regional GVC hub (figure 1.15).[17] Even if imported inputs sourced from the Latin America and Caribbean region and from North America were combined, the 43 percent share would be lower than in comparator regions.

Latin America and the Caribbean's greater dependence on extraregional inputs reflects the absence of a regional GVC hub and the fact that only Mexico and a few Central American countries depend on imported inputs from the United States, while

Figure 1.15   Distribution of total imported inputs in exports, by source region, 2005 versus 2015

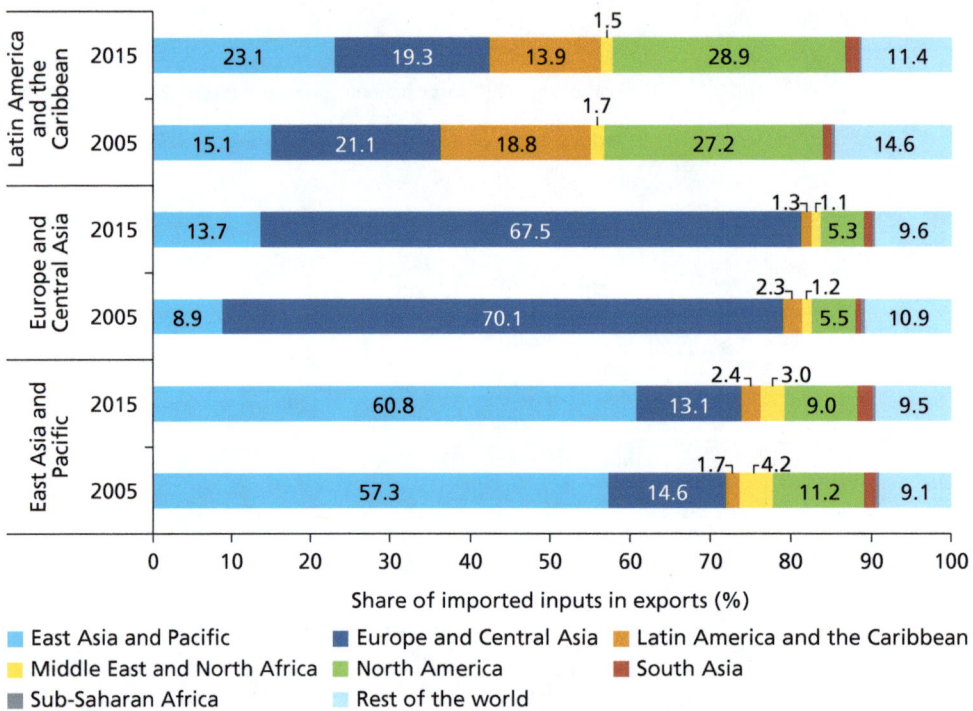

Share of imported inputs in exports (%)

- ■ East Asia and Pacific
- ■ Europe and Central Asia
- ■ Latin America and the Caribbean
- ■ Middle East and North Africa
- ■ North America
- ■ South Asia
- ■ Sub-Saharan Africa
- ■ Rest of the world

Source: World Bank, based on the Trade in Value Added (TiVA) database of the Organisation for Economic Co-operation and Development.

Note: The figure shows simple averages of the distribution across countries and includes only TiVA countries that are part of the global value chain (GVC taxonomy) and were eligible for World Bank lending as of 2000. Source regions include only 64 TiVA countries. Source countries that are missing from the TiVA database are classified as "rest of the world." "Latin America and Caribbean" covers only seven countries: Argentina, Brazil, Chile, Colombia, Costa Rica, Mexico, and Peru.

all European and Central Asian countries depend strongly on Europe (centered on Germany) and all East Asian and Pacific countries rely strongly on Asia (centered on China) as sources for imported inputs.

At the firm level, GVC participating firms in Latin America and the Caribbean depend much less on intraregional markets as sources of inputs and capital goods than their Europe and Central Asia comparators do. GVC participating firms in Chile, Colombia, the Dominican Republic, Ecuador, El Salvador, Guatemala, Peru, and Uruguay import 12–51 percent of their intermediate inputs and capital goods from the Latin America and Caribbean region (figure 1.16).

Mexico stands out for its extremely low sourcing from intraregional markets (only 5 percent of imports) owing to its strong GVC integration with the United States (which belongs to the "rest of the world" category in figure 1.16). Paraguay stands out for its much higher intraregional dependence, but even its 51 percent share of intermediate inputs and capital goods sourced from intraregional markets pales against the 77–92 percent sourced by GVC participating firms in Europe and Central Asia.

Countries also depend much less on intraregional destination markets

The share of domestic value added exported to intraregional markets in 2015 was still less than 38 percent in the Latin America and Caribbean region and is much higher in Europe and Central Asia at 82 percent and in East Asia and Pacific at 63 percent (figure 1.17). The low share of intraregional markets reflects the absence of large consumer markets in geographic proximity to the Latin America and Caribbean region (except Mexico), while European and Central Asian countries benefit from the European Union (EU) market and East Asian and Pacific countries from their proximity to large consumer markets in China, Japan, and the Republic of Korea. But if Latin America and the Caribbean and North America are combined to capture the large US consumer market, two-thirds of Latin American and Caribbean exports are accounted for. The share of intraregional markets increased by 6 percentage points between 2000 and 2015 in the Latin America and Caribbean region and now exceeds that of North America, whose role as export destination sharply declined. The share of intraregional export markets also expanded in East Asia and Pacific at the expense of export shares to North America (and, to a lesser extent, to Europe and Central Asia).

For exporter-only and GVC participating firms in Mexico, the Latin America and Caribbean region accounts for less than 27 percent of their exports. But intraregional markets account for more than half the exports of GVC participating firms in Colombia, El Salvador, Guatemala, Paraguay, Peru, and Uruguay. Whereas in Europe and Central Asia the intraregional market dominates as the destination for any type of exporter, intraregional markets are more important for GVC participating firms than exporter-only firms in all Latin American and Caribbean countries.

Figure 1.16   Sources of imported inputs for GVC participating firms in Latin American and Caribbean countries and selected European and Central Asian countries

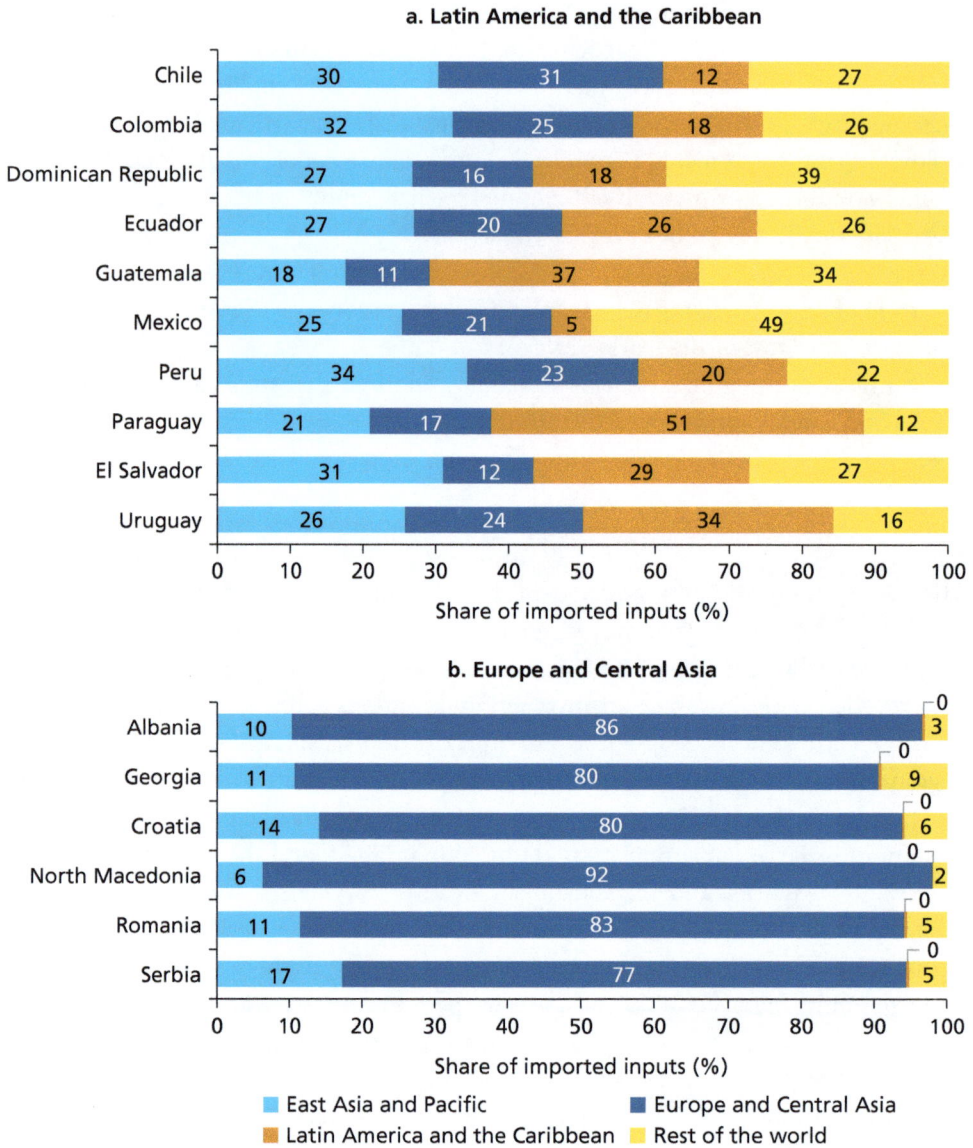

a. Latin America and the Caribbean

Country	East Asia and Pacific	Europe and Central Asia	Latin America and the Caribbean	Rest of the world
Chile	30	31	12	27
Colombia	32	25	18	26
Dominican Republic	27	16	18	39
Ecuador	27	20	26	26
Guatemala	18	11	37	34
Mexico	25	21	5	49
Peru	34	23	20	22
Paraguay	21	17	51	12
El Salvador	31	12	29	27
Uruguay	26	24	34	16

Share of imported inputs (%)

b. Europe and Central Asia

Country	East Asia and Pacific	Europe and Central Asia	Latin America and the Caribbean	Rest of the world
Albania	10	86	0	3
Georgia	11	80	0	9
Croatia	14	80	0	6
North Macedonia	6	92	0	2
Romania	11	83	0	5
Serbia	17	77	0	5

Share of imported inputs (%)

- ■ East Asia and Pacific
- ■ Europe and Central Asia
- ■ Latin America and the Caribbean
- ■ Rest of the world

Source: Updates to World Bank's Exporter Dynamics database (described in Fernandes, Freund, and Pierola 2016).

Note: For each country, shares of imported inputs and capital goods are computed based on the most recent year of customs data. GVC = global value chain.

Figure 1.17 Distribution of total domestic value added in exports, by partner region, 2000 versus 2015

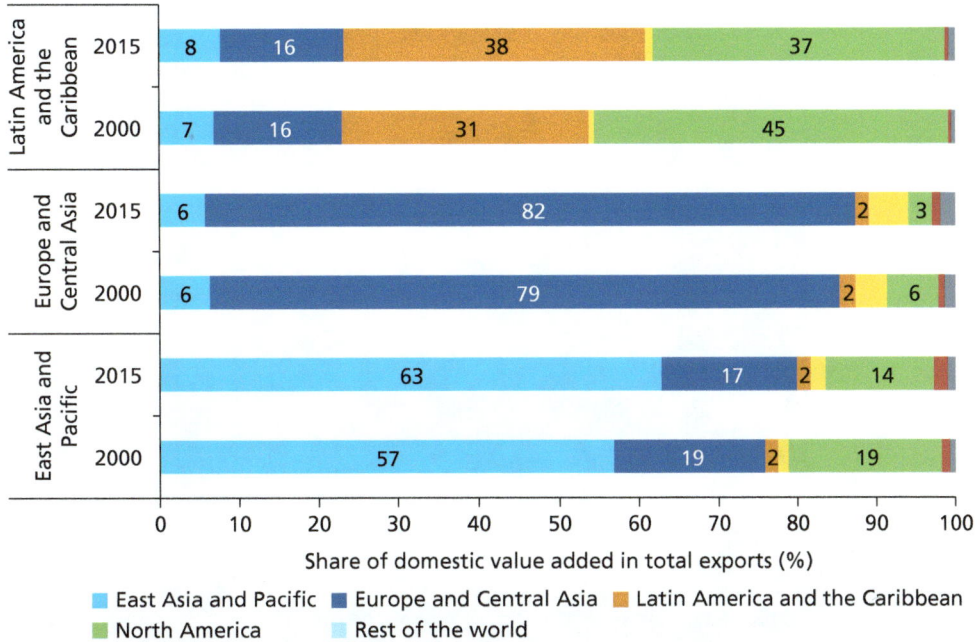

Source: World Bank, based on the Eora global supply chain database (https://worldmrio.com/).

Note: The figure shows simple averages of the distribution across countries and includes only countries that are part of the global value chain (GVC) taxonomy and were eligible for World Bank lending as of 2000. Partner regions include all countries.

WHAT DETERMINES GVC PARTICIPATION?

GVC participation is determined by four fundamentals: geography, market size, factor endowments, and institutions. Latin America and the Caribbean is disadvantaged in the first three (World Bank 2020b).

Fundamentals of GVC participation

Geography. Longer distances to the major GVC hubs—China, Germany, and the United States—greatly reduce both backward and forward GVC participation (Fernandes, Kee, and Winkler 2020). Latin America and the Caribbean is, on average, more than 29,000 kilometers from the major GVC hubs, farther than any other region (table 1.3). In contrast, Europe and Central Asia is, on average, 17,000 kilometers from those hubs. Although East Asian and Pacific countries are also far from major GVC hubs, many of them are connected to Asian manufacturing countries and the GVC hubs in China and Japan—the high average of their distance to GVC hubs—28,383 kilometers—is biased by their great distance to the United States. Countries specializing in advanced

Table 1.3 Fundamental GVC participation determinants using selected indicators, by region and taxonomy group, 2010–15

Region or taxonomy group	Geography	Market size	Endowments			Institutions
	Distance to GVC hubs (km)	Manufacturing value added (US$, billions)	Rents from natural resources (% of GDP)	Labor costs[a] (US$)	Capital stock or GDP (logs)	Political stability index[b]
Lending-eligible region						
East Asia and Pacific	28,383	6.0	7.7	4,495	−11.8	−0.16
Europe and Central Asia	16,951	5.7	7.2	9,855	−12.0	−0.23
Latin America and the Caribbean	29,089	4.8	6.7	8,356	−12.0	−0.17
Middle East and North Africa	19,837	7.4	13.3	6,515	−11.8	−1.31
South Asia	23,064	4.1	1.7	4,217	−11.7	−1.05
Sub-Saharan Africa	27,583	0.8	13.7	3,084	−12.0	−0.55
GVC taxonomy group						
Commodities	25,233	2.9	15.9	8,807	−12.1	−0.58
Limited manufacturing	24,288	6.1	3.0	11,530	−11.8	−0.31
Advanced manufacturing and services	19,545	45.0	2.0	16,192	−12.0	0.08
Innovative activities	16,865	140.6	0.5	53,203	−12.4	0.76

Sources: World Bank, based on Center for Prospective Studies and International Information (CEPII) data; Penn World Table 9.0 data from data from Feenstra, Inklaar, and Timmer 2015; World Development Indicators; World Governance Indicators, and global value chain (GVC) taxonomy data from World Bank (2020b).

Note: Simple averages shown cover the period 2010–15. Dark blue shading designates the highest value in that part of a column; dark red, the lowest value; and lighter shades, intermediate values. In each region, averages are based only on World Bank client countries. The listed (regional and taxonomy) groups include only countries that were eligible for World Bank lending as of 2000 and are part of the Eora global supply chain database (https://worldmrio.com/). GVC = global value chain; km = kilometer.

a. Labor costs were obtained by multiplying a country's (deflated) gross domestic product (GDP) by its labor share and dividing by the number of employees.

b. Political stability (and absence of violence and terrorism) index values are from the World Bank's Worldwide Governance Indicators, measuring perceptions of the likelihood of political instability or politically motivated violence, including terrorism. The estimate gives the country's score on the aggregate indicator, in units of a standard normal distribution (ranging from approximately −2.5 to 2.5).

manufacturing and services or innovative GVCs, by contrast, show a lower geographical distance to the GVC hubs.

Market size. Countries with larger domestic markets have a larger industrial capacity and are thus less likely to use imported inputs in their exports, reducing backward GVC participation, while they are also characterized by higher forward GVC participation (Fernandes, Kee, and Winkler 2020). The size of the manufacturing sector in Latin America and the Caribbean fell into the middle range between 2010 and 2015, at US$4.8 billion. Although that is larger than the markets in South Asia and especially in Sub-Saharan Africa, it is smaller than those in the Europe and Central Asia and East Asia and Pacific regions as well as those in countries specializing in limited manufacturing GVCs (table 1.3).

Factor endowments. Factor endowments strongly matter for a country's GVC participation. Around the world, stronger endowments of land and abundant extractive resources (such as copper, iron ore, and other minerals) are linked to higher forward participation (Fernandes, Kee, and Winkler 2020). In countries specializing in commodities, 16 percent of GDP originated from natural resources between 2010 and 2015 (table 1.3). In Latin America and the Caribbean, that share was 6.7 percent—substantially lower than the shares in Sub-Saharan Africa or the Middle East and North Africa, where average rents from natural resources exceed 13 percent of GDP, but more than four times the average share in countries worldwide specializing in limited manufacturing GVCs.

Abundant low-cost labor in lower-income countries is often an entry point for participation in the labor-intensive manufacturing segments of GVCs, as suggested by the low annual labor costs of less than US$12,000 for countries specialized in limited manufacturing GVCs over 2010–15 (table 1.3). But upgrading skills becomes necessary for integrating into more complex GVCs, as reflected in increasing labor costs as GVC taxonomy groups ascend from commodities to advanced manufacturing and services.

Although average annual labor costs in the Latin America and Caribbean region are only around US$8,400 (excluding countries ineligible for World Bank lending), that is the second highest regional average globally, below Europe and Central Asia's but almost twice East Asia and Pacific's. Similarly, whereas higher capital endowments stimulate backward GVC participation—so they matter especially for countries in the limited manufacturing GVC group—the Latin America and Caribbean region shows the lowest capital stock in relation to GDP (Fernandes, Kee, and Winkler 2020), as shown in table 1.3.

Services matter at all stages of GVC participation but become increasingly important once countries move from limited manufacturing GVC activities to advanced manufacturing and services and especially to innovative GVC activities. Inefficient transportation and logistics services and weak competition in these services amplify trade costs in many manufacturing GVCs with multiple border crossings—and can offset other competitive advantages such as low labor costs. Better logistics performance is related to higher backward GVC participation, as is a higher internet density (World Bank 2020b).

Institutions. Finally, institutional quality matters for the type of GVC participation. Greater political stability enhances backward GVC participation and lowers forward GVC participation (Fernandes, Kee, and Winkler 2020). Stability is also important for foreign direct investment, which often acts as a catalyst for GVC entry. Upgrading along the GVC taxonomy is associated with higher political stability (table 1.3).

Among countries eligible for World Bank lending, the Latin America and Caribbean region performs fairly well on political stability, on par with the East Asia and Pacific region and lagging only the Europe and Central Asia region.

Ways forward for Latin America and the Caribbean

In sum, Latin America and the Caribbean is disadvantaged by its geographical distance from GVC hubs, average domestic market size, and endowments of low-skilled labor and capital. It obtains only a medium-average share of GDP from natural resources. These characteristics, along with the region's sectoral specialization in commodities and food exports, explain the region's low backward GVC participation, on average, and several Latin American and Caribbean countries' high forward GVC participation, though different patterns exist within the region.

Latin America and the Caribbean has not fully taken advantage of policy options that could help it overcome disadvantages and upgrade its GVC participation. Trade agreements in the EU and the Association of Southeast Asian Nations (ASEAN) have fostered backward GVC participation, but Southern Common Market (MERCOSUR) membership has not (Fernandes, Kee, and Winkler 2020; World Bank 2020b).

Deep trade agreements present an avenue to overcome geographical remoteness, expand effective market size, and increase access to imported services that could support GVC participation and upgrading in Latin America and the Caribbean. They can also improve domestic institutions by importing reforms and technical and financial assistance, further strengthening GVC participation.

ANNEX 1A SUPPLEMENTARY FIGURES AND TABLES

Figure 1A.1   Exports and imports of goods and services as a share of GDP in Latin America and the Caribbean and comparator regions, by country, 2018

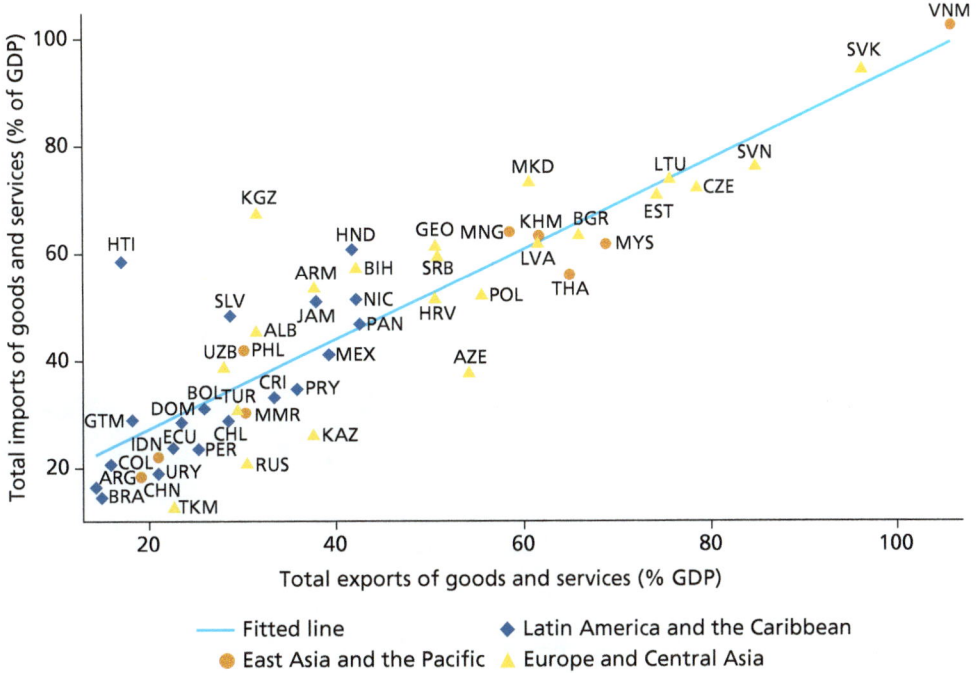

Source: World Bank, based on World Development Indicators database.

Note: The figure includes only countries that are part of the GVC taxonomy and are eligible for World Bank lending. Countries are labeled by ISO alpha-3 code. GDP = gross domestic product.

Figure 1A.2   Share of top exporters versus GDP per capita in Latin America and the Caribbean and comparator regions, by country

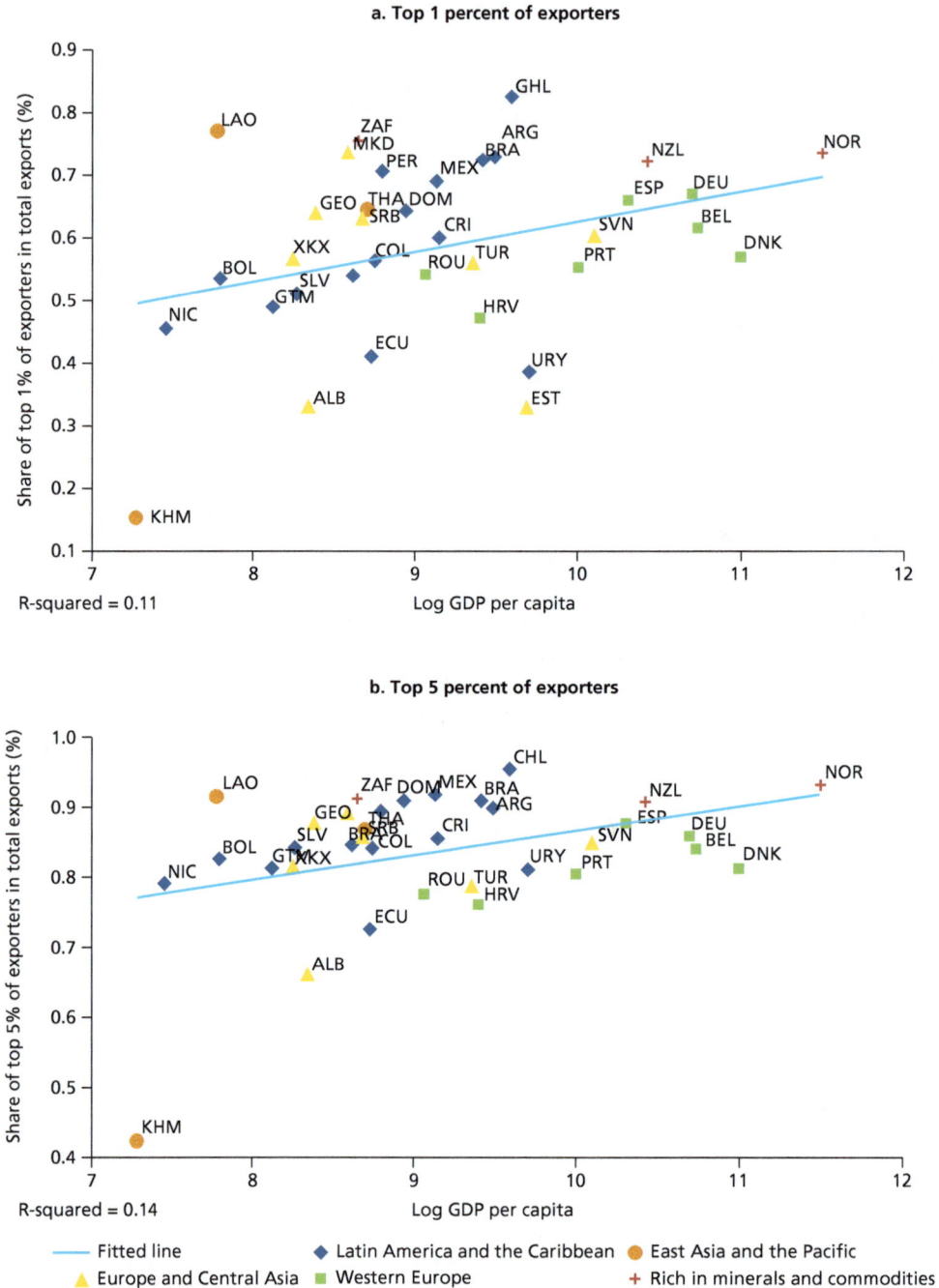

Source: Updates to World Bank's Exporter Dynamics database (described in Fernandes, Freund, and Pierola 2016).

Note: The figure shows averages for available years in 2015–19, except for Guatemala and Romania, whose averages are for available years in 2010–14. Countries are labeled by ISO alpha-3 code. GDP = gross domestic product.

Figure 1A.3   Export share of high-tech goods versus export sophistication in Latin America and the Caribbean and comparator regions, by country, 2018

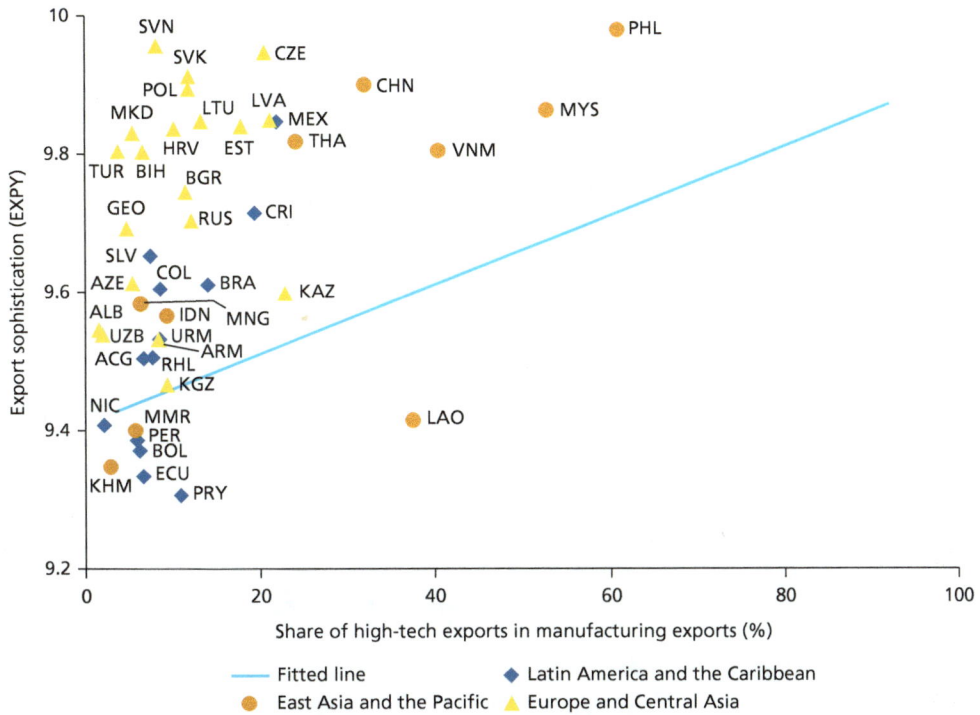

Source: World Bank, based on World Development Indicators database.

Note: The figure includes only countries that are part of the global value chain (GVC) taxonomy and are eligible for World Bank lending. Countries are labeled by ISO alpha-3 code. High-technology exports are products with high research and development intensity, such as in aerospace, computers, pharmaceuticals, scientific instruments, and electrical machinery. A country's expected gross domestic product (GDP) per capita, or EXPY (measured in logs), is given by summing all the PRODY values for the products exported by the country, each weighted by the product's share in total exports. PRODY is an outcome-based measure of sophistication: if a product is mostly produced by rich countries, then it is treated as a "rich," or sophisticated, product. PRODY is calculated as a weighted average of the per capita GDP of countries producing that product, with weights derived from revealed comparative advantage.

Figure 1A.4   Decomposition of sectoral contributions to GVC participation in Latin America and the Caribbean, by country, 2015

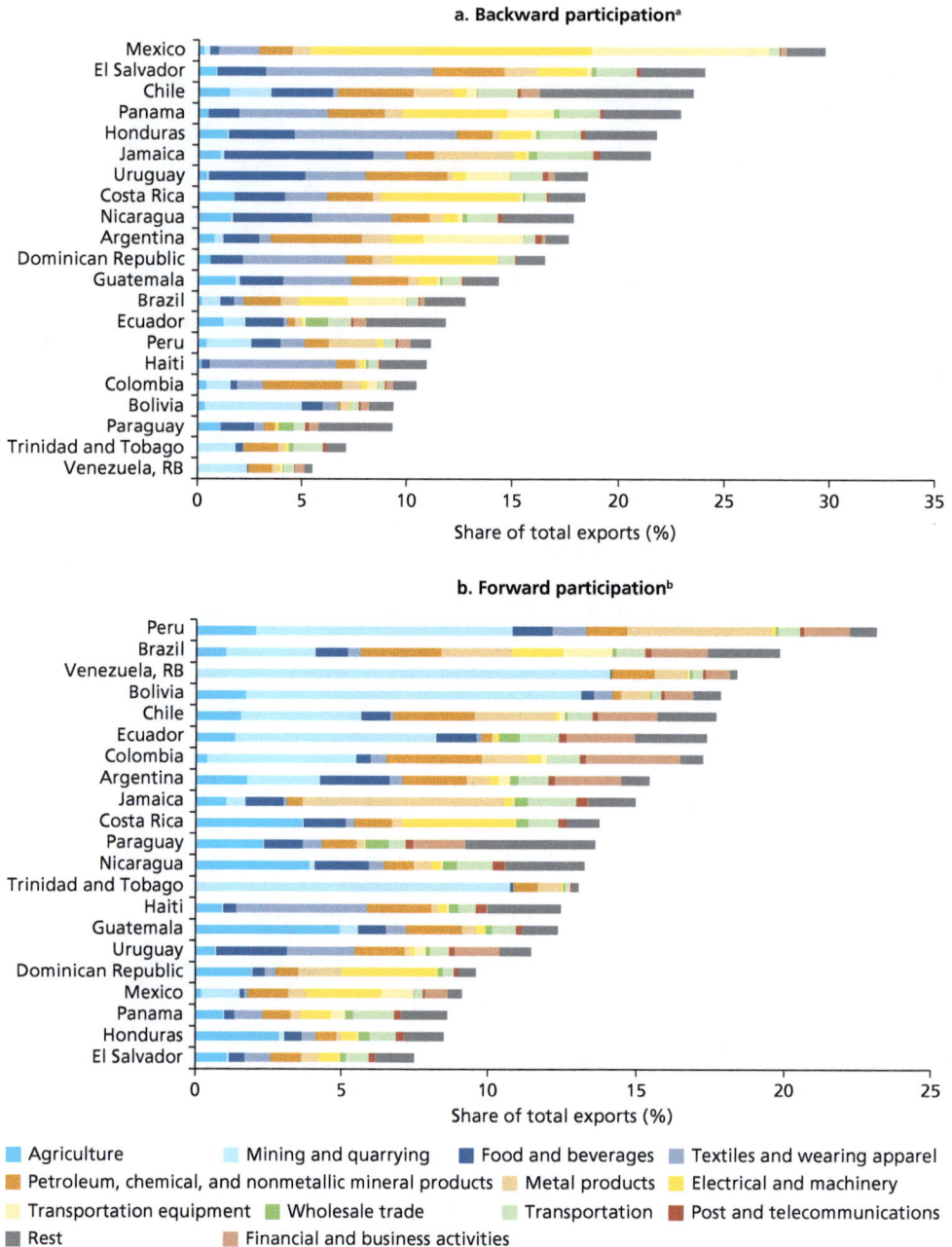

a. Backward participation[a]

b. Forward participation[b]

Agriculture — Mining and quarrying — Food and beverages — Textiles and wearing apparel — Petroleum, chemical, and nonmetallic mineral products — Metal products — Electrical and machinery — Transportation equipment — Wholesale trade — Transportation — Post and telecommunications — Rest — Financial and business activities

Source: Eora global supply chain database (https://worldmrio.com/).

Note: The figures show the sectoral contribution to total backward and forward participation by country in 2015. "Rest" refers to the rest of the sectors. GVC = global value chain.

a. Backward GVC participation refers to the share of imported inputs in a sector's exports.
b. Forward GVC participation refers to the share of exports that are inputs for another country's production of exports.

Figure 1A.5 Backward and forward GVC participation in Latin America and the Caribbean and comparator regions, by sector, 2000

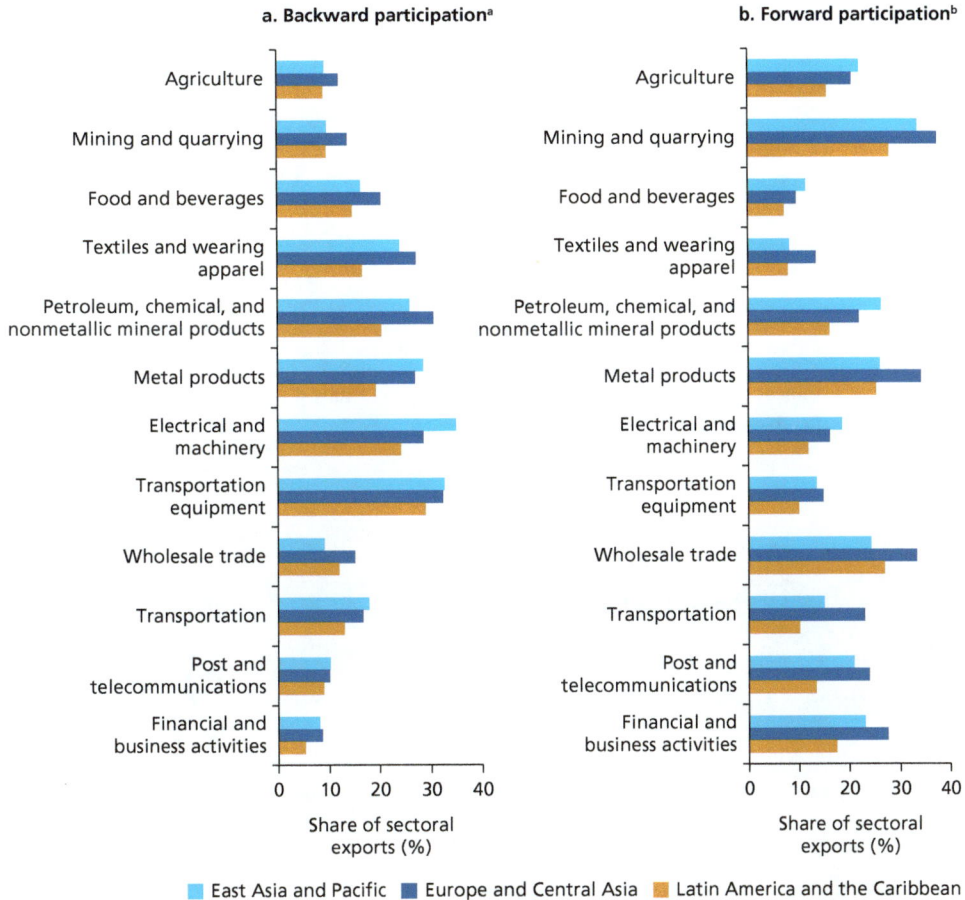

a. Backward participation[a]

b. Forward participation[b]

East Asia and Pacific   Europe and Central Asia   Latin America and the Caribbean

Source: World Bank, based on Eora global supply chain database (https://worldmrio.com/); Borin and Mancini 2019; World Development Indicators database; and global value chain (GVC) taxonomy data from World Bank 2020b.

Note: The figures show simple averages across countries and include only countries that are part of the GVC taxonomy and were eligible for World Bank lending as of 2000.

a. Backward GVC participation refers to the share of imported inputs in a sector's exports.
b. Forward GVC participation refers to the share of exports that are inputs for another country's production of exports.

Table 1A.1   High- and low-performing Latin American and Caribbean countries along selected trade indicators

Growth	Export growth	Import growth	
High	Nicaragua, Panama, Peru	Colombia, Peru, Chile, Ecuador	
Low	Argentina, Guatemala, El Salvador	Haiti, El Salvador, Dominican Republic, Guatemala	
Performance	**Trade openness**	**Exporters per capita**	**Exporter size of GVC firms**
High	Honduras, Nicaragua, Panama, Mexico, Jamaica	Costa Rica, Chile	Mexico, Chile, Peru
Low	Argentina, Brazil, Colombia, Guatemala, Uruguay	Brazil, Bolivia, Paraguay	El Salvador, Guatemala
Diversification	**Concentration of firm export shares**	**Number of destinations per GVC firms**	**Number of products per GVC firms**
High	Ecuador, Bolivia, Colombia, Peru, Paraguay	Ecuador, Peru, Chile, Colombia, Uruguay	Mexico, Dominican Republic, El Salvador
Low	Mexico, El Salvador, Nicaragua, Costa Rica	Dominican Republic, El Salvador, Paraguay, Guatemala	Paraguay, Uruguay, Ecuador
Sophistication	**Manufactures (% of goods exports)**	**EXPY**[a]	**High-tech goods (% of goods exports)**
High	Mexico, El Salvador, Costa Rica, Nicaragua	Mexico, Costa Rica, El Salvador	Mexico, Costa Rica, Brazil
Low	Bolivia, Ecuador, Peru, Chile, Paraguay	Paraguay, Ecuador, Bolivia, Peru, Nicaragua	Ecuador, Bolivia, Peru, Nicaragua
Survival	**Survival of GVC firms**	**Entrant survival of GVC firms**	
High	Guatemala, Mexico, El Salvador	Mexico, Paraguay, El Salvador	
Low	Ecuador, Chile, Peru	Chile, Dominican Republic, Uruguay, Ecuador	

Source: World Bank, based on analysis in this chapter.

Note: Dark blue indicates countries in the "backward" global value chain (GVC) participation group; green, countries in the "balanced" group; red, countries in the "forward" group; and light blue, countries in the "low" group (see table 1.2). The table excludes some Latin American and Caribbean countries that are not covered by the World Bank's Exporter Dynamics Database.

a. EXPY is a country's expected gross domestic product (GDP) per capita, measured in logs, which is given by summing all the PRODY values for the products exported by the country, each weighted by the product's share in total exports. PRODY is an outcome-based measure of sophistication: if a product is mostly produced by rich countries, then it is treated as a "rich," or sophisticated, product. PRODY is calculated as a weighted average of the per capita GDP of countries producing that product, with weights derived from revealed comparative advantage.

NOTES

1. Earlier national input-output–based studies have also found positive productivity effects from offshoring (Amiti and Wei 2009; Egger and Egger 2006; Winkler 2010).

2. East Asia and the Pacific and Europe and Central Asia are emerging market regions but with higher average income per capita than Latin America and the Caribbean and thus providing good aspirational benchmarks. Besides countries eligible for lending that the World Bank includes in the Europe and Central Asia region, our analysis also includes the Czech Republic, Estonia, Latvia, and Lithuania because they reached high-income status after 2005 and thus were still eligible for World Bank lending in 2000, when some of our analysis starts.

3. In this chapter, the Latin American and Caribbean countries covered are part of the GVC taxonomy discussed later in this section and listed in table 1.1. Most small islands are excluded. But the exact set of countries in each figure may vary depending on the availability of data for the specific indicator.

4. Regional averages in this analysis (and in what follows) include all countries in annex 1A, figure 1A.1. Simple rather than weighted averages are computed throughout this chapter to avoid a bias toward large trading economies, particularly Mexico.

5. Whereas figure 1.3, panel a, shows a simple correlation, Fernandes, Freund, and Pierola (2016) also provide evidence of a positive relationship between the number of exporters and GDP per capita even after controlling for country size (captured by GDP).

6. This evidence is shown for Chile and Colombia by Gutiérrez de Piñeres and Ferrantino (1997, 1999).

7. For an approximate distribution of backward and forward GVC participation across the four taxonomy groups, by country, see figure 1.10.

8. Fernandes, Kee, and Winkler (2020) show that a higher share of rents from natural resources is positively associated with forward GVC participation (but negatively associated with backward GVC participation).

9. There is evidence of a positive relationship between forward GVC participation and domestic value added (Stolzenburg, Taglioni, and Winkler 2019). Two reasons might explain a smaller impact of backward participation relative to forward participation: First, the study's country sample excludes lower-income countries, for which stronger growth gains from backward participation are expected (as shown by Pahl and Timmer 2020). Second, because the study's country sample is biased toward countries with more sophisticated types of GVC participation, higher forward GVC participation reflects higher value-added services and inputs rather than commodities. So, the gains are higher than they would be in a country sample including many commodity exporters. The gains from forward GVC participation in this study are larger than those from backward GVC participation because of the exclusion of low-income and most lower-middle-income countries characterized by high forward GVC participation.

10. All countries in our sample in the East Asia and Pacific region except Vietnam have reduced their backward GVC participation since 2000, particularly Indonesia, Malaysia, the Philippines, and Thailand.

11. Although these measures allow for assessment of a country's extent of backward and forward GVC participation, they mask what determines it, including a country's endowments and sector specialization, geography, market size, foreign direct investment, trade policy, connectivity, the quality of institutions, and other macroeconomic factors (Fernandes, Kee, and Winkler 2020). This explains, for example, why Brazil, China, and Mongolia have similar positions in figure 1.12, though they differ strongly in these determinants.

12. A caveat in using customs data for measuring GVC participation at the firm level is that such data do not trace firm-to-firm transactions across countries; that would require an unrealistic degree of global cooperation across customs agencies to have linked datasets and linked firm identifiers (World Bank 2020b). Without such linked datasets, it is not feasible to construct firm-level measures of forward GVC participation. Even if a firm is identified as an exporter of intermediate inputs (instead of final goods), it is not possible to establish whether those inputs are fully absorbed in the importing country or whether they are reexported to third markets by the importing firms after having added value to them.

13. The logarithmic average exporter size shown in the figure corresponds to exports of about US$10 million per firm for GVC participating firms and US$1.7 million per firm for exporter-only firms in Peru.

14. The findings in this paragraph draw on the longer background paper by Fernandes, Nievas, and Winkler (2021).

15. This question is related to a similar inconclusive debate on whether exporters perform better because of self-selection into the exporting market or because of learning by exporting. Self-selection refers to advance differences in performance across firms, while learning by exporting refers to recognizing actual performance gains of exporters versus nonexporters (Wagner 2007).

16. Sophistication is measured by how many exported goods are largely produced by wealthy countries (as further explained in the note to annex figure 1A.3).

17. The macro-level analysis decomposes the imported inputs used in overall or sectoral exports by source regions, drawing on the Trade in Value Added (TiVA) database of the Organisation for Economic Co-operation and Development, which enables identification of the source countries of value added in exports. One caveat in using the TiVA database is that it covers only 64 countries, including only 7 Latin American and Caribbean countries (Argentina, Brazil, Chile, Colombia, Costa Rica, Mexico, and Peru), while unidentified sources of imported inputs are classified under rest of world (RoW). So, the RoW includes inputs originating in other Latin American and Caribbean countries that are not part of the TiVA database.

REFERENCES

Aghion, P., and P. Howitt. 1998. *Endogenous Growth Theory*. Cambridge, MA: MIT Press.

Agosin, M. 2007. "Export Diversification and Growth in Emerging Economies." Working Paper No. 233, Department of Economics, Universidad de Chile, Santiago.

Amiti, M., and S.-J. Wei. 2009. "Service Offshoring and Productivity: Evidence from the US." *The World Economy* 32 (2): 203–20.

Autor, D., D. Dorn, L. F. Katz, C. Patterson, and J. Van Reenen. 2020. "The Fall of the Labor Share and the Rise of Superstar Firms." *Quarterly Journal of Economics* 135 (2): 645–709.

Banh, H., P. Wingender, and C. Gueye. 2020. "Global Value Chains and Productivity: Micro Evidence from Estonia." Working Paper No. 20/11, International Monetary Fund, Washington, DC.

Borin, A., and M. Mancini. 2019. "Measuring What Matters in Global Value Chains and Value-Added Trade." Policy Research Working Paper 8804, World Bank, Washington, DC.

Constantinescu, C., A. Mattoo, and M. Ruta. 2019. "Does Vertical Specialisation Increase Productivity?" *The World Economy* 42 (8): 2385–402.

Dodaro, S. 1991. "Comparative Advantage, Trade and Growth: Export-Led Growth Revisited." *World Development* 19 (9): 1153–65.

Dollar, D., and A. Kraay. 2004. "Trade, Growth, and Poverty." *Economic Journal* 114 (493): F22–F49.

Egger, H., and P. Egger. 2006. "International Outsourcing and the Productivity of Low-Skilled Labour in the EU." *Economic Inquiry* 44 (1): 98–108.

Espitia, A., A. Mattoo, N. Rocha, M. Ruta, and D. Winkler. 2021. "Pandemic Trade: Covid-19, Remote Work and Global Value Chains." Policy Research Working Paper 9508, World Bank, Washington, DC.

Ethier, W. J. 1982. "National and International Returns to Scale in the Modern Theory of International Trade." *American Economic Review* 72 (3): 389–405.

Feenstra, R. C., R. Inklaar, and M. P. Timmer. 2015. "The Next Generation of the Penn World Table." *American Economic Review* 105 (10): 3150–82.

Fernandes, A., C. Freund, and M. D. Pierola. 2016. "Exporter Behavior, Country Size and Stage of Development: Evidence from the Exporter Dynamics Database." *Journal of Development Economics* 119: 121–37.

Fernandes, A., H.-L. Kee, and D. Winkler. 2020. "Determinants of Global Value Chain Participation: Cross-Country Evidence." Policy Research Working Paper 9197, World Bank, Washington, DC.

Fernandes, A., G. Nievas, and D. Winkler. 2021. "Trade and Global Value Chain Integration in Latin America: Stylized Facts." Working Paper, Report No. 159028, World Bank, Washington, DC.

Freund, C., and M. Pierola. 2015. "Export Superstars." *Review of Economics and Statistics* 97 (5): 1023–32.

Grossman, G., and E. Helpman. 1991. *Innovation and Growth in the Global Economy.* Cambridge, MA: MIT Press.

Gutiérrez de Piñeres, S. A., and M. Ferrantino. 1997. "Export Diversification and Structural Dynamics in the Growth Process: The Case of Chile." *Journal of Development Economics* 52 (2): 375–91.

Gutiérrez de Piñeres, S. A., and M. Ferrantino. 1999. "Export Sector Dynamics and Domestic Growth: The Case of Colombia." *Review of Development Economics* 3 (3): 268–80.

Harrison, A., and A. Rodríguez-Clare. 2009. "Trade, Foreign Investment, and Industrial Policy for Developing Countries." Working Paper 15261, National Bureau of Economic Research, Cambridge, MA.

Helpman, E., and P. Krugman. 1985. *Market Structure and Foreign Trade. Increasing Returns, Imperfect Competition, and the International Economy.* Cambridge, MA: MIT Press.

Kasahara, H., and B. Lapham. 2013. "Productivity and the Decision to Import and Export: Theory and Evidence." *Journal of International Economics* 89 (2): 297–316.

Lederman, D., and W. F. Maloney, eds. 2007. "Trade Structure and Growth." In *Natural Resources: Neither Curse nor Destiny*, edited by D. Lederman and W. F. Maloney, 15–39. Palo Alto, CA: Stanford University Press.

Méndez-Chacón, E., and D. Van Patten. 2021. "Multinationals, Monopsony and Local Development: Evidence from the United Fruit Company." Unpublished manuscript, Princeton University, Princeton, NJ.

Muûls, M., and M. Pisu. 2009. "Imports and Exports at the Level of the Firm: Evidence from Belgium." *The World Economy* 32 (5): 692–734.

Pahl, S., and M. P. Timmer. 2020. "Do Global Value Chains Enhance Economic Upgrading? A Long View." *Journal of Development Studies* 56 (9): 1683–705.

Pierola, M., A. Fernandes, and T. Farole. 2018. "The Role of Imports for Exporter Performance in Peru." *The World Economy* 41 (2): 550–72.

Romer, P. M. 1987. "Growth Based on Increasing Returns Due to Specialization." *American Economic Review* 77 (2): 56–62.

Romer, P. 1990. "Endogenous Technological Change." *Journal of Political Economy* 98 (5): 71–102.

Stolzenburg, V., D. Taglioni, and D. Winkler. 2019. "Economic Upgrading through Global Value Chain Participation: Which Policies Increase the Value-Added Gains?" In *Handbook on Global Value Chains,* edited by S. Ponte, G. Gereffi, and G. Raj-Reichert, 483–505. Northampton, MA: Edward Elgar Publishing.

Taglioni, D., and D. Winkler. 2016. *Making Global Value Chains Work for Development.* Washington, DC: World Bank.

Wagner, J. 2007. "Exports and Productivity: A Survey of the Evidence from Firm-level Data." *World Economy* 30 (1): 60–82.

Wagner, J. 2012. "International Trade and Firm Performance: A Survey of Empirical Studies since 2006." *Review of World Economics* 148: 235–67.

Winkler, D. 2010. "Services Offshoring and Its Impact on Productivity and Employment: Evidence from Germany, 1995–2006." *The World Economy* 33 (12): 1672–701.

World Bank. 2019. *Trade Integration as a Pathway to Development?* Semiannual Report of the Latin America and Caribbean Region (October). Washington, DC: World Bank.

World Bank. 2020a. "COVID-19 Trade Watch." Monthly note series by the Global Trade and Integration unit, World Bank, Washington, DC. https://www.worldbank.org/en/topic/trade/brief /trade-watch.

World Bank. 2020b. *World Development Report 2020: Trading for Development in the Age of Global Value Chains.* Washington, DC: World Bank.

2 Deep Trade Agreements: Promoting Trade and GVC Integration

Alvaro Espitia, Nadia Rocha, Michele Ruta, and Deborah Winkler

KEY MESSAGES

- Latin American and Caribbean countries have signed increasing numbers of preferential trade agreements since the 1990s.
- Most trade under Latin American and Caribbean trade agreements is with partner countries outside the region.
- Larger Latin American and Caribbean countries would benefit more from deepening existing trade agreements than from signing agreements with new partners. The reverse is true for the region's small countries.
- The deepening of trade agreements is likely to expand a country's global value chain trade and raise the sophistication of the products it trades.

INTRODUCTION

In the 1980s, Latin American and Caribbean countries saw trade agreements as an instrument to protect regional markets and a complement to import substitution strategies. After the 1990s, "open regionalism" became prevalent, which emphasized trade agreements as promoting global integration rather than closing regional markets. The most recent literature on regional integration in Latin America and the Caribbean stresses the role of deep trade agreements (DTAs) in the context of open regionalism. This chapter builds on that long-standing policy debate, using recent data on the content of trade agreements and providing new evidence that deepening trade agreements in areas beyond market access can support trade and global value chain (GVC) integration.

Deeper trade agreements would promote GVC links. For GVCs to operate efficiently, cooperation on border and behind-the-border policies is needed for several reasons: First, international fragmentation of production can create new forms of cross-border policy spillovers that require cooperation to be managed. Second, without such cooperation, governments might face credibility problems over behind-the-border measures in the context of GVCs. And third, heterogeneous regulations might create higher costs in the presence of cross-border production.

DTAs in Latin America and the Caribbean are associated with more GVC participation and with upgrading to more-advanced GVC participation. Globally, deep provisions in trade agreements facilitate and promote GVCs, thus contributing to increased participation in them. GVC-related trade between countries after signing a DTA is 12 percent higher than it was before signing the agreement. The positive link between DTAs and GVC participation also appears in the Latin American and Caribbean region: the value of GVC-related trade in 2017 (proxied by trade in parts and components) was higher on average for the region's countries that had signed deeper agreements with their trading partners than for countries with shallower agreements. There is also evidence that DTAs are associated with GVC upgrading, though causation is more difficult to establish.

THE RISING TREND IN PREFERENTIAL TRADE AGREEMENTS

Countries around the world have increased their participation in preferential trade agreements (PTAs), especially in the past two decades (figure 2.1). From the 1950s onward, the number of active PTAs increased steadily to almost 50 in 1990. Thereafter, PTA activity accelerated noticeably, with the number of new PTAs more than doubling over the next five years and more than quadrupling by 2010, reaching well over 300 PTAs in force by 2019.

What are the drivers of the global increase in PTAs?

Factors such as lack of progress in multilateral trade negotiations, together with the fear of losing market share by being excluded from existing PTAs, partly explain the increase in the number of PTAs between countries with the objective of increasing market access. The global trend toward tariff liberalization from the 1940s, both multilateral and preferential, has been essential to expanding GVCs. Firms participating in increasingly fragmented production needed access to production inputs at competitive international prices, and they needed better access to destination markets for their products. Latin America and the Caribbean entered this trend at a later stage, when trade reforms in the late 1990s allowed countries to reverse the protectionist excesses of the preceding decades (box 2.1).

But the rise of PTAs and their changing content are also closely linked with the growing importance of GVCs in world trade. Toward the end of the 1990s, more

Figure 2.1   Globally, PTAs accelerated in the 1990s, reaching more than 300 by 2019

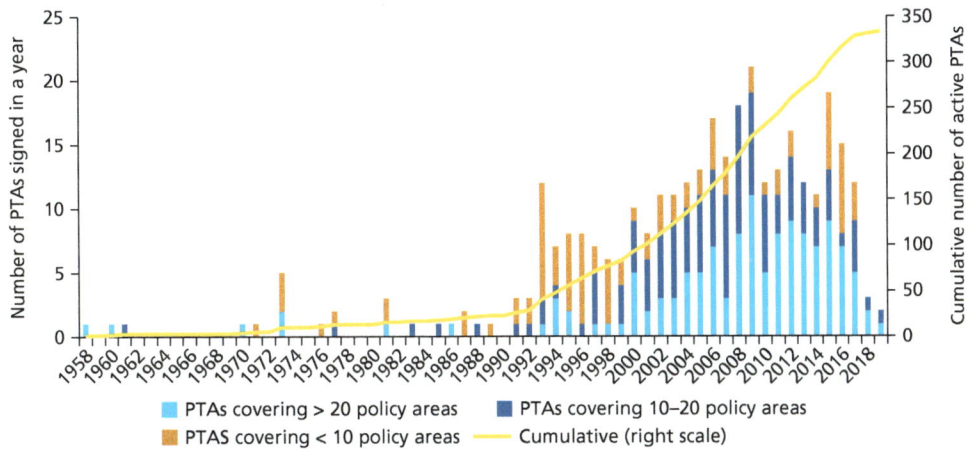

PTAs covering > 20 policy areas   PTAs covering 10–20 policy areas
PTAS covering < 10 policy areas   Cumulative (right scale)

Sources: World Bank's Deep Trade Agreements database; Mattoo, Rocha, and Ruta 2020.

Note: Bars designate the number of new preferential trade agreements (PTAs) in a given year (left scale). The yellow line indicates the cumulative number of active PTAs (right scale). Colors within the bars indicate the number of policy areas addressed within those PTAs. In 1973, for example, five PTAs were signed, of which two had more than 20 provisions and three had fewer than 10 provisions.

Box 2.1   Preferential tariff liberalization in Latin America and the Caribbean

Globally, trade-weighted nondiscriminatory (most-favored-nation, or MFN) tariffs fell from 11.1 percent to 8.1 percent over 2000–18. Latin American and Caribbean tariffs fell from 13.3 percent to 6.6 percent, South Asian rates from 21.4 percent to 6.6 percent, and Sub-Saharan African rates from 9.8 percent to 8.7 percent. Other regions had even lower rates by 2018: Europe and Central Asia, 4.1 percent; East Asia and Pacific, 3.9 percent; and North America, 3.2 percent.

The extent of preferential liberalization varies across Latin American and Caribbean countries. Around 60 percent of them have reduced trade-weighted average tariffs to less than 5 percent (figure B2.1.1). Whereas Argentina, Chile, and El Salvador have applied trade-weighted preferential tariffs more than 5 percentage points below their trade-weighted MFN rates, Brazil, Mexico, and Peru have applied trade-weighted preferential tariffs less than 3 percentage points below their trade-weighted MFN rates.

Preferential tariff liberalization by the region's governments varies by the kind of partner in a trade agreement—with other Latin American and Caribbean partners getting lower tariffs than extraregional partners. The trade-weighted preferential margins applied to imports from Latin American and Caribbean countries are 8.7 percent, while those applied to extraregional partners are 2.3 percent (figure B2.1.2). In other words, the trade-weighted preferential tariffs on imports from Latin American and Caribbean partners is 1.3 percent, or 8.7 percentage points lower than

Continued

Box 2.1   Preferential tariff liberalization in Latin America and the Caribbean *(continued)*

Figure B2.1.1   Trade-weighted average tariffs in Latin America and the Caribbean, by country, 2018

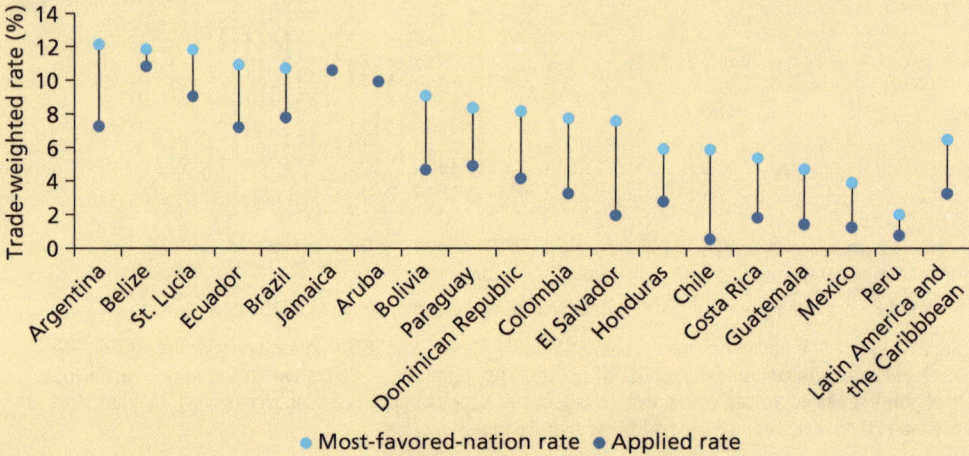

● Most-favored-nation rate ● Applied rate

Source: World Integrated Trade Solution (WITS) data, https://wits.worldbank.org/.

Note: Data are from 2018 except for most-recent data for the Dominican Republic (2017), Guatemala (2015), Honduras (2015), Jamaica (2016), and St. Lucia (2016).

Figure B2.1.2   Trade-weighted average tariffs in Latin America and the Caribbean, by partner location, 2018

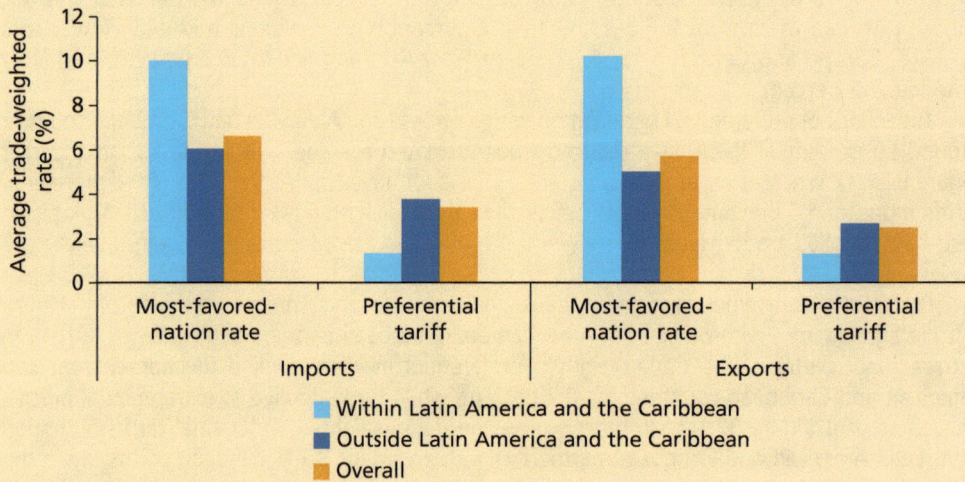

■ Within Latin America and the Caribbean
■ Outside Latin America and the Caribbean
■ Overall

Sources: World Bank's Deep Trade Agreements database; Mattoo, Rocha, and Ruta 2020.

Continued

> **Box 2.1**   **Preferential tariff liberalization in Latin America and the Caribbean** *(continued)*
>
> the 10 percent trade-weighted MFN rate, and those on imports from partners outside the region is 3.8 percent, or 2.3 percentage points lower than the 6.6 percent trade-weighted MFN rate (see annex 2A, table 2A.1).
>
> The tariffs of countries in the region also have been reduced across sectors but are still relatively high for agricultural products. Tariff rates for imports of foodstuffs and animals and animal products have been cut by more than half, but average applied trade-weighted foodstuff rates remain near 5 percent, and MFN trade-weighted average foodstuff rates are over 15 percent. (For all MFN and applied rates by sector, see annex 2A, table 2A.2.) Similarly, exports of agricultural products from Latin American and Caribbean countries face trade-weighted preferential tariffs of 7.5–10.7 percent.
>
> Rates have been cut far less for imports of textiles and apparel, where trade-weighted preferential tariffs rates remain at about 13 percent for footwear and headgear, 9.5 percent for textiles, and 8.7 percent for raw hides, leather, and furs.

countries began signing bilateral and regional PTAs that went beyond preferential tariffs and simple market access. The new "deep trade agreements" (DTAs) increasingly covered a wider set of border and behind-the-border policy areas: investment, services trade, customs procedures, competition policy, technical barriers to trade (TBT), sanitary and phytosanitary (SPS) measures, intellectual property rights (IPR), and more (Mattoo, Rocha, and Ruta 2020).

Relative to a situation of goods produced in a single location and final products traded internationally, GVCs imply an increase in trade flows involving customized inputs, incomplete contracts, and search costs to find suitable foreign input suppliers. GVC trade thus creates new forms of cross-border external effects as government actions spill over the value chain in more complex ways, requiring new forms of policy cooperation. And DTAs are instruments to promote international cooperation in policy areas that allow cross-border production to operate efficiently.

What is the extent of Latin America and the Caribbean's participation in PTAs?

Although Latin America and the Caribbean's participation in PTAs has increased over time, it varies widely across individual countries. By 2019, the region's countries took part in 84 agreements, a third of the total in force globally. Chile, with 27 agreements, is among the countries with the most, after the European Union (EU), with 38. Colombia, Mexico, and Peru are members of 13, 15, and 17 agreements, respectively (map 2.1). Argentina and Brazil are members of 4, and Ecuador and Bolivia are members of only 3.

The partner countries in Latin American and Caribbean PTAs also vary. The five States Parties of the Southern Common Market (MERCOSUR)[1] have so far not participated in any agreements with other regions—particularly with any

Map 2.1   Country participation in PTAs varies widely, 2019

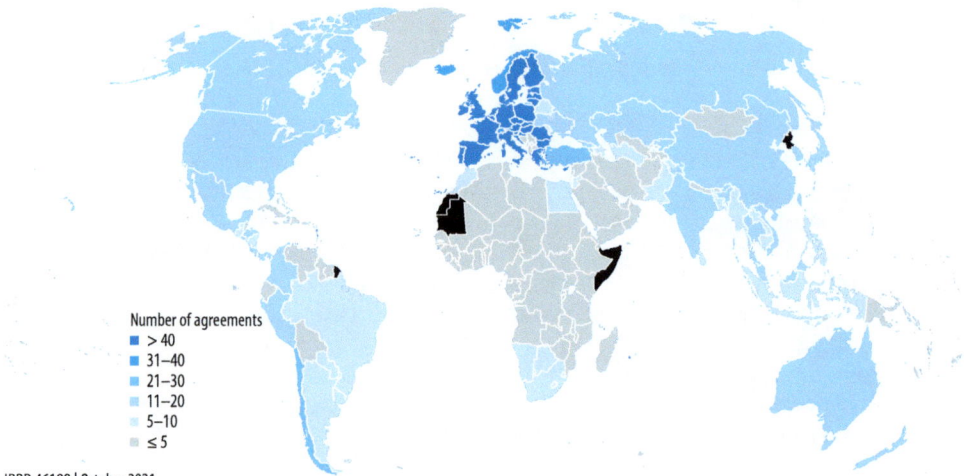

Number of agreements
- > 40
- 31–40
- 21–30
- 11–20
- 5–10
- ≤ 5

IBRD 46198 | October 2021

Sources: Calculations based on the World Bank's Deep Trade Agreements database; Mattoo, Rocha, and Ruta 2020. © World Bank. Further permission required for reuse. No data are available for French Guiana, the People's Democratic Republic of Korea, Mauritania, Somalia, and Western Sahara.

high-income economy.[2] In contrast, the Pacific Alliance members—Chile, Colombia, Mexico, and Peru—have agreements with an increasing number of high-income economies. (For a full list of the region's PTAs, years entered into force, and coverage ratios, see annex 2A, table 2A.3.)

As for the depth of these agreements, PTAs signed by Latin American and Caribbean countries include 16 enforceable policy areas on average (map 2.2).[3] The Pacific Alliance members' PTAs include the most: Mexico and Peru each averaging 18, followed by Colombia with 17 and Chile with 15. Caribbean country PTAs, such as those of Costa Rica, Dominican Republic, and Jamaica, have 16 on average. MERCOSUR countries have less depth in their PTAs, whether with other members (only 6 policy areas being effectively implemented) or with the rest of the world.

PTAs among Latin American and Caribbean countries usually include policy areas that currently fall in the World Trade Organization (WTO) mandate (referred to as WTO+ provisions): antidumping, export taxes, countervailing measures, customs and trade facilitation, TBT, SPS measures, tariff reductions on industrial and agricultural goods, and services trade areas covered by the WTO. Latin American and Caribbean PTAs with countries outside the region are typically deeper in content, covering policy areas beyond the WTO mandate (WTO-X provisions) such as investment, movement of capital, and competition policy more often than PTAs among Latin American and Caribbean countries (table 2.1). The detailed coverage of

Map 2.2   Average depth of active PTAs in Latin American and Caribbean countries, 2019

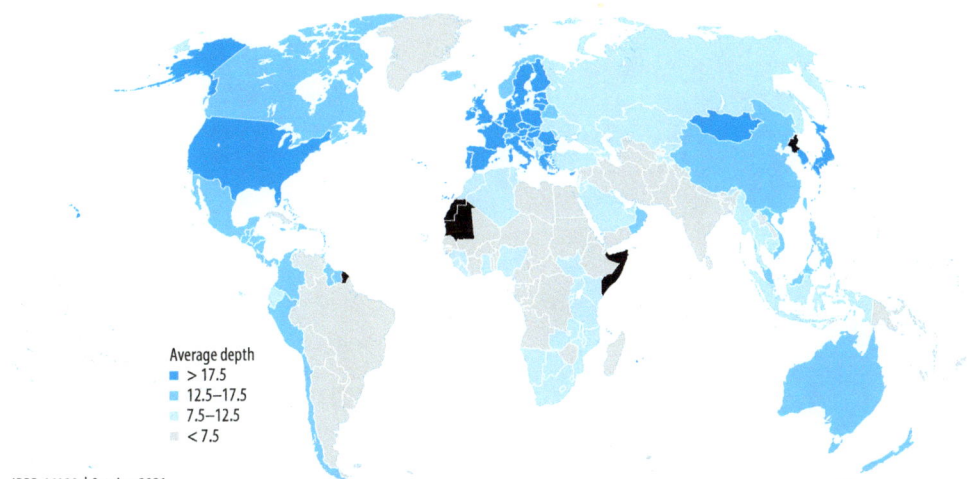

Average depth
- \> 17.5
- 12.5–17.5
- 7.5–12.5
- < 7.5

IBRD 46199 | October 2021

Sources: Calculations based on the World Bank's Deep Trade Agreements database; Hofmann, Osnago, and Ruta 2017. © World Bank. Further permission required for reuse.

Note: Depth of preferential trade agreements (PTAs) refers to the number of enforceable policy areas in an agreement. No data are available for French Guiana, the People's Democratic Republic of Korea, Mauritania, Somalia, and Western Sahara.

these policy areas in PTAs and the ways they translate into reforms in national laws vary widely.

The number of extraregional Latin American and Caribbean PTAs has increased since 2000 (figure 2.2). In 2000, only 5 were in force,[4] but by 2017, there were 50 (compared with 32 intraregional PTAs). And the coverage ratio—the share of provisions in each agreement relative to the maximum number of possible provisions—has risen. In agreements signed in the 1980s and 1990s, coverage ratios were below 15 percent and in many cases below 5 percent. But in most PTAs signed after 2000, the ratio is above 25 percent.

Extraregional agreements typically include more essential provisions than intra-regional agreements. "Essential" provisions are those including a set of substantive commitments plus the complementary procedural, transparency, and enforcement regulations or objectives viewed as indispensable to achieving the substantive commitments. Agreements between Latin American and Caribbean countries and countries in other regions tend on average to have a higher share of essential provisions and a higher share of provisions to achieve substantive commitments (figure 2.3). In other words, the commitments in intraregional PTAs tend to support shallower regional integration than the commitments in extraregional PTAs.

Table 2.1 Most common provisions in selected PTAs, Latin America and the Caribbean

Policy area	Comprehensive and Progressive Agreement for Trans-Pacific Partnership (CPTPP)	United States–Mexico–Canada Agreement (USMCA)	European Community–Caribbean Forum (EC–CARIFORUM)	Southern Common Market (MERCOSUR)	Pacific Alliance	Caribbean Community and Common Market (CARICOM)	Central American Common Market (CACM)
Tariffs on manufacturing goods	✓	✓	✓	✓	✓	✓	✓
Tariffs on agricultural goods	✓	✓	✓	✓	✓	✓	✓
General Agreement on Trade in Services	✓	✓	✓	✓	✓	✓	✗
Export taxes	✓	✓	✓	✓	✓	✓	✗
Movement of capital	✓	✓	✓	✓	✓	✓	✗
Customs	✓	✓	✓	✓	✓	✗	✗
TBT	✓	✓	✓	✓	✓	✗	✗
SPS	✓	✓	✓	✓	✓	✗	✗
Public procurement	✓	✓	✓	✓	✓	✗	✗
Competition policy	✓	✓	✓	✓	✗	✓	✓
State aid	✓	✓	✓	✓	✗	✓	✓
Antidumping	✓	✓	✓	✓	✗	✓	✗
Countervailing measures	✓	✓	✓	✓	✗	✓	✗
State trading enterprises	✓	✓	✓	✓	✗	✓	✗

Continued

Table 2.1 Most common provisions in selected PTAs, Latin America and the Caribbean *(continued)*

Policy area	Comprehensive and Progressive Agreement for Trans-Pacific Partnership (CPTPP)	United States–Mexico–Canada Agreement (USMCA)	European Community–Caribbean Forum (EC–CARIFORUM)	Southern Common Market (MERCOSUR)	Pacific Alliance	Caribbean Community and Common Market (CARICOM)	Central American Common Market (CACM)
Trade-related aspects of intellectual property rights	✓	✓	✓	✓	✗	✗	✗
Intellectual property rights	✓	✓	✓	✓	✗	✗	✗
Trade-related investment measures	✓	✓	✗	✓	✗	✗	✗
Investment	✓	✓	✓	✗	✓	✗	✗
Environmental laws	✓	✓	✓	✗	✗	✗	✗
Labor market regulations	✓	✓	✓	✗	✗	✗	✗

Sources: Calculations based on the World Bank's Deep Trade Agreements database; Hofmann, Osnago, and Ruta 2017.

Note: ✓ = Included and legally enforceable. ✗ = Not included or legally enforceable. SPS = sanitary and phytosanitary; TBT = Technical Barriers to Trade.

Figure 2.2   Number and coverage ratios of PTAs in Latin America and the Caribbean, selected years

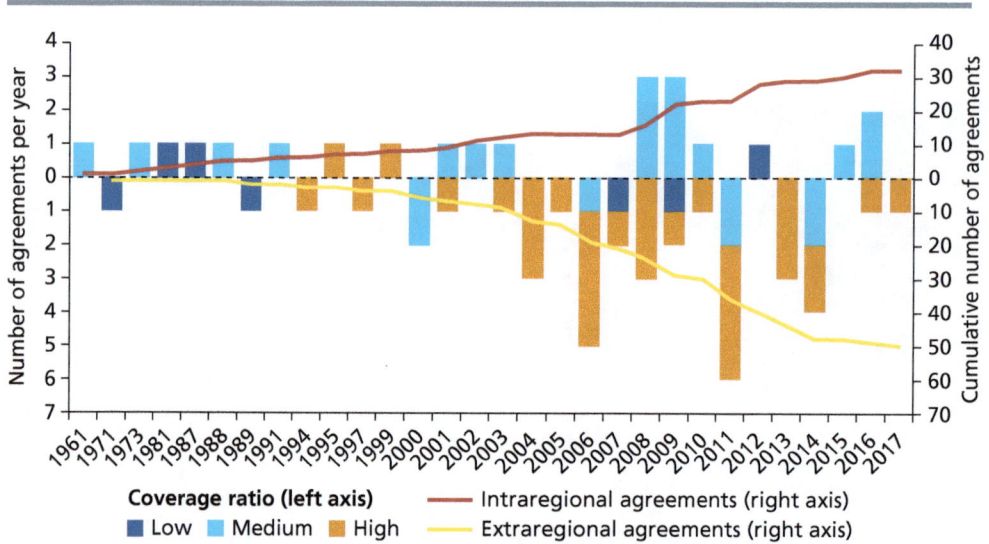

Sources: World Bank Deep Trade Agreements database; Mattoo, Rocha, and Ruta 2020.

Note: The left axis indicates the number of preferential trade agreements (PTAs) signed in a single year; the right axis indicates the cumulative number of PTAs. The bars' color intensity indicates the coverage ratio—that is, the number of provisions in an agreement relative to the maximum number of possible provisions. The bars and red line above the rule at zero pertain to intraregional partners; bars and the yellow line below the rule are for extraregional partners.

Figure 2.3   Intraregional PTAs of Latin American and Caribbean countries tend to be shallower in both essential and complementary provisions than the extraregional PTAs, 2017

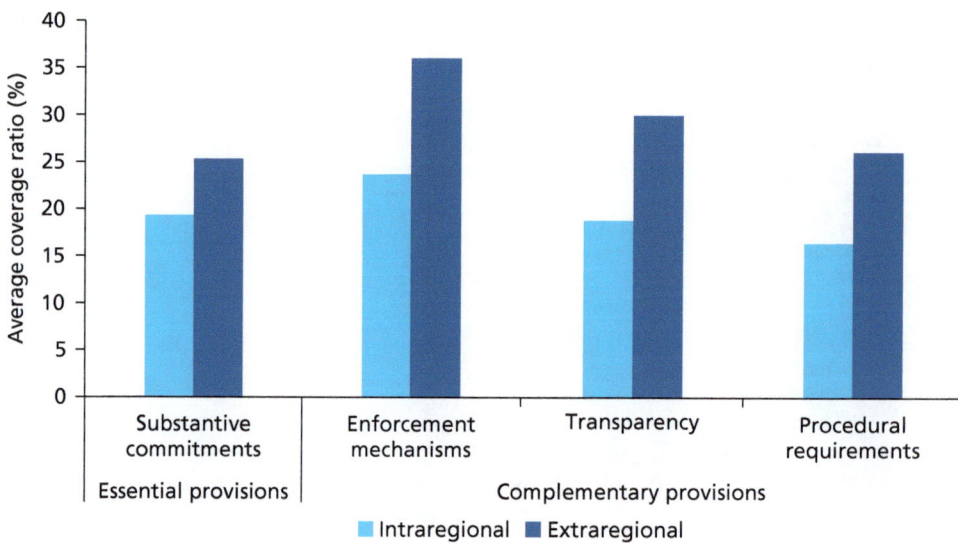

Sources: World Bank's Deep Trade Agreements Database; Mattoo, Rocha, and Ruta 2020.

Note: The coverage ratio is the share of provisions contained in each preferential trade agreement (PTA) divided by the maximum number of possible provisions. No data are available for French Guiana.

PATTERNS OF DEEP INTEGRATION IN LATIN AMERICA AND THE CARIBBEAN

Trade under DTAs

More than two-thirds of exports from Latin America and the Caribbean in 2017–19 took place under agreements. For instance, more than 95 percent of exports from Chile, Honduras, Mexico, Nicaragua, and Peru went to a partner country (map 2.3). But fewer exports from MERCOSUR members went to partners under an agreement—less

Map 2.3 Average share of exports under a trade agreement in Latin American and Caribbean countries, 2017–19

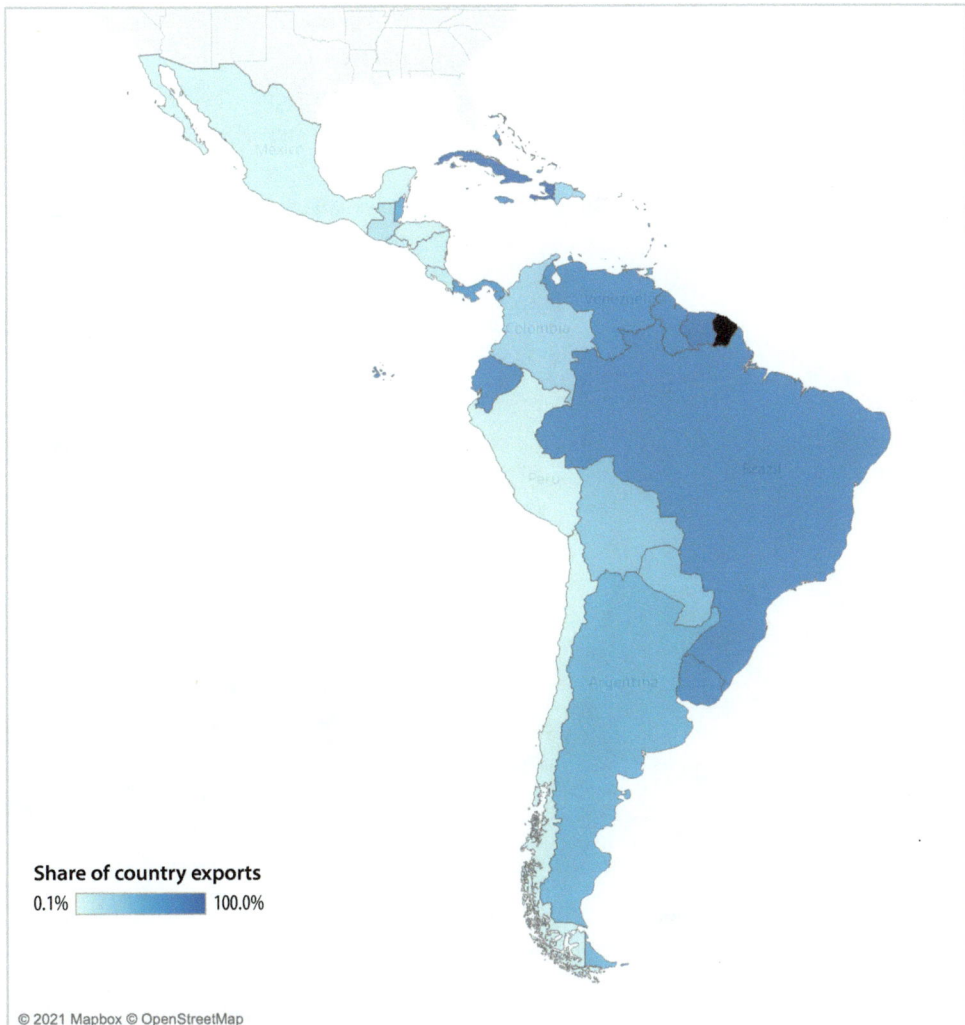

Share of country exports
0.1% — 100.0%

© 2021 Mapbox © OpenStreetMap

Sources: Calculations based on the World Bank's Deep Trade Agreements database; Mattoo, Rocha, and Ruta 2020. © World Bank. Further permission required for reuse.

Note: Total exports are calculated using mirror data for the average of 2017, 2018, and 2019 (where data were available). No data are available for French Guiana.

than 25 percent for Brazil and Uruguay—whereas those shares exceeded 75 percent of exports from Colombia (of the Pacific Alliance) and Costa Rica (of the Central American Common Market [CACM]).

Intraregional agreements tend to cover smaller shares of trade than extra-regional trade agreements. Only 16.2 percent of exports from Latin America and the Caribbean represent intraregional trade under an agreement. Of the trading blocs, the Pacific Alliance has the fewest intraregional trade links under a trade agreement, and MERCOSUR has the most. Only 7.1 percent of exports from Pacific Alliance countries go to a regional partner under an agreement, but 57.1 percent of exports from MERCOSUR economies do—as do 41.2 percent of exports from members of the Caribbean Community and Common Market (CARICOM) and 26.5 percent of exports from CACM countries.[5]

The United States receives 52.2 percent of the exports that fall under PTAs with Latin American and Caribbean countries—mainly from Colombia, Mexico, and Central American and Caribbean countries under the Dominican Republic–Central America Free Trade Agreement (CAFTA–DR). But China and other East Asia and Pacific countries are the primary destinations of exports from Chile and Peru (figure 2.4), in those cases under the Comprehensive and Progressive Agreement for Trans-Pacific Partnership (CPTPP).

Figure 2.4   Of all Latin American and Caribbean exports under a PTA in 2017–19, less than a fifth went to a regional partner

Sources: Calculations based on the World Bank's Deep Trade Agreements database; Mattoo, Rocha, and Ruta 2020. © World Bank. Further permission required for reuse.

Note: Total exports calculated using mirror data for the average of 2017, 2018, and 2019 (where data were available). EU-28 comprises the 28 European Union (EU) member states preceding the February 1, 2020, exit of the United Kingdom. PTA = preferential trade agreement.

PTA partner countries matter more than nonpartners as export destinations for Latin American and Caribbean countries, especially those with high backward GVC participation (use of imported inputs for export production) and low forward GVC participation (production of inputs for other countries' exports). On average, two-thirds of exported domestic value added from the region's countries in 2015 went to countries with which they had a PTA (figure 2.5, panel a). That share had expanded substantially from only 30 percent in 2000 (figure 2.5, panel b).

But those countries with high backward and low forward GVC participation—Dominican Republic, El Salvador, Honduras, Mexico, and Panama (termed the "backward" group under the GVC participation typology discussed in chapter 1)—sent at least 90 percent of their exported domestic value added to PTA partners (often the United States) in 2015. And although Chile, Colombia, Costa Rica, Nicaragua, and Peru participate differently in GVCs, they also now export the bulk of exported domestic value added to PTA partners. Firm-level analysis confirms this pattern (see annex 2A, figure 2A.1). Note the big change by 2015 from 2000, when the region's only countries with high intra-PTA export shares were Mexico and several MERCOSUR members (Argentina, Paraguay, and Uruguay), whereas other countries exported at least two-thirds of exports to trade partners with whom they had no PTA (figure 2.5, panel b).

Today, PTA partners, including nonregional partners, tend to be more important than nonpartners for the region's exports. Recent PTAs include the Mexico–Central America Free Trade Agreement (Costa Rica, El Salvador, Guatemala, Honduras, and Nicaragua), which entered into force in 2012; the EU–Colombia–Peru trade agreement, signed in 2012; the Pacific Alliance (Chile, Colombia, Mexico, and Peru), signed in 2016; and the CPTPP (Chile, Mexico, Peru, Canada, and seven East Asian and Pacific countries), signed in 2017.

The CPTPP and EU–Colombia–Peru agreements are characterized by smaller shares of domestic value added in intra-PTA exports (18 percent and 16 percent, respectively)—as are the Pacific Alliance and Mexico–Central America agreements (both less than 5 percent)—than in non-PTA exports (figure 2.6, panel a).

Although the relative importance of domestic value added in exports to partners in the CPTPP and Pacific Alliance in recent years has not yet been assessed, a preliminary analysis suggests two issues: (a) that PTAs with countries outside Latin America and Caribbean are deeper, and (b) that PTAs within the region are generally shallow (Mattoo, Rocha, and Ruta 2020). The smaller role of the Pacific Alliance and Mexico–Central America agreement areas as export destinations for exporter-only firms (which export products but do not import inputs and so do not participate in GVCs) in their member countries is confirmed, though to a lesser extent (see annex 2A, figure 2A.2).

The reliance of the CPTPP's Latin American and Caribbean member countries on CPTPP destinations for their exported domestic value added is highest in

Figure 2.5   Percentage of exported domestic value added going from Latin American and Caribbean countries to PTA partners and nonpartners, 2000 to 2015

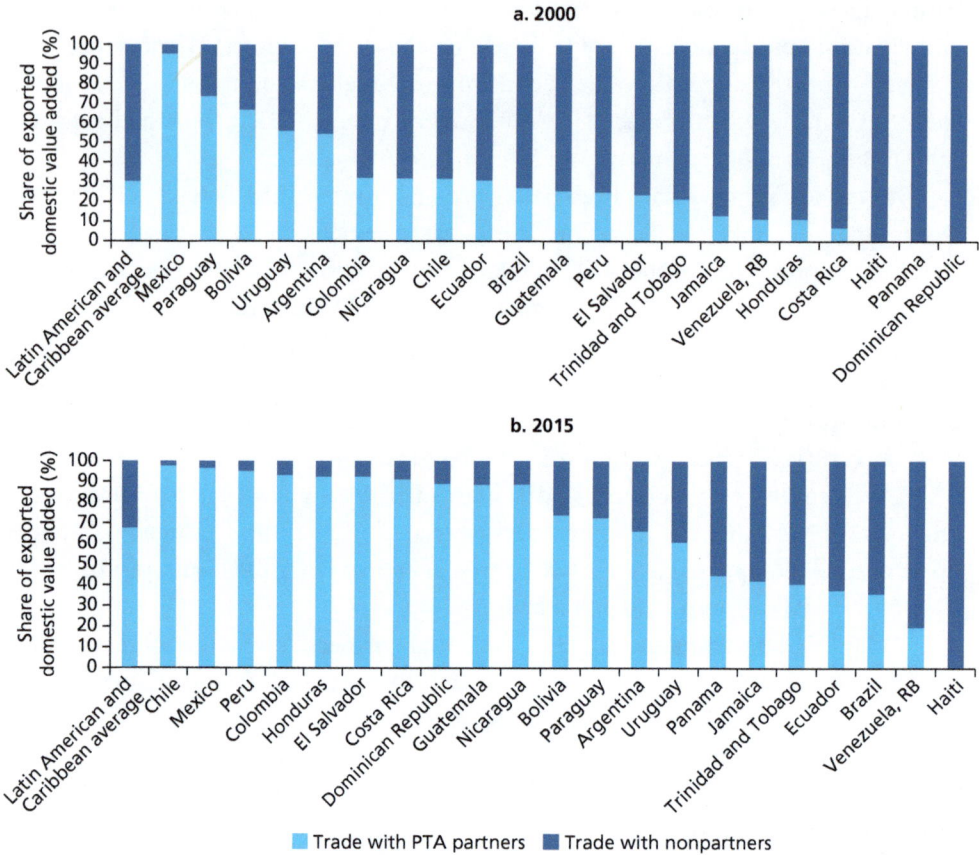

Sources: Eora global supply chain database (https://worldmrio.com/); World Bank's Deep Trade Agreements database; Fernandes, Nievas, and Winkler 2021.

Note: PTA = preferential trade agreement.

Chile (25 percent) and Peru (19 percent) but lower in Mexico (less than 10 percent), which depends more heavily on exports to the United States (figure 2.6, panel b). Peru also relies strongly on other EU–Colombia–Peru members as export destinations (see figure 2.6, panel b; and annex 2A, figure 2A.3).

MERCOSUR, despite its large role as a destination market for its own member countries, has not fostered GVC participation among them. The average share of domestic value added in exports from MERCOSUR members to other MERCOSUR destinations exceeds 35 percent (figure 2.6, panel a), a scale confirmed by firm-level analysis (see annex 2A, figure 2A.2). The high intra-PTA reliance in MERCOSUR is driven by Paraguay, with a share exceeding 60 percent; Uruguay, above 50 percent; and Argentina, above 40 percent; and less by Brazil, with a share of 18 percent (figure 2.6, panel b).

Figure 2.6 Share of domestic value added exported to PTA partners, by agreement and by member country, 2015

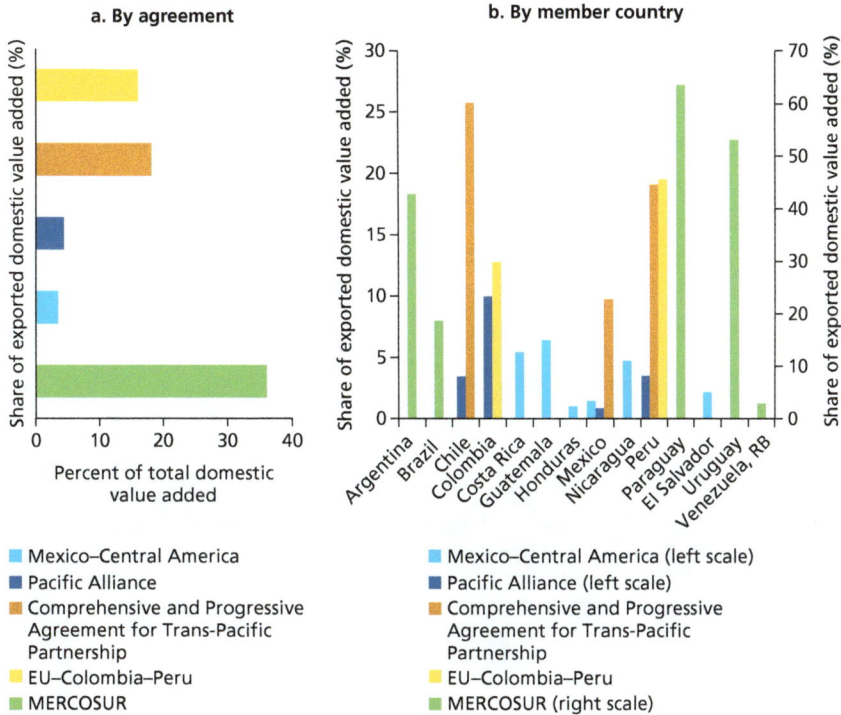

a. By agreement

b. By member country

Sources: Eora global supply chain database (https://worldmrio.com/); World Bank's Deep Trade Agreements database; Fernandes, Nievas, and Winkler 2021.

Note: The EU–Colombia–Peru agreement was signed in 2012. Comprehensive and Progressive Agreement for Trans-Pacific Partnership (CPTPP) members (signed in 2017): Australia, Brunei Darussalam, Canada, Chile, Japan, Malaysia, Mexico, New Zealand, Peru, Singapore, and Vietnam. Pacific Alliance members (signed in 2016): Chile, Colombia, Mexico, and Peru. Mexico–Central America members: Costa Rica, El Salvador, Guatemala, Honduras, and Nicaragua. MERCOSUR (Southern Common Market) members in 2015: Argentina, Brazil, Paraguay, Uruguay, and República Bolivariana de Venezuela. EU = European Union; PTA = preferential trade agreement.

Although EU and Association of Southeast Asian Nations (ASEAN) membership have fostered backward GVC participation, MERCOSUR membership has not (Fernandes, Kee, and Winkler 2020). Argentina's backward integration into GVCs is low because of restrictive trade policies, but its forward integration into GVCs is high because of its rich natural resources. Its GVC integration would advance substantially if MERCOSUR added such deep integration provisions as commitments to investment, removal of entry barriers, and deterrence of anticompetitive business practices (Martínez Licetti et al. 2018). The other MERCOSUR giant, Brazil, could also realize large gains in GVC participation by deepening existing PTAs and by engaging in new DTAs (Hollweg and Rocha 2018).

DTAs, imported inputs, and exports

Exporters in Latin American and Caribbean countries vary widely in how much they rely on inputs imported from PTA partner countries. Those countries with high backward GVC participation (Chile, the Dominican Republic, El Salvador, and Mexico) tend to rely strongly on inputs from PTA partners (figure 2.7). But those with low backward GVC participation (Colombia, Guatemala, and Peru) also source most of their imported inputs from their PTA partners. Only Ecuador, Paraguay, and Uruguay source most imported inputs from nonpartners.

Intra-PTA imported inputs from the Pacific Alliance matter more for Colombia's and Peru's exports than for Chile's or, especially, Mexico's (figure 2.8). This finding is confirmed by analysis of GVC participating firms (see annex 2A, figure 2A.4).

Figure 2.7   Percentage of GVC firms' imported inputs from PTA partners or nonpartners, by Latin American and Caribbean importing country

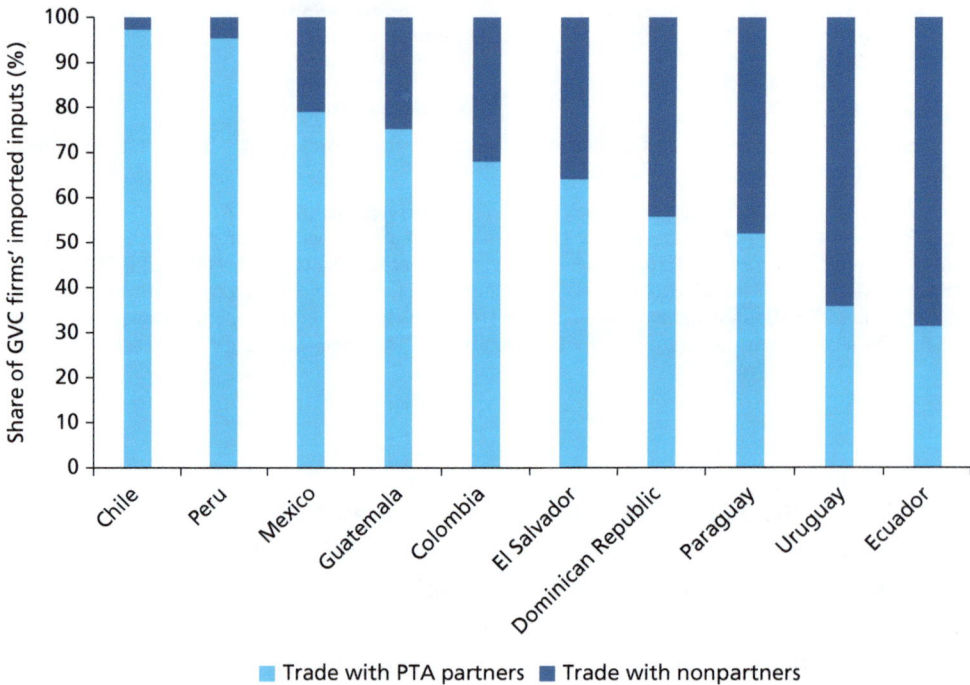

Sources: Fernandes, Nievas, and Winkler 2021, based on updates to the Exporter Dynamics database (described in Fernandes, Freund, and Pierola 2016); World Bank's Deep Trade Agreements database.

Note: Percentages of imported inputs and capital goods for each country are based on the most recent year of customs data. GVC = global value chain; PTA = preferential trade agreement.

Nonregional PTA partners matter more than regional partners for Latin American and Caribbean countries as a source of imported inputs for exports. The 10–12 percent share of CPTPP as a source of imported inputs for exports for Chile, Mexico, and Peru is much larger than that of the Pacific Alliance (figure 2.8). Evidence for GVC participating firms confirms that larger shares of intra-PTA inputs are sourced from CPTPP partners than from Pacific Alliance partners (see annex 2A, figure 2A.4).

Colombia and Peru's PTA with the EU is a major source of imported inputs. Colombia sources 12 percent of imported inputs used in exports from within that PTA, and Peru sources 14 percent (figure 2.8). GVC participating firms in Colombia and Peru source on average more than 20 percent of their imported inputs from within the PTA (see annex 2A, figure 2A.4). This could, again, indicate that PTAs with countries outside Latin America and the Caribbean are deeper than the intraregional PTAs (Mattoo, Rocha, and Ruta 2020).

Figure 2.8 Percentage of imported inputs for production of exports coming to Latin American and Caribbean countries from within selected PTAs, 2015

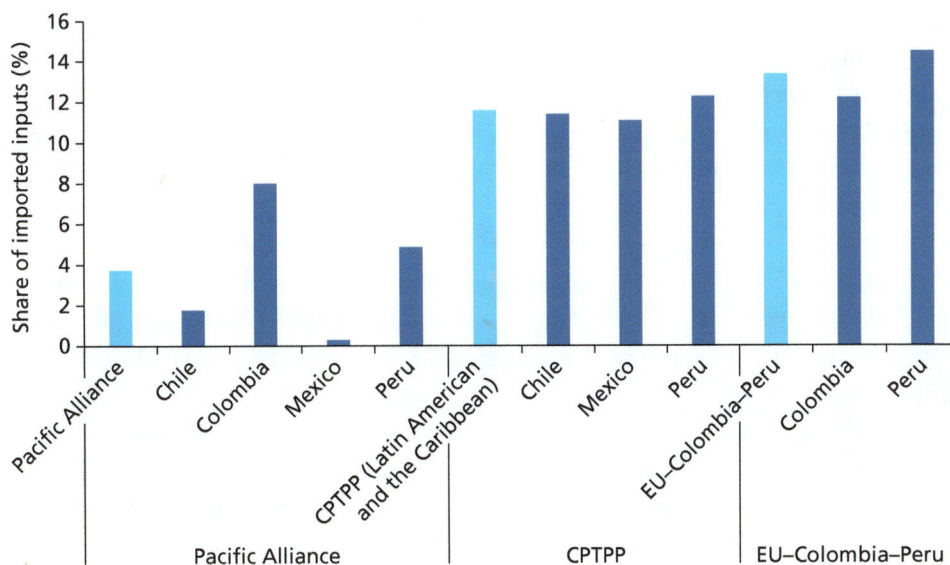

Sources: Fernandes, Nievas, and Winkler 2021; Trade in Value Added (TiVA) database of the Organisation for Economic Co-operation and Development; World Bank's Deep Trade Agreements database.

Note: Comprehensive and Progressive Agreement for Trans-Pacific Partnership (CPTPP) members (signed in 2017) include Australia, Brunei Darussalam, Canada, Chile, Japan, Malaysia, Mexico, New Zealand, Peru, Singapore, and Vietnam. Pacific Alliance members (signed in 2016) include Chile, Colombia, Mexico, and Peru. The EU–Colombia–Peru agreement was signed in 2012. EU = European Union; PTA = preferential trade agreement.

ECONOMIC IMPACT OF DEEP TRADE AGREEMENTS IN LATIN AMERICA AND THE CARIBBEAN

The potential economic impact of deepening integration

The following analysis explores the potential trade and welfare impacts of DTAs in Latin America and the Caribbean. It combines network analysis to quantify the depth of existing trade agreements with a general equilibrium gravity model to simulate (a) the deepening of existing PTAs within the region (intensive margin), and (b) a scenario in which the region's countries sign new DTAs with each other (extensive margin) (Fontagné et al. 2021).

Assessing the depth of the region's trade agreements

Assessing the overall depth of PTAs is challenging because of the richness of their content and the variety of disciplines they include.[6] This analysis uses a statistical procedure to classify the region's PTAs into an optimal set of groups (map 2.4) where the PTAs present both the maximum similarity of provisions within groups and the maximum difference between groups.

Six Latin American and Caribbean PTAs, classified in a first cluster, have the largest impact on trade, so they are recognized as DTAs. They are European Free Trade Agreement–Chile; Canada–Chile; Chile–Japan; Peru–Mexico; the Andean Community (CAN); and the North American Free Trade Agreement (NAFTA).[7]

Twenty-eight agreements are classified in a second cluster of medium-deep PTAs. Of those, 7 are intraregional agreements (including such trading blocs as the Caribbean Community and Common Market [CARICOM]), and 21 are extraregional (such as CPTPP, European Free Trade Association–Central American States, and EU–Colombia–Peru).

Forty-eight remaining agreements are classified in the third cluster as shallow PTAs. Of those, 24 are intraregional (including Dominican Republic–Central America, the Latin American Integration Association [LAIA], MERCOSUR, and the Pacific Alliance); and 24 are extraregional (such as Chile–China, MERCOSUR–India, and United States–Chile).

Antidumping and competition provisions play a more important role in the first cluster than provisions in such areas as labor regulation. So, transforming a third-cluster PTA into a first-cluster PTA would, on average, require putting more emphasis on antidumping, competition, and technical regulation.

Assessing the trade and welfare impact of deeper integration

To assess the impact of deepening existing PTAs, this exercise assumes that all the currently shallow and medium-deep agreements become deep. As expected, intensifying cooperation enhances trade among participating countries, with only marginal diversion from countries in the rest of the world and from isolated Caribbean countries (figure 2.9).

Map 2.4   Number and depth of PTAs in Latin American and Caribbean countries, 2017

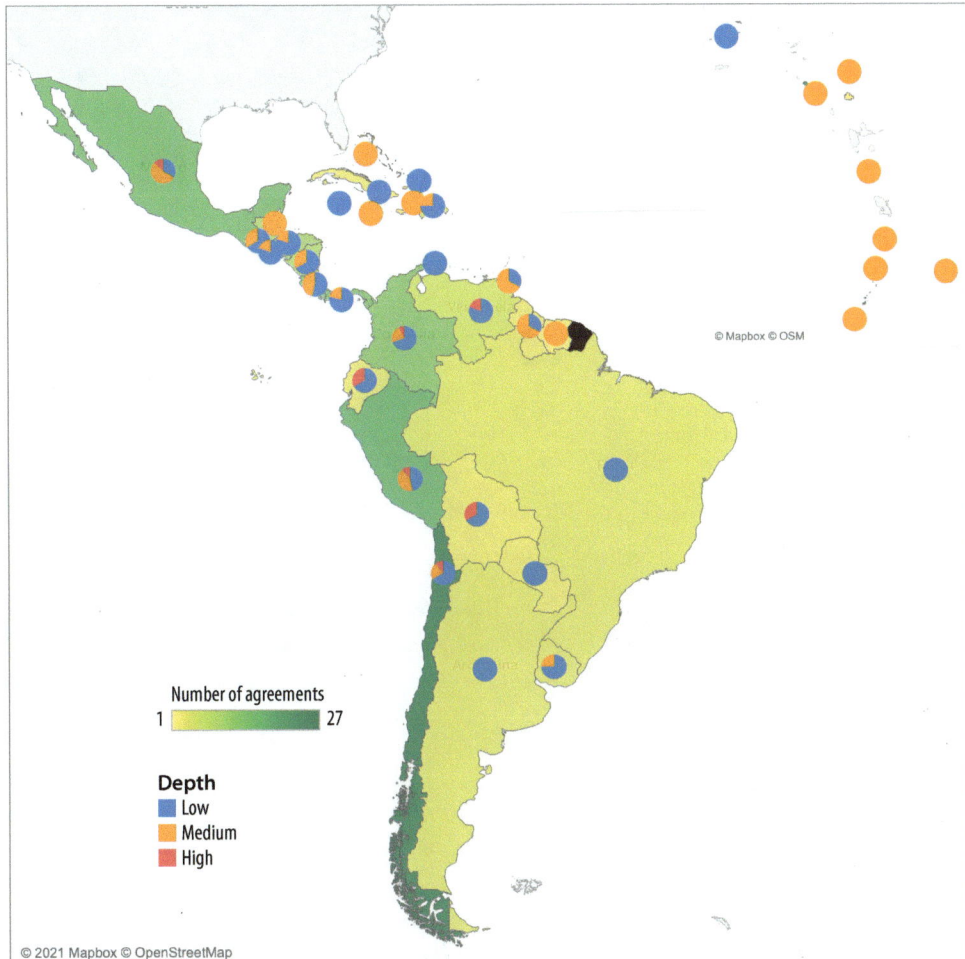

Source: Fontagné et al. 2021. © World Bank. Further permission required for reuse.

Note: The pie chart in each country depicts the country's distribution of agreements between low, medium, and high depth. "Depth" refers to the number or share of essential, legally enforceable provisions (substantive commitments) in a preferential trade agreement (PTA) to deepen economic integration between the trading partners. No data are available for French Guiana.

A good illustration of the impact of deepening integration in Latin America and the Caribbean comes from the Pacific Alliance partners. Colombia's exports within the region grow by 8.9 percent and its gross domestic product (GDP) by 0.4 percent; Peru's exports by 4.1 percent and GDP by 0.4 percent; Chile's exports by 2.9 percent and GDP by 0.6 percent; and Mexico's exports by 0.2 percent and GDP by 0.3 percent.

If the measured impact extends to relations between Pacific Alliance members and the rest of the world, Colombia's exports grow by 19.7 percent and its GDP by

Figure 2.9   Economic effects of deepening existing PTAs in Latin America and the Caribbean, by country

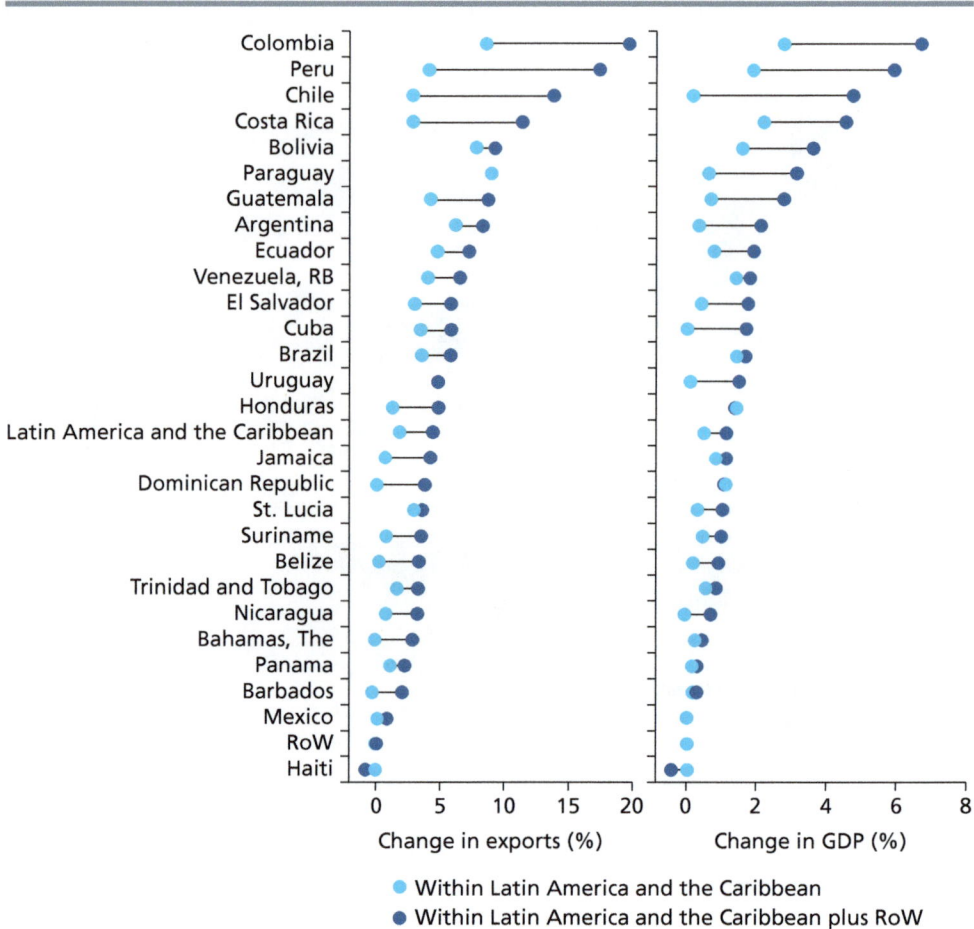

Source: Fontagné et al. 2021.

Note: The figure presents general equilibrium effects of deepening existing preferential trade agreements (PTAs) for Latin American and Caribbean countries in 2017. GDP = gross domestic product; RoW = rest of the world.

1.0 percent; Peru's exports by 17.4 percent and GDP by 1.8 percent; Chile's exports by 13.8 percent and GDP by 3.2 percent; and Mexico's exports by 0.9 percent and GDP by 2.1 percent.

But diversion effects are present, concentrated in relatively disconnected and small economies in the region such as The Bahamas, Belize, Haiti, Jamaica, St. Lucia, and Suriname. Because these countries participate only in one agreement—CARICOM, which already belongs to the cluster of medium cooperation agreements—the main effect on them in the simulation comes from indirect effects induced by third-country adjustments.

To assess the impact of signing new agreements, a second exercise assumes that each country within the region signs a shallow agreement with every other country. As a result, small Latin American and Caribbean countries that sign with large countries see their trade and GDP increase substantially (figure 2.10). Barbados is an extreme example, with exports increasing by 3.5 percent and GDP by 1.1 percent. But large countries (such as Argentina) that sign with small ones gain little.

If countries signed deep new agreements, small country gains would be magnified. Again, Barbados is an extreme example, with exports increasing by 8.0 percent and GDP by 2.6 percent.

Figure 2.10 Economic effects of new intraregional PTAs in Latin America and the Caribbean, by country and PTA depth level, 2017

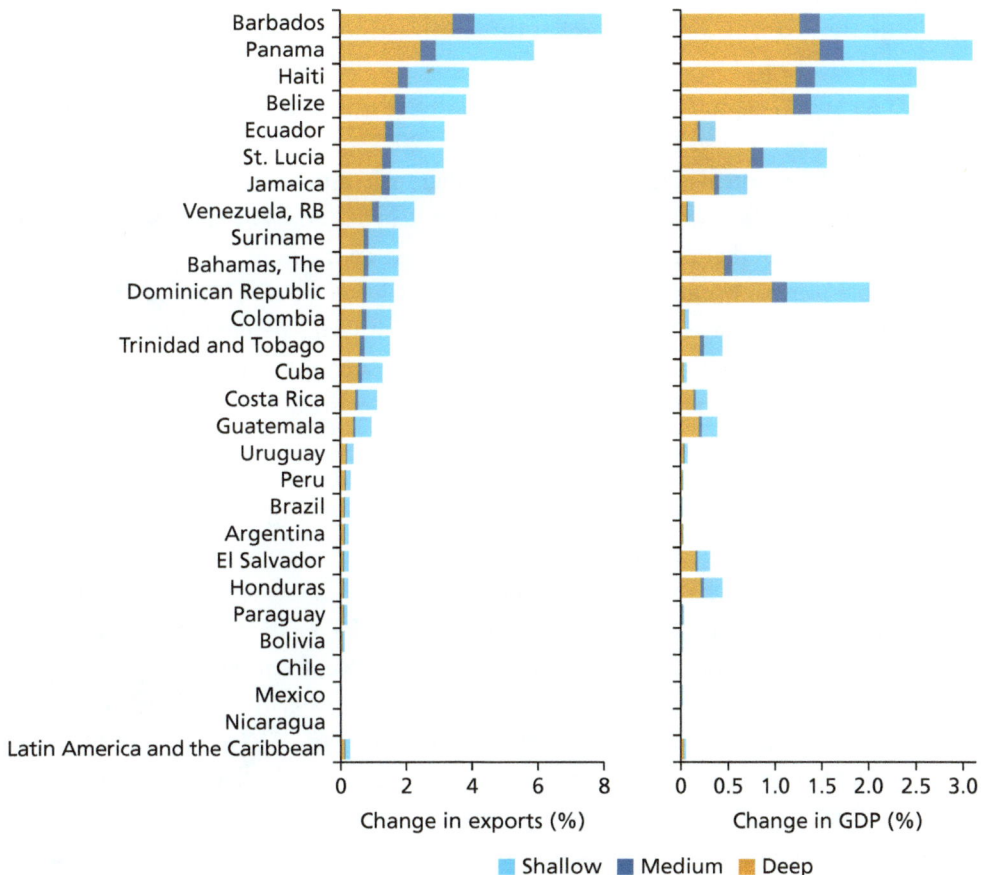

Source: Fontagné et al. 2021.

Note: The figure presents general equilibrium effects of Latin American and Caribbean countries signing new preferential trade agreements (PTAs) of varying depth (shallow, medium, or deep) with other Latin American and Caribbean countries in 2017. GDP = gross domestic product.

These results have two main policy implications for regional integration in Latin America and the Caribbean: First, the region's larger countries already engaged in PTA networks would benefit more from deepening existing agreements than from extending their networks to new partners. Second, the region's smaller countries would gain from signing new agreements, even shallow ones. (Deeper agreements would lead to higher gains but might be out of reach at first.)

DTAs as a vehicle for trade and GVC integration

DTAs present an avenue for promoting trade and GVC integration in Latin America and the Caribbean. Globally, deep provisions in trade agreements contribute to increases in GVC-related trade (Mattoo, Mulabdic, and Ruta 2017; Orefice and Rocha 2012; and Osnago, Rocha, and Ruta 2017). DTAs are also related to the way firms internationalize (inside the firm's national boundary through vertical integration or outside it through arm's-length transactions). And specific provisions in DTAs are linked with vertical foreign direct investment (Osnago, Rocha, and Ruta 2017, 2019).

DTAs and GVC integration are also positively linked in Latin America and the Caribbean. The value of GVC-related trade in 2017 (proxied by trade in parts and components)[8] was on average higher for the region's countries that had signed deeper agreements with their trading partners (figure 2.11). And estimates using a gravity framework suggest that deeper agreements, defined by the number or share of legally enforceable provisions, are associated with higher levels of GVC-related trade.[9] One additional provision in an agreement is correlated with a 0.3 percent increase in GVC-related trade. Similarly, GVC-related trade between countries that had signed the deepest agreements (with 30 or more provisions) was 12 percent higher than it had been before signing.

DTAs can also help countries upgrade the kinds of GVCs they participate in. The average numbers of a country's DTA partners and DTA provisions both increase as countries advance along the GVC taxonomy, from participating in commodity GVCs to participating in innovation GVCs (see chapter 1 on the taxonomy). This suggests that deeper integration in PTAs is associated with GVC upgrading. Across countries worldwide, the average number of PTA partners between 2015 and 2017 was 22 for countries specializing in "commodity" GVCs, 35 for countries participating in "limited manufacturing" GVCs, but more than 60 for the "advanced manufacturing and services" and "innovative activities" GVC groups (figure 2.12). The latter two groups of countries had more than 200 provisions on average in their DTAs. The countries specializing in "innovative activities" GVCs had 100 more provisions on average than countries specializing in commodity GVCs (233 versus 128).

Figure 2.11 Average value of GVC-related trade in 2017 was higher for Latin American and Caribbean countries that had signed DTAs

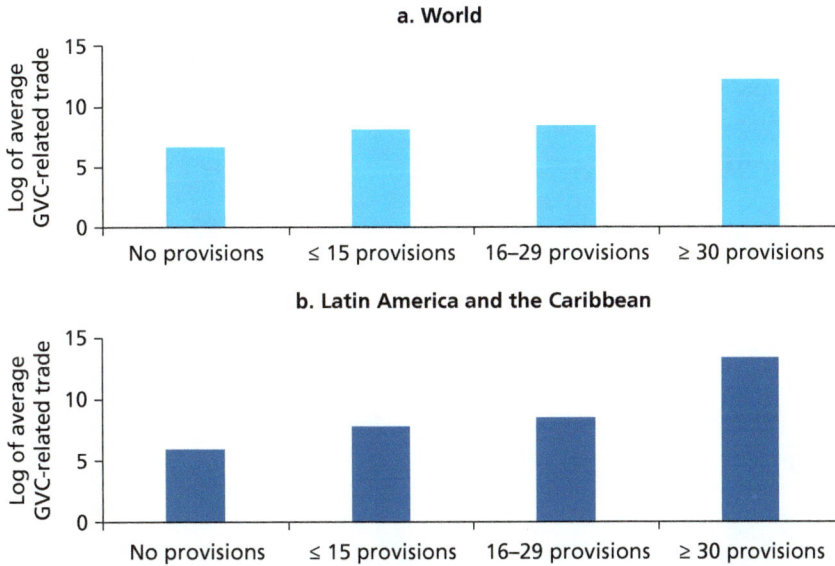

a. World

b. Latin America and the Caribbean

Source: Laget et al. 2018.

Note: The figure presents simple correlations between preferential trade agreements (PTAs) of varying depth and global value chain (GVC)-related trade. GVC-related trade is represented by trade in parts and components, defined as all nonfuel intermediates from the Broad Economic Categories (BEC) classification (codes 111, 121, 21, 22, 42, and 53). Here, deep trade agreements (DTAs) are defined as agreements containing at least 30 legally enforceable provisions.

Figure 2.12 Deeper integration in PTAs is associated with GVC upgrading

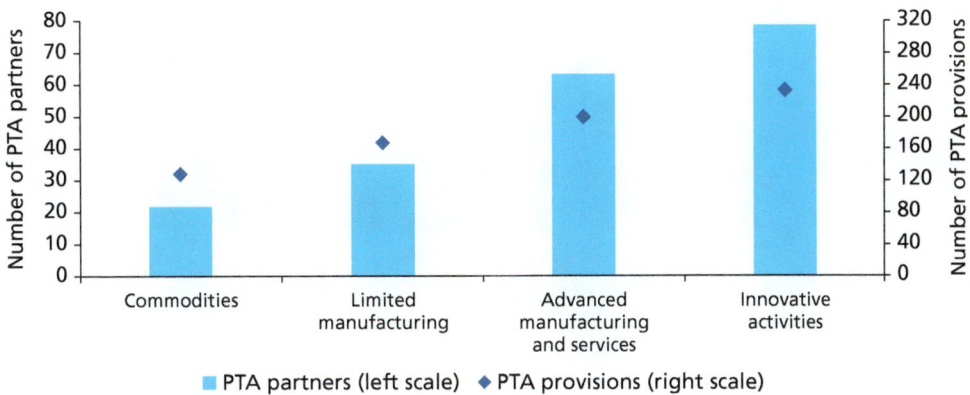

■ PTA partners (left scale) ◆ PTA provisions (right scale)

Sources: Winkler 2021; World Bank's Deep Trade Agreements database; global value chain (GVC) taxonomy data from World Bank 2020.

Note: The figure presents the average number of preferential trade agreement (PTA) partners and provisions for countries across regions globally, grouped by World Bank GVC taxonomy. It shows averages for 2015–17 and includes only countries that appear in the World Bank GVC taxonomy. Regions include only countries eligible for World Bank lending.

DTA CONTENT AND GVC INTEGRATION IN LATIN AMERICA AND THE CARIBBEAN

Global analysis suggests that the increased role of GVCs in recent decades has been accompanied by an increase in PTAs regulating trade facilitation, nontariff measures such as SPS and TBTs, and services (figure 2.13). This is not surprising, given that these policy priorities could potentially help countries to overcome disadvantages related to geography, market size, factor endowments, and institutions that limit their participation in GVCs (as further discussed in chapter 1).

The depth and content of those regulations tend to be higher in agreements signed by countries that are integrated into more sophisticated GVCs (figure 2.14). This suggests that the agreements might serve as a mechanism for countries to undertake domestic reforms in policy areas that are key to the fundamental determinants of GVC integration. The next chapters of this report analyze in depth the links between geography, market size, factor endowments, institutions and trade, and GVC integration in Latin America and the Caribbean.

Figure 2.13   Average coverage ratio of selected policy areas in new PTAs globally, by decade

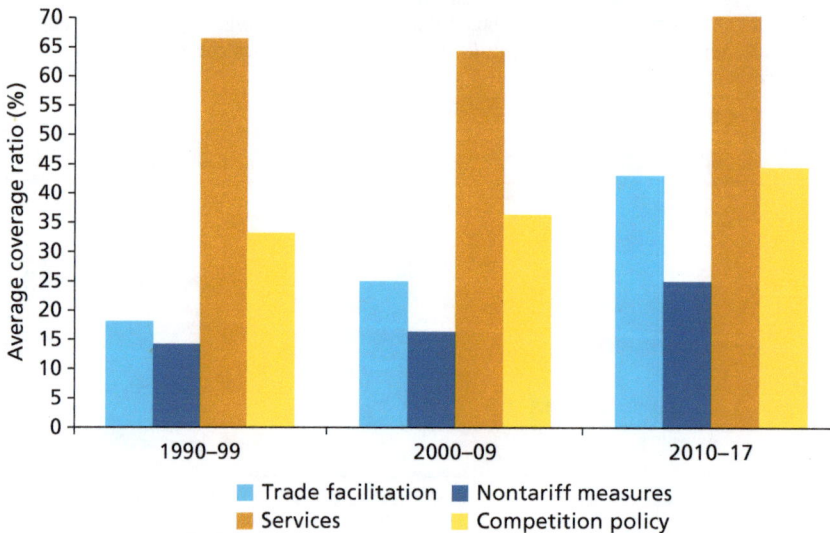

Source: World Bank's Deep Trade Agreements database.

Note: Coverage ratio refers to the share of provisions for each policy area contained in a given preferential trade agreement (PTA) divided by the maximum number of provisions in that policy area. Years refer to entry-into-force date. The figure excludes partial scope agreements, as well as the European Union agreement and enlargements.

Figure 2.14   Average coverage ratio of selected policy areas in new PTAs globally, by GVC taxonomy group, 2017

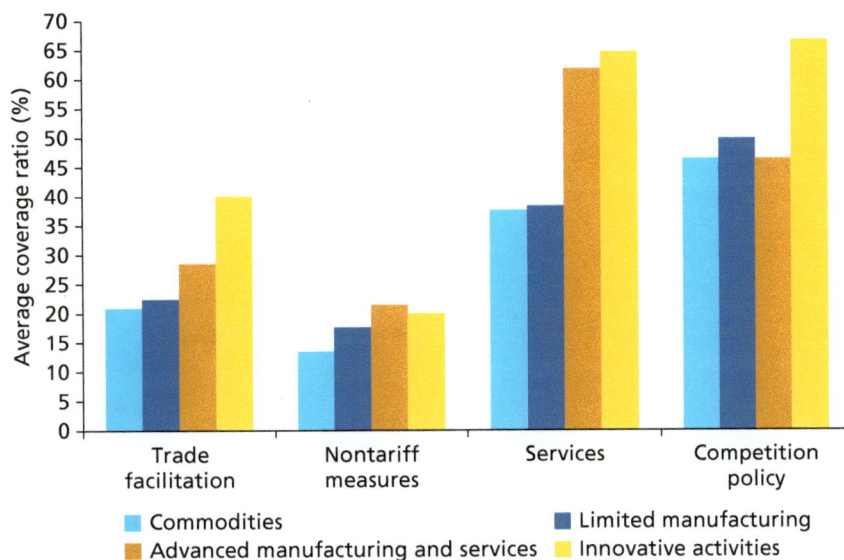

Source: World Bank's Deep Trade Agreements database; World Bank 2020.

Note: Coverage ratio refers to the share of provisions for each policy area contained in a given preferential trade agreement (PTA) divided by the maximum number of provisions in that policy area. The European Union agreement and enlargements are excluded. GVC = global value chain.

ANNEX 2A SUPPLEMENTARY TABLES AND FIGURES

Table 2A.1   Trade-weighted average of MFN and applied tariffs in Latin America and the Caribbean, by country

Tariff rate, percent

Country	Imports		Exports	
	MFN rate	Applied tariff	MFN rate	Applied tariff
Argentina	12.3	7.5	10.1	6.1
Aruba	8.4	8.4	5.2	5.1
Belize	23.3	21.1	15.4	9.8
Bolivia	9.3	4.9	3.2	0.4
Brazil	10.2	8.0	8.5	6.6
Chile	5.7	0.4	3.8	0.8
Colombia	7.2	4.9	3.7	1.1
Costa Rica	5.0	1.6	5.3	1.3

Continued

Table 2A.1   Trade-weighted average of MFN and applied tariffs in Latin America and the Caribbean, by country *(continued)*

Country	Imports		Exports	
	MFN rate	Applied tariff	MFN rate	Applied tariff
Dominican Republic	7.8	4.6	6.2	1.7
Ecuador	9.4	6.7	6.8	3.1
El Salvador	7.5	1.9	11.7	1.4
Guatemala	5.2	1.6	8.4	1.6
Honduras	6.9	3.2	8.8	0.4
Jamaica	11.5	9.8	4.4	1.8
Mexico	4.7	1.3	4.0	0.5
Panama	4.9	4.9	4.5	1.8
Paraguay	7.7	4.2	14.6	10.3
Peru	2.1	1.6	3.4	0.5
St. Lucia	11.8	8.9	6.4	0.5
Uruguay	9.4	5.7	10.5	6.8
Overall average	**6.6**	**3.4**	**5.7**	**2.5**

Sources: World Bank's Deep Trade Agreements database; Mattoo, Rocha, and Ruta 2020.

Note: The table excludes two countries—Trinidad and Tobago and República Bolivariana de Venezuela—for lack of data. MFN = most-favored-nation.

Table 2A.2   Trade-weighted average of MFN and applied tariffs in Latin America and the Caribbean, by sector

Tariff rate, percent

Sector	Imports		Exports	
	MFN rate	Applied tariff	MFN rate	Applied tariff
Agriculture				
Animal and animal products	25.67	4.59	14.63	10.67
Vegetable products	10.28	3.28	10.27	7.54
Foodstuffs	15.02	4.66	12.42	8.36
Natural resources				
Mineral products	1.36	0.48	0.57	0.19
Manufacturing				
Chemicals and allied industries	4.80	2.87	4.56	1.38
Plastics/rubbers	6.63	3.18	6.21	1.09

Continued

Table 2A.2 Trade-weighted average of MFN and applied tariffs in Latin America and the Caribbean, by sector *(continued)*

Sector	Imports		Exports	
	MFN rate	Applied tariff	MFN rate	Applied tariff
Raw hides, skins, leather, and furs	11.17	8.69	4.43	3.23
Wood and wood products	5.04	1.88	2.12	0.52
Textiles	13.74	9.53	11.92	1.07
Footwear/headgear	16.96	13.02	12.15	3.45
Stone/glass	8.17	4.19	2.39	0.74
Metals	4.55	2.62	2.61	0.54
Machinery/electrical	3.95	2.77	1.92	0.31
Transportation	12.38	4.99	9.24	0.84
Miscellaneous	6.94	4.76	1.81	0.41
Overall	**6.63**	**3.39**	**5.71**	**2.48**

Sources: World Bank's Deep Trade Agreements database; Mattoo, Rocha, and Ruta 2020.

Note: MFN = most-favored-nation.

Table 2A.3 PTAs of Latin American and Caribbean countries

Agreement	Year entered into force	Intra–Latin America and the Caribbean?	Coverage ratio (%)
Andean Community (CAN)	1988	Yes	13.9
Australia–Chile	2009	No	37.2
Canada–Chile	1997	No	32.8
Canada–Colombia	2011	No	45.1
Canada–Costa Rica	2002	No	18.6
Canada–Honduras	2014	No	40.4
Canada–Panama	2013	No	38.8
Canada–Peru	2009	No	42.0
Caribbean Community and Common Market (CARICOM)	1973	Yes	16.5
Central American Common Market (CACM)	1961	Yes	18.2
Chile–China	2006	No	15.9
Chile–Colombia	2009	Yes	30.2
Chile–Costa Rica (Chile–Central America)	2002	Yes	19.0

Continued

Table 2A.3   PTAs of Latin American and Caribbean countries *(continued)*

Agreement	Year entered into force	Intra–Latin America and the Caribbean?	Coverage ratio (%)
Chile–El Salvador (Chile–Central America)	2002	Yes	19.0
Chile–Guatemala (Chile–Central America)	2010	Yes	18.7
Chile–Honduras (Chile–Central America)	2008	Yes	18.5
Chile–India	2007	No	9.4
Chile–Japan	2007	No	27.7
Chile–Malaysia	2012	No	11.8
Chile–Mexico	1999	Yes	30.1
Chile–Nicaragua (Chile–Central America)	2012	Yes	18.6
Chile–Vietnam	2014	No	10.1
China–Costa Rica	2011	No	20.5
Colombia–Mexico	1995	Yes	28.9
Colombia–Northern Triangle (El Salvador, Guatemala, Honduras)	2009	Yes	25.6
Comprehensive and Progressive Agreement for Trans-Pacific Partnership (CPTPP)	2017	No	54.2
Costa Rica–Colombia	2016	Yes	20.3
Costa Rica–Peru	2013	Yes	34.7
Costa Rica–Singapore	2013	No	33.5
Dominican Republic–Central America	2001	Yes	22.5
Dominican Republic–Central America–United States Free Trade Agreement (CAFTA-DR)	2006	No	33.8
El Salvador–Cuba	2012	Yes	7.2
El Salvador–Honduras–Taiwan, China	2008	No	26.6
European Free Trade Agreement (EFTA)–Central America (Costa Rica and Panama)	2014	No	40.0
European Free Trade Agreement (EFTA)–Chile	2004	No	26.9
European Free Trade Agreement (EFTA)–Colombia	2011	No	37.6
European Free Trade Agreement (EFTA)–Mexico	2001	No	27.1

Continued

Table 2A.3 PTAs of Latin American and Caribbean countries *(continued)*

Agreement	Year entered into force	Intra–Latin America and the Caribbean?	Coverage ratio (%)
European Free Trade Agreement (EFTA)–Peru	2011	No	33.0
European Union–European Community–Caribbean Forum States Economic Partnership Agreement	2008	No	37.2
European Union–Central America	2013	No	43.9
European Union–Chile	2003	No	34.4
European Union–Colombia and Peru	2013	No	44.6
European Union–Mexico	2000	No	14.9
European Union–Overseas Countries and Territories (OCT)	1971	No	8.1
Global System of Trade Preferences among Developing Countries (GSTP)	1989	No	1.5
Guatemala–Taiwan, China	2006	No	26.5
Hong Kong SAR, China–Chile	2014	No	22.1
Israel–Mexico	2000	No	17.0
Japan–Mexico	2005	No	28.9
Japan–Peru	2012	No	36.9
Korea, Rep.–Chile	2004	No	37.4
Korea, Rep.–Colombia	2016	No	30.6
Latin American Integration Association (LAIA)	1981	Yes	4.6
Mexico–Central America	2012	Yes	28.1
Mexico–Panama	2015	Yes	20.4
Mexico–Uruguay	2004	Yes	26.8
Nicaragua–Taiwan, China	2008	No	37.6
North American Free Trade Agreement (NAFTA)	1994	No	40.7
Pacific Alliance	2016	Yes	13.8
Panama–Chile	2008	Yes	17.3
Panama–Taiwan, China	2004	No	30.8

Continued

Table 2A.3   PTAs of Latin American and Caribbean countries *(continued)*

Agreement	Year entered into force	Intra–Latin America and the Caribbean?	Coverage ratio (%)
Panama–Costa Rica (Panama–Central America)	2008	Yes	20.4
Panama–Dominican Republic	1987	Yes	3.9
Panama–El Salvador (Panama–Central America)	2003	Yes	23.6
Panama–Guatemala (Panama–Central America)	2009	Yes	20.0
Panama–Honduras (Panama–Central America)	2009	Yes	20.2
Panama–Nicaragua (Panama–Central America)	2009	Yes	19.3
Panama–Peru	2012	Yes	35.2
Panama–Singapore	2006	No	31.1
Peru–Chile	2009	Yes	29.2
Peru–China	2010	No	29.7
Peru–Korea, Rep.	2011	No	45.3
Peru–Mexico	2012	Yes	27.2
Peru–Singapore	2009	No	34.8
Southern Common Market (MERCOSUR)	1991	Yes	18.5
Southern Common Market (MERCOSUR)–India	2009	No	6.7
Trans-Pacific Strategic Economic Partnership	2006	No	29.9
Turkey–Chile	2011	No	11.8
United States–Chile	2004	No	39.1
United States–Colombia	2012	No	39.7
United States–Panama	2012	No	36.8
United States–Peru	2009	No	39.7

Sources: World Bank's Deep Trade Agreements database; Mattoo, Rocha, and Ruta 2020.

Note: The coverage ratio is the share of provisions contained in each agreement divided by the maximum number of possible provisions. PTA = preferential trade agreement.

Figure 2A.1 Average share of exporting firms' exports to PTA partners versus nonpartners, selected Latin American and Caribbean countries

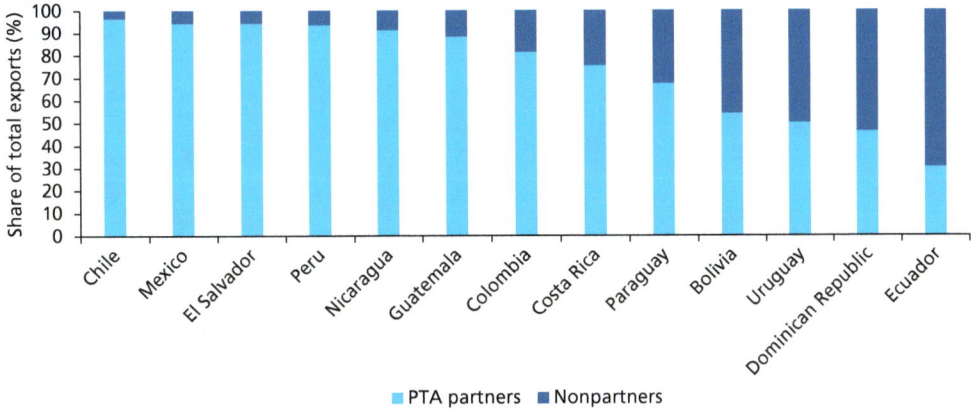

Sources: Fernandes, Nievas, and Winkler 2021, based on updates to the World Bank's Exporter Dynamics database (described in Fernandes, Freund, and Pierola 2016) and the World Bank's Deep Trade Agreements database.

Note: PTA = preferential trade agreement.

Figure 2A.2 Average share of exports to PTA partners for GVC participating firms versus exporter-only firms in Latin American and Caribbean PTAs

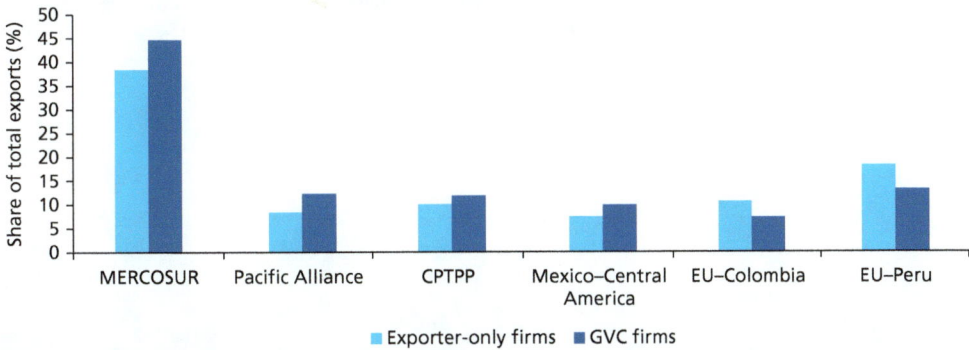

Sources: Fernandes, Nievas, and Winkler 2021, based on updates to the World Bank's Exporter Dynamics database (described in Fernandes, Freund, and Pierola 2016); World Bank's Deep Trade Agreements database.

Note: Global value chain (GVC) participating firms are exporters that import inputs and capital goods, while exporter-only firms do not import them. For each country, shares of imported inputs and capital goods are computed based on the most recent year of customs data. The Southern Common Market (MERCOSUR) averages include Paraguay and Uruguay only, because customs data are inaccessible for the other two current members (Argentina and Brazil). The EU–Colombia and EU–Peru figures measure only the European Union (EU) share of exports and imported inputs and not the other Latin American and Caribbean country shares in the EU–Colombia–Peru preferential trade agreement (PTA). CPTPP = Comprehensive and Progressive Agreement for Trans-Pacific Partnership.

Figure 2A.3   Share of exports to PTA partners for GVC participating firms versus exporter-only firms in selected Latin American and Caribbean countries, by PTA

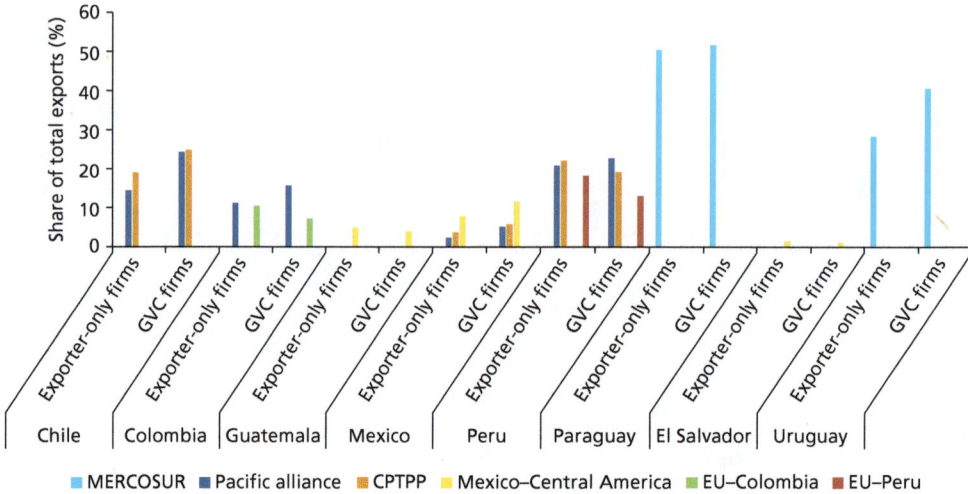

Sources: Fernandes, Nievas, and Winkler 2021, based on updates to the World Bank's Exporter Dynamics database (described in Fernandes, Freund, and Pierola 2016); World Bank's Deep Trade Agreements database.

Note: Global value chain (GVC)-participating firms are exporters that import inputs and capital goods, while exporter-only firms do not import them. For each country, shares of imported inputs and capital goods are computed based on the most recent year of customs data. The EU–Colombia and EU–Peru figures measure only the European Union (EU) share of exports and imported inputs and not the other Latin American and Caribbean country shares in the EU–Colombia–Peru preferential trade agreement (PTA). CPTPP = Comprehensive and Progressive Agreement for Trans-Pacific Partnership.

Figure 2A.4   Average shares of imported inputs from within selected PTA areas across GVC participating firms in Latin America and the Caribbean

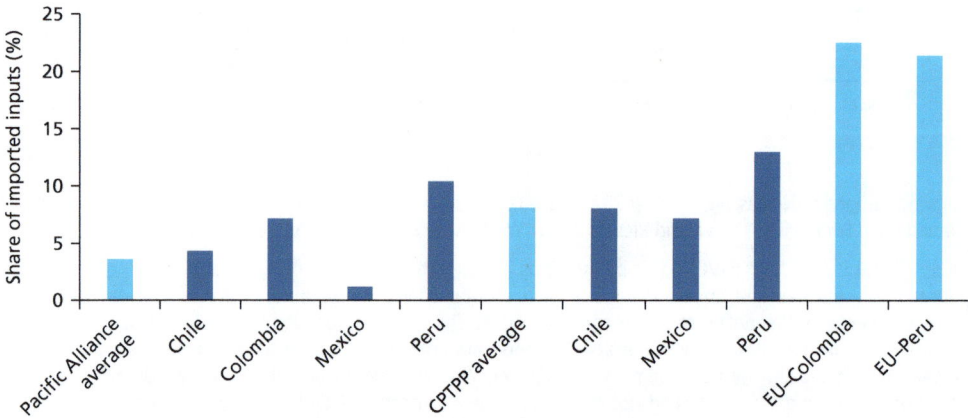

Sources: Fernandes, Nievas, and Winkler 2021, based on updates to the World Bank's Exporter Dynamics database (described in Fernandes, Freund, and Pierola 2016; World Bank's Deep Trade Agreements database.

Note: Global value chain (GVC)-participating firms are exporters that import inputs and capital goods. For each country, shares of imported inputs and capital goods are computed based on the most recent year of customs data. The EU–Colombia and EU–Peru figures measure only the European Union (EU) share of exports and imported inputs and not the other Latin American and Caribbean country shares in the EU–Colombia–Peru preferential trade agreement (PTA). CPTPP = Comprehensive and Progressive Agreement for Trans-Pacific Partnership.

NOTES

1. The MERCOSUR States Parties include Argentina, Brazil, Paraguay, Uruguay, and República Bolivariana de Venezuela (the latter of which has been suspended indefinitely since December 2016). Bolivia has been in the process of accession to MERCOSUR since July 2015.

2. After 20 years of negotiations, an agreement for a free trade area between the European Union (EU) and MERCOSUR was reached in 2019. Despite an agreement in principle, the final texts have not been finalized, signed, or ratified, so the PTA has not entered into force.

3. The language in a PTA is considered "enforceable" if it is sufficiently precise from a legal point of view and if the agreement for a specific policy area includes a dispute settlement mechanism to resolve disagreement.

4. The five extraregional Latin American and Caribbean PTAs in force in 2000 were EU–Overseas Countries and Territories (OCT); the Global System of Trade Preferences among Developing Countries (GSTP); the North American Free Trade Agreement (NAFTA); Canada–Chile; and EU–Mexico.

5. The Caribbean Community and Common Market (CARICOM) has 15 member states: Antigua and Barbuda, The Bahamas, Barbados, Belize, Dominica, Grenada, Guyana, Haiti, Jamaica, Montserrat, St. Kitts and Nevis, St. Lucia, St. Vincent and the Grenadines, Suriname, and Trinidad and Tobago. The Central American Common Market (CACM) includes five countries: Costa Rica, El Salvador, Guatemala, Honduras, and Nicaragua.

6. Different approaches can be contemplated from the simple count, or the coverage ratio, of the provisions included in an agreement, where it is assumed that the relative importance of each provision is the same across policy areas and agreements to alternative methods to assign different weights to different provisions according to their commonality or explanatory power across agreements.

7. Because not enough information is yet available on trade flows under the United States–Mexico–Canada Agreement (USMCA), it is excluded from this analysis.

8. Following Yeats (1998) and Hummels, Ishii, and Yi (2001), we use trade in parts and components to proxy for global production sharing.

9. Similar results are obtained using data from the Trade in Value Added (TiVA) database of the Organisation for Economic Co-operation and Development. However, results using a gravity equation for trade in value added should be considered cautiously because they do not take into account third-country effects through (a) inputs used in final exports of third countries, and (b) inputs of third countries used in other countries.

REFERENCES

Fernandes, A., C. Freund, and M. D. Pierola. 2016. "Exporter Behavior, Country Size and Stage of Development: Evidence from the Exporter Dynamics Database." *Journal of Development Economics* 119: 121–37.

Fernandes, A., H.-L. Kee, and D. Winkler. 2020. "Determinants of Global Value Chain Participation: Cross-Country Evidence." Policy Research Working Paper 9197, World Bank, Washington, DC.

Fernandes, A., G. Nievas, and D. Winkler. 2021. "Trade and Global Value Chain Integration in Latin America: Stylized Facts." Working Paper, Report No. 159028, World Bank, Washington, DC.

Fontagné, L., N. Rocha, M. Ruta, and G. Santoni. 2021. "A General Equilibrium Assessment of the Economic Impact of Deep Trade Agreements." Policy Research Working Paper 9630, World Bank, Washington, DC.

Hofmann, C., A. Osnago, and M. Ruta. 2017. "Horizontal Depth: A New Database on the Content of Preferential Trade Agreements." Policy Research Working Paper 7981, World Bank, Washington, DC.

Hollweg, C. H., and N. Rocha. 2018. "GVC Participation and Deep Integration in Brazil." Policy Research Working Paper 8646, World Bank, Washington, DC.

Hummels, D. L., J. Ishii, and K.-M. Yi. 2001. "The Nature and Growth of Vertical Specialization in World Trade." *Journal of International Economics* 54 (1): 75–96.

Laget, E., A. Osnago, N. Rocha, and M. Ruta. 2018. "Deep Trade Agreements and Global Value Chains." Policy Research Working Paper 8491, World Bank, Washington, DC.

Martínez Licetti, M., M. Iootty, T. Goodwin, and J. Signoret. 2018. *Strengthening Argentina's Integration into the Global Economy: Policy Proposals for Trade, Investment, and Competition.* International Development in Focus Series. Washington, DC: World Bank.

Mattoo, A., A. Mulabdic, and M. Ruta. 2017. "Trade Creation and Trade Diversion in Deep Agreements." Policy Research Working Paper 8206, World Bank, Washington, DC.

Mattoo, A., N. Rocha, and M. Ruta, eds. 2020. *Handbook of Deep Trade Agreements.* Washington, DC: World Bank.

Orefice, G., and N. Rocha. 2012. "Deep Integration and Production Networks: An Empirical Analysis." Staff Working Paper ERSD-2011-11, World Trade Organization, Geneva.

Osnago, A., N. Rocha, and M. Ruta. 2017. "Do Deep Trade Agreements Boost Vertical FDI?" *The World Bank Economic Review* 30 (Suppl 1): S119–S125.

Osnago, A., N. Rocha, and M. Ruta. 2019. "Deep Trade Agreements and Vertical FDI: The Devil Is in the Details." *Canadian Journal of Economics* 52 (4): 1558–99.

Winkler, D. 2021. "Policy Constraints to Global Value Chain Participation in Latin America: Which Areas Can Be Addressed through Deep Trade Agreements?" Background paper for this volume, World Bank, Washington, DC.

World Bank. 2020. *World Development Report 2020: Trading for Development in the Age of Global Value Chains.* Washington, DC: World Bank.

Yeats, A. J. 1998. "Just How Big Is Global Production Sharing?" Policy Research Working Paper 1871, World Bank, Washington, DC.

3 Trade Facilitation: Simplifying and Harmonizing Procedures

Woori Lee, Ernani Checcucci, and Mayra Alfaro de Morán

KEY MESSAGES

- Trade facilitation (TF) commitments in deep trade agreements can help Latin American and Caribbean countries better integrate into regional and global value chains. Evidence for Peru suggests that they help the export performance of global value chain (GVC)-participating firms by reducing the trade costs and uncertainty associated with importing in both the home and destination countries.
- Latin American and Caribbean countries should establish robust governance frameworks to drive reform and create coordinating committees to promote international cooperation and alignment in implementing agreements.
- TF activities should engage the private sector, enhance program and project management capacities, implement integrated risk management systems, and recognize certificates from accredited agencies in other countries with similar or higher standards.

INTRODUCTION

Trade facilitation (TF) is particularly important in Latin America and the Caribbean, where the time and cost of trading across borders are high. Border inefficiency and regulatory uncertainty are key barriers to boosting trade in low- and middle-income countries, even when tariffs are low. Completing the documents to import a standard container takes 108 hours in Latin American and Caribbean countries, on average—on par with countries participating in commodity global value chains (GVCs) but more than three times as long as in European and Central Asian countries and almost seven times as long as in countries specializing in advanced manufacturing and services GVCs. TF can reduce tangible and intangible costs in the region by improving, simplifying, and harmonizing the procedures and controls governing the cross-border movement of goods.

Deep trade agreements (DTAs) can push TF reforms forward, advancing the free movement of goods between member countries by stipulating more advanced and sophisticated solutions than multilateral agreements typically contain.[1] The DTA provisions promote coordination, collaboration, and information sharing between relevant agencies; harmonize processes and procedures that reduce transaction costs; and establish governance structures to pursue continuous improvement of border procedures as well as compliance and enforcement.

GVCs, in which goods cross borders multiple times, often magnify the impact of TF provisions. Because firms involved in GVCs rely on the timely and reliable delivery of foreign inputs, their export competitiveness is enhanced by more efficient import procedures. Because many border improvements are nondiscriminatory, TF commitments in a DTA generate positive spillovers for GVC firms that import inputs from countries that are not partners to the DTA.

Commitments to TF require an effective governance structure to support implementation. TF reforms entail major investments of time and resources over several years, especially if the political environment is volatile. And preferential trade agreement (PTA) partners' different levels of development necessitate coordinated efforts to identify solutions suitable to national contexts. For Latin American and Caribbean countries to overcome the implementation challenges and reap the full benefits of TF, provisions must promote coordination among agencies and establish a clear governance structure such as through a TF committee.

THE BENEFITS OF TRADE FACILITATION

Border inefficiency and regulatory uncertainty are barriers to boosting trade in low- and middle-income countries, even when tariffs are low (WTO 2015). The problem has prompted renewed efforts to improve TF by simplifying and harmonizing the procedures and controls governing the movement of goods across borders.

TF measures reduce tangible and intangible costs at and behind the border. Although TF is often associated with the activities of a national customs administration, it also involves other agencies at the border and beyond.[2] TF defined in this way includes measures aimed at not only facilitating trade directly but also promoting compliance and customs cooperation. For example, TF provisions in DTAs often include measures to promote cooperation between border agencies or information exchange on best practices. In addition, DTA provisions that require the publication or internet publication of regulatory information before implementation enhance the transparency of trade-related regulations. Implementing such measures helps enable easier and quicker flows of imports and exports and reduces the uncertainty associated with international trade.

The impact of TF and uncertainty is usually magnified by trade through GVCs, whereby goods cross borders multiple times along a production chain (World Bank 2020b). Firms participating in GVCs not only export but also import intermediate inputs used in their production and exports. Increased efficiency in import procedures directly improves firms' export performance and GVC participation (Fontagné, Orefice, and Piermartini 2017; Moïsé and Sorescu 2013; World Bank 2020a). Because TF can enhance border efficiency on both the exporting and importing sides, it is particularly important for GVC firms that import and export. And when competitiveness along GVCs relies on the timely and reliable supply of foreign inputs, high uncertainty is costly (Fernandes, Hillberry, and Berg 2016).

The TF agenda is particularly important in Latin America and the Caribbean, where the time and cost of trading across borders are high. TF indicators show a large gap between Latin America and the Caribbean and other, more-developed regions in export and import costs. The gap implies that TF improvements offer opportunities for better integrating Latin America and the Caribbean economically—and for the region's countries to increase their participation in regional and global value chains.

Although TF reforms use various channels—including multilateral agreements, PTAs, and domestic reforms—DTAs can push TF forward. DTA provisions related to customs and TF advance the free movement of goods between member countries by including more advanced and sophisticated solutions beyond multilateral commitments. They harmonize processes and procedures that reduce transaction costs in imports and exports. They promote coordination, collaboration, and information sharing between relevant agencies of member countries. And they establish governance structures to pursue ongoing improvement of border procedures and facilitation and to improve trade compliance and enforcement.

DTAs in Latin America and the Caribbean contain a wide range of TF provisions, from those specifying rules of origin requirements to those addressing customs cooperation and information sharing. The region's agreements have high numbers of TF provisions, exceeded only by those in North America and the European Union (EU). But DTAs vary across partner regions and countries. DTAs of mostly high-income regions (including East Asia and Pacific, the EU, and North America) tend to include more TF provisions than do the agreements of other regions. Intraregional DTAs within Latin America and the Caribbean include, on average, fewer TF provisions than those with extraregional partners—a notable difference for a region characterized by high intraregional trade and transportation costs.

As Latin American and Caribbean countries seek to integrate further into regional and global value chains, TF provisions in DTAs can reduce trade costs and times for GVC participating firms. In a recent study using firm-level data from Peru,

TF provisions boosted the export performance of GVC firms through efficiency enhancements at the country's own borders (Lee, Rocha, and Ruta 2021). Because GVC firms rely on the timely and reliable delivery of foreign inputs, their export competitiveness is enhanced when import procedures are made more efficient. And TF commitments in DTAs have nondiscriminatory aspects (as well as preferential ones), generating positive spillovers for GVC firms that import inputs from countries other than the DTA partner country.

Despite recognizing that the TF provisions of DTAs enhance GVC firms' export performance, governments cannot always secure the benefits easily. Many TF commitments require a large investment of time and resources over a span of several years. Negotiating and implementing the TF provisions of DTAs can also be challenging because of differences in the maturity of partner countries. Successful implementation requires coordination of efforts between the partners to identify the most suitable solutions given their national contexts. Even so, successfully implementing TF reforms driven by DTAs can increase border efficiency and promote trade, as exemplified by the Guatemala–Honduras case study discussed later in this chapter.

REGIONAL CONTEXT

Trade facilitation indicators

Indicators for TF—such as the World Bank's *Doing Business* indicators for trading across borders, the Bank's Logistics Performance Index, and the Organisation for Economic Co-operation and Development (OECD) TF Index—show a large gap in export and import costs between Latin America and the Caribbean and other regions.

Doing Business indicators on trading across borders

Latin America and the Caribbean's overall score on the World Bank's *Doing Business 2020* indicator set on trading across borders, which assesses the time and costs required for border compliance and documentary compliance, was lower than the scores for East Asia and Pacific, Europe and Central Asia, the Middle East and North Africa, and the OECD high-income countries (table 3.1). The average cost of border compliance for exports and imports was higher in Latin America and the Caribbean than in most other regions, second only to Sub-Saharan Africa.

The time required for border compliance for exports in Latin America and the Caribbean was more than 4 times that in the OECD (55.3 versus 12.7 hours), while importing was 6.5 times more time consuming (55.6 versus 8.5 hours).[3] The time required for export document compliance was more than 15 times higher than in OECD countries (35.7 versus 2.3 hours), while that for import document compliance was more than 12 times higher (43.2 versus 3.4 hours). The cost of document compliance to export from Latin America and the Caribbean was triple that of the OECD countries (US$100.30 versus US$33.40), whereas the cost to import was 4.5 times higher (US$107.30 versus US$23.50).

Table 3.1 Latin America and the Caribbean's weak performance relative to other regions on the *Doing Business* trading across borders indicators, 2020

Region	Trading across borders score	Border compliance				Documentary compliance			
		Time to export (hours)	Cost to export (US$)	Time to import (hours)	Cost to import (US$)	Time to export (hours)	Cost to export (US$)	Time to import (hours)	Cost to import (US$)
East Asia and Pacific	71.6	57.5	381.1	68.4	422.8	55.6	109.4	53.7	108.4
Europe and Central Asia	87.3	16.1	150.0	20.4	158.8	25.1	87.6	23.4	85.9
Latin America and the Caribbean	**69.1**	**55.3**	**516.3**	**55.6**	**628.4**	**35.7**	**100.3**	**43.2**	**107.3**
Middle East and North Africa	61.8	52.5	441.8	94.2	512.5	66.4	240.7	72.5	262.6
OECD high-income	94.3	12.7	136.8	8.5	98.1	2.3	33.4	3.4	23.5
South Asia	65.3	53.4	310.6	85.7	472.9	73.7	157.9	93.7	261.7
Sub-Saharan Africa	53.6	97.1	603.1	126.2	690.6	71.9	172.5	96.1	287.2

Source: World Bank *Doing Business 2020* database, https://openknowledge.worldbank.org/bitstream/handle/10986/32436/9781464814402.pdf.

Note: The *Doing Business* indicators on trading across borders measure the time and cost to clear official procedures, including customs controls. OECD = Organisation for Economic Co-operation and Development.

Logistics Performance Index

Latin America and the Caribbean ranked similarly on the World Bank's Logistics Performance Index for 2018 (table 3.2). Its performance was lower than that of East Asia and Pacific, Europe and Central Asia, the Middle East and North Africa, and OECD members but higher than that of South Asia and Sub-Saharan Africa on the ability to track and trace consignments, the competence and quality of logistics services, the frequency of on-time shipments, and the quality of trade- and transport-related infrastructure. Latin America and the Caribbean's indicators for the efficiency of customs clearance and the ease of arranging competitively priced shipments were at the same level as those of the Middle East and North Africa.

Trade Facilitation Index

Latin America and the Caribbean's relative weakness in TF is also evident on the OECD Trade Facilitation Index (table 3.3). The region's average TF performance in 2019 was lower than that of all other regions except Sub-Saharan Africa. It lags particularly in such areas as advance rulings, fees and charges, and border agency cooperation, though it performs relatively well in automation, documents, and procedures.

Border thickness

A new World Bank measure of border "thickness" also indicates high bilateral trade costs in Latin America and the Caribbean. Bilateral border thickness measures the additional cost incurred when trading internationally versus domestically, calculated

Table 3.2   Latin America and the Caribbean was similarly weak on the Logistics Performance Index, 2018

Region	Overall	Customs	Infrastructure	International shipments	Logistics quality and competence	Tracking and tracing	Timeliness
East Asia and Pacific	3.1	3.0	3.1	3.0	3.1	3.2	3.5
Europe and Central Asia	3.2	3.0	3.1	3.1	3.2	3.3	3.6
Latin America and the Caribbean	**2.7**	**2.5**	**2.5**	**2.7**	**2.6**	**2.7**	**3.0**
Middle East and North Africa	2.8	2.5	2.8	2.7	2.7	2.8	3.2
OECD members	3.6	3.4	3.6	3.4	3.6	3.7	3.9
South Asia	2.5	2.3	2.3	2.5	2.5	2.6	2.9
Sub-Saharan Africa	2.4	2.3	2.2	2.5	2.4	2.5	2.8

Source: World Bank's Logistics Performance Index 2018, https://lpi.worldbank.org/.

Note: 1 = low to 5 = high. OECD = Organisation for Economic Co-operation and Development.

Table 3.3 Latin America and the Caribbean was also weak on the Trade Facilitation Index, 2019

Region	Average TF performance	Information availability	Involvement of the trade community	Advance rulings	Appeal procedures	Fees and charges	Documents	Automation	Procedures	Internal border agency cooperation	External border agency cooperation	Governance and impartiality
Asia and Pacific	1.2	1.2	1.3	1.2	1.3	1.5	1.2	1.1	1.2	1.0	0.9	1.5
Europe and Central Asia	1.5	1.5	1.6	1.7	1.5	1.7	1.6	1.5	1.5	1.1	1.2	1.7
Latin America and the Caribbean	**1.1**	**1.2**	**1.3**	**1.1**	**1.3**	**1.4**	**1.2**	**1.1**	**1.3**	**0.7**	**0.7**	**1.2**
Middle East and North Africa	1.2	1.2	1.2	1.2	1.3	1.5	1.2	1.1	1.2	0.9	0.7	1.2
Sub-Saharan Africa	0.8	0.8	0.9	0.5	0.8	1.3	0.9	0.7	1.0	0.5	0.5	0.7
OECD members	1.7	1.7	1.7	1.8	1.6	1.9	1.7	1.8	1.7	1.4	1.6	1.9

Source: OECD Trade Facilitation Index, http://www.compareyourcountry.org/trade-facilitation.

Note: The Trade Facilitation (TF) Index takes values from 0 to 2, where 2 designates the best performance that can be achieved. Regions follow Organisation for Economic Co-operation and Development (OECD) classifications, wherein Asia and Pacific includes East Asia and Pacific as well as South Asia.

as the ad valorem equivalent "wedge" between international trade and domestic commerce. The border thickness measure captures a wider range of trade costs than those related only to TF—including tariffs, trade finance, border delays, insurance costs, and logistics and regulatory barriers. It shows that cross-border trade in the Latin America and the Caribbean region faces significant costs beyond those of domestic trade. The three thickest borders in the region are between Brazil and Suriname, Brazil and Guyana, and Mexico and Belize (map 3.1).

The ongoing trade facilitation agenda

Latin America and the Caribbean's weak TF performance provides a motivation for advancing the TF agenda in the region. As in other regions, the agenda in Latin America and the Caribbean is defined by four complementary driving forces: (a) implementation of commitments in multilateral agreements such as the Trade Facilitation Agreement (TFA) of the World Trade Organization (WTO); (b) regional economic integration and plurilateral agreements; (c) bilateral agreements, notably between neighboring countries; and (d) the domestic TF agenda.

Map 3.1   Thick borders mean high bilateral trading costs in Latin America and the Caribbean

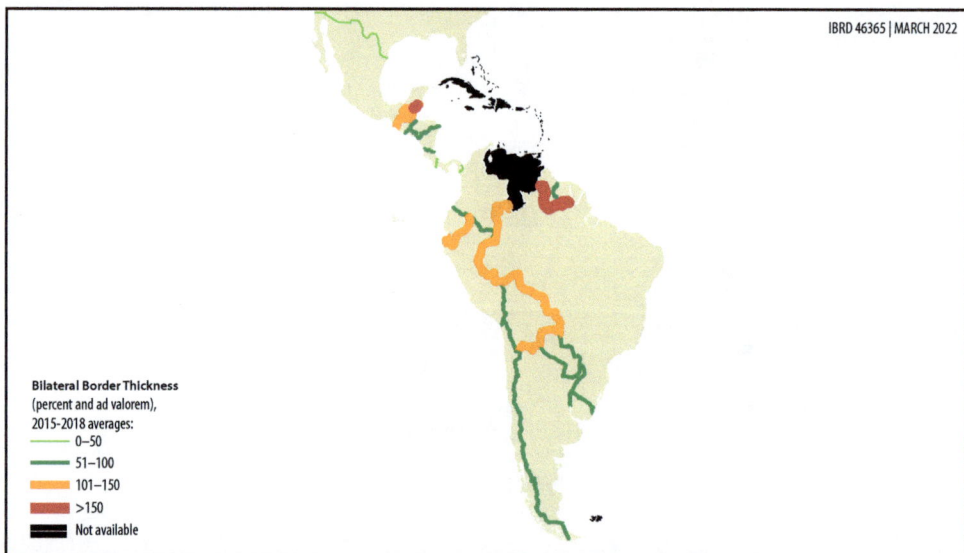

IBRD 46365 | MARCH 2022

Bilateral Border Thickness
(percent and ad valorem),
2015-2018 averages:
— 0–50
— 51–100
— 101–150
— >150
■ Not available

Sources: World Bank estimates using the United Nations Economic and Social Commission for Asia and the Pacific (ESCAP)–World Bank Trade Cost Database (2018); World Bank's Deep Trade Agreements database; Mattoo, Rocha, and Ruta 2020.

Note: Bilateral border "thickness" here measures the additional cost of trading internationally versus domestically, calculated as the percentage ad-valorem-equivalent "wedge" between international trade and domestic commerce. Thickness measures are 2015–18 averages. Black denotes countries without data. km = kilometers.

WTO Trade Facilitation Agreement. The WTO TFA establishes global standards for TF, and countries continue their efforts to implement it. The main projects and initiatives under development include national single window trade solutions, information sharing and transparency, risk management solutions for customs administrations and other cross-border regulatory agencies, and authorized economic operators (AEOs).[4] For instance, almost all countries in Latin America and the Caribbean have ongoing development processes related to national single windows for trade, though at varying stages of development and speeds of implementation. Some TFA multilateral commitments are reinforced and further advanced through corresponding provisions in DTAs, as discussed in detail below.

Regional and plurilateral economic integration agreements. One of the biggest such efforts in Latin America and the Caribbean is the Central America regional integration agenda, reflected in the 2017 TF strategy of the Secretariat for Central American Economic Integration (SIECA). The strategy prioritizes the use of prearrival declarations, coordination of immigration controls, electronic zoo and phytosanitary certificates, cargo tracking through radio frequency identification technology, and video surveillance cameras at border crossings.[5]

The Latin American Integration Association (ALADI) promotes the automatic exchange of electronic certificates of origin, while the Southern Common Market (MERCOSUR) Trade Facilitation Strategy includes automatic exchange of information, interoperability of information systems, and improved risk management. The Pacific Alliance includes single window interoperability and the mutual recognition of AEOs (Mejia Rivas and Maday 2019). In addition, the Pacific Alliance and MERCOSUR signed an agreement to explore the harmonization of AEO programs, mutual recognition agreements, and the interoperability of single windows for trade.

Bilateral agreements. Pairs of countries reach bilateral agreements, either DTAs or specific border reform projects, to facilitate trade. For example, the Enabling Protocol for the Process of Deep Integration toward the Free Transit of Goods and Natural Persons between the Republics of Guatemala and Honduras (hereafter referred to as Guatemala–Honduras) was signed in 2015 and began operations in 2018. As further discussed later in the chapter, this bilateral agreement establishes an institutional framework that defines policies, regulations, and procedures for deep integration between the two countries. It introduces the Central American Invoice and Single Declaration (FYDUCA) and creates integrated border posts at the land borders between the two countries.

In addition, Costa Rica and El Salvador are pursuing a ferry project, in collaboration with the World Bank, that would allow multimodal logistics companies to offer full transportation services and reduce risks and time on the road (box 3.1).

Box 3.1   The Costa Rica–El Salvador ferry project

Most intraregional trade in Central America travels by land. The main route is the Pacific Corridor, or CA1 (2,461 kilometers). It begins in Tecún Umán, on the border between Mexico and Guatemala, and ends in the Colón Free Zone in Panama. This journey involves a dozen border controls (immigration, customs, quarantine, police, and so on) at six borders.

The average freight speed on CA1 is 18 kilometers per hour, which makes intraregional trade expensive and hinders regional competitiveness. Poor roads, safety problems, manual procedures, physical border controls, incomplete documentation, and uncoordinated processes among public institutions cause bottlenecks at border crossings that reduce the average speed. But multimodal transportation adding short sea shipping by ferry could skirt most of these regional transit problems.

Technical assistance

In September 2019, the government of El Salvador requested technical assistance from the World Bank to facilitate the preparation of a road map for a ferry project between Costa Rica and El Salvador. The project would allow multimodal logistics companies to offer full transportation service and substantially reduce the time spent on the road and the risks of intraregional trade.

In October 2019, the World Bank organized and facilitated a technical workshop for the governments of Costa Rica and El Salvador, with the participation of all entities involved in clearing cargo in both countries. The workshop defined a binational action plan and established a binational working group. The Bank facilitated weekly meetings between the two countries and provided technical assistance to El Salvador to design a contingency program for all border agencies and an integrated operational process at Puerto de la Unión Centroamericana (in La Unión, El Salvador).

The technical assistance has also helped develop an integrated risk management mechanism that specifies, before the arrival of a ferry, the types of integrated physical inspections and controls that all border agencies will carry out in El Salvador. The integrated oversight would avoid delays at the port, increase efficiency, and improve trade facilitation (TF) without affecting fiscal controls. This practice could be replicated in the rest of Central America or in other regions.

Expected benefits

During recent border blockades—such as the one between Costa Rica and Nicaragua in May 2020—a ferry could have allowed trade to continue between the southern and northern countries of Central America. The May 2020 blockade meant daily million-dollar losses to the Guatemalan food and beverage sector because of blocked exports to Costa Rica and Panama.

The World Bank expects a wide range of benefits in regional integration, increased exports, and reduced time and costs of transportation, together with impacts on employment, especially for the population living in the extremely poor areas near the ports. The Bank will measure progress against a baseline of the time it takes to transport freight between El Salvador and Costa Rica; it has preliminarily estimated a possible reduction from about 3 days to less than 24 hours. Various Bank studies have found that a 1 percent reduction in the time to export increases exports by roughly 0.4 percent (Subramanian 2012, 3). The development might also create market opportunities for International Finance Corporation investments in infrastructure and transportation.

Domestic trade facilitation agendas. Finally, national TF may be affected by domestic reforms that address customs agency and other border agency needs. For example, initiatives just launched by Costa Rica and Colombia will replace their customs management systems and improve interoperability between their tax administrations and existing single windows for trade. Those developments will have a major impact on the future implementation of TF measures.

TRADE FACILITATION THROUGH DTAs

TF, like tariff liberalization, takes place at both the multilateral and the preferential level. The WTO TFA entered into force in 2017, after two-thirds of the WTO members completed domestic ratification.[6] Countries have also included TF provisions in regional and bilateral trade agreements—commonly for free trade and customs unions. TF provisions in DTAs can support complementary policies that improve TF.

How DTAs promote trade facilitation

Although the WTO TFA established global standards for TF, DTAs can promote more advanced and sophisticated solutions to advance the free circulation of goods and people and improved means of transportation beyond the TFA's scope. For example, the TFA requires members to establish advance ruling services for the classification and origin of goods and encourages advance rulings on other subjects: customs valuation, tax relief or exemption, quota application, and any other relevant subject. DTAs may also facilitate the advance ruling process, such as by waiving the need for legal representation or registration of applicant in the national territory.

DTAs can support implementation of TF measures by harmonizing compliance requirements for goods to access markets (on a variety of subjects, such as tariffs, nontariff measures, consumer standards, health requirements, and sanitary and phytosanitary requirements); coordinating control processes and procedures; aligning data requirements; and reducing transaction costs. That harmonization paves the way to reduce or lift border controls, significantly reducing costs and times for transactions. And DTAs often include provisions on cooperation, collaboration, and information sharing between partner countries to simplify, harmonize, and modernize the export and import processes.

TF provisions in DTAs typically establish governance structures to pursue ongoing improvement of border procedures and facilitation, to address any trade constraints later identified, and to improve trade compliance and enforcement. For example, MERCOSUR, SIECA, and other agreements establish customs technical committees that also engage other cross-border regulatory agencies. The committees are responsible for implementing commitments and advancing TF.

Trade facilitation provisions in Latin American and Caribbean trade agreements

Latin America and the Caribbean has 82 trade agreements in force—including an average of 16.4 TF provisions each.[7] This simple count of provisions cannot accurately capture the degree of TF commitments in a DTA because some provisions (such as rules of origin requirements) do not directly translate into enhanced TF. But the count serves as a proxy for the aggregate level of TF commitments in each DTA. The region's agreements have high numbers of TF provisions, exceeded only by those in North America and the EU (figure 3.1).

There is, however, much heterogeneity of TF provisions in Latin America and the Caribbean trade agreements. PTAs with mostly high-income regions, including East Asia and Pacific, the EU, and North America, tend to include more provisions than PTAs with other regions (figure 3.2). Latin America and the Caribbean PTAs with South Asia and the Middle East and North Africa have the fewest TF provisions on average. Agreements with North America include an average of 24.7 TF provisions, while agreements with South Asia include an average of 2.3. DTAs inside Latin America and the Caribbean include on average fewer TF provisions than interregional agreements. Intraregional trade agreements include an average of 13.8 TF provisions, compared with the overall Latin America and the Caribbean average of 16.4. That sparseness is notable in a region characterized by high intraregional trade and transportation costs.

Figure 3.1 Latin America and the Caribbean DTAs have relatively high numbers of TF provisions

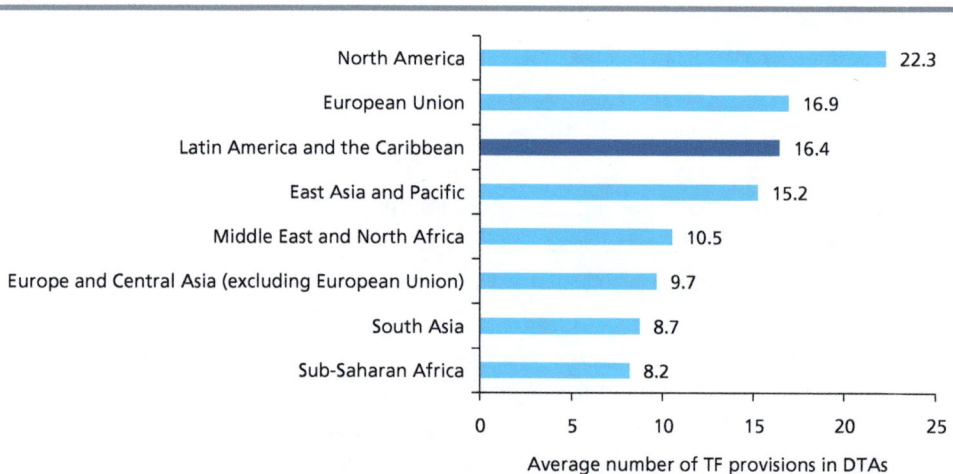

Region	Average number of TF provisions in DTAs
North America	22.3
European Union	16.9
Latin America and the Caribbean	16.4
East Asia and Pacific	15.2
Middle East and North Africa	10.5
Europe and Central Asia (excluding European Union)	9.7
South Asia	8.7
Sub-Saharan Africa	8.2

Sources: World Bank's Deep Trade Agreements database; Mattoo, Rocha, and Ruta 2020.

Note: Deep trade agreements (DTAs) refer to regional or preferential trade agreements (PTAs) that are "deep" in terms of content and cover a broad range of behind-the-border policy areas. The dataset covers the content of 18 policy areas that are most frequently covered in all PTAs that were in force and notified to the World Trade Organization by 2017. "North America" includes Canada and the United States. TF = trade facilitation.

Figure 3.2   Latin America and the Caribbean DTAs with mostly high-income regions tend to include more TF provisions

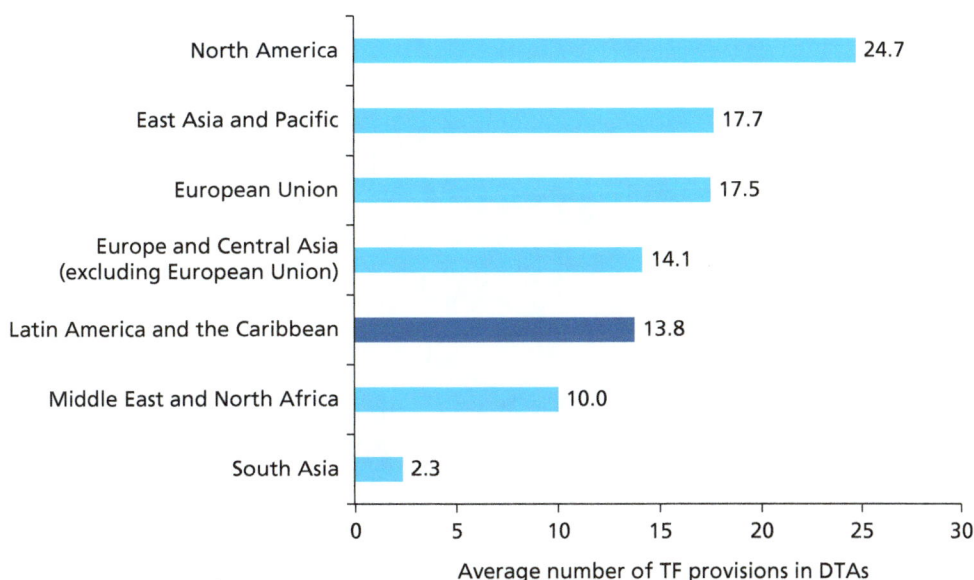

Sources: World Bank's Deep Trade Agreements database; Mattoo, Rocha, and Ruta 2020.

Note: Deep trade agreements (DTAs) refer to regional or preferential trade agreements that are "deep" in terms of content and cover a broad range of behind-the-border policy areas. The dataset covers the content of 18 policy areas that are most frequently covered in all DTAs that were in force and notified to the World Trade Organization by 2017. Latin America and the Caribbean had no DTAs with Sub-Saharan Africa. "North America" includes Canada and the United States. TF = trade facilitation.

The inclusion of TF provisions in PTAs also varies substantially across countries (figure 3.3). Countries with the most PTAs tend also to have the most TF provisions. Even so, notable differences remain, with Mexico's 14 agreements having an average of 10.3 TF provisions and Peru's 16 agreements having an average of 22.1 TF provisions.

Besides provisions concerning rules of origin, which are specific to free trade agreements, the TF provisions most often included in Latin American and Caribbean DTAs are related to information sharing and cooperation (figure 3.4). For example, "publication and availability of information," included in 65 of the region's DTAs, requires states to promptly publish information on their regulations in a nondiscriminatory and accessible manner. Sixty-one agreements require states to provide for administrative or judicial appeals of customs administrative decision. Such measures enhance the transparency of customs processes and so reduce the uncertainty that firms face in importing and exporting.

Fifty-nine of the region's DTAs have provisions committing states to cooperate in additional customs and economic and TF activities (such as risk management and simplification of processes). Such cooperation provisions—unlike the transparency

Figure 3.3   The inclusion of trade facilitation provisions in DTAs varies substantially across Latin American and Caribbean countries

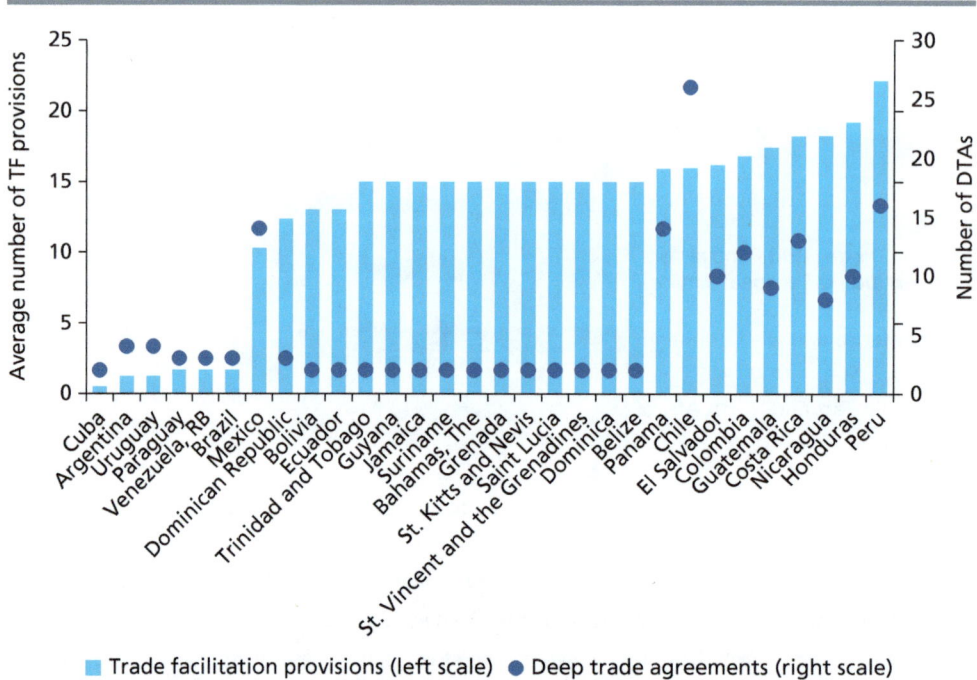

■ Trade facilitation provisions (left scale)   ● Deep trade agreements (right scale)

Sources: World Bank's Deep Trade Agreements database; Mattoo, Rocha, and Ruta 2020.

Note: The figure includes countries that have more than one deep trade agreement (DTA) in force. DTAs refer to regional or preferential trade agreements that are "deep" in terms of content and cover a broad range of behind-the-border policy areas. TF = trade facilitation.

provisions described above, which often promote nondiscriminatory measures—tend to be restricted to PTA partners.

The provisions in Latin America and the Caribbean's DTAs have advanced TF in the region. For example, the provisions on the exchange of customs-related information, risk management solutions, and institutional cooperation among customs and other cross-border regulatory agencies have reduced border inspections and transaction costs and boosted regional integration.

Even so, more modern and advanced TF measures are not always incorporated into the region's DTA provisions. Among such measures are prearrival processing, the separation of customs release from clearance,[8] development and interoperability of single windows for trade, requirements for coordinated border management, deployment of postclearance audit, and mutual recognition of AEOs. Many measures are under negotiation between customs administrations and other governmental agencies or have been included in regional TF development agendas (such as SIECA and MERCOSUR). But they lack a higher level of commitment and a legal framework to

Figure 3.4   Most frequently included TF provisions in Latin American and Caribbean DTAs

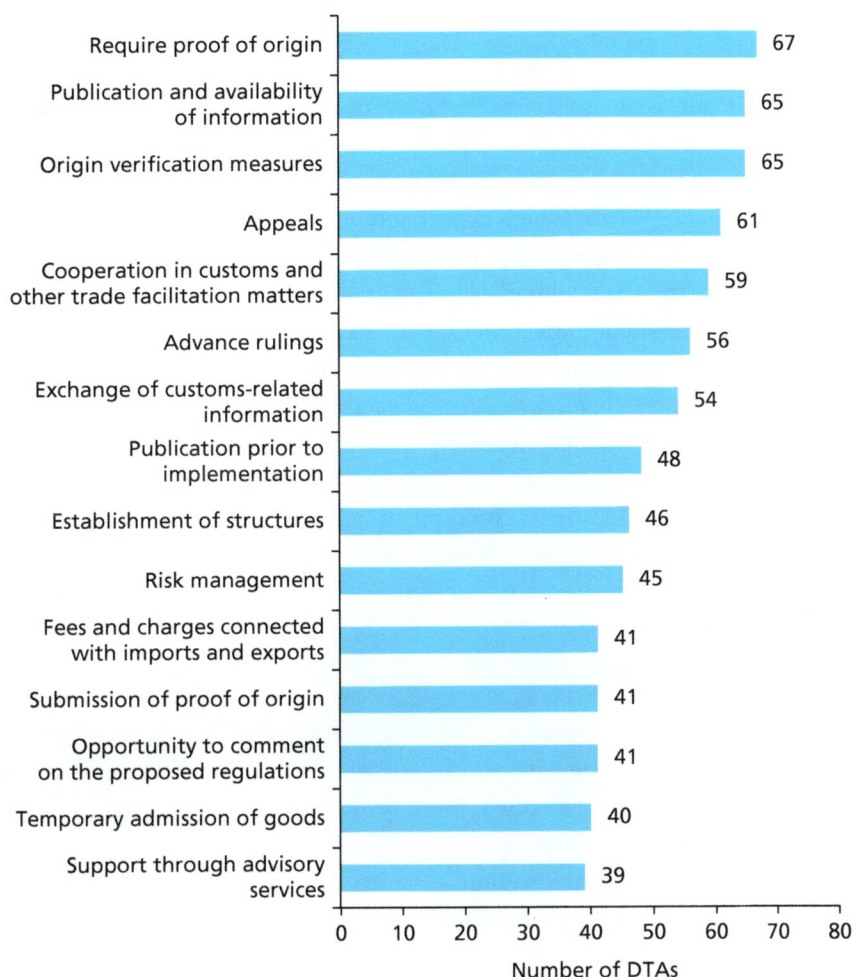

Provision	Number of DTAs
Require proof of origin	67
Publication and availability of information	65
Origin verification measures	65
Appeals	61
Cooperation in customs and other trade facilitation matters	59
Advance rulings	56
Exchange of customs-related information	54
Publication prior to implementation	48
Establishment of structures	46
Risk management	45
Fees and charges connected with imports and exports	41
Submission of proof of origin	41
Opportunity to comment on the proposed regulations	41
Temporary admission of goods	40
Support through advisory services	39

Sources: World Bank's Deep Trade Agreements database; Mattoo, Rocha, and Ruta 2020.

Note: Deep trade agreements (DTAs) refer to regional or preferential trade agreements that are "deep" in terms of content and cover a broad range of behind-the-border policy areas. TF = trade facilitation.

underpin their development. Including them in DTAs can strengthen partner country commitments and make political, legal, and financial resources more available to push implementation forward.

The impact of the DTA provisions depends on how various parties implement them. Establishing governance structures, such as customs or TF committees, has boosted coordination and the exchange of experiences to address discrepancies in interpretation and further align the understanding of provisions. Such governance structures harmonize and prompt the mutual recognition of requirements and formalities. They also support the establishment of an ongoing development process.

IMPACT OF TRADE FACILITATION PROVISIONS ON GVCs: AN ECONOMETRIC ANALYSIS

A recent analysis investigated the impact of TF provisions on GVC firms' export decisions at the extensive margin (whether trade occurs) and intensive margin (the level of trade, once it occurs) (Lee, Rocha, and Ruta 2021). It used detailed firm-level data from Peru, collected by the World Bank's Exporter Dynamics Database (Fernandes, Freund, and Pierola 2016), for which export and import records of all firms were available for 2000–17. The information on the import side of exporting firms—whether they import, what, and from where—allowed an econometric analysis of whether TF provisions had a differential impact on GVC firms through the importing channel.

To capture differential impacts, the analysis distinguished three types of firms: (a) traditional exporters that relied on domestic inputs for their exports; (b) GVC firms that imported intermediate inputs from other countries as well as exporting; and (c) bilateral GVC firms, a subset of GVC firms that imported inputs from and exported to the same countries. GVC firms could presumably achieve larger gains than traditional exporters from enhanced TF through both the importing and exporting channels as PTA provisions improved border efficiency and transparency at both Peru's and the partner's borders.

The study had three main findings:

- First, the effect of PTAs on export performance varied across different types of firms, at both the extensive and intensive margins. GVC firms that imported intermediate inputs benefited more, especially when they imported inputs from PTA partner countries.
- Second, TF provisions promoted the export performance of GVC firms by reducing trade costs and uncertainty associated with import processes at both the home country's border and the destination country's border. For Peru, the main benefit of TF provisions in PTAs seemed to result from efficiency enhancements at its own border, which allow GVC firms to get their inputs faster and more predictably.
- Third, the evidence supported both preferential and nondiscriminatory benefits of the TF provisions of PTAs, because gains were observed for GVC firms whether they imported inputs from PTA partner countries or from elsewhere.

These findings support policies to include TF provisions in DTAs. As Latin America and the Caribbean countries seek to integrate further into regional and global value chains, TF reforms can reduce trade costs and times for GVC firms. DTAs can encourage such reforms through TF provisions, which often go beyond partners' multilateral commitments.

The trade-promoting impact of those provisions in DTAs is particularly strong for GVC firms, increasing the region's competitiveness and promoting further regional integration into GVCs. GVC firms that import and export from DTA partner countries benefit the most, boosting intraregional trade and supply chain development in Latin America and the Caribbean. And the nondiscriminatory benefits of some DTA TF commitments spill over to GVC firms that import inputs from countries other than the partner country, boosting a more general integration into regional and global value chains.

Trade facilitation provisions in DTAs and their impacts on GVC firms

TF provisions of PTAs have characteristics that differentiate them from unilateral reforms or from implementation of the WTO TFA. First, because PTAs take place between two (or more) partner countries, the provisions affect import and export procedures in both partner countries. For example, the TF provisions in a country's agreement with its partner could enhance the efficiency of border procedures in both countries. The bilateral nature of PTAs means that increased efficiency at the destination country's border can promote the home country's exports, even when efficiency gains only affect import procedures.

Second, some provisions tend to be nondiscriminatory, while others grant preferential treatment to PTA partner countries. For example, establishing a single window for firms to submit documentation for import, export, or transit of goods can enhance border efficiency. Single windows are typically nonpreferential, so even if a PTA provision triggered the establishment of the single window, the gain spreads beyond the PTA partner country because all trade flowing across the border becomes more efficient. But other provisions (such as the exchange of information or the mutual recognition of AEOs) may provide preferential gains to PTA partners, with few spillover effects to other trading partners.

To capture these different characteristics, figure 3.5 illustrates the effect of TF provisions on the three types of exporters described in the last section, using as an example the US–Peru PTA. TF provisions in this agreement can affect import procedures at the borders of both Peru and the United States. On both sides, some provisions will affect imports from all countries in the same way; we refer to these provisions as most-favored-nation (MFN) provisions. Other provisions provide preferential treatment to imports from the partner country only. These elements will generate specific effects of the PTA on Peruvian exporters to the United States.

TF provisions will affect traditional exporters and GVC firms in different ways. First, consider the traditional exporter, which relies only on domestic inputs to export. TF provisions in the US–Peru PTA promote Peruvian exports to the United States by simplifying import procedures at the US border. Peruvian exporters thus benefit from TF measures at the US destination, whether the measures are MFN or applied preferentially. In figure 3.5, imports by the United States correspond to channels (c) and (d).

Second, consider the GVC firm that imports intermediate inputs from a third country and exports to the United States. This firms benefits both from improved

Figure 3.5   Effect through different channels of trade facilitation provisions in the US–Peru PTA

Peruvian exporters benefit from channels

- (c) + (d) if they (only) export to the United States (traditional exporters);
- (a) + (c) + (d) if they import inputs from rest of the world and export to the United States (GVC firms); or
- (a) + (b) + (c) + (d) if they import inputs from the United States and reexport to the United States (bilateral GVC firms).

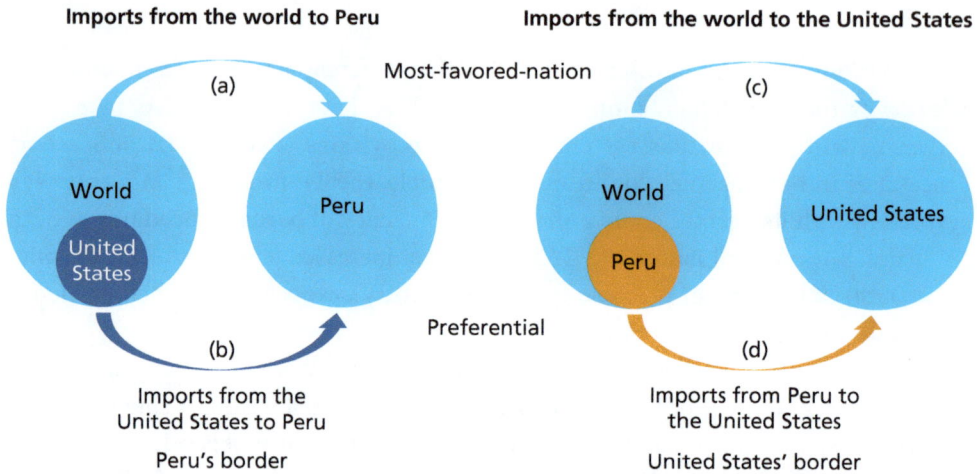

Source: World Bank.

Note: GVC = global value chain; PTA = preferential trade agreement.

procedures at the US border for processing its shipments and from expedited or more predictable import procedures at the Peruvian border. To the extent that the TF measures in the PTA affect import shipments from all countries (MFN provisions), GVC firms will gain from the enhanced efficiency in their supply chains regardless of where they import inputs from. Those gains are represented by (a) + (c) + (d) in figure 3.5.

Finally, consider the bilateral GVC firms, which both import intermediates from the United States and export to the United States. Those firms benefit from the most channels because their import shipments of intermediate inputs from the United States gain from both nondiscriminatory and preferential provisions. Their potential gains are characterized by (a) + (b) + (c) + (d).

Between 2000 and 2017, Peru entered 12 PTAs, with 38 countries represented in the agreements. The agreements vary in depth and in TF provisions (figure 3.6). Although deeper trade agreements tend to cover more TF provisions on average, the correlation is not perfect. For example, the Peru–Republic of Korea (2011) and EU–Colombia–Peru (2013) PTAs have the most provisions overall among Peru's PTAs, but the Canada–Peru (2009) and Panama–Peru (2012) PTAs have the most TF provisions. The imperfect correlation allows identifying the TF provisions' effects while controlling for the overall depth of agreements.

Figure 3.6 TF provisions in Peru's PTAs vary in depth

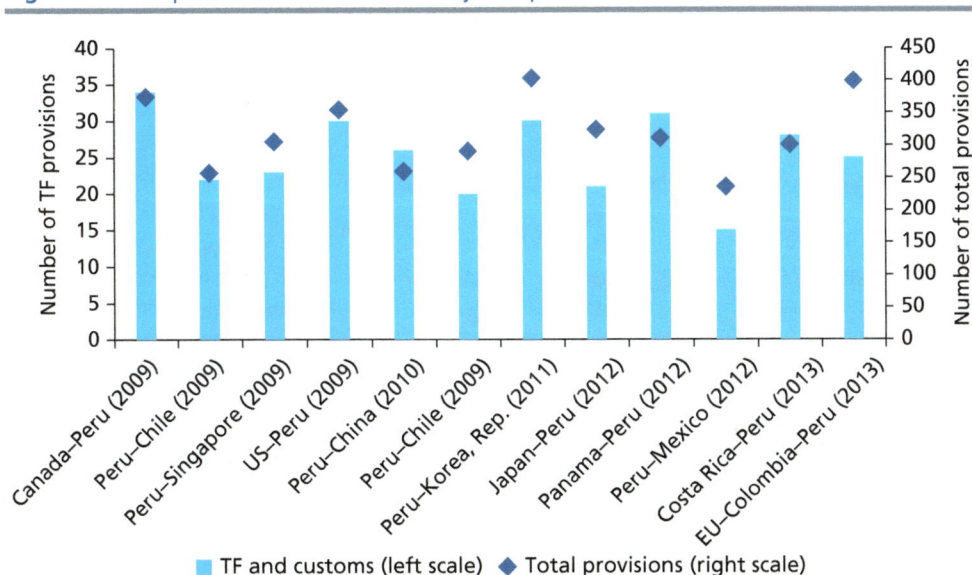

■ TF and customs (left scale) ◆ Total provisions (right scale)

Sources: World Bank's Deep Trade Agreements database; Mattoo, Rocha, and Ruta 2020.

Note: The figure includes all of Peru's preferential trade agreements (PTAs) that entered into force between 2000 and 2017. "Depth" refers to the number of enforceable policy areas in a PTA. EU = European Union; TF = trade facilitation.

Econometric analysis of the impact of PTAs and TF provisions on firms

The econometric analysis examined the impact of PTAs and TF provisions on the three types of firms based on their GVC participation status (Lee, Rocha, and Ruta 2021). Before delving into TF, the analysis tested whether regional trade agreements themselves had a differential impact on the export performance of GVC firms. If PTA provisions, including those related to TF and customs, had heterogeneous effects on firms that participate in GVCs, a regression using interaction terms for different types of firms would capture that (box 3.2).

Impact of PTAs on firms' export participation and export value

Estimation results confirmed that PTAs had a differential effect on GVC firms at both the extensive and intensive margins (figure 3.7; see annex 3A, table 3A.2). Having a PTA in force increased the likelihood that a firm would export to the partner country by an average of 0.3 percent (figure 3.7, panel a), but the effects were significantly different for GVC firms that imported intermediate inputs and exported. The positive impact of a PTA on exporting was significantly larger for firms that imported inputs, with a small negative coefficient on firms that only exported. For GVC firms, a PTA increased the likelihood of exports by 1.8 percent on average. Furthermore, for bilateral GVC firms—those that both imported inputs from the PTA partner country and exported to that country—the effect was even larger, averaging 6.3 percent.

Box 3.2 Empirical specification for the impact of PTA trade facilitation provisions on trade

The following equation estimates the heterogeneous impact of preferential trade agreements (PTAs) on export performance of different types of firms (Lee, Rocha, and Ruta 2021):

$$y_{ijt} = \beta_1 \, PTA_{jt} + \beta_2 \, (PTA_{jt} \times GVCfirm_{i(j)}) + \beta_3 \, \log(GDP_{jt}) + \alpha_{it} + \alpha_j + \varepsilon_{ijt}. \qquad \text{(B3.2.1)}$$

The baseline outcome variable y_{ijt} is the export participation and log export value of firm i's exports to country j in year t. PTA_{jt} is a dummy variable, equal to 1 if Peru has a PTA in force with country j in year t. This variable is then interacted with $GVCfirm_{i(j)}$, which is a time-invariant dummy variable, equal to 1 if exporter i imports intermediate inputs (for a GVC firm) or if exporter i imports inputs from country j (for a bilateral GVC firm). With this specification, β_1 would capture the average effect of the PTA with country j across exporters that do not import (traditional exporters), and β_2 would capture the differential impact on GVC firms, if any.

The estimation also includes a rich set of fixed effects to control for a wide range of other factors that can affect firms' exports to a particular country. Firm-year fixed effects, α_{it}, control for time-varying firm characteristics, such as productivity shocks, that might affect a firm's export performance to all countries. Destination fixed effects, α_j, capture destination country characteristics, including standard gravity variables—such as distance from Peru, shared language, or cultural or regulatory similarities—that could also affect Peru's exports to the country j. In addition, all regressions include the gross domestic product (GDP) of country j in year t to control for demand shocks.

Equation (B3.2.2) includes the key variable of interest, TF_{jt}, which captures the extent of TF commitments in the PTA by counting the number of provisions included. As was shown in figure 3.6, the number of TF provisions in Peru's PTAs ranges between 15 and 34. For ease of interpretation, this is normalized to between 0 and 1 in the regressions. The interaction terms allow the effect of TF provisions to vary by firm type.

$$y_{ijt} = \beta_1 \, RTA_{jt} + \beta_2 \, TF_{jt} + \beta_3 \, (TF_{jt} \times GVCfirm_{i(j)}) + \beta_4 \, Depth_{jt} + \beta_5 \, \log(GDP_{jt})$$
$$+ \alpha_{it} + \alpha_j + \varepsilon_{ijt}. \qquad \text{(B3.2.2)}$$

A key challenge in identifying the effect of specific provisions in DTAs is that modern PTAs increasingly cover many policy areas, and agreements that are deep overall typically include many commitments across all chapters. The large number of possible provisions and the multicollinearity pose econometric challenges to perfectly control for the commitments in various chapters. The econometric specification takes the simplest intuitive approach to control for the overall depth of the agreement by counting the number of policy areas it covers (like the construction of the TF variable). The variable $Depth_{jt}$ in equation (B3.2.2), therefore, captures the "horizontal" depth of PTAs, which represents the inclusion of 52 policy areas in DTAs (Hofmann, Osnago, and Ruta 2017). The depth variable is constructed by counting the number of strictly enforceable provisions.[a]

a. For detailed information on the legal enforceability of provisions, see Hofmann, Osnago, and Ruta (2017).

Figure 3.7   Heterogeneous effects of PTAs on GVC firms

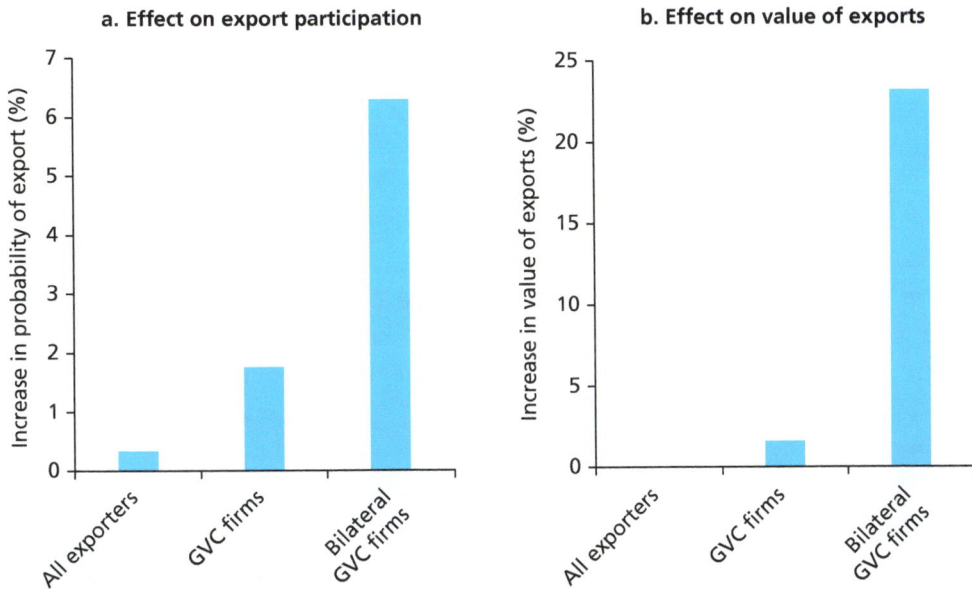

Source: Illustrated based on Lee, Rocha, and Ruta 2021.

Note: To represent the impact of preferential trade agreements (PTAs) for different types of firms, estimates were calculated using equation (B3.2.1) in box 3.2. Results are reported only when they are statistically significant at $p \leq .05$. All regressions control for GDP in the destination country and include firm-year and destination fixed effects. "All exporters" include those that rely on domestic inputs for their exports as well as those that import inputs. Global value chain (GVC) firms are exporters that also import intermediate inputs from other countries. Bilateral GVC firms are those that that import inputs from and exported to the same countries. For exact coefficients and standard errors, see annex 3A, table 3A.2.

Similarly, at the intensive margin (figure 3.7, panel b), although the average effect of PTAs was not statistically significant, the value of GVC firm exports to destination countries was larger once a PTA entered into force.

Impact of trade facilitation provisions on firms' export participation and export value

PTAs' differential impact on GVC firms shows their role in facilitating both exports and imports. Understanding the mechanisms for PTAs to facilitate imports is crucial, because the reduction of import costs directly affects the export competitiveness of GVC firms. Administrative and regulatory procedures at the border and beyond are often major barriers to importing in low- and middle-income countries, especially in Latin America and the Caribbean. The TF indicators presented earlier in tables 3.1–3.3 showed that trading across borders tends to be costly and time consuming in Latin America and the Caribbean.

So, did TF provisions in PTAs increase export participation and the value of exports for GVC firms? The results showed a positive and significant effect, on average, if other provisions in the PTA were controlled for (figure 3.8 and annex 3A, table 3A.3) (Lee, Rocha, and Ruta 2021). If the effects are examined by firm type, the positive impact of TF provisions was driven by GVC firms that imported intermediate inputs. Although TF provisions had no significant impact on firms that only exported (traditional exporters), they had a positive and significant effect for exporters that imported intermediate inputs.

The interpretation of magnitude is not completely straightforward, given the multiple interaction terms and the construction of the TF and depth variables from counting the number of provisions. For GVC firms, a PTA with average overall depth (0.661) that included TF provisions at the deepest level (that is, included the largest number of provisions) increased the probability of export participation by about 3.4 percent (figure 3.8, panel a).[9] For bilateral GVC firms that imported inputs from the PTA partner country, that effect was larger, at 9.9 percent. Qualitatively similar results held at the intensive margin, where TF provisions in PTAs increased the value of exports to the partner country significantly for GVC firms and the most for bilateral GVC firms (figure 3.8, panel b).[10]

Figure 3.8 Heterogeneous effects of TF provisions on GVC firms

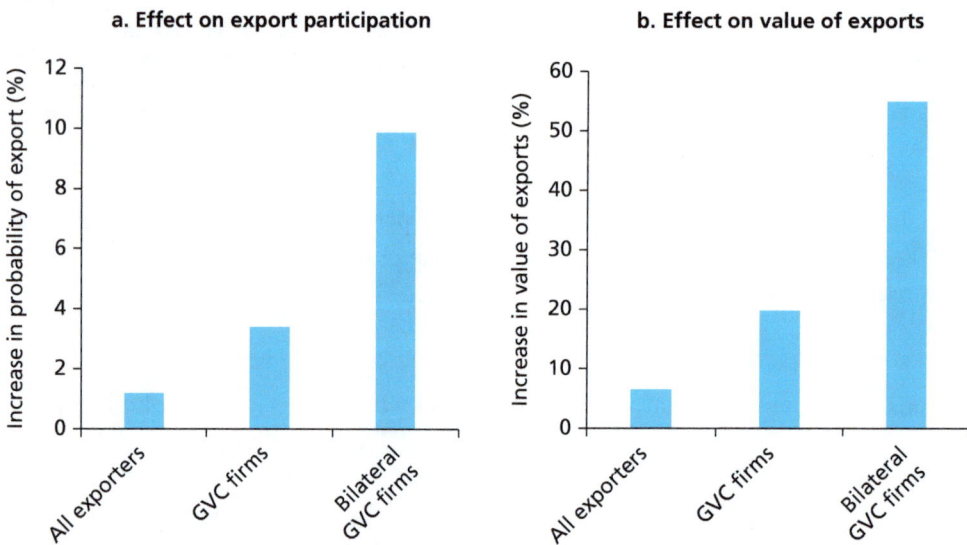

Source: Illustrated based on Lee, Rocha, and Ruta 2021.

Note: The bars represent the impact of preferential trade agreements (PTAs) with average depth that included trade facilitation (TF) provisions at the deepest level (that is, included the largest number of provisions) for different types of firms, estimating equation (B3.2.2) in box 3.2. Results are reported only when they are statistically significant at $p < .05$. All regressions control for gross domestic product (GDP) in the destination country and include firm-year and destination fixed effects. "All exporters" include those that rely on domestic inputs for their exports as well as those that import inputs. Global value chain (GVC) firms are exporters that also import intermediate inputs from other countries. Bilateral GVC firms are those that import inputs from and exported to the same countries. Exact coefficients and standard errors are available in annex 3A, table 3A.3.

In summary, the effects of PTAs vary across firm types depending on their GVC links. TF provisions particularly help the export performance of GVC firms by reducing the trade costs and uncertainty associated with importing in both the home country and the destination country. In Peru, the main benefits of TF provisions in PTAs seem to be realized through efficiency enhancements at Peru's own border, allowing the GVC firm to get its inputs faster and more predictably. So, Peruvian GVC firms are more likely to export and are likely to export goods and services with larger values to countries with which Peru has a PTA containing TF provisions.

The findings underscore the role of TF commitments in PTAs in enhancing Latin America and the Caribbean countries' export competitiveness through importing by GVC firms, thus promoting countries' further integration into GVCs. Moreover, bilateral GVC firms that import from and export to PTA partner countries benefit the most—with an extra boost from back-and-forth trade that could increase intraregional trade and regional supply chain development. And the econometric evidence demonstrates nondiscriminatory as well as preferential gains from PTAs' TF commitments, because benefits are observed for GVC firms that import inputs, whether from partner or from nonpartner countries. That finding implies positive spillover effects on shipments from nonpartner countries due to TF commitments in PTAs, while preferential benefits are still provided to shipments from partner countries.

Although the firm-level analysis in this section provides empirical evidence that PTAs' TF provisions enhance GVC firms' exports, the benefits are not always easily secured. Many TF commitments require considerable investment of time and resources, because full implementation of major reforms can take several years. And the negotiation and implementation of TF in regional trade agreements can face challenges owing to differences in the partner countries' maturity. Successfully implementing PTAs requires coordinating the partners' efforts to identify and articulate the most suitable solutions, given their national contexts.

IMPLEMENTATION CHALLENGES AND CASE STUDY

Although Latin America and the Caribbean countries recognize that implementing TF commitments can reduce trade transaction costs and promote economic integration, doing so creates challenges.

Implementation challenges for trade facilitation commitments

Competing priorities. A national reform agenda typically faces competing priorities because of national expectations as well as commitments in multilateral, plurilateral, and bilateral agreements. This situation obliges the agencies engaged in implementation (such as the trade, health, customs, standards, immigration, sanitary and phytosanitary, and other cross-border regulatory agencies) to prioritize, plan, and sequence reform projects in a coordinated manner while managing expectations and maintaining schedules. A coordinated effort is particularly important for complex TF reforms that take several years to implement because they require continued commitment across multiple agencies.

Lengthy implementation process. Some TF reforms imply major undertakings by governments, entail years of implementation efforts, and eventually involve multiple political and governmental mandates. For example, a full-fledged single window for trade demands huge effort and takes several years. Such projects need to mitigate the risks associated with maintaining political commitment and allocating resources throughout development and can be affected by changes of leadership and staff at the agencies responsible for the reform.

Need for strong governance and political commitment. TF projects also demand that governments secure buy-in and political commitment from multiple ministries and agencies. A robust governance framework must drive the reform to ensure adequate resource allocation and mitigate challenges to sustainability. Project implementation usually requires legal reforms (or completion of the legal process for internalizing international agreements); business process mapping and reengineering; infrastructure development at land borders, ports, airports, or inland facilities; procurement, development, or updates of information technology systems; review of operational procedures and regulations; adoption and integration of new technologies; promotion of adequate communication and coordination with stakeholders; effective change management; and capacity building for both public and private sectors affected by the reforms.

Private sector engagement. In addition, TF reforms depend on aligning solutions with business practices and procedures to minimize the private sector's effort to comply with requirements for imports, exports, and the movement of cargo. One challenge is to properly engage the private sector at all stages: project inception and diagnosis; assessment of constraints and opportunities for improvement; design, development, and piloting of solutions; and rollout and implementation. Without trust, appropriate consultative and engagement mechanisms, and mutual understanding of the contributions needed from the public and private sectors, country capacity to successfully implement TF measures can be constrained.

Different levels of maturity in TF development. In PTAs, the negotiation of TF provisions must consider the different maturity of TF in each country. Jointly implementing PTAs can require coordinating the partners' efforts, in view of their national contexts, to clearly identify and articulate the most suitable solutions. For instance, almost all customs administrations have already implemented some risk management solutions for targeting cargo for border inspection. Some administrations might be in early development, relying on human analysis of results and profiling, with border inspections disconnected from other compliance controls beyond the borders. Other administrations might be much more advanced, with comprehensive risk-based compliance management strategies, border inspections complemented by compliance controls beyond the borders (desk monitoring, and automatic data analysis and audits), sophisticated intelligence using modern technologies such as artificial intelligence and machine learning, and advanced domestic and international cooperation and coordination.

Timeline coordination. Agreement on a timeline, also a challenge in negotiating and implementing DTAs, must consider the status of each measure in the partner countries. For instance, the parties may agree on the mutual recognition of AEOs and on corresponding benefits. Even so, the benefit to operators and the mutual recognition agreement's impact on transactional costs can vary greatly depending on the feasibility and stage of implementation. At the initial stage, benefits might be limited to some services, such as the designation of contacts for guidance, orientation, and response to consultations as well as normal prioritization in carrying out processes. Later, the parties may implement exchanges of information and automatic recognition of AEOs, with treatment by the parties' respective risk management engines, enabling border inspections to be reduced, measured, and jointly monitored with performance indicators. In an even more sophisticated arrangement, the parties might agree on implementing dedicated express trade lanes and procedures for mutually recognized AEOs, eventually with infrastructure changes at borders and specific logistics treatment (such as an automatic release upon arrival).

Case study: The Guatemala–Honduras deep integration agreement

The deep integration agreement between Guatemala and Honduras, also referred to as the customs union agreement, demonstrates good practices in which the parties have overcome the implementation challenges just described. The bilateral agreement led to establishing integrated border posts and a single electronic document that serves as both invoice and declaration—the Central American Invoice and Single Declaration (FYDUCA). The implementation of the agreement substantially reduced border-crossing times between the two countries (SIECA, n.d.).

The origin of the agreement can be traced to the General Treaty on Central American Economic Integration, signed in 1960. That agreement, besides creating a common market, established a permanent secretariat to ensure the correct application of the treaty. Now called the Secretariat for Central American Economic Integration (SIECA), it acted as the forum for the Guatemala–Honduras bilateral agreement.

Since the beginning of Central American economic integration, one of its central objectives has been to gradually and progressively form and operate a customs union. Although major political and legal integration instruments repeatedly mentioned that goal for more than 60 years, it faced major implementation challenges. For instance, the numerous agencies that would participate (health, trade, customs, agriculture, immigration, and others) were uncoordinated both within and between countries and had priorities other than implementing trade agreements. There were many attempts to achieve concrete progress on the customs union, but resources were lacking to implement reforms or improve infrastructure. And limited private sector pressure for reforms hindered implementation.

In 2015, aiming at a deep integration agreement, the region adopted new legal instruments for Guatemala and Honduras. The instruments contain TF measures such as border agency cooperation within each country and with its neighbor country, simplified formalities using information and communications technology, collection of duties and taxes at the final destination, and an institutional framework to coordinate implementation. In June 2017, the deep integration between the two countries began operation, although mandatory FYDUCA use started in March 2018. In 2021, the countries implemented other TF measures such as anticipated electronic transmission of sanitary and phytosanitary certificates, and prearrival processing.[11]

Legal framework

The regulatory framework of the deep integration between Honduras and Guatemala comprises six legal instruments:

- The Enabling Protocol for the Deep Integration Process (2015) establishes the central aspects of the deep integration model.
- The Agreement for the Compatibility of Internal Taxes Applicable to Trade between the States Parties to the Central American Customs Union (2006), which creates the FYDUCA, concerns value added taxes (VAT) and income taxes, which are collected at the destination.
- The Framework Agreement for the Central American Customs Union (2007) established the model and the stages for the construction of the customs union.
- Regulation of the Organization and Operation of the Ministerial Agency (2017) defines the main functions and attributions of the ministerial body in charge of implementing, managing, and constantly improving the customs union.
- Regulation for the Operation of Deep Integration (2017) develops the operational procedures of the customs union both for goods under free movement and goods that are exempted.
- Protocol for the Accession of El Salvador to the Customs Union (2018) ratified the protocol of El Salvador's accession, but the free movement of goods to and from El Salvador has not yet begun. However, in December 2021, Guatemala, Honduras, and El Salvador jointly approved a road map for the implementation of the customs union for El Salvador.

Operational details and implementation

The main concept in the customs union is free movement of goods as the regime applicable to community goods. Community goods are those obtained, collected, produced, elaborated, or transformed in the single customs territory, as well as goods from third countries that have been nationalized in any of the countries in the customs union, complying with tax and nontax obligations.

Guatemala and Honduras established three integrated border posts: Agua Caliente, Corinto, and El Florido. At each integrated border post, officials from the tax administrations (customs and internal taxes) and immigration from both countries operate two types of control posts: the TF post and the integrated control center post. Each post has a unique purpose:

- The TF Center simplifies and uses technology for formalities. Tax officials use FYDUCA, a single electronic document that serves as both invoice and declaration (box 3.3). Tax officials validate that the FYDUCA tax payments have been made, and immigration officials check truck drivers' immigration documents without exerting any physical controls on the transportation unit. Value added tax is paid electronically so that the funds go to the destination country.
- The Integrated Control Center simplifies formalities. For goods that are not in free circulation, both countries' customs, immigration, and quarantine authorities are in a single area to carry out import and export controls.[12]

Faster border crossings, more trade

The customs union using the FYDUCA was launched on March 1, 2018. About 75 percent of bilateral trade enjoys free movement. Although not enough data are yet available for a thorough impact evaluation of this reform, the World Bank prepared a baseline and measured the preliminary results (Alfaro de Morán and Sarmiento 2019).

By early 2018, the time to cross land borders between Guatemala and Honduras had dropped from 10 hours to 15 minutes during pilot exercises. More-recent measurements at the end of 2018 showed even better results: a border crossing time of only 6 minutes on average. According to data from the Banco de Guatemala, bilateral trade between Guatemala and Honduras grew by 10.9 percent from 2017 to 2018, from US$1,352.0 million to US$1,498.8 million.

The major reduction in border-crossing time and the resulting increase in bilateral trade between Guatemala and Honduras is likely to tighten the GVC links between the two countries. As discussed earlier, reducing the time and costs of cross-border trade is particularly important for GVC firms that rely on the timely delivery of foreign inputs. Inputs represent a substantial share of bilateral

Box 3.3   The single-document FYDUCA process

The single-document Central American Invoice and Single Declaration (FYDUCA) is a best practice for simplifying formalities and using e-government practices to improve services and reduce costs. Under the Guatemala–Honduras deep integration agreement, the FYDUCA is the only legal or fiscal document used for trading between the countries. It constitutes both (a) an invoice supporting the transfer and acquisition of goods or the provision of services between economic agents of the countries in the customs union, and (b) a declaration of the withholding or liquidation and payment of taxes. The export process using FYDUCA is reduced to the following steps:

1. The transferor (exporter) accesses the electronic platform of its tax administration and fills out the FYDUCA with data about its company, the acquirer (importer), the merchandise traded, and the transportation that will carry the merchandise.
2. Once the FYDUCA has been completed and validated in the computer system, it is transmitted to the tax administration of the acquiring country (importer), where the tax obligation is determined and a value added tax (VAT) or sales tax payment slip is generated. From that moment, 24 hours is allowed for the acquirer to pay the tax obligation electronically to the tax administration of the acquiring country. The VAT must be paid before goods enter the territory of the acquiring country.
3. Once that tax payment has been made, the transporter carries the goods to the TF Center (fast-track lane) at the border, where the tax authority of the acquiring country electronically validates that the tax has been paid and registers in the system that the goods have entered the country.
4. Immigration exit and entry processes are carried out in the same center.
5. Once both validation and immigration procedures have been completed, the transport leaves the border post and goes to its destination, where the acquirer records in the electronic system that the merchandise has been received.

Source: World Bank.

Guatemala–Honduras trade, with cotton, paper articles, iron and steel, and plastic and plastic articles among the main products crossing the border. Enhanced border efficiency could boost the competitiveness of these supply chains and accelerate a deeper regional integration.

The Guatemala–Honduras agreement shows how a DTA can enhance TF between two countries despite challenges that had kept an earlier regional trade agreement from achieving the free movement of goods. The bilateral agreement included measures to promote border agency cooperation between the partner countries, simplify formalities using information and communications technology, and establish an institutional framework to coordinate implementation. The success in this case study highlights the importance of DTA provisions for cooperation and institutional arrangements to establish structures for implementation and mechanisms to involve the private sector.

Among other specific lessons is the need to provide sufficient funds to implement TF reforms. The Enabling Protocol for the Deep Integration Process between Guatemala and Honduras established a Structural and Investment Fund, which has been crucial to the reforms. According to the regulations of the fund, each country was to contribute an initial US$5 million and to provide annual contributions to be determined. The fund could be further supported by reimbursable and nonreimbursable funds. The Central American Bank for Economic Integration, part of the Central American Integration System, provided funds for infrastructure needed at the borders between Guatemala and Honduras. Other collaborators, such as the Spanish Agency for International Development Cooperation (AECID) and the Inter-American Development Bank, provided technical assistance for many of the information technology developments, and the World Bank formally consulted with both partners.

Another lesson is the need to involve the private sector to push for TF reforms. Private sector involvement was critical during implementation. The World Bank organized pilot exercises with regional companies, which demonstrated dramatic reductions of border-crossing time—key to project buy-in as companies saw the benefits. It also organized training for more than 150 companies.

CONCLUSION AND POLICY RECOMMENDATIONS

Trade facilitation commitments in PTAs can help Latin American and Caribbean countries better integrate into regional and global value chains. Additional efforts in the region to simplify and harmonize export and import processes, through deep integration agreements as well as unilateral reforms, can further reduce trade costs and so boost participation in regional and global value chains. But many countries in the region face multidimensional challenges that might undermine the effectiveness of DTAs.

Key trade facilitation provisions for PTAs

Lessons from regional experiences, including the Guatemala–Honduras customs union, suggest that PTAs in Latin America and the Caribbean that aim at promoting GVC integration should include provisions related to modern and advanced TF measures.

Integrated risk management and postclearance audit

Most customs administrations already have processes for adopting risk-based compliance management strategies, though they are at different levels of maturity. Countries should implement integrated risk management systems across the various border agencies that control goods. To achieve more efficient clearance, border agencies should integrate risk criteria, concentrate controls and focused inspections on high-risk consignments, and expedite the release of low-risk consignments. For imports requiring inspection, nonintrusive inspection should be the first option. Border agencies should also explore complementary controls beyond the borders, such as postclearance audits, inspections, and inventory controls.

Cooperation between neighboring border agencies, including mutual recognition of compliance controls

The working hours of all public and private entities necessary for managing imports or exports and international transit in partner countries should be standardized, along with other measures and activities. Joint processes and operations to recognize certificates from accredited agencies in countries with similar or higher standards, especially for low-risk goods, should be developed. Implementing Mutual Recognition of Authorized Economic Operators between subregions, such as Central America and MERCOSUR, is another crucial point that will allow granting benefits to all AEO companies in the region, improving fiscal and parafiscal control at borders.

Prearrival processing and separation of customs release from final clearance.

Prearrival processing allows for the submission of import documents and a declaration to initiate the clearance, with the risk assessment conducted before goods arrive and release taking place immediately upon arrival. The procedure significantly decreases logistics costs.

Development and interoperability of national single windows for trade

Most countries are developing national single windows for trade. A DTA can establish the requirements for automatic exchange of information; the redesign, automation, and digitization of business processes and procedures; and the interoperability of single windows, reducing formalities and requirements considerably.

Reduction of forms and documents and increased security using information technology

Particularly given the COVID-19 pandemic, forms and physical contact should be reduced using information and communications technologies. Countries should simplify and automate processes gradually, implementing back-office and customer-facing systems, especially mobile technologies, as well as interoperable national and regional information systems. Electronic payment gateways should be used for fees, duties, taxes, and charges collected by all border agencies. And countries should incorporate technologies for more expeditious and secure cargo processing, such as nonintrusive inspection equipment, cargo tracking systems, biometrics in driver identification, surveillance cameras, and monitoring of cargo inspections (eventually with remote inspection).

Authorized economic operator programs and single government solutions

Based on risk management and compliance records, benefits to AEOs should be extended. An AEO program enables regulatory and control agencies to manage compliance much more effectively, replacing costly transaction inspections at borders with voluntary compliance by operators through a certification process and submission to regular monitoring and compliance verification. For example, AEOs could pass through green channels or not be required to present physical documents, complementing these measures with postaudit practices.

Establishment of effective governance structures

The impact of the DTA provisions depends on their implementation by various parties. So, the establishment of governance structures such as customs or TF committees is instrumental to coordinating and exchanging experiences to address discrepant interpretations and better align how provisions are understood. Such governance structures also have roles in harmonizing or developing mutual recognition of requirements and formalities, and in implementing ongoing development.

Policy recommendations

PTAs face a variety of challenges. The following broad recommendations could advance TF in Latin American and Caribbean PTAs:

- *Establish a robust governance framework to drive reform and ensure the commitment and participation of all agencies and the private sector.* Since the approval of the WTO TFA, the national committees on TF are the main forum for developing public policies and coordinating related reform initiatives. It is recommended that a committee report to or establish an interministerial coordinating body. And the design of policies and projects must encompass commitments and buy-ins by all relevant ministries and agencies. The governance framework might also support the process of prioritizing and sequencing reforms, mobilizing and allocating resources, and establishing ongoing improvement, with milestones and deliverables clearly articulated and communicated to all stakeholders.
- *Establish coordinating committees to promote international cooperation and alignment in implementing agreements.* Customs and other cross-border regulatory agencies would particularly benefit. For regional integration, governance structures have harmonized the legal frameworks, standards, and procedures while also continuously advancing TF. DTAs can prompt the establishment of such governance structures, as in the MERCOSUR and SIECA TF and customs committees. The joint governance structures could conduct diagnostics and assessments, identify best practices and exchange experiences, establish an appropriate results and monitoring framework, and support the development agenda.

- *Enhance program and project management capacities to implement complex projects and initiatives.* Such developments as the single window for trade exploit agile, phased, and incremental implementation strategies. Sustained political support, continuous improvement, and timely deliverables are essential throughout the process.
- *Engage the private sector from inception in implementing TF projects and initiatives.* Reforms should go beyond changing customs and other border agencies' legal frameworks, systems, and procedures. They must engage the private sector in adopting and embracing development. Private sector involvement was critical in implementing deep integration between Guatemala and Honduras. The pilot exercises the World Bank organized with regional companies, which demonstrated dramatic reductions of border-crossing time, were crucial to building companies' buy-in of the project, and the World Bank also organized training for more than 150 companies.
- *Design projects and TF solutions based on comprehensive analyses and diagnostics.* Such analyses should cover all aspects and constraints identified, including the legal framework, operational policies and procedures, existing information and communications technologies, other technologies adopted or available, infrastructural constraints, and potential environmental or social impact. A thorough analysis of the financial needs for investment and for sustainability after implementation is imperative to mobilize the necessary technical and financial resources.

ANNEX 3A SUPPLEMENTARY TABLES

Table 3A.1 Trade facilitation provisions in DTAs

No.	Provision	Section
1	Publication and availability of information	Transparency
2	Internet publication	Transparency
3	Enquiry points	Transparency
4	Publication prior to implementation	Transparency
5	Obligation to consult traders/business	Transparency
6	Opportunity to comment on the proposed regulations	Transparency
7	Advance rulings	Transparency
8	Appeals	Transparency
9	Fees and charges connected with import/export	Fees and formalities
10	Penalty disciplines	Fees and formalities

Continued

Table 3A.1 Trade facilitation provisions in DTAs *(continued)*

No.	Provision	Section
11	Prearrival processing	Fees and formalities
12	Separation of release from clearance	Fees and formalities
13	Risk management	Fees and formalities
14	Postclearance audits	Fees and formalities
15	Release times	Fees and formalities
16	Authorized operators	Fees and formalities
17	Expedited shipments	Fees and formalities
18	Cooperation in customs and other TF matters	Fees and formalities
19	Simplification/harmonization of formalities/procedures	Fees and formalities
20	Use of international standards	Fees and formalities
21	Single window	Fees and formalities
22	Destination inspection/postshipment inspections	Fees and formalities
23	Customs brokers	Fees and formalities
24	Temporary admission of goods	Fees and formalities
25	Freedom of transit for goods	Transit
26	Exchange of customs-related information	Customs and other forms of cooperation
27	Technical assistance and capacity building	Technical assistance/capacity building
28	Specific disciplines for customs processing fees	Fees and formalities
29	Advance lodging in electronic format	Fees and formalities
30	Electronic payment of duties	Fees and formalities
31	Release goods within prescribed time limits	Fees and formalities
32	Mutual recognition of authorized economic operators	Fees and formalities
33	World Customs Organization immediate release guidelines	Fees and formalities
34	Special arrangements for release—perishable goods	Fees and formalities
35	Cooperation between border agencies	Fees and formalities
36	Copies of supporting documents	Fees and formalities
37	Interconnected/compatible customs/software systems	Customs and other forms of cooperation
38	Cooperation on law enforcement	Customs and other forms of cooperation
39	Exchange of information on best practices	Customs and other forms of cooperation
40	Cooperation in international fora	Customs and other forms of cooperation
41	Harmonization and common legal framework	Customs union specific
42	Customs and other duties collection	Customs union specific

Continued

Table 3A.1   Trade facilitation provisions in DTAs *(continued)*

No.	Provision	Section
43	Sharing of customs revenue	Customs union specific
44	Require proof of origin	FTA specific
45	Issuance of proof of origin	FTA specific
46	Proof of origin: paper/electronic format	FTA specific
47	Submission of proof of origin	FTA specific
48	Origin verification measures	FTA specific
49	Support through advisory services and so on	Technical assistance/capacity building
50	Establishment of structures	Institutional arrangements
51	Establishment of a mechanism	Institutional arrangements
52	Interoperability of single window	Fees and formalities

Source: Mattoo, Rocha, and Ruta 2020.

Note: DTA = deep trade agreement. FTA = free trade agreement; TF = trade facilitation.

Table 3A.2   Heterogeneous effects of preferential trade agreements on GVC firms

	Export participation			Log (exp value)		
Dependent variable	(1)	(2)	(3)	(4)	(5)	(6)
PTA	0.00332**	−0.0104***	−0.00286*	−0.0701	−0.494***	−0.306***
	(0.00161)	(0.00298)	(0.00153)	(0.0433)	(0.0718)	(0.0574)
PTA × GVC firm		0.0280***			0.510***	
		(0.00610)			(0.0920)	
PTA × bilateral GVC firm			0.0658***			0.538***
			(0.0133)			(0.0801)
Observations	39,685,492	39,685,492	39,685,492	226,280	226,280	226,280
R-squared	0.093	0.096	0.099	0.496	0.497	0.499

Source: World Bank.

Note: Robust standard errors, clustered at destination country level, are in parentheses. All regressions control for gross domestic product (GDP) in destination country and include firm-year and destination fixed effects. GVC = global value chain; PTA = preferential trade agreement.

* $p < 0.1$; ** $p < 0.05$; *** $p < 0.01$

Table 3A.3 Heterogeneous effects of TF provisions on GVC firms

Dependent variable	Export participation			In (exp value)		
	(1)	(2)	(3)	(4)	(5)	(6)
PTA	−0.0172**	−0.0172**	−0.0141**	−0.0677	−0.0728	−0.0430
	(0.00709)	(0.00709)	(0.00614)	(0.119)	(0.119)	(0.0878)
… TF provisions	0.0247***	0.00334	0.0149	0.309**	−0.335**	0.0962
	(0.00900)	(0.0101)	(0.00909)	(0.134)	(0.161)	(0.158)
… TF provisions × GVC firm		0.0434***			0.774***	
		(0.00913)			(0.139)	
… TF provisions × bilateral GVC firm			0.0960***			0.775***
			(0.0194)			(0.111)
… Depth	0.00661	0.00661	0.00284	−0.267	−0.255	−0.421***
	(0.0125)	(0.0125)	(0.0106)	(0.171)	(0.172)	(0.158)
Observations	39,685,492	39,685,492	39,685,492	226,280	226,280	226,280
R-squared	0.094	0.096	0.099	0.496	0.497	0.499

Source: World Bank.

Note: Robust standard errors, clustered at destination country level, in parentheses. All regressions control for gross domestic product (GDP) in destination country and include firm-year and destination fixed effects. GVC = global value chain; ln = natural logarithm; PTA = preferential trade agreement; TF = trade facilitation.

* $p < 0.1$; ** $p < 0.05$; ***; $p < 0.01$.

ANNEX 3B TASK FACILITATION PROVISIONS IN DEEP TRADE AGREEMENTS: DETAILED QUESTIONS

I. **TRANSPARENCY**

A. **Publication and Availability of Information**
- Does the agreement require states to promptly publish information in a nondiscriminatory and easily accessible manner?
- Does the agreement require states to publish import–export-related information through the internet?
- Does the agreement require states to establish/maintain enquiry points to answer queries on importation, exportation, and transit procedures, forms, and documents?

B. **Opportunity to Comment, Information before Entry into Force, and Consultations**
- Does the agreement require states to provide an opportunity to traders and other interested parties to comment on laws and regulations related to the movement, release, and clearance of goods (including transit) before entry into force?

- Does the agreement require states to publish/make available information on laws and regulations related to the movement, release, and clearance of goods (including transit) prior to entry into force?
- Does the agreement require states to provide for regular consultations between border agencies and traders or other stakeholders?

C. Advance Rulings

- Does the agreement require states to issue advance rulings?

D. Procedures for Appeal or Review

- Does the agreement require states to provide for
  - Administrative appeal/review against a decision of customs administration?
  - Judicial appeal/review of a decision of customs administration?

II. FEES AND FORMALITIES

A. Requirements on Fees and Charges Imposed on or in Connection with Importation and Exportation and Penalties

- Does the agreement require states to apply the following general disciplines on fees and charges for importation and exportation:
  - Publish information on fees and charges (amount, reasons, responsible authority, when and how to pay)?
  - Accord an adequate time between publication of new or amended fees and charges and entry into force?
  - Review, periodically, fees and charges with a view to reducing their number and diversity, where practicable?
- Does the agreement require states to apply the following specific disciplines for customs processing fees and charges:
  - Limited to approximate cost of services/specific operation?
  - Not required to be linked to a specific operation if they are levied for services connected to customs processing?
- Does the agreement provide any rules for penalties imposed by customs administration for a breach of customs laws, regulations, or procedural requirements?

B. Release and Clearance of Goods

- Does the agreement require states to adopt/maintain prearrival processing procedures (submission of import documentation and other required information, including manifests)?
- Does the agreement require states to provide for advance lodging of such documentation in electronic format?
- Does the agreement require states to adopt/maintain electronic payment of duties, taxes, fees, and charges collected by customs administration? If this requirement is extended to other agencies, please describe.

- Does the agreement require states to adopt/maintain procedures for separation of release from final determination of customs duties, taxes, fees, and charges?
- Does the agreement require states to adopt/maintain a risk management system for customs control?
- Does the agreement require states to adopt/maintain postclearance audit to ensure compliance?
- Does the agreement require states to release goods within prescribed time limits (please describe if for all and/or specific categories of goods)?
- Does the agreement require states to extend additional TF measures for authorized operators (AOs) who meet specified criteria related to compliance?
- Does the agreement provide for mutual recognition of AOs?
- Does the agreement provide for the expedited release of goods entered through air cargo facilities (at least)?
- Does the agreement provide for the application of the World Customs Organization immediate release guidelines?
- Does the agreement provide special arrangements for the release of perishable goods?

C. **Border Agency Cooperation**
- Does the agreement require states to ensure cooperation between national border agencies and coordination of their activities?

D. **Formalities Connected with Importation, Exportation, and Transit**
- Does the agreement require states to review formalities and documentation requirements?
- Does the agreement require states to accept copies of supporting documents for import, export, or transit formalities?
- Does the agreement encourage states to use relevant international standards as a basis for import, export, or transit formalities and procedures?
- Does the agreement encourage states to establish/maintain a single window to submit documentation for importation, exportation, or transit of goods through a single entry point?
- Does the agreement encourage/commit states to provide for the interoperability of their single window systems or to establish a single window between them?
- Does the agreement prohibit states from requiring the use of preshipment inspections for classification and valuation?
- Does the agreement prohibit states from requiring the use of customs brokers (that is, there should not be such a requirement)?
- Does the agreement require states to allow for temporary admission of goods and inward and outward processing?

III. TRANSIT

A. Freedom of Transit

- Does the agreement contain any provisions on freedom of transit?

IV. CUSTOMS AND OTHER FORMS OF TF COOPERATION

A. Exchange of Information

- Does the agreement provide for mutual administrative assistance through the exchange of information to verify an import and export declaration in identified cases?
- Does the agreement encourage states to:
  - Exchange information and data on a secure and rapid basis such as automatically and/or in advance of arrival of goods?
  - Develop common data elements, unique consignment reference numbers, processes, and common risk rules?
  - Adopt interconnected/compatible customs/software systems?
- Does the agreement require states to cooperate on law enforcement (prevent smuggling, fraud, and other illicit trade-related activities) such as:
  - Risk management?
  - Exchange of data and intelligence?
  - Joint law enforcement actions?
  - Please describe other activities.
- Does the agreement require states to exchange information on best practices or share expertise generally, or specifically on:
  - Procedures, techniques?
  - Technology?
  - Please describe other areas.
- Does the agreement require states to cooperate in international fora? If more than a general commitment, please describe.
- Does the agreement commit the states to cooperate in additional customs and other economic and TF activities (such as risk management, simplification, and so on)? If yes, please describe.

V. CUSTOMS UNION-SPECIFIC

- In case of a customs union, does the agreement require states to:
  - Harmonize/standardize some of their legal provisions (please describe the elements)?
  - Adopt and apply a common customs legal framework?
- Does the agreement provide for customs and other duties and taxes to be collected at:
  - First port of entry?
  - Destination?
- Does the agreement provide for sharing customs revenue or another revenue distribution mechanism (please describe)?

VI. FREE TRADE AGREEMENT-SPECIFIC

A. Rules of Origin

- Does the agreement require any of the following types of proof of origin:
  - Certificate of origin?
  - Commercial invoice declaration?
  - "Self-certification" or declaration (by approved exporter)?
  - Waiver if below prescribed value?
- Does the agreement specify who is responsible for issuing the proof of origin:
  - Customs?
  - Business association (such as chamber of commerce designated by a ministry responsible for trade or customs)?
  - Exporter/importer?
- Does the agreement require that proof of origin should be in:
  - Paper format?
  - Electronic format?
- Does the agreement provide for submission of proof of origin:
  - On a transactional basis?
  - To cover multiple transactions?
- Does the agreement provide for origin verification measures and channels?

VII. TECHNICAL ASSISTANCE/CAPACITY BUILDING

- Does the agreement require states to assist each other in implementation of the agreement or specific elements thereof? Please describe.
- Does the agreement provide for states to support each other with:
  - Advisory services?
  - Training?
  - Study visits?
  - Exchange/secondment of officers?
  - Infrastructure?
  - Financial support?

VIII. INSTITUTIONAL ARRANGEMENTS

- Does the agreement provide for the establishment of structures (such as working group/committee or other body) to:
  - Develop a customs or TF work program?
  - Guide and/or monitor implementation of customs or TF provisions?

Source: Mattoo, Rocha, and Ruta 2020.

Note: DTA = deep trade agreement; TF = trade facilitation.

NOTES

1. Deep trade agreements (DTAs) refer to regional trade agreements (RTAs) or preferential trade agreements (PTAs) that are "deep" in terms of content and cover a broad range of behind-the-border policy areas.

2. The World Trade Organization (WTO) defines trade facilitation as the simplification, modernization, and harmonization of export and import processes. The WTO Trade Facilitation Agreement (TFA) recognizes the central role of customs but, in article 8, also acknowledges other government agencies through the concept of border agency cooperation (Kieck 2020).

3. All data on the *Doing Business* trading across border scores are from the World Bank's *Doing Business* report: https://openknowledge.worldbank.org/bitstream/handle/10986/32436/97814648 14402.pdf.

4. An AEO is a party involved in the international movement of goods that has been approved by, or on behalf of, a national customs administration as complying with World Customs Organization (WCO) or equivalent supply chain security standards.

5. The SIECA TF strategy also contains three cross-cutting initiatives (development of the Central American Digital Trade Platform, piloting and implementing bilateral solutions and borders, and strengthening the national TF committees) with seven medium-term measures focused on data interoperability and exchange of information, comprehensive risk management, trusted operators, quarantine control, integration of control procedures, infrastructure and equipment, and border community and security.

6. High-income countries committed to immediately implement the TFA upon its entry into force, while low- and middle-income countries were to apply only those substantive provisions of the agreement that they indicated they were able to do from the date of its entry into force.

7. This section provides a descriptive analysis of TF provisions in the region's trade agreements, based on a new database of deep trade agreements (Mattoo, Rocha, and Ruta 2020). The dataset presents detailed data on the content of 18 policy areas that are most frequently covered in PTAs and that were in force and notified to the WTO by 2017. This entailed the coding of 937 provisions by experts in each area, of which 52 provisions are in the TF and customs policy area (annex 3A, table 3A.1).

8. "Separating release from clearance means that goods are released by Customs prior to the payment of duties and taxes in cases where final classification of the goods, assessment of value, and other transactions are pending. A security for the applicable duties and taxes in the form of a deposit or bond is usually required" (WCO and UNCTAD 2011).

9. Calculated by $-0.0172 + 0.00334 + 0.0434 + (0.00661 * 0.661) = 0.0335721$, based on coefficients available in annex 3A, table 3A.3.

10. Other provisions in DTAs may also have differential impacts on GVC firms. As a sensitivity analysis, we include additional interaction terms allowing the effect of PTAs and overall depth to vary across firm type. The positive and significant effect of TF provisions on GVC firms remain robust. The results are also robust to an alternative estimation using a Poisson pseudo maximum likelihood (PPML) model. See Lee, Rocha, and Ruta (2021) for more details.

11. Prearrival processing refers to procedures allowing for the submission of import documentation and other required information, including manifests, to begin processing before the arrival of goods with a view to expediting the release of goods upon arrival.

12. For exceptions to the free movement regime, the following circumstances are considered, among others, (a) goods contained in part II of the Central American Import Tariff, (b) goods subject to tariff quotas by preferential agreements, (c) goods subject to safeguards, (d) goods with a different phyto or sanitary zoo regime, and (e) goods subject to substantially different tax regimes. See the list of goods exempted from free movement at https://www.ua.sieca.int/FYDUCA/Pages /_ConsultaListados.aspx.

REFERENCES

Alfaro de Morán, M., and A. Sarmiento. 2019. "Análisis de la medición de tiempos de la operación de los pasos de frontera entre Guatemala y Honduras." Unpublished discussion paper, World Bank, Washington, DC.

Fernandes, A., C. Freund, and M. D. Pierola. 2016. "Exporter Behavior, Country Size and Stage of Development: Evidence from the Exporter Dynamics Database." *Journal of Development Economics* 119: 121–37. doi:10.1016/j.jdeveco.2015.10.007.

Fernandes, A. M., R. H. Hillberry, and C. N. Berg. 2016. "Expediting Trade: Impact Evaluation of an In-House Clearance Program." Policy Research Working Paper 7708, World Bank, Washington, DC.

Fontagné, L., G. Orefice, and R. Piermartini. 2017. "Making (Small) Firms Happy. The Heterogeneous Effect of Trade Facilitation Measures." Working paper available on HAL open archive, https://hal .archives-ouvertes.fr/hal-01476546.

Hofmann, C., A. Osnago, and M. Ruta. 2017. "Horizontal Depth: A New Database on the Content of Preferential Trade Agreements." Policy Research Working Paper 7981, World Bank, Washington, DC.

Kieck, E. 2020. "Trade Facilitation and Customs." In *Handbook of Deep Trade Agreements*, edited by A. Mattoo, N. Rocha, and M. Ruta, 293–317. Washington, DC: World Bank.

Lee, W., N. Rocha, and M. Ruta. 2021. "Trade Facilitation Provisions in Preferential Trade Agreement: Impact on Peru's Exporters." Policy Research Working Paper 9674, World Bank, Washington, DC.

Mattoo, A., N. Rocha, and M. Ruta, eds. 2020. *Handbook of Deep Trade Agreements*. Washington, DC: World Bank.

Mejia Rivas, I., and M. Maday. 2019. "Así conectó la Alianza del Pacífico sus Ventanillas Únicas de Comercio Exterior." *Más Allá de las Fronteras* [Beyond Borders] (blog), August 2. https://blogs.iadb .org/integracion-comercio/es/conecto-alianza-del-pacifico-ventanillas-unicas-comercio/.

Moïsé, E., and S. Sorescu. 2013. "Trade Facilitation Indicators: The Potential Impact of Trade Facilitation on Developing Countries' Trade." Trade Policy Paper No. 144, Organisation for Economic Co-operation and Development (OECD) Publishing, Paris.

SIECA (Secretariat for Central American Economic Integration). n.d. "Unión Aduanera Guatemala-Honduras." Video on the Central American Invoice and Single Declaration (FYDUCA), SIECA General Secretariat, Guatemala City. https://www.sieca.int/index.php/integracion -economica/integracion-economica/integracion-profunda-guatemala-honduras-elsalvador /informacion-general/.

Subramanian, U. 2012. "Trade Logistics Reforms: Linking Business to Global Markets." *Viewpoint* Note No. 335 of the Investment Climate Impact Project, World Bank and International Finance Corporation, Washington, DC.

World Bank. 2020a. *The African Continental Free Trade Area: Economic and Distributional Effects*. Washington, DC: World Bank.

World Bank. 2020b. *World Development Report 2020: Trading for Development in the Age of Global Value Chains*. Washington, DC: World Bank. doi:10.1596/978-1-4648-1457-0.

WCO and UNCTAD (World Customs Organization and United Nations Commission for Trade and Development). 2011. "Separating Release from Clearance Procedures." Technical Note No. 19, UNCTAD Trust Fund for TF Negotiations, Geneva.

WTO (World Trade Organization). 2015. *World Trade Report 2015. Speeding Up Trade: Benefits and Challenges of Implementing the WTO TF Agreement*. Geneva: WTO.

4 Regulatory Cooperation: Reducing the Trade Costs of Nontariff Measures

Ana Fernandes and Kevin Lefebvre, with inputs from
Hiau Looi Kee and Anabel González

KEY MESSAGES

- Nontariff measures (NTMs)—such as sanitary and phytosanitary (SPS) measures and technical barriers to trade (TBT)—have gained importance as obstacles to trade.
- Although Latin American and Caribbean countries impose fewer SPS measures and TBT on imports than other regions, they face such measures in destination markets. Preferential trade agreements (PTAs) that integrate SPS and TBT rules play a key role in reduction of NTM costs.
- The inclusion of certain SPS and TBT provisions in Latin American and Caribbean PTAs promotes regulatory convergence, which boosts bilateral exports, particularly of intermediate inputs by the region's countries.
- Firm-level evidence for Chile, Colombia, and Peru shows that the boost to exports from including SPS and TBT provisions in PTAs is largest for small firms because such PTAs reduce the fixed entry costs of exporting created by NTMs, which are especially onerous for small exporters.
- Some PTAs have been more successful than others in implementation of SPS and TBT provisions, but some countries have found other innovative approaches for regulatory cooperation.

INTRODUCTION

Over the past three decades, as multilateral and preferential import tariffs have been reduced, nontariff measures (NTMs)—such as sanitary and phytosanitary (SPS) measures and technical barriers to trade (TBT)—have gained importance as obstacles to trade.

NTMs may raise trade costs in Latin American and Caribbean countries and reduce opportunities to exploit economies of scale. In the region, 42 percent of imported products and 53 percent of import value are covered by NTMs. The resulting high trade costs limit Latin American and Caribbean firms' ability to exploit economies of scale from regional markets. Countries in Europe, North America, and East Asia impose even more costly NTMs on their imports—particularly SPS and TBT measures, whose prevalence in those important destination markets can hamper Latin American and Caribbean exporting firms' trade and growth prospects.

Although regulatory cooperation can reduce trade costs, Latin American and Caribbean trade agreements have a mixed record of achieving such cooperation. SPS and TBT rules in trade agreements require members to increase NTM transparency, promote forms of regulatory cooperation such as harmonization or mutual recognition of standards, and improve enforcement of those commitments. Including SPS and TBT rules in preferential trade agreements (PTAs) reduces the potential negative impact of NTMs and lowers the trade costs of regulatory divergence. Trade agreements involving Latin American and Caribbean countries have increasingly included SPS and TBT rules, though implementation remains a challenge. And important differences persist: SPS provisions in Latin American and Caribbean agreements tend to have more binding commitments than TBT provisions have. The SPS provisions sometimes require mutual recognition or harmonization but are less stringent regarding transparency.

SPS AND TBT MEASURES: THE ROLE OF PTAs IN PROMOTING REGULATORY CONVERGENCE

SPS and TBT measures are often imposed to pursue noneconomic objectives for legitimate reasons, such as protecting the safety, public health, and well-being of consumers. But the measures create information, compliance, and procedural costs, and they can be used to protect domestic producers from import competition.

A couple of examples illustrate the complexity and diversity of NTMs as well their purpose: An SPS measure that many countries impose is a testing requirement to check for pesticide residue on oranges. The objective is to protect consumer health from toxins added to food. A TBT that many countries impose is a labeling requirement on imported products, such as refrigerators and air conditioning units, to indicate their size, weight, and electricity consumption. The objective is to protect consumers from deceptive practices by providing consumers with information.

Regulatory heterogeneity across countries in the SPS and TBT areas can increase foreign market entry costs, but international regulatory cooperation can help reduce them (Ederington and Ruta 2016; Hoekman 2015).[1] For exporting firms, regulatory heterogeneity may bring information and compliance costs (OECD 2017; Stone and Lejárraga 2018; Van Tongeren, Bastien, and von Lampe 2015). For firms engaged in global value chains (GVCs), differences in domestic regulations result in frictions and delays in access to imported inputs, generating disruptions across the chain, especially for smaller firms (WTO 2012). Empirical evidence shows that SPS measures have a stronger impact on the extensive margin of trade (expanding into new products or new markets) than on the intensive margin of trade (expanding volumes of existing products or markets), and they act as a stronger barrier for small exporting firms relative to large ones (Fernandes, Ferro, and Wilson 2019; Fontagné et al. 2015; Reyes 2011).

International regulatory cooperation may take different forms, ranging from informal information exchanges to formal mechanisms (including impact assessments and mutual recognition agreements or determinations of regulatory equivalence) as well as efforts to increase coherence across regulatory regimes (Goldberg 2019; Hoekman 2018; OECD 2013; Polanco and Sauvé 2018). The World Trade Organization (WTO) SPS and TBT agreements include regulations that address the preparation, adoption, and application of domestic regulations; provide a framework for transparency and deliberation; and require regulations not to be discriminatory or more trade restrictive than necessary (WTO and OECD 2019).[2]

PTAs increasingly include provisions that regulate the use of SPS and TBT measures between member countries, and PTAs can be useful vehicles for minimizing regulatory divergence.[3] Some PTAs include a large number of SPS and TBT provisions (such as the Comprehensive and Progressive Agreement for Trans-Pacific Partnership, or CPTPP), while others include few (such as the 1997 Canada–Chile PTA). But not all provisions matter equally. Essential provisions—those that require specific liberalization and integration commitments and obligations; relate to procedures, transparency, and enforcement; or relate to the objectives to achieve SPS and TBT integration—are more critical.

The integration of SPS and TBT measures into PTAs can follow different approaches. One approach to addressing regulatory diversity is to harmonize SPS and TBT to require common policy objectives and the standards and regulations to achieve those objectives. Common standards to harmonize SPS and TBT can be existing international standards (such as the Codex Alimentarius Commission standards for food safety) or new regional standards developed by the PTA's members. This approach could, at least initially, increase the costs for firms of complying with the new harmonized standards. But it subsequently lowers information costs for producers and consumers trading within the PTA. A challenge for the harmonization approach is that it requires a high degree of coordination across countries, especially if regional standards are developed, because the standards must integrate the preferences and specifics of all member countries.

Another approach for addressing regulatory diversity is the mutual recognition of SPS and TBT measures across member countries.[4] An advantage of this approach is that it eliminates additional costs for firms of complying with PTA partners' standards and regulations. A limit is that it tends to be adopted by high-income countries, where there is a higher degree of trust. In several PTAs, both the harmonization and mutual recognition approaches are used.[5]

Both harmonization and mutual recognition of SPS and TBT measures can enhance trade. These integration approaches affect the fixed costs of exporting for firms in different ways. Mutual recognition of member countries' regulations reduces costs for firms because they do not have to comply with a multiplicity of regulations (Baldwin 2000). Firms only need to comply with their domestic regulations to have their products accepted in PTA partner markets.

Although harmonizing member countries' regulations could initially increase the fixed costs, the use of common standards, especially international standards, could also increase demand if harmonized rules are based on consumer preferences and on compatibility between products across countries. Such an increase in market size could then allow firms to exploit economies of scale and increase exports.

But there is theoretical ambiguity on whether harmonization or mutual recognition is more beneficial for trade.[6] Although mutual recognition is expected to increase trade with PTA member countries, harmonization can have a positive spillover effect on trade with non-PTA countries that use similar standards. Empirically, harmonization and mutual recognition of standards among high-income countries increase trade, with a larger effect for mutual recognition (Chen and Mattoo 2008). But harmonizing TBT standards in PTAs between high-income countries and low- and middle-income countries has a detrimental effect on trade when the harmonization is based on regional standards (Disdier, Fontagné, and Cadot 2015). From a firm perspective, harmonizing standards fosters the entry of new exporters and encourages higher exports by existing firms (Reyes 2011; Schmidt and Steingress 2019).

Provisions for transparency in SPS and TBT can also foster trade integration. Given the complexity of SPS and TBT measures and the potential regulatory divergence across PTA partners, information asymmetries generate uncertainty about the measures and can result in additional importing and exporting costs for firms (Ing, Cadot, and Walz 2017). Transparency provisions in PTAs cover the publication and notification of measures, making available the information—often of a scientific nature—on which SPS or TBT measures are based. PTAs with deeper mechanisms for enhancing transparency promote trade more strongly than those with shallower commitments to transparency (Lejárraga and Shepherd 2013).

NONTARIFF MEASURES IN LATIN AMERICA AND THE CARIBBEAN

The Latin America and Caribbean region imposes fewer NTMs on its imports than higher-income regions, and this is particularly true for SPS and TBT measures. NTMs are diverse and complex, as illustrated by Colombia (box 4.1). Unlike tariffs, most NTMs are qualitative, and it is not easy to quantify their impact on trade. In fact, NTMs can affect trade by changing prices, quantities traded, or both (UN 2019).

Many studies quantify the impact of NTMs by estimating their ad valorem tariff equivalents (AVEs) and thus taking into account the responsiveness of import demand to the measures.[7] But the discussion here focuses on the prevalence of NTMs, not on their trade restrictiveness.

Box 4.1   Nontariff measures in Colombia

In the 1990s, after decades of protectionism, Colombia liberalized its trade. Tariffs were substantially reduced, and import prohibitions were eliminated. But in response to economic conditions and political pressure, especially from the agriculture and food processing sectors, the Colombian government introduced several nontariff measures (NTMs). This was done because World Trade Organization (WTO) commitments made increasing tariffs unfeasible.

Wine imports are one example of the results of NTMs. As of 2020, every time a wine import shipment arrives in Colombia, eight forms must be submitted to different agencies, and 15 days are spent obtaining clearance. Colombia imposes NTMs on 60 percent of Harmonized System (HS) 6-digit imports. But this high frequency index (the share of imported products subject to NTMs) is lower than that of Argentina and Brazil, which both impose NTMs on more than 75 percent of HS 6-digit imported products. Compared with other Latin American and Caribbean countries, Colombia's imports of food products and consumption goods face the most NTMs, while capital goods face the fewest. Nearly 100 percent of food products face at least one NTM in Colombia, while that frequency index averages close to 90 percent for the region overall. In addition, intermediate products and raw agricultural materials face more NTMs in Colombia than in the rest of the region.

To reduce cross-border smuggling from special economic zones, imports of textiles and apparel products face an NTM that requires products to enter Colombia through authorized ports only. To ensure proper inspection, some agriculture and food products also face similar port-of-entry requirements. More than 1,700 products have port-of-entry requirements, a number seen nowhere else in the region.

Processed food and industrial, chemical, or metal products that are inputs into the production of pesticides or fertilizers face registration and inspection requirements in Colombia, with the sanitary and phytosanitary (SPS) and technical barriers to trade (TBT) measures aimed at safeguarding public health. More broadly, SPS or TBT inspection and certification requirements in Colombia are the most commonly used NTMs, while authorizations for SPS and TBT reasons are also prevalent. For example, the TBT inspection requirements are imposed on more than 1,900 imported products.

Source: Economist 2020; Kee and Forero 2020.

Measuring the prevalence of NTMs

One way to establish the prevalence of NTMs is to examine each country's share of imported products subject to NTMs (the frequency index) as well as the share of import value subject to NTMs (the import coverage ratio) using data collected from official sources (UNCTAD 2017).[8] In Latin America and the Caribbean, 42 percent of imported products and 53 percent of import value are covered by NTMs (figure 4.1, panel a).

Higher-income regions in Europe and Central Asia and North America, but also East Asia and the Pacific, have much higher NTM frequency indexes and import coverage ratios than Latin America and the Caribbean. In Europe and Central Asia and North America, about 90 percent of imported products and trade value are covered by NTMs, while in East Asia and the Pacific, close to 70 percent of imported products and trade value are covered. As for SPS and TBT measures specifically, the evidence shows a lower prevalence in Latin America and the Caribbean than in some higher-income regions (figure 4.1, panel b).

The SPS frequency index in the region is 22 percent of imported products, and the TBT frequency is 31 percent. Higher frequency indexes characterize both Europe and Central Asia (28 percent for SPS and 87 percent for TBT) and East Asia and the Pacific (24 percent for SPS and 52 percent for TBT).

In Latin America and the Caribbean, the import coverage ratio for SPS is 21 percent of import value, and for TBT it is 39 percent. The import coverage ratios for TBT are much higher for East Asia and the Pacific (at 60 percent) and for Europe and Central Asia and North America (at 88 percent). These regional variations are ascribed to some degree to societal differences in preferences for noneconomic objectives, namely health and safety, that increase as countries develop.

Note that although the evidence in figure 4.1 shows that the coverage ratios in Latin America and the Caribbean are lower than those of other regions, this does not imply that such measures are not restrictive. On the contrary, evidence in a 2019 regional flagship report based on AVEs for NTMs imposed across different regions shows that the NTMs in the Latin America and Caribbean region are more restrictive than those imposed by countries in other regions (World Bank 2019).[9]

A higher prevalence of SPS and TBT in destination markets can hurt the region's exporters. The higher frequency indexes and import coverage ratios of SPS and TBT in major destination markets (North America and Europe and Central Asia) are a potential source of concern for Latin American and Caribbean exporters. Those in the East Asia and Pacific region—a crucial destination market for Latin American and Caribbean countries since the 2000s as China's centrality in world trade has grown—are also a concern. (Latin American and Caribbean exporters express particular concerns about SPS and TBT measures that limit benefits from tariff liberalization under PTAs [Mowatt 2017].)

Figure 4.1   Import coverage ratios are lower in Latin America and the Caribbean than in other regions

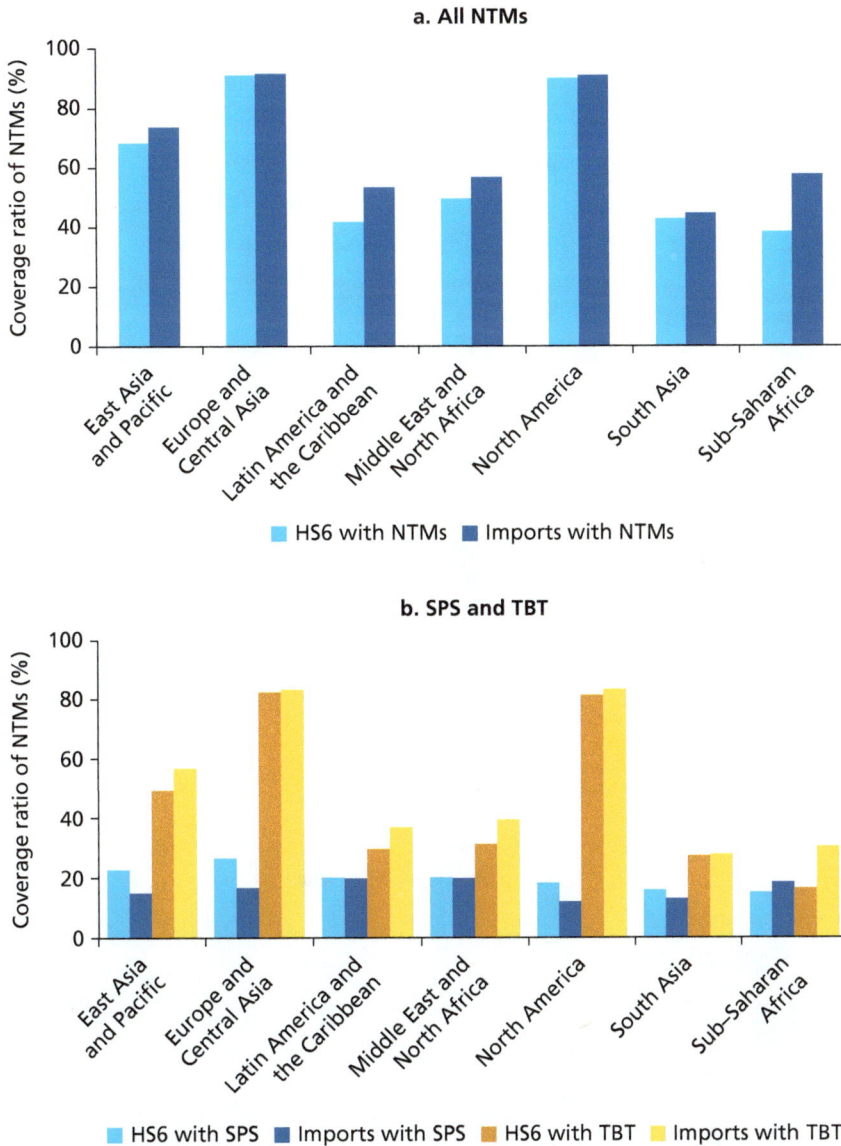

a. All NTMs

b. SPS and TBT

Source: United Nations Conference on Trade and Development (UNCTAD) Trade Analysis Information System (TRAINS) database, https://trainsonline.unctad.org/.

Note: The "coverage ratio" is the share of import value subject to nontariff measures (NTMs). The regional averages are based on data for all available countries (listed in annex 4A, table 4A.2) for the most recent year. The years range from 2012 to 2018 and differ across countries. Products are classified according to the international Harmonized System (HS). HS6 refers to HS classification at the 6-digit code level. "HS6 with NTMs," "HS6 with SPS," and "HS6 with TBT" refer to the number of products covered by NTMs, SPS measures, and TBT, respectively. "Imports with NTMs," "Imports with SPS," and "Imports with TBT" refer to the import value covered by NTMs, SPS measures, and TBT, respectively. "North America" includes Canada and the United States. SPS = sanitary and phytosanitary measures; TBT = technical barriers to trade.

There is a potential role for deep PTAs within the Latin America and Caribbean region to integrate SPS and TBT measures. This will further enhance GVC participation through improved market access for export goods and better access to imports of intermediate inputs.

Examining SPS and TBT notifications to the WTO

A second way to establish the importance of SPS and TBT for WTO members is to examine the number of yearly notifications of new SPS and TBT measures that each country makes to the WTO.[10] Notifications in Latin America and the Caribbean have grown more slowly than they have outside the region.

Notifications about new SPS measures have hovered around 300 per year for all Latin American and Caribbean countries, growing slightly since 2005 (figure 4.2, panel a). Notifications about new TBT measures average about 200 a year for the region's countries and have also grown slightly since 2005 (figure 4.2, panel b). Since 1995, there has been a stronger growth in new SPS and TBT notifications outside the region.

Until 2000, richer countries were the biggest notifiers of SPS and TBT measures in Latin America and the Caribbean. Since then, many other countries in the region have become important notifiers. But a shift is observed over the past two decades in individual country notifications of new SPS and TBT measures to the WTO: up to 2000,

Figure 4.2 Notifications to the WTO of SPS measures and TBT provisions have grown more slowly from Latin American and Caribbean countries than from the rest of the world

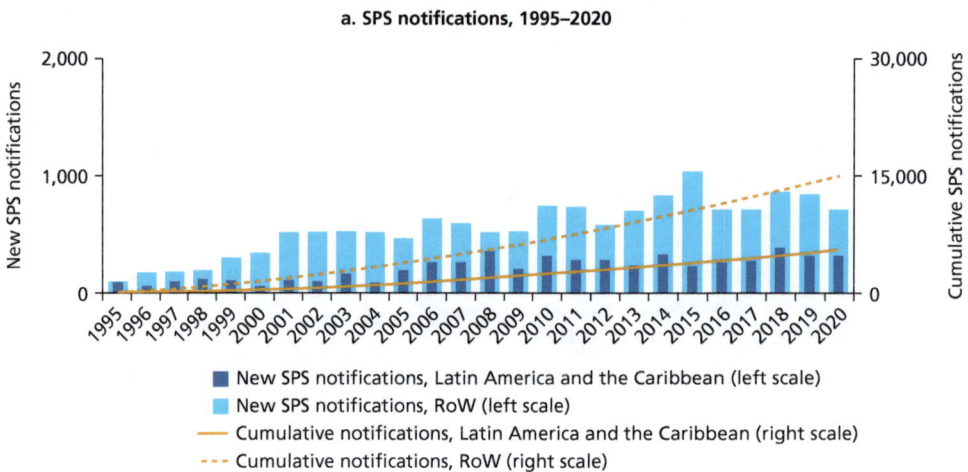

a. SPS notifications, 1995–2020

- New SPS notifications, Latin America and the Caribbean (left scale)
- New SPS notifications, RoW (left scale)
- —— Cumulative notifications, Latin America and the Caribbean (right scale)
- --- Cumulative notifications, RoW (right scale)

Continued

Figure 4.2   Notifications to the WTO of SPS measures and TBT provisions have grown more slowly from Latin American and Caribbean countries than from the rest of the world *(continued)*

b. TBT notifications, 1995–2020

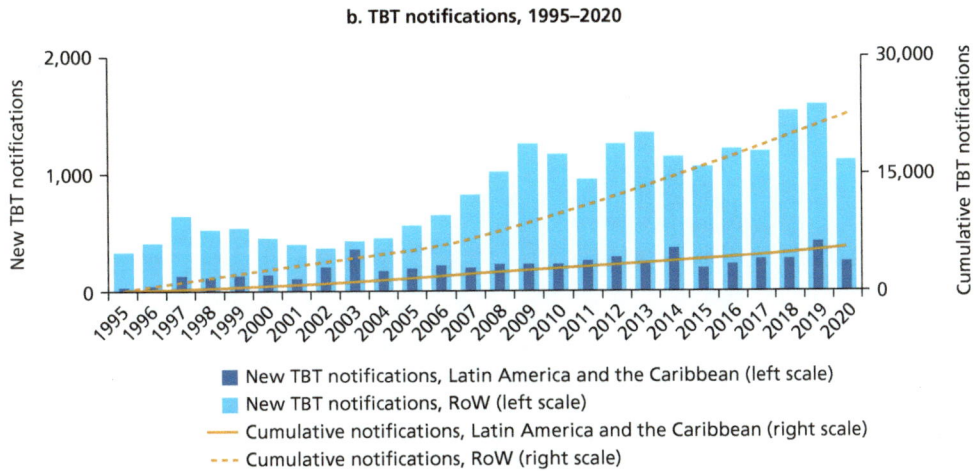

■ New TBT notifications, Latin America and the Caribbean (left scale)
■ New TBT notifications, RoW (left scale)
— Cumulative notifications, Latin America and the Caribbean (right scale)
--- Cumulative notifications, RoW (right scale)

Source: World Trade Organization (WTO) database of official notifications of sanitary and phytosanitary (SPS) measures and technical barriers to trade (TBT).

Note: The figures show the number of regular and emergency notifications of SPS and TBT measures made to the WTO by Latin America and Caribbean countries versus all other countries from 1995 to 2020. RoW = rest of the world.

Argentina, Brazil, Chile, and Mexico were the countries that had notified the largest cumulative number of new SPS and TBT measures to the WTO. But by 2020, almost all Latin American and Caribbean countries were notifying new SPS and TBT measures to the WTO.[11]

Examining concerns raised in WTO committees

A third way to establish the importance of SPS and TBT is to examine the number of concerns raised by members of the WTO committees on SPS and TBT about measures imposed by particular countries. These SPS- and TBT-specific trade concerns are viewed as capturing de facto trade barriers (Fontagné et al. 2015). These WTO committee members raise more concerns about TBT measures in Latin American and Caribbean countries than about the region's SPS measures (figure 4.3, panels a and b).

Fewer concerns have been reported since 2010 about the imposition of SPS in the region. In contrast, there has been faster growth in specific trade concerns about both SPS and TBT measures imposed by countries outside the region.

Figure 4.3   WTO trade concerns about SPS and TBT measures in Latin America and the Caribbean versus the rest of the world

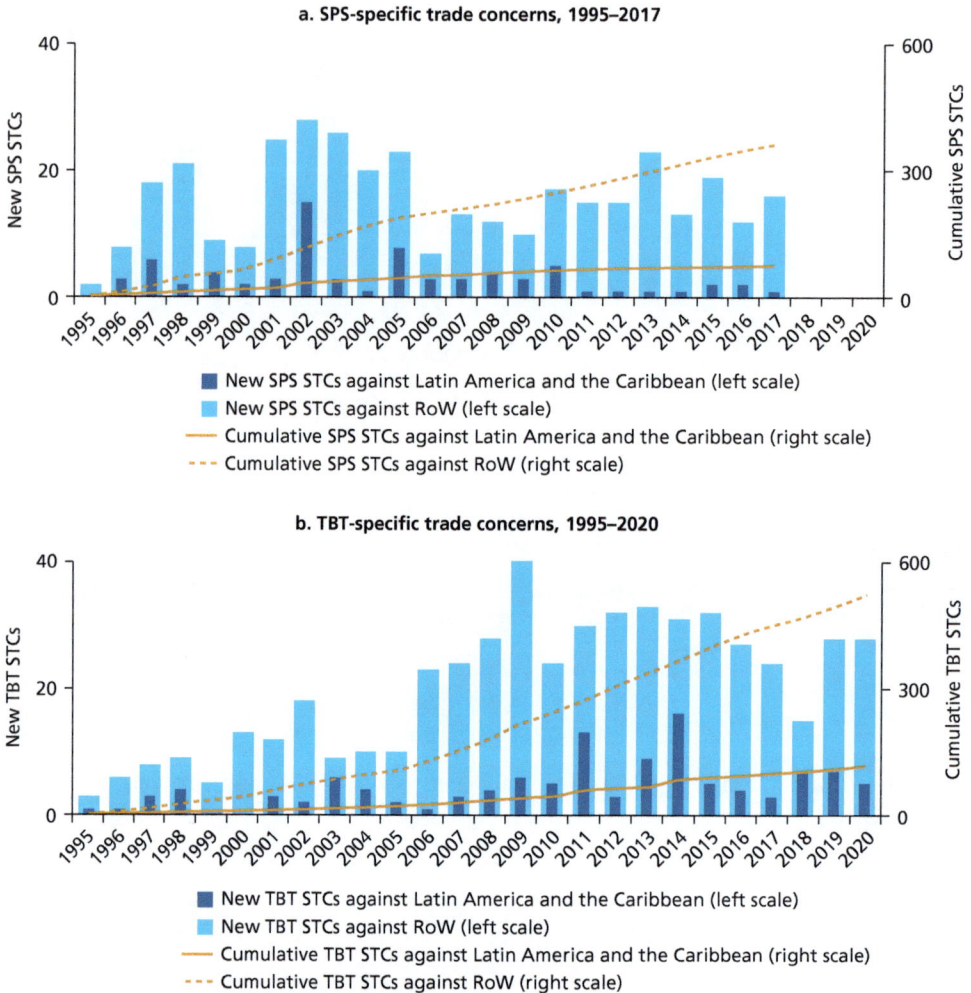

a. SPS-specific trade concerns, 1995–2017

■ New SPS STCs against Latin America and the Caribbean (left scale)
■ New SPS STCs against RoW (left scale)
— Cumulative SPS STCs against Latin America and the Caribbean (right scale)
--- Cumulative SPS STCs against RoW (right scale)

b. TBT-specific trade concerns, 1995–2020

■ New TBT STCs against Latin America and the Caribbean (left scale)
■ New TBT STCs against RoW (left scale)
— Cumulative TBT STCs against Latin America and the Caribbean (right scale)
--- Cumulative TBT STCs against RoW (right scale)

Source: World Trade Organization (WTO) data on specific trade concerns (STCs) about sanitary and phytosanitary (SPS) measures and technical barriers to trade (TBT).

Note: The figures show the number of STCs raised in WTO SPS and TBT committees against Latin American and Caribbean countries' markets and against all other country markets from 1995 to 2020. RoW = rest of the world.

SPS AND TBT MEASURES IN PTAs: INTEGRATION PATTERNS IN LATIN AMERICA AND THE CARIBBEAN

The World Bank's Deep Trade Agreements database covers 59 SPS and 34 TBT provisions in PTAs—encompassing standards as well as technical and procedural regulations (conformity and risk assessments) (Mattoo, Rocha, and Ruta 2020)—and captures aspects such as the following:[12]

- Reference to WTO rules
- Type of integration approach for standards (harmonization versus mutual recognition), technical regulations, and conformity assessment procedures
- Transparency
- Institutions or mechanisms to administer agreements and solve disputes
- Cooperation among regional partners on standards-related issues.

Essential SPS and TBT provisions

In practice, countries include a substantially smaller number of SPS and TBT measures in the PTAs they sign. The deepest PTAs in the database include 30 SPS provisions and 18 TBT provisions. To assess the depth of PTAs, it is useful to focus only on essential provisions (Mattoo, Rocha, and Ruta 2020). "Essential provisions" require specific liberalization and integration commitments and obligations; relate to procedures, transparency, enforcement, or objectives; and are viewed as indispensable and complementary to achieving SPS and TBT integration across member countries.[13]

Essential provisions that aim at further integrating SPS and TBT into PTAs include those that promote the international standards set out in the 2011 Canada–Colombia PTA (article 605). Essential provisions focusing on procedures include the right of an importing country to audit an exporting party's competent authorities, inspection systems, and the production procedures that were included in the 2013 European Union (EU)–Colombia and Peru PTA (article 93).

PTAs with SPS and TBT provisions have grown tremendously over recent decades, particularly for Latin American and Caribbean countries (figure 4.4). The increasing prevalence of TBT and SPS provisions in PTAs signed by the region's countries is noticeable (figure 4.4, panels a and c). In fact, the share of PTAs that include more than 25 percent of the total possible SPS or TBT provisions is higher for countries in Latin America and the Caribbean than outside the region (figure 4.4, panels b and d).

Of the 78 PTAs signed by Latin American and Caribbean countries over the past 40 years, 38 include more than 25 percent of the total possible SPS provisions, 58 include more than 25 percent of the total possible TBT provisions, and 16 include no SPS or TBT provisions at all. Within the region, the Pacific Alliance (PA) agreement includes the largest number of SPS provisions (28), while the 1995 Colombia–Mexico PTA and the 2009 Peru–Chile PTA include the largest number of TBT provisions (18), as shown in table 4.1.

Essential SPS provisions are frequent in Latin American and Caribbean PTAs. But essential TBT provisions are less prevalent in the region's PTAs than in PTAs from outside the region. The share of PTAs that include more than 25 percent of the essential SPS provisions is high for Latin American and Caribbean countries (figure 4.5, panel a, dark blue bars). Of the 78 PTAs signed by Latin American and Caribbean countries over the past four decades, 30 include more than 25 percent of the essential

Figure 4.4 SPS and TBT provisions in PTAs of the Latin America and Caribbean region and the rest of the world, 1958–2017

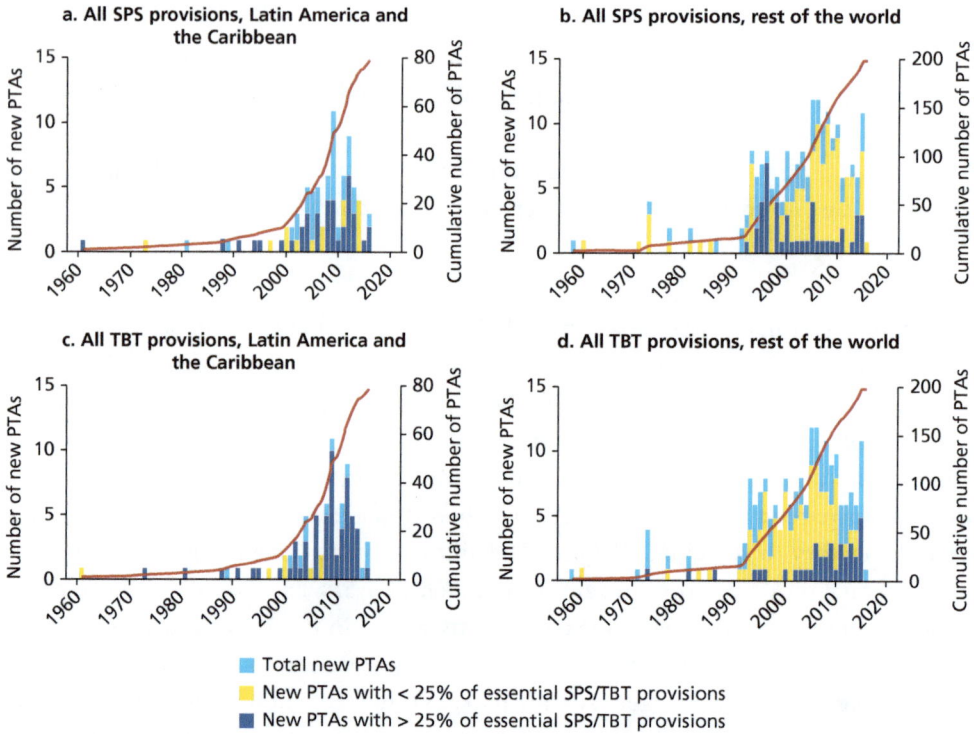

a. All SPS provisions, Latin America and the Caribbean

b. All SPS provisions, rest of the world

c. All TBT provisions, Latin America and the Caribbean

d. All TBT provisions, rest of the world

■ Total new PTAs
■ New PTAs with < 25% of essential SPS/TBT provisions
■ New PTAs with > 25% of essential SPS/TBT provisions

Sources: World Bank's Deep Trade Agreements database; Mattoo, Rocha, and Ruta 2020.

Note: The bars (left scale) show the number of new preferential trade agreements (PTAs) entering into force from 1958 to 2017. The red lines (right scale) show the cumulative number of PTAs. SPS = sanitary and phytosanitary; TBT = technical barrier to trade.

SPS provisions (and of the 31 signed since 2010, 10 include more than 25 percent of those provisions). The prevalence of PTAs with high percentages of essential SPS provisions is much greater in the Latin America and Caribbean region than in the rest of the world (figure 4.5, panels a and b).

However, PTAs with more than 25 percent of the essential TBT provisions are less frequent in the Latin America and Caribbean region than outside the region (see figure 4.5, panels c and d). Of the 78 PTAs signed by Latin American and Caribbean countries over the last four decades, only 11 include more than 25 percent of the essential TBT provisions. The PTAs with very large numbers of SPS and TBT provisions also include fewer essential provisions. The 1995 Colombia–Mexico PTA includes 10 essential SPS provisions and 7 essential TBT provisions, while the 1999 Chile–Mexico PTA and the 2009 Peru–Chile PTA include 9 essential SPS provisions and 6 essential TBT provisions (see table 4.1).[14]

The lower prevalence of essential SPS and especially TBT provisions in Latin American and Caribbean PTAs is of some concern, because these provisions capture the regulatory changes most likely to bring about deeper integration of SPS and TBT provisions among member countries and thus potentially enhance trade.

REGULATORY COOPERATION: REDUCING THE TRADE COSTS OF NONTARIFF MEASURES

Table 4.1 Top 30 Latin American and Caribbean PTAs in number of SPS measures and TBT provisions

Agreements	Entry in force	SPS					TBT				
		Total	Essential	MR	Harm.	Transp.	Total	Essential	MR	Harm.	Transp.
Andean Community (CAN)	1988	22	13	Yes	Yes	2	14	5	No	No	1
Colombia–Mexico	1995	25	10	Yes	Yes	6	18	7	No	No	2
North American Free Trade Agreement (NAFTA)	1994	21	10	Yes	Yes	5	15	6	No	No	3
Peru–Chile	2009	20	9	No	Yes	1	18	6	No	No	2
Chile–Mexico	1999	21	9	No	Yes	6	17	6	No	No	2
Nicaragua–Taiwan, China	2008	27	12	Yes	Yes	5	11	2	No	No	2
Pacific Alliance	2016	28	9	No	Yes	7	14	5	No	No	1
Mexico–Uruguay	2004	19	8	No	Yes	3	15	5	No	No	1
Chile–Colombia	2009	18	7	No	Yes	0	16	6	No	No	2
Central American Common Market (CACM)	1961	24	11	No	Yes	3	6	1	No	No	0
Panama–Taiwan, China	2004	23	11	No	Yes	5	11	1	No	No	2
Peru–Mexico	2012	17	6	No	Yes	4	16	6	No	No	2
EU–Chile	2003	26	10	Yes	Yes	4	8	2	No	No	0
Dominican Republic–Central America	2001	22	10	No	Yes	3	13	2	No	No	2
Southern Common Market (MERCOSUR)	1991	16	6	No	Yes	3	14	5	No	No	1

Continued

Table 4.1 Top 30 Latin American and Caribbean PTAs in number of SPS measures and TBT provisions *(continued)*

Agreements	Entry in force	SPS						TBT			
		Total	Essential	MR	Harm.	Transp.	Total	Essential	MR	Harm.	Transp.
Panama–El Salvador (Panama–Central America)	2003	19	11	No	Yes	1	9	0	No	No	2
Guatemala–Taiwan, China	2006	20	9	No	Yes	4	10	1	No	No	2
Korea, Rep.–Chile	2004	22	8	No	Yes	5	8	2	No	No	1
Mexico–Central America	2012	25	7	No	No	6	13	2	No	No	2
Chile–China	2006	20	7	No	Yes	4	12	2	No	No	2
EU–Central America	2013	24	8	No	Yes	3	11	1	No	No	1
Panama–Peru	2012	23	7	No	Yes	4	11	2	No	No	2
El Salvador–Honduras–Taiwan, China	2008	17	8	No	Yes	2	11	1	No	No	2
Costa Rica–Peru	2013	22	7	No	Yes	5	13	2	No	No	2
El Salvador–Cuba	2012	22	9	No	Yes	2	8	0	No	No	0
Peru–Singapore	2009	21	7	No	Yes	5	13	2	No	No	2
Panama–Chile	2008	19	6	No	Yes	4	10	2	No	No	2
Canada–Peru	2009	15	5	Yes	No	2	12	2	No	No	2
Peru–China	2010	22	6	No	Yes	6	11	1	No	No	2

Sources: World Bank's Deep Trade Agreements database; Mattoo, Rocha, and Ruta 2020.

Note: Preferential trade agreements (PTAs) are ranked by the cumulative number of "essential" sanitary and phytosanitary (SPS) and technical barrier to trade (TBT) provisions they include, from the largest to the smallest. "Essential" provisions are those that require specific liberalization and integration commitments and obligations; relate to procedures, transparency, and enforcement; or relate to achievement of SPS and TBT integration. The Comprehensive and Progressive Agreement for Trans-Pacific Partnerships (CPTPP) is excluded from the analysis. EU = European Union; Harm. = harmonization; MR = mutual recognition; Transp. = transparency provisions.

Figure 4.5 Essential SPS and TBT provisions in PTAs for Latin America and the Caribbean and the rest of the world, 1958–2017

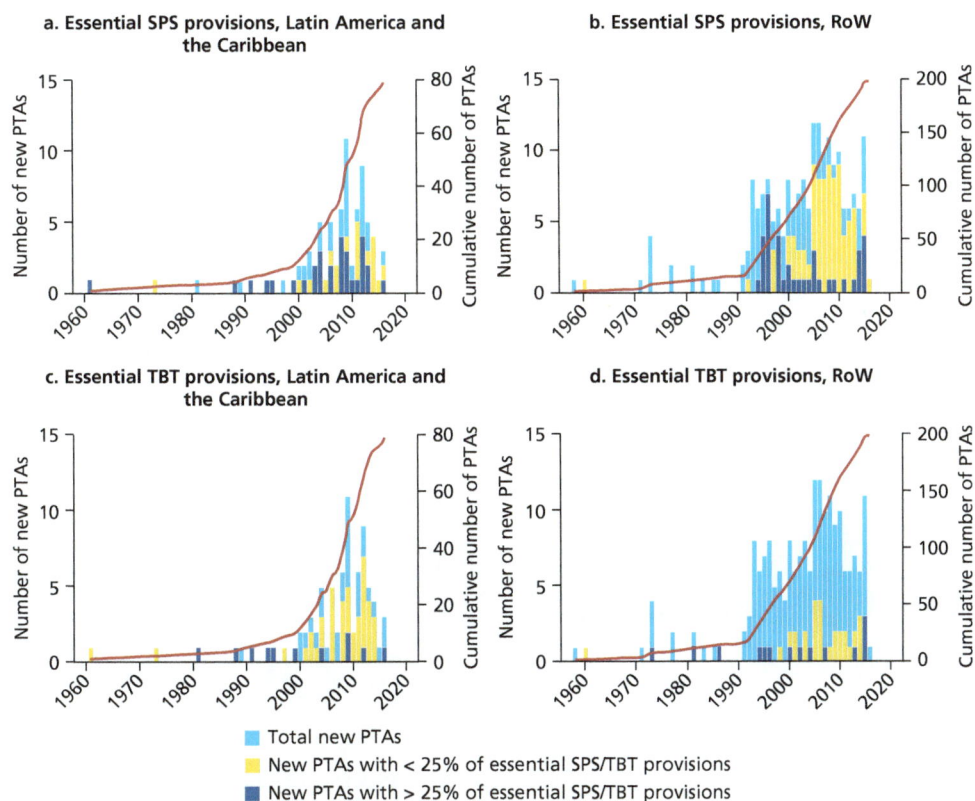

a. Essential SPS provisions, Latin America and the Caribbean

b. Essential SPS provisions, RoW

c. Essential TBT provisions, Latin America and the Caribbean

d. Essential TBT provisions, RoW

■ Total new PTAs
■ New PTAs with < 25% of essential SPS/TBT provisions
■ New PTAs with > 25% of essential SPS/TBT provisions

Sources: World Bank's Deep Trade Agreements database; Mattoo, Rocha, and Ruta 2020.

Note: The bars (left scale) plot the number of new preferential trade agreements (PTAs) entering in force from 1958 to 2017 and differentiate between those including essential sanitary and phytosanitary (SPS) provisions (panels a and b) and those with technical barrier to trade (TBT) provisions (panels c and d) signed by Latin American and Caribbean countries (panels a and c) and countries in the rest of the world (RoW) (panels b and d). The red lines (right scale) show the cumulative number of PTAs. "Essential" provisions are those that require specific liberalization and integration commitments and obligations; relate to procedures, transparency, and enforcement; or relate to achievement of SPS and TBT integration. There are a total of 24 essential SPS and 19 essential TBT provisions. The deepest PTAs include 13 essential SPS provisions and 9 essential TBT provisions.

Mutual recognition of SPS and TBT provisions

The integration of SPS measures into PTAs signed by Latin American and Caribbean countries often follows the mutual recognition approach, which is totally absent for TBT provisions. Since the 2000s, a large number of PTAs signed by the region's countries include mutual recognition provisions for SPS (figure 4.6, panel a), but no PTAs include mutual recognition provisions for TBT (figure 4.6, panel c).

Moreover, the region's share of new PTAs with mutual recognition provisions for SPS is larger than that in the rest of the world (figure 4.6, panels a and b). The rarity of using mutual recognition as an approach to integrate TBT provisions into PTAs is also seen outside the Latin America and Caribbean region (figure 4.6, panels c and d).

Figure 4.6   Mutual recognition of SPS and TBT provisions in PTAs of Latin America and the Caribbean and the rest of the world, 1958–2017

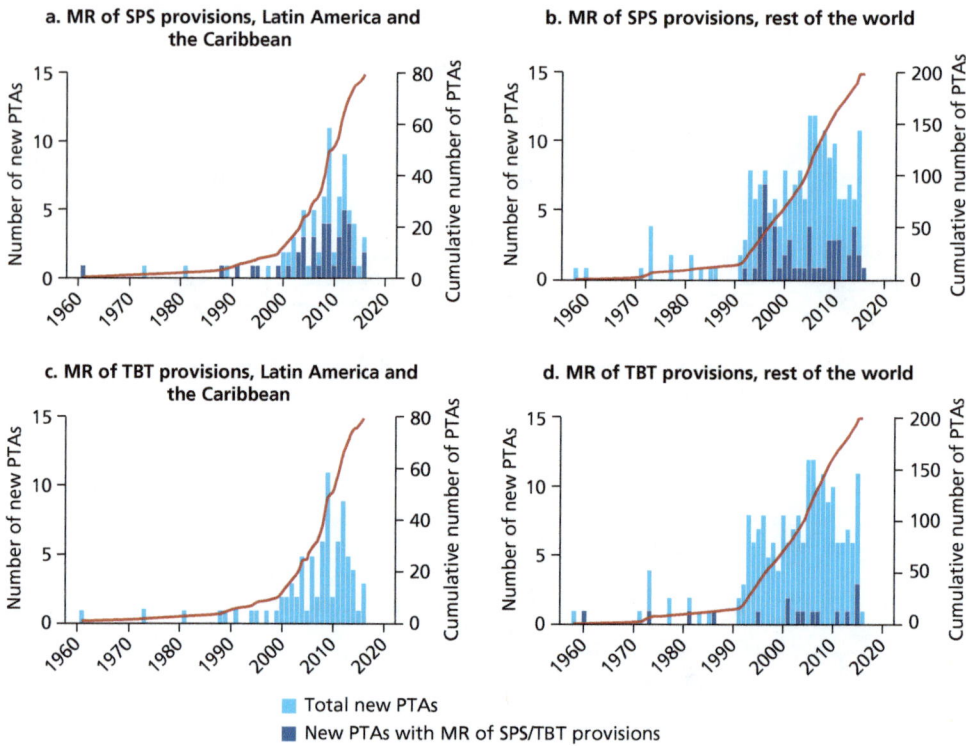

Sources: World Bank's Deep Trade Agreements database; Mattoo, Rocha, and Ruta 2020.

Note: The bars (left scale) plot the number of new preferential trade agreements (PTAs) entering in force from 1958 to 2017 and differentiate between the total number of PTAs and those that include at least one provision on mutual recognition (MR) of sanitary and phytosanitary (SPS) measures (panels a and b) and at least one provision on MR of technical barriers to trade (TBT) provisions (panels c and d) signed by Latin American and Caribbean countries (panels a and c) and countries of the rest of the world (RoW) (panels b and d). The red lines (right scale) show the cumulative number of PTAs.

Of the 78 PTAs signed by Latin American and Caribbean countries over the past four decades, 40 include mutual recognition provisions for SPS measures. Among the region's 30 PTAs with the highest number of essential SPS and TBT provisions, those that include mutual recognition provisions for SPS measures are the Canada–Peru PTA (2009), the Nicaragua–Taiwan, China PTA (2008), the EU–Chile PTA (2003), the Colombia–Mexico PTA (1995), the North American Free Trade Agreement (1994), and the Andean Community (1988), as shown in table 4.1.

Harmonization of SPS and TBT provisions

The harmonization approach is used for the integration of SPS measures in several PTAs signed by Latin American and Caribbean countries but rarely for the integration of TBT provisions. In most years since 2000, about half of the new PTAs signed by the region's countries include harmonization provisions for SPS (figure 4.7, panel a), but only one (European Free Trade Agreement [EFTA]–Peru in 2011) includes harmonization provisions for TBT (figure 4.7, panel c). Of the 78 PTAs signed by the region's countries over the last four decades, 29 include harmonization provisions for SPS.

Latin America and the Caribbean's share of new PTAs with harmonization provisions for SPS is larger than the share for PTAs in the rest of the world (figure 4.7, panel b). The rare inclusion in PTAs of harmonization provisions for TBT is also verified outside the Latin America and Caribbean region (figure 4.7, panel d).

Among the 30 Latin American and Caribbean PTAs with the highest number of essential SPS and TBT provisions, 28 include harmonization provisions for SPS. The only exceptions are the Mexico–Central America PTA (2012) and the Canada–Peru PTA (2009), as shown in table 4.1.

Figure 4.7 Harmonization of SPS and TBT measures in PTAs for Latin America and the Caribbean and the rest of the world, 1958–2017

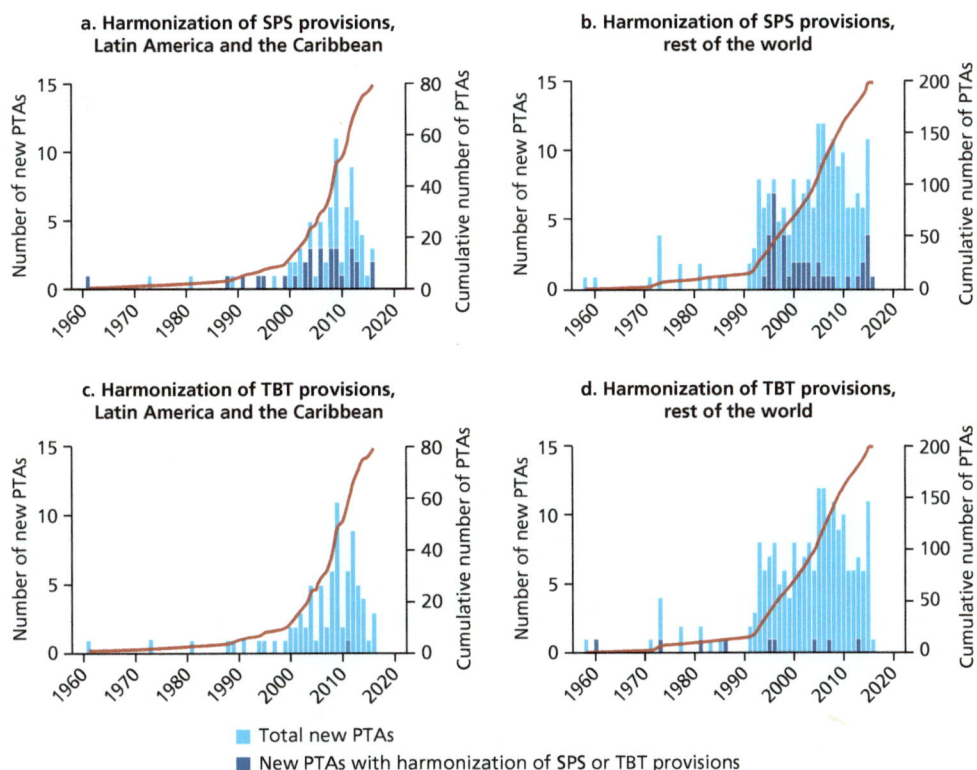

Sources: World Bank's Deep Trade Agreements database; Mattoo, Rocha, and Ruta 2020.

Note: The bars (left scale) plot the number of new preferential trade agreements (PTAs) entering in force from 1958 to 2017 and differentiate between the total number of PTAs and those that include at least one provision on harmonization of sanitary and phytosanitary (SPS) measures (panels a and b) and at least one provision on harmonization of technical barrier to trade (TBT) provisions (panels c and d) signed by Latin American and Caribbean countries (panels a and c) and countries of the rest of the world (RoW) (panels b and d). The red lines (right scale) show the cumulative number of PTAs.

Transparency and enforceability of SPS and TBT provisions

Transparency provisions for TBT are prevalent in Latin American and Caribbean PTAs but less common for SPS measures. The bulk of PTAs signed by the region's countries since 2000 include more than 25 percent of the transparency provisions for TBT, while relatively few PTAs include more than 25 percent of the transparency provisions for SPS (figure 4.8, panels a and c).[15] The prevalence of PTAs intensive in transparency provisions for TBT is much higher in the region than in the rest of the world (figure 4.8, panels c and d). Of the 78 PTAs signed by Latin American and Caribbean countries over the past four decades, 49 include more than 25 percent of the transparency provisions for TBT and 27 include more than 25 percent of the transparency provisions for SPS.

Figure 4.8   Transparency provisions of SPS measures and TBT provisions in PTAs for Latin America and the Caribbean and the rest of the world, 1958–2017

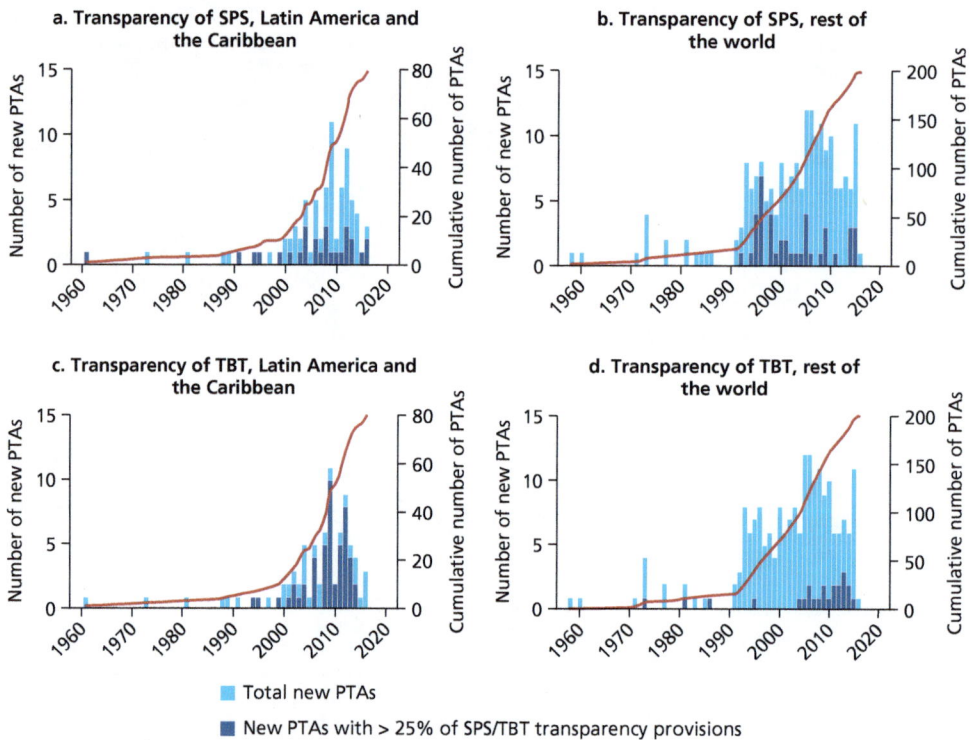

■ Total new PTAs

■ New PTAs with > 25% of SPS/TBT transparency provisions

Sources: World Bank's Deep Trade Agreements database; Mattoo, Rocha, and Ruta 2020.

Note: The bars (left scale) plot the number of new preferential trade agreements (PTAs) entering in force from 1958 to 2017 and differentiate between the total number of PTAs and those that include sanitary and phytosanitary (SPS) transparency provisions (panels a and b) and technical barrier to trade (TBT) transparency provisions (panels c and d) signed by Latin American and Caribbean countries (panels a and c) and countries of the rest of the world (panels b and d). There are a total of 12 SPS transparency provisions and 3 TBT transparency provisions. The deepest PTAs include 8 SPS transparency provisions and 3 TBT transparency provisions. The red lines (right scale) shows the cumulative number of PTAs.

Despite the prevalence of SPS and TBT provisions in Latin American and Caribbean PTAs, knowledge about their enforceability is limited. The World Bank's Deep Trade Agreements database collects information on only one general question about enforceability: whether SPS and TBT chapters are excluded from the PTA's dispute settlement. For most PTAs, these chapters are excluded from the dispute settlement mechanism.

THE IMPACTS ON TRADE AND GVCs OF INTEGRATING SPS AND TBT PROVISIONS

Impacts on countries' exports

Agricultural and food exports increase substantially for Latin American and Caribbean countries that sign PTAs with more overall or essential SPS provisions (box 4.2 and annex 4E).[16] Signing a PTA with the maximum number of total SPS provisions (such as the 2009 Peru–Chile PTA) increases the value of agricultural and food exports by

---

Box 4.2   The impact on aggregate trade of SPS measures and TBT provisions in PTAs

The trade and global value chain (GVC) impacts of sanitary and phytosanitary (SPS) measures and technical barriers to trade (TBT) provisions in preferential trade agreements (PTAs) can be estimated based on a gravity regression framework. The framework relies on Database for International Trade Analysis (BACI) bilateral trade data for all countries in the world from 1995 to 2015 (Gaulier and Zignago 2010). The gravity equation predicts the value of trade between two countries to be positively related to the size of their economies and negatively related to the distance and other trade costs between them (Piermartini and Yotov 2016). To capture GVC trade, two different outcomes are considered: exports and imports of intermediate inputs—defined according to the United Nations' Broad Economic Categories (BEC) classification. The gravity equation for trade between country i and country j in year t is given by

$$y_{ijt} = exp\,(\alpha_{ij} + \alpha_{it} + \alpha_{jt} + \beta_1\,ln\,(1 + \tau_{ijt}) + \beta_2\,Prov_{ijt} \times LAC_i + \beta_3\,Depth_{ijt} \times LAC_i$$
$$+\,\beta_4\,Prov_{ijt} \times ROW_i + \beta_5\,Depth_{ijt} \times Row_i) + \epsilon_{ijt}, \qquad (B4.2.1)$$

where y_{ijt} is either bilateral exports or bilateral imports of intermediate inputs; $Prov_{ijt}$ is, separately for SPS and for TBT, either (a) the number of total, essential, or transparency provisions in a PTA (normalized as described in annex 4C), or (b) a dummy variable for harmonization or mutual recognition; and $Depth_{ijt}$ is the number of provisions in all non-SPS non-TBT chapters (normalized as described in annex 4C). Equation (B4.2.1) includes bilateral country-pair dummy variables (α_{ij}) that account for gravity forces (such as distance) in explaining bilateral trade and import country–year, and export country–year dummy variables (α_{it} and α_{jt}) that account for the size of the countries and other macroeconomic factors affecting trade.

Equation (B4.2.1) also controls for a measure of trade costs: tariffs imposed by each importing country on a given exporting country, averaged across all Harmonized System (HS) 6-digit products (τ_{ijt}) (Teti 2020). To understand whether the Latin American and Caribbean region differs in its trade response, equation (B4.2.1) allows the coefficients on SPS and TBT provisions and on PTA depth to be separately estimated for the region by a dummy variable (LAC_i) and for outside the region by

---

Continued

Box 4.2   The impact on aggregate trade of SPS measures and TBT provisions in PTAs
(continued)

a dummy variable (*Row*). The dataset used for the estimation is the BACI bilateral data expanded along the year (panel) dimension so that each country pair has an observation in each year from 1995 to 2015. If trade does not occur between a country pair in a year, the trade flow is equal to 0.

Equation (B4.2.1) is estimated using the Poisson pseudo maximum likelihood (PPML) methodology introduced by Santos Silva and Tenreyro (2006) with the recent command of Correia, Guimarães, and Zylkin (2019).

The estimated trade impacts shown graphically for all essential and transparency provisions are based on the following thought experiment: How different would the impact on bilateral trade be for countries signing a PTA with the maximum number of SPS or TBT provisions (say, the 2009 Peru–Chile PTA) compared with countries signing a PTA with a small number of SPS or TBT provisions (say, the 2001 Mexico–EFTA PTA)? For a PTA with the maximum number of provisions, the variable *Prov*$_{ijt}$ moves from 0 to 1. If the estimated coefficient β_2 is 0.5, the resulting change in trade is 65 percent (exp(0.5) − 1). For harmonization or mutual recognition, the estimated trade impact is based on the comparison between PTAs that include such provisions and those that do not. For the corresponding tables with all estimated coefficients, see annex 4D.

22 percent on average for the region's countries, after accounting for the depth of other provisions and for any tariff liberalization brought about by the PTA (figure 4.9, first bar). Signing a PTA with the maximum number of *essential* SPS provisions increases the countries' agricultural and food exports even more—by close to 30 percent (figure 4.9, second bar). However, exports do not increase as much for Latin American and Caribbean PTAs with more SPS provisions than they do for such PTAs outside the region (annex 4D, table 4D.1).

Mutual recognition provisions for SPS foster significant growth in agricultural and food exports for Latin American and Caribbean countries, whereas harmonization plays no role. Agricultural and food exports increase by 15 percent on average for the region's countries that sign PTAs including mutual recognition provisions for SPS (figure 4.9, third bar). This increase in agricultural and food exports is significantly larger for the region than for the rest of the world (annex 4D, table 4D.2). Exports do not increase significantly for countries signing PTAs with harmonization provisions for SPS (figure 4.9, fourth bar). This could be because few PTAs in the region, or in the rest of the world, include such provisions.

Overall exports also increase for Latin American and Caribbean countries that sign PTAs with larger numbers of overall TBT provisions. A PTA that includes the maximum number of total TBT provisions (the 2009 Peru–Chile PTA) increases overall exports of the region's countries by 17 percent on average (figure 4.9, sixth bar). However, the impact of PTAs with larger numbers of *essential* TBT provisions is not statistically significant (figure 4.10, second bar). The increase in exports from PTAs that include a larger number of overall TBT provisions is similar in the Latin America and Caribbean region to PTAs outside the region (annex 4E, table 4E.1). The weaker trade impacts of TBT provisions in PTAs could partly be explained by the relatively

Figure 4.9   Estimated impacts of SPS and TBT provisions, by type, on Latin American and Caribbean agricultural and food exports

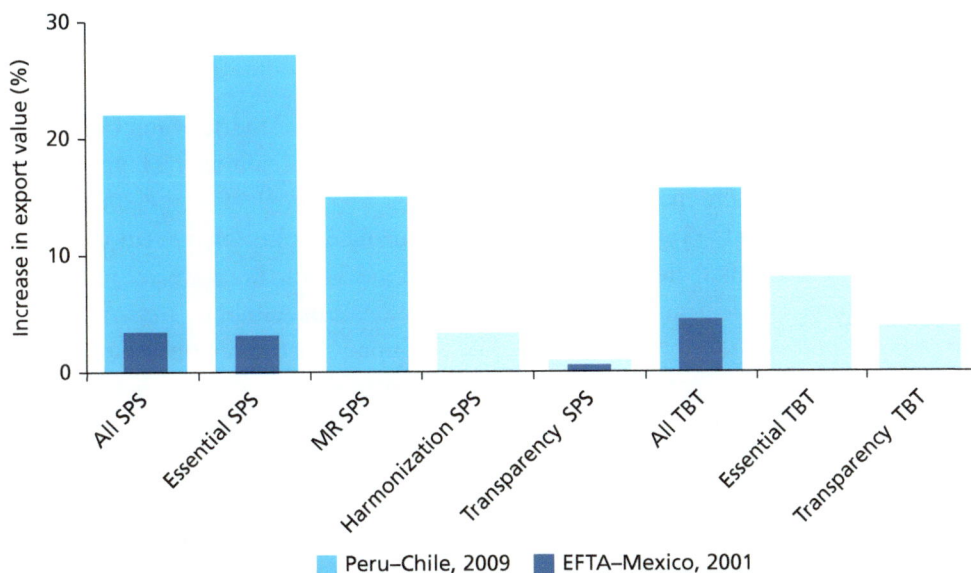

Peru–Chile, 2009   EFTA–Mexico, 2001

Source: World Bank calculations.

Note: The figure shows the calculated magnitude of added export value from increasing the number of specific sanitary and phytosanitary (SPS) and technical barrier to trade (TBT) provisions to the levels in two different preferential trade agreements (PTAs): the 2009 Peru–Chile PTA (considered a deep PTA in SPS and TBT provisions) and the 2001 European Free Trade Agreement (EFTA)–Mexico PTA (considered a shallow PTA in SPS and TBT). The bars indicate increases in export value—of agricultural and food exports (in the case of SPS provisions) and of overall exports (in the case of TBT provisions)—after accounting for the depth of other provisions and for any tariff liberalization brought about by the PTA. "Essential" provisions are those that require specific liberalization and integration commitments and obligations; relate to procedures, transparency, and enforcement; or relate to achievement of SPS and TBT integration. Light-shaded bars indicate insignificant effects in the case of the Peru–Chile PTA. The figure does not include the impacts of mutual recognition (MR) and harmonization provisions for TBT because none of the Latin American and Caribbean PTAs includes those provisions.

smaller prevalence of PTAs that include those provisions relative to those that include SPS provisions.[17]

Harmonization provisions for TBT play no role in fostering Latin American and Caribbean countries' exports. (Exports of the region's countries do not respond to the presence of PTAs that include harmonization provisions for TBT.) This finding is also obtained outside the region (annex 4E, table 4E.2). For the region, the lack of effects is because there is only one Latin American and Caribbean PTA with such provisions—the 2011 EFTA–Peru PTA—possibly combined with a weak export response by Peru.

There is no evidence that transparency provisions for SPS and TBT benefit bilateral exports. Although the inclusion of transparency provisions for SPS and for TBT does increase exports (figure 4.9, fifth and eighth bars), the increase is not statistically significant. This finding is consistent with the slow growth in notifications to the WTO about SPS and TBT measures by countries in the region (see figure 4.2). The weak role of transparency could be because of poor enforcement of such provisions in Latin American and Caribbean PTAs.

Impacts on countries' imports of intermediate inputs

Imports of intermediate inputs increase significantly for Latin American and Caribbean countries that sign PTAs with larger numbers of overall or essential TBT provisions. Signing a PTA with the maximum number of total TBT provisions (the 2009 Peru–Chile PTA) increases the value of imports of intermediate inputs for the region's countries by 70 percent, after the depth of the PTA and tariff reductions are accounted for (figure 4.10, first bar). Signing a PTA with the maximum number of *essential* TBT provisions increases the imports of intermediate inputs for the region's countries by more than 80 percent (figure 4.10, second bar). Imports of intermediate inputs respond substantially less for the countries signing PTAs with small numbers of provisions (figure 4.10, darker small rectangle in the first bar).

The increases in imports of intermediate inputs when PTAs include more TBT provisions are significantly larger for Latin American and Caribbean countries than for countries outside the region (annex 4D, table 4D.1). These findings on the impact on imports of intermediate inputs highlight the importance of SPS and TBT integration in a world of GVCs where intermediate inputs flow across borders and trade costs accumulate across the supply chain.

Figure 4.10   Estimated impacts of TBT provisions, by type, on Latin American and Caribbean imports of intermediate inputs

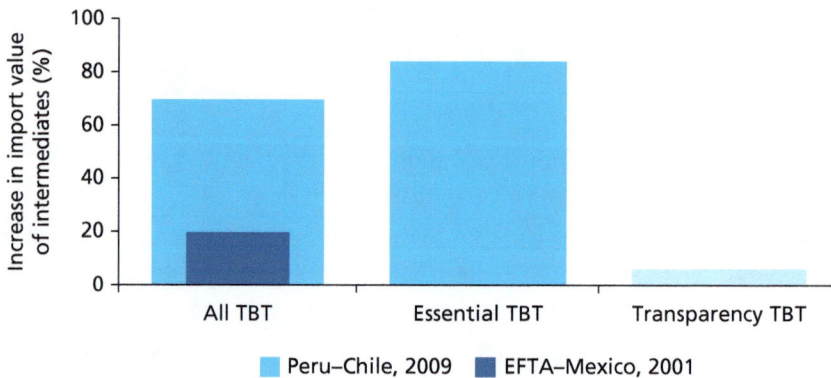

Peru–Chile, 2009   ■ EFTA–Mexico, 2001

Source: World Bank calculations.

Note: The figure shows the calculated magnitude of added value of imports of intermediate inputs from increasing the number of specific technical barrier to trade (TBT) provisions to the levels in two different preferential trade agreements (PTAs): the 2009 Peru–Chile PTA (considered a deep PTA in sanitary and phytosanitary [SPS] and TBT provisions) and the 2001 European Free Trade Agreement (EFTA)–Mexico PTA (considered a shallow PTA in SPS and TBT). The figure shows increases in import value after the depth of the PTA and tariff reductions are accounted for. "Essential" provisions are those that require specific liberalization and integration commitments and obligations; relate to procedures, transparency, and enforcement; or relate to achievement of SPS and TBT integration. The light-shaded bar indicates insignificant effects in the case of the Peru–Chile PTA.

Firm-level trade impacts

SPS and TBT integration in PTAs can have heterogeneous effects on trade across firms depending on firm size, but the aggregate impacts of SPS and TBT provisions in PTAs on bilateral exports can mask significant differences across firms.

SPS and TBT regulations require firms to make changes to their production processes or to other investments to comply with destination country regulations that differ from those of the home country. Increasing these fixed costs to trade can be prohibitive for small firms (Macedoni and Weinberger 2020). Business surveys from the multilateral International Trade Center consistently show that the costs of complying with NTMs are a barrier to trade for small firms (WTO 2012). Background work for this report focused on firms in Chile, Colombia, and Peru from 1996 to 2015, examining whether integrating regulatory trade barriers in PTAs alleviated burdens and benefited small firms (Fernandes, Lefebvre, and Rocha 2021).[18]

For small firms (in the lowest tercile of firm export value), agricultural and food exports increase substantially in Latin American and Caribbean countries that sign PTAs with larger numbers of overall or essential SPS provisions. A PTA with the maximum number of total SPS provisions (the 2009 Peru–Chile PTA) increases these firms' agricultural and food exports by close to 30 percent on average in Chile, Colombia, and Peru (figure 4.11, panel a). A substantially larger increase—50 percent—is estimated for small firms' agricultural and food exports if the PTA includes the maximum number of *essential* SPS provisions (figure 4.11, panel b). The benefits of SPS provisions in PTAs for exports of larger firms (those in the middle and highest terciles of firm export value) are not statistically significant (figures 4.11, panels a and b).

In contrast to evidence at the aggregate level, both mutual recognition and harmonization provisions for SPS foster significant increases in agricultural and food export value for small firms. Such exports for small firms in Chile, Colombia, and Peru increase by 40 percent on average if a PTA includes mutual recognition provisions for SPS, relative to PTAs without such provisions (figure 4.11, panel c). If the PTAs include harmonization provisions for SPS, they boost the export response even higher for small firms—with an average increase in export value of 50 percent (figure 4.11, panel d).

As for large firms, exports do not change significantly if their countries sign PTAs with mutual recognition provisions for SPS (annex 4E, table 4E.2), but they do increase by about 15 percent in response to the entry into force of a PTA with harmonization provisions for SPS (figure 4.11, panel d).

Small firms' exports also increase substantially in Latin American and Caribbean countries that sign PTAs with larger numbers of overall or essential TBT provisions. Signing a PTA with the maximum number of total TBT provisions (the Peru–Chile PTA of 2009) leads to a 40 percent average increase in exports for small firms in Chile, Colombia, and Peru (figure 4.12, panel a).[19] A substantially larger response—more than 60 percent—is estimated on smaller-firms' exports if the PTA includes the maximum number of *essential* TBT provisions (figure 4.12, panel b). These strong micro-level

Figure 4.11   Estimated impacts of SPS provisions on agricultural and food export value of firms in Chile, Colombia, and Peru, by provision type and firm size

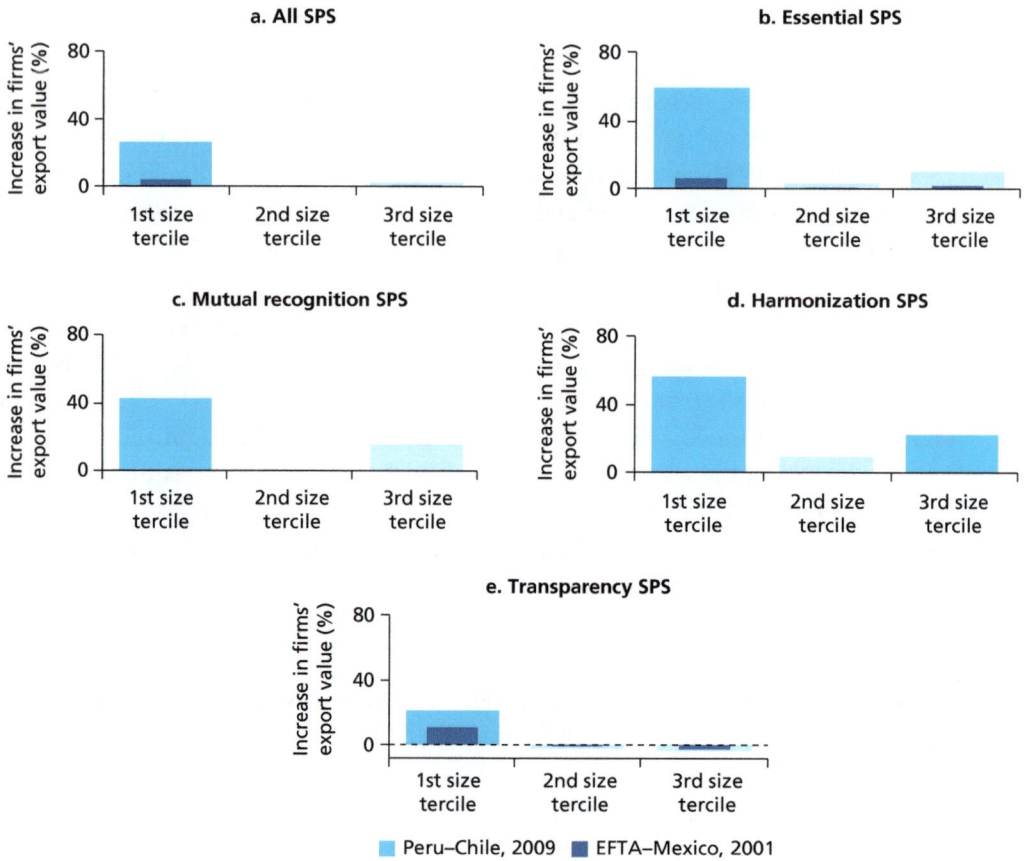

Source: World Bank calculations.

Note: The figure shows the calculated magnitude of added firm-level agricultural and food export value from increasing the number of specific sanitary and phytosanitary (SPS) provisions to the levels in two different preferential trade agreements (PTAs): the 2009 Peru–Chile PTA (considered a deep PTA in the area of SPS) and the 2001 European Free Trade Agreement (EFTA)–Mexico PTA (considered a shallow PTA in SPS). The bars indicate increases in firm-level export value after accounting for the depth of other provisions and for any tariff liberalization brought about by the PTA. Firm size is by tercile of firm export value, from first (lowest) to third (highest). "Essential" provisions are those that require specific liberalization and integration commitments and obligations; relate to procedures, transparency, and enforcement; or relate to achievement of SPS and TBT integration. The light-shaded bars indicate insignificant effects in the case of the Peru–Chile PTA.

findings for small firms are surprising, given the small number of PTAs that include many TBT provisions compared with those including many SPS provisions (see figure 4.5).

Although transparency provisions for SPS and TBT play no role in increasing exports at the aggregate level, they do foster exports for small firms in Chile, Colombia, and Peru. Signing a PTA with the maximum number of transparency provisions for SPS (the 2009 Peru–Chile PTA) increases exports of small firms in Chile, Colombia, and Peru by close to 20 percent on average (figure 4.11, panel e). A PTA with the

Figure 4.12   Estimated impacts of TBT provisions on export value of firms in Chile, Colombia, and Peru, by provision type and firm size

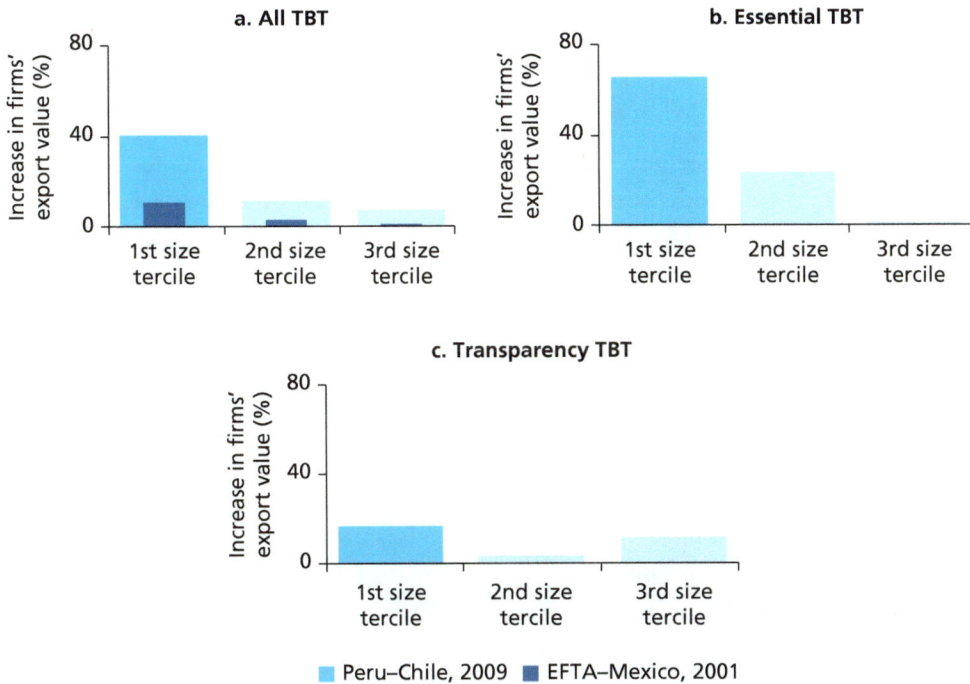

a. All TBT

b. Essential TBT

c. Transparency TBT

■ Peru–Chile, 2009   ■ EFTA–Mexico, 2001

Source: World Bank calculations.

Note: The figure shows the calculated magnitude of added firm-level export value from increasing the number of technical barrier to trade (TBT) provisions to the levels in two different preferential trade agreements (PTAs): the 2009 Peru–Chile PTA (considered a deep PTA in the area of TBT) and the 2001 European Free Trade Agreement (EFTA)–Mexico PTA (considered a shallow PTA in TBT). The bars indicate increases in firm-level export value after accounting for the depth of other provisions and for any tariff liberalization brought about by the PTA. Firm size is by tercile of firm export value, from first (lowest) to third (highest). "Essential" provisions are those that require specific liberalization and integration commitments and obligations; relate to procedures, transparency, and enforcement; or relate to achievement of SPS and TBT integration. The light-shaded bars indicate insignificant effects in the case of the Peru–Chile PTA.

maximum number of transparency provisions for TBT elicits a smaller but still significant increase in exports—about 10 percent—for small firms (figure 4.12, panel c). Transparency provisions for SPS and TBT do not significantly affect large firms' exports (annex 4E, table 4E.2).

IMPLEMENTING DEEP REGULATORY COOPERATION IN SELECTED LATIN AMERICAN AND CARIBBEAN PTAs

This section focuses on the steps and challenges in implementing regulatory cooperation on SPS and TBT provisions in three PTAs signed by Latin American and Caribbean countries: the US–Panama agreement on recognition of equivalence systems for meats and dairy products; the Pacific Alliance's sectoral TBT annexes; and Central America's commitments to regulatory harmonization under its Association Agreement with the EU. These three examples showcase different approaches to integrating SPS and TBT provisions into PTAs in the region, identifying not only the drivers of success but also the challenges of international regulatory cooperation in the context of deep PTAs.[20]

The US–Panama PTA as a catalyst for equivalence agreements

Panama's stringent inspection, sanitary, and registration requirements for imports of meat and dairy were addressed in the negotiations of the US–Panama PTA (which entered into force in 2012) when Panama recognized the equivalence of US regulatory systems and conformity assessment procedures. The requirements were raised as a concern by the United States and other countries at the WTO's SPS Committee in 2005 (WTO 2005).[21] In the context of the negotiation of a free trade agreement in 2006, the United States requested that Panama recognize its meat inspection system and that Panama address other regulatory barriers imposed on meat and dairy product imports (Hornbeck 2012). Panama agreed to recognize US regulatory systems as equivalent and accepted the results of US conformity assessment procedures.

In 2006, both countries entered into the far-reaching United States–Panama Agreement regarding Certain Sanitary and Phytosanitary Measures and Technical Standards Affecting Trade in Agricultural Products. Panama recognized the equivalence of the US food safety inspection system for meat and poultry and the US regulatory system for processed foods, including dairy products. In addition, Panama brought its sanitary requirements on imports of meat products into conformity with international standards, thus reopening its market to US exports of those products. Panama also committed to streamlining import documentation requirements, including its product registration system for agricultural products and processed foods, and it formalized its recognition of the US beef grading system and cuts nomenclature (USTR 2011).

To implement the US–Panama regulatory agreement, Panama established a new institution and adopted domestic resolutions that had spillovers—recognizing meat and dairy as equivalent—for other countries' sanitary systems. In 2006, to implement the US–Panama regulatory agreement, Panama created a new Panamanian Food Safety Authority (AUPSA) and adopted seven domestic resolutions to implement the agreement. AUPSA was responsible for SPS and certain other measures related to imports and food products. Panama also later recognized as equivalent the sanitary systems for meat and dairy products of other countries (Argentina, Australia, Canada, Chile, the Netherlands, and Spain), significantly simplifying sanitary measures for imports.[22]

The Pacific Alliance as an instrument to promote regulatory improvement and cooperation

The PA countries—Chile, Colombia, Mexico, and Peru—agreed to establish and implement international good regulatory practices. To advance their regulatory performance, they agreed to use international good regulatory practices, including the establishment and systemic application of tools such as review, simplification of procedures, use of transparency and public consultation, and before-and-after measurement of the impact of regulations (Polanco and Sauvé 2018).

Each PA country committed to determining which measures were to be covered by the agreement's regulatory chapter (chapter 15BIS) before three years had elapsed after the PA entry into force. They also committed to achieving broad coverage. However, since the chapter's entering into force on April 1, 2020, covered measures have yet to be identified. To provide for effective implementation, chapter 15BIS establishes a committee on regulatory improvement, provides for cooperation among the parties, and commits them to the issuance of regular implementation reports. The regulatory chapter is not subject to the PA dispute settlement mechanism.

The PA countries established a framework to facilitate, increase, and promote regulatory cooperation. The PA includes a chapter on TBT measures (chapter 7) whose content goes beyond the WTO's TBT Agreement by including a commitment by members to identify, develop, and promote trade-facilitating initiatives, including mutual understanding of their respective systems and promoting equivalence and harmonization with international standards. Mechanisms to help increase regulatory coherence and eliminate unnecessary technical obstacles to trade within the PA are also identified. Additional transparency provisions are included. For example, a provision requires a party blocking an import from another party (because of noncompliance with a technical regulation) to notify the importer or customs agent as soon as possible and give the reason for the action. The parties in the PA also agree to exchange information on the use of standards in connection with technical regulations. The provisions and mechanisms in chapter 7 are subject to the PA dispute settlement mechanism.

The PA countries also agreed to engage in regulatory cooperation at the sectoral level. The committee on TBT, established by chapter 7, is supposed to foster sectoral cooperation among the parties on standards, technical regulations, and conformity assessment procedures as well as to facilitate mutual recognition agreements and equivalence of technical regulations. Even before the TBT provisions were agreed on, the PA countries established a "regulatory cooperation pathway" for identifying sectors of interest for cooperation. The pathway is based on a public consultation process, with priorities identified by the private sector.[23] Biannual work plans will include agreed-on sectors, and a free trade commission has the authority to approve the sectoral annexes negotiated under the TBT chapter.

PA members made substantial progress on regulatory cooperation in the cosmetic sector but less so in other sectors. The PA countries agreed to eliminate technical barriers to the trade of pharmaceutical and cosmetic products. In June 2013, the member countries' sanitary authorities signed the Inter-Institutional Cooperation Agreement on Pharmaceutical Products, which facilitates the sanitary registration processes and the certification of good manufacturing practices. For cosmetics, a specific annex was adopted by PA members that included commitments to streamlining procedures, adopting international good regulatory practices, and harmonizing technical regulations based on international standards (box 4.3).

Box 4.3   Eliminating technical obstacles to trade for cosmetic products in the Pacific Alliance

The Pacific Alliance (PA) parties (Chile, Colombia, Mexico, and Peru) committed to the following:[a]

- Take the necessary steps to harmonize the definition of cosmetic products based on the European Union (EU) definition
- Establish a market surveillance system based on international good regulatory practices and eliminate the need for prior sanitary authorization or replace it with an automatic notification
- Eliminate the free sale certificate
- Use the EU and US lists of prohibited and recognized ingredients as a reference and adopt expedited mechanisms to include, prohibit, or restrict ingredients in the PA lists
- Harmonize labeling requirements for cosmetic products, basing them on international standards and having only one format so as to protect consumers
- Harmonize the requirements and application of good manufacturing practices, based on international standards.

a. The listed provisions are from the Pacific Alliance Free Trade Agreement's chapter on Technical Barriers to Trade, annex 7.11.

Source: González 2020.

Regulatory cooperation in other sectors—medical devices, food supplements, household cleaning products, and pharmaceutical and organic products—is under negotiation or in implementation, but progress has been slow (Dorantes 2020; Fatat Romero 2020). In 2018, the PA Business Council urged governments to prioritize and move forward quickly on regulatory cooperation.

The EU–Central America PTA as a tool to foster the development and adoption of regional technical regulations

The inclusion of technical standards in the EU–Central American Association Agreement (EU–Central America PTA) was crucial for the integration of goods trade across the two regions. Regional economic integration in technical standards was essential for goods to circulate freely within the EU and the Central American countries of Costa Rica, El Salvador, Guatemala, Honduras, Nicaragua, and Panama. In the context of this agreement (article 303), member countries agreed to adopt provisions to allow for the free circulation of goods.

The EU could comply by applying the mutual recognition principle governing trade to the areas of standards, technical regulations, and conformity assessments. But Central America does not apply the mutual recognition principle to intraregional trade. Instead, it harmonizes technical requirements and conformity assessment procedures, and countries can recognize the requirements or procedures of another Central American country as equivalent to their own.

The Central American countries committed to developing regional technical regulations and harmonizing a set of technical regulations. In the context of the EU–Central

America PTA, they agreed to adopt, within five years of the entry into force of the agreement in 2012, regional technical regulations and conformity assessment procedures prepared in accordance with international standards for the list of products in annex XX to the agreement.[24] For products not yet harmonized and not included in annex XX, the Association Committee—the agreement's top governance body—will establish a future work program. Although the Central American countries committed to submitting regular progress reports on implementation, these commitments are not subject to the agreement's dispute settlement mechanism.

Harmonizing technical regulations among Central American countries in the context of the PTA with the EU has been achieved in several sectors. Most of the technical regulations that Central American countries committed to in the context of the agreement have been harmonized. These are in the areas of foods and beverages, drugs and related products, textiles and footwear, and agricultural inputs. The technical regulations predominantly relate to the adoption of harmonized good manufacturing practices and labeling and registration requirements. Because these regulations and procedures are mostly based on international standards, they should eventually facilitate Central American trade with countries outside the agreement (Molina and Khoroshavina 2015). In the context of the Central American integration process, the region has identified 22 additional technical regulations for harmonization.

Success factors and challenges in implementing SPS and TBT regulatory cooperation in PTAs

The three cases show how countries have explored ways to build and advance regulatory cooperation on SPS and TBT chapters in PTAs, particularly at the sectoral level. The cases provide examples of deeper regulatory cooperation, but they use different mechanisms to foster convergence, including equivalence, harmonization, and mutual recognition. Albeit in different ways, the regulatory cooperation provisions have moved member countries closer to international standards, which can then facilitate market access and reduce trade costs by addressing TBT and SPS frictions. Table 4.2 compares the main features of each of these mechanisms.

The US–Panama PTA is an example of success in implementing agreed-upon commitments on recognizing the equivalence of SPS. It implemented commitments on sanitary and technical standards for trade in agricultural products, and Panama adopted domestic legal and administrative provisions even before the free trade agreement's negotiations were concluded.[25] Effective implementation was facilitated by

- The focus on Panama's unilateral actions on recognizing equivalence, accepting the results of conformity assessment procedures, and streamlining processes so that no long or complex negotiations on new or harmonized regulations were needed; and
- The inclusion of detailed provisions and expedited mechanisms for notification and consultation.

Table 4.2   The main SPS measures and TBT regulatory cooperation features under selected Latin American and Caribbean trade agreements

Feature	US–Panama Agreement	Pacific Alliance	EU–Central American Association Agreement
Parties' level of development	Advanced and developing	Developing	Advanced and developing
Scope of regulatory cooperation	Meat (included but not limited to beef and pork), poultry, and products thereof, and all processed products, including but not limited to dairy products	Cosmetics, medical devices, food supplements, pharmaceutical products, organic products and household cleaning products; others to be defined	Foods and beverages, drugs and related products, textiles and footwear, and agricultural inputs; others to be defined
Regulatory cooperation mechanisms	• Recognition of equivalence by Panama of US technical regulations and SPS measures • Acceptance by Panama of results of US conformity assessment procedures • Streamlining of procedures by Panama	• Regulatory improvement • Harmonization of technical regulations based on international standards • Adoption of international good regulatory practices • Streamlining of procedures	• Harmonization among Central American countries of technical regulations to international standards • Acceptance by Central American countries of the results of conformity assessment procedures from other Central American countries
Monitoring and follow-up mechanisms	• Panama's commitment to speedy notification to the United States in case of shipment detentions • Panama's commitment to notify new SPS measures applicable to US products before implementation	• TBT committee to facilitate cooperation among regulatory authorities • High-level officials to monitor progress	• Central America to provide detailed yearly progress reports and working programs until implementation is completed • TBT subcommittee to review progress in detail
Enforceability	Separate agreement not subject to the FTA dispute settlement mechanism	• Exclusion of chapter on regulatory improvement from the dispute settlement mechanism • Inclusion of sectoral regulatory cooperation agreements as annexes to the TBT chapter, which is subject to the dispute settlement mechanism	Exclusion from the dispute settlement mechanism

Source: González 2020.

Note: EU = European Union; FTA = free trade agreement; SPS = sanitary and phytosanitary; TBT = technical barrier to trade.

The US–Panama agreement supported a top-down system change in Panama toward greater alignment with international standards, acceptance of conformity assessments, streamlining of procedures in meat and dairy products, and improved transparency on SPS and TBT measures on agricultural products. This was done to prevent SPS and TBT provisions from hindering market access for the covered products. However, the approach taken by the US–Panama agreement was limited in scope, and there is no formal mechanism in place to effectively promote similar processes for other types of products.

The EU–Central America PTA is an example of an agreement that fosters regional harmonization of standards and regulations. In a different but also successful way, it energized the bottom-up harmonization drive in Central America, providing guidance and support to existing convergence initiatives and helping to facilitate the free circulation of goods in the region for all partners, including from countries in the region. As regulatory rulemakers, the United States and the EU brought their respective preferred approaches to regulatory cooperation to the negotiations. Panama and Central America both gained from the process. In the case of the EU–Central America PTA, although a provision was made for Central America to harmonize additional areas in the future, it is not clear that future results will have the same outcomes, because there is an absence of the political dynamism needed for PTA negotiation and implementation.

The Pacific Alliance is an example of regulatory convergence among members with similar levels of development. The PA is a different story in that it is a bottom-up regulatory convergence process among members with no prior significant regulatory cooperation experience. Political commitment was thus critical in supporting early engagement by regulators and in ensuring results. In the face of political deceleration, the lack of a structured framework to support regulatory cooperation has hindered progress toward the originally planned sectoral regulatory convergence. Continued engagement from the private sector could help reenergize the process—if governments refocus their efforts.

Countries can leverage PTAs to foster regulatory improvement and regulatory convergence, but such processes can be challenging to implement. In the PA, parties engaged in a longer-term process of fostering regulatory improvement and regulatory convergence, but implementation has proven to be challenging. In accordance with the regulatory improvement chapter, the PA members have until 2023 to identify the scope of application. Regarding regulatory cooperation at the sectoral level, since 2012, priority products for collaboration were identified—with input from the private sector. But a specific annex was adopted only for the cosmetics sector. In the annex on harmonization, the commitments are phrased in broad and imprecise terms (for example, the steps necessary to harmonize). On process streamlining, the commitments are precise (see box 4.3), but they have no time frame for adoption. Despite private sector interest, lack of experience on regulatory cooperation among PA countries has hindered collaboration. So has diminished political attention.

By building on previous regulatory cooperation among Central American countries, and because of political support and regular monitoring from the EU, the implementation of the regulatory commitments in the EU–Central America PTA is on track. Of the 22 technical regulations that Central American countries agreed to harmonize, 20 have been implemented. These are detailed regulations agreed upon by the respective regulatory authorities of the Central American countries. Once agreed upon, domestic regulations are replaced by regional regulations, and countries merely need to publish them in their official gazettes. No further steps are required to put them into practice.

Because of opposition from vested interests and bureaucratic resistance, adopting some of the regulations has been challenging. But several factors have contributed to the high rate of implementation: Central American countries have established a framework for putting negotiation of technical regulations on the political agenda. In addition, twice a year, the rotating Central American presidency of the trade ministers' council identifies the biannual work plan, reviews priorities, negotiates calendars, and so on. And vice-ministers work with technical authorities to monitor progress. Regular reports are submitted, and the private sector follows the process closely. Finally, detailed monitoring by the TBT subcommittee of the Association Agreement—including regular monitoring reports and plans on next steps presented by the Central American Association to the EU—have significantly energized the process.

The US–Panama agreement, the PA, and the EU–Central America agreement confirm that advancing international regulatory cooperation via PTAs is difficult but feasible. Some of the challenges arise because trade negotiations differ from regulatory cooperation discussions (Goldberg 2019; Hoekman 2018). If the regulatory process extends beyond the trade negotiation time frame—as is often the case when searching for broader regulatory convergence—collaboration among regulators can lose steam. In addition,

- Weak domestic regulatory institutional and administrative capacity, or a lack of common interests and incentives to cooperate among regulators, will make it harder to deliver;
- Broad and complex agendas, with overambitious regulatory objectives, could overwhelm collaboration efforts. Vested interests could capture the regulation process;
- Mistrust from the public on the objectives of regulatory cooperation could affect the possibility of achieving results; and
- Finally, because most international cooperation mechanisms are nonbinding in nature, even when they are part of PTAs, a lack of effective monitoring and follow-up mechanisms can result in partial or defective implementation.

Even when successful in the context of a specific agreement, PTA-driven regulatory cooperation entails risks, including risks on how to define the optimal level of regulation for the parties and whether results in different contexts could lead to regulatory conflict. But although there is no single approach to delivering results, several factors can help effectively advance international regulatory cooperation in deep PTAs (box 4.4).

> **Box 4.4   Factors that can help effectively advance regulatory cooperation in PTAs**
>
> - Define clear mandates at the political level to empower and guide regulators
> - Aim at concrete and binding outcomes at the measure, product, or sectoral level
> - Align levels of ambition with starting conditions in the parties (for example, institutional and administrative capacities, previous experience in cooperation, and so on)
> - Focus cooperation on moving toward international standards to support global trade integration and maximize welfare
> - Embed continuous regulatory cooperation in effective institutional setups, with oversight from high-level trade officials and with appropriate resources
> - Establish regular work programs to provide structure and a time frame to the discussions
> - Put in place consultative mechanisms with the private sector and other stakeholders to prioritize sectoral cooperation, collect inputs, and guard against regulatory capture
> - Formalize cooperation among regulators and provide opportunities for deliberation, learning, and building trust
> - Institute monitoring and follow-up mechanisms in preferential trade agreements (PTAs), with transparency and accountability built in
> - Define a methodology to determine the economic impact of regulatory cooperation at the measure, product, or sectoral level to inform and support collaboration efforts
>
> *Source:* González 2020.

CONCLUSION

Latin American and Caribbean countries impose fewer SPS and TBT provisions on imports than other regions, but they face significant SPS and TBT provisions in destination markets. Regulatory convergence is an important tool to reduce trade costs and support trade and GVC integration. The inclusion of SPS and TBT provisions in PTAs, which has grown tremendously in Latin American and Caribbean PTAs, is a step toward that convergence.

SPS and TBT integration is important in a world of GVCs where intermediate inputs flow across borders and trade costs accumulate across the supply chain. The inclusion of certain SPS and TBT provisions in Latin American and Caribbean PTAs boosts bilateral exports and boosts bilateral imports of intermediate inputs by the region's countries. Firm-level evidence for Chile, Colombia, and Peru shows a boost to exports from such inclusion that is larger for small firms, and this is consistent with the hypothesis that the provisions help reduce the fixed-entry costs of exporting.

The implementation of SPS and TBT integration in PTAs is an issue of concern. Some PTAs have been more successful than others in implementation (for example, PTAs outside Latin America and the Caribbean), and more-similar groups of countries have found innovative approaches for regulatory cooperation (for example, the Pacific Alliance). Factors that can help drive regulatory cooperation include the following:

- Clear political mandates;
- Emphasis on concrete and binding outcomes;

- Ambitions aligned with the parties' initial conditions;
- Cooperation focused on moving toward international standards;
- Effective institutional setups;
- Structured discussions based on work programs;
- Consultative mechanisms with the private sector;
- Formalized cooperation and experience sharing among regulators;
- Follow-up mechanisms in PTAs; and
- Defined methodologies to determine the economic impact of regulatory cooperation.

ANNEX 4A A CLASSIFICATION OF NONTARIFF MEASURES

The chapter uses the United Nations Commission on Trade and Development (UNCTAD)–World Bank database to construct frequency indexes and import coverage ratios of NTMs. The database contains information on NTMs by country and HS 6-digit product and year, following the international classification of NTMs listed in table 4A.1 (UN 2019).

Table 4A.1   Classification of nontariff measures, by chapter

Type	Chapter	Title
Imports: Technical measures	A	Sanitary and phytosanitary measures
	B	Technical barriers to trade
	C	Preshipment inspection and other formalities
Imports: Nontechnical measures	D	Contingent trade-protective measures
	E	Nonautomatic import licensing, quotas, prohibitions, quantity-control measures, and other restrictions not including sanitary and phytosanitary measures or measures relating to technical barriers to trade
	F	Price-control measures, including additional taxes and charges
	G	Finance measures
	H	Measures affecting competition
	I	Trade-related investment measures
	J	Distribution restrictions
	K	Restrictions on postsales services
	L	Subsidies and other forms of support
	M	Government procurement restrictions
	N	Intellectual property
	O	Rules of origin
Exports	P	Export-related measures

Source: UN 2019.

The data used in this chapter cover the countries listed in table 4A.2. The authors rely on the latest year of data for each country, ranging from 2012 to 2018.

Table 4A.2   Economies with available NTM data

Code	Economy name	Code	Economy name	Code	Economy name
AFG	Afghanistan	FRA	France	NZL	New Zealand
DZA	Algeria	GMB	Gambia, The	NIC	Nicaragua
ATG	Antigua and Barbuda	DEU	Germany	NER	Niger
ARG	Argentina	GHA	Ghana	NGA	Nigeria
AUS	Australia	GRC	Greece	OMN	Oman
AUT	Austria	GRD	Grenada	PAK	Pakistan
BHS	Bahamas, The	GTM	Guatemala	PAN	Panama
BHR	Bahrain	GIN	Guinea	PNG	Papua New Guinea
BGD	Bangladesh	GUY	Guyana	PRY	Paraguay
BRB	Barbados	HND	Honduras	PER	Peru
BLR	Belarus	HKG	Hong Kong SAR, China	PHL	Philippines
BEL	Belgium	HUN	Hungary	POL	Poland
BEN	Benin	IND	India	PRT	Portugal
BOL	Bolivia	IDN	Indonesia	QAT	Qatar
BWA	Botswana	IRL	Ireland	ROM	Romania
BRA	Brazil	ISR	Israel	RUS	Russian Federation
BRN	Brunei Darussalam	ITA	Italy	SAU	Saudi Arabia
BGR	Bulgaria	JAM	Jamaica	SEN	Senegal
BFA	Burkina Faso	JPN	Japan	SGP	Singapore
KHM	Cambodia	JOR	Jordan	SVK	Slovak Republic
CMR	Cameroon	KAZ	Kazakhstan	SVN	Slovenia
CAN	Canada	KOR	Korea, Rep.	ESP	Spain
CPV	Cabo Verde	KWT	Kuwait	LKA	Sri Lanka
CHL	Chile	KGZ	Kyrgyz Republic	SUR	Suriname
CHN	China	LAO	Lao PDR	SWE	Sweden
COL	Colombia	LVA	Latvia	CHE	Switzerland
CRI	Costa Rica	LBN	Lebanon	TJK	Tajikistan
CIV	Côte D'Ivoire	LBR	Liberia	THA	Thailand
HRV	Croatia	LTU	Lithuania	TGO	Togo
CUB	Cuba	LUX	Luxembourg	TTO	Trinidad and Tobago

Continued

Table 4A.2 Economies with available NTM data *(continued)*

Code	Economy name	Code	Economy name	Code	Economy name
CYP	Cyprus	MYS	Malaysia	TUN	Tunisia
CZE	Czech Republic	MLT	Malta	TUR	Turkey
DNK	Denmark		EU	ARE	United Arab Emirates
DMA	Dominica	MRT	Mauritania	GBR	United Kingdom
ECU	Ecuador	MUS	Mauritius	USA	United States
SLV	El Salvador	MEX	Mexico	URY	Uruguay
EST	Estonia	MAR	Morocco	VEN	Venezuela, RB
ETH	Ethiopia	MMR	Myanmar	VNM	Vietnam
FIN	Finland	NPL	Nepal	PSE	West Bank and Gaza
		NLD	Netherlands	ZWE	Zimbabwe

Source: United Nations Conference on Trade and Development (UNCTAD) Non-Tariff Measures (NTM) Database, https://unctad.org/topic/trade-analysis/non-tariff-measures/NTMs-data.

Note: Codes are ISO alpha-3 country codes. SAR = Special Administrative Region.

The NTM chapters from UN (2019) are further described as follows:

- *Chapter A* deals with sanitary and phytosanitary (SPS) measures. The chapter outlines measures, such as those restricting substances, ensuring food safety, and preventing the dissemination of diseases or pests. Chapter A also includes all conformity assessment measures related to food safety, such as certification, testing and inspection, and quarantine.

- *Chapter B* provides a collection of technical measures, also called technical barriers to trade (TBT). The chapter describes measures relating to product characteristics such as technical specifications and quality requirements; related processes and production methods; and measures such as labeling and packaging in relation to environmental protection, consumer safety, and national security. As in the case of SPS measures, chapter B includes all conformity-assessment measures related to technical requirements, such as certification, testing, and inspection.

- *Chapter C*, the last chapter in the technical measures section, classifies the measures related to preshipment inspections and other customs formalities.

- *Chapter D* groups contingent measures—that is, those measures implemented to counteract the adverse effects of imports in the market of the importing country, including measures aimed at tackling unfair foreign trade practices. These include antidumping, countervailing, and safeguard measures.

- *Chapters E and F* feature the "hard" measures that are traditionally used in trade policy. Chapter E includes licensing, quotas, and other quantity-control measures, including tariff rate quotas. Chapter F lists the price control measures that are implemented to control or affect the prices of imported goods. Among the examples are measures designed to support the domestic prices of certain products when the import prices of the goods are lower, to establish the domestic prices of certain products because of price fluctuation in domestic markets or price instability in a foreign market, and to increase or preserve tax revenue. This category also includes measures other than tariffs that increase the cost of imports in a similar manner (para-tariff measures).

- *Chapter G* outlines finance measures restricting the payments for imports—for example, when the access and cost of foreign exchange is regulated. It also includes measures imposing restrictions on terms of payment.
- *Chapter H* includes those measures affecting competition—those that grant exclusive or special preferences or privileges to one or more limited group of economic operators. They are mainly monopolistic measures, such as state trading, sole importing agencies, or compulsory national insurance or transportation.
- *Chapter I* deals with trade-related investment measures and groups the measures that restrict investment by requiring local content or requesting that investment be related to export in order to balance imports.
- *Chapters J and K* relate to the way products—or services connected to the products—are marketed after being imported. They are considered nontariff measures (NTMs) because they could affect the decision to import such products or services. Chapter J, on distribution restrictions, describes restrictive measures related to the internal distribution of imported products. Chapter K deals with restrictions on postsales services—for example, restrictions on the provision of accessory services.
- *Chapter L* contains measures that relate to the subsidies that affect trade.
- *Chapter M*, on government procurement restrictions, describes the restrictions that bidders may find when trying to sell their products to a foreign government.
- *Chapter N* contains restrictions related to intellectual property measures and rights.
- *Chapter O*, on rules of origin, groups the measures that restrict the origin of products or their inputs.
- *Chapter P*, the last chapter, is on export measures. The chapter groups the measures applied by a country to its exports, inter alia, export taxes, export quotas, and export prohibitions.

Frequency index and coverage ratio of NTMs

For each country *i* in a given year (time subscript is ignored below), the frequency index of NTMs is defined as

$$F_i = \frac{\sum_s D_s M_s}{\sum_s M_s} * 100,$$ (4A.1)

where s designates a Harmonized System (HS) 6-digit product, D_s is a dummy variable indicating the presence of an NTM (in any of the chapters A through O in table 4A.1), and M_s is a dummy variable equal to 1 if there are imports of product s. The denominator is, therefore, the total number of HS 6-digit products imported.

The frequency index for SPS measures is defined analogously but restricting D_s to cover only NTMs in chapter A. The frequency index for technical barriers to trade is defined analogously but restricting D_s to cover only NTMs in chapter B.

For each country i in a given year (time subscript is ignored below), the import coverage ratio of NTMs is defined as

$$C_i = \frac{\sum_s D_s V_s}{\sum_s V_s}, \tag{4A.2}$$

where V_s is the imported value for HS 6-digit product s and all else is defined as above.

Restrictiveness of trade policies

Figure 4A.1   Restrictiveness of tariffs and nontariff barriers, by region

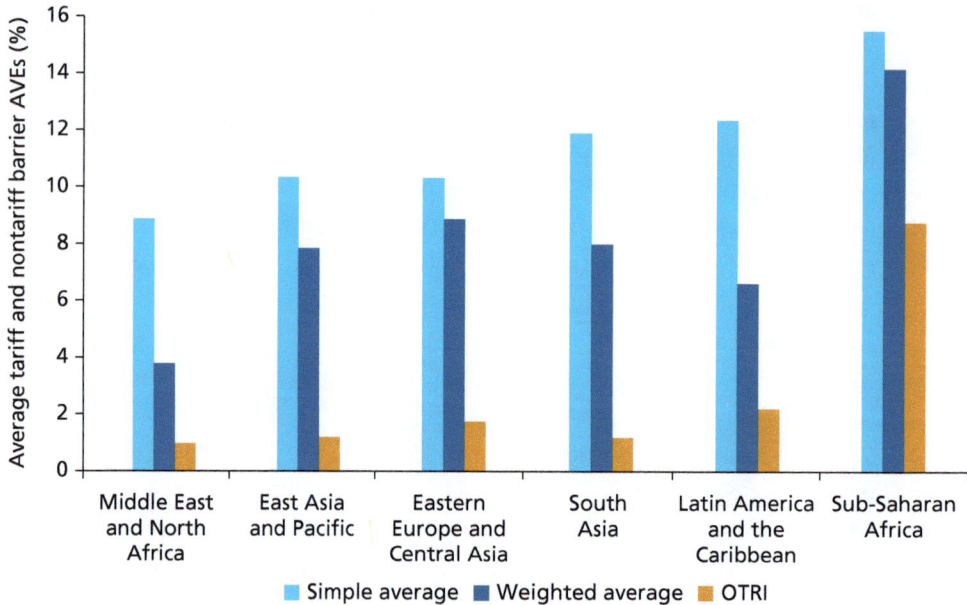

Source: World Bank 2019, 31.

Note: The figure shows simple average and weighted average of tariffs and ad valorem equivalents (AVEs) of nontariff measures (NTMs) as well as overall trade restrictiveness indexes (OTRI), expressed as percentages, that take into account the responsiveness of import demand, taken from Kee (2019). The NTM data for each country (entering the regional average) are the most recent available data from the years 2013–18.

ANNEX 4B SPS AND TBT NOTIFICATIONS TO THE WORLD TRADE ORGANIZATION

Map 4B.1   SPS and TBT notifications to the WTO, by country, 1995–2000 and 1995–2020

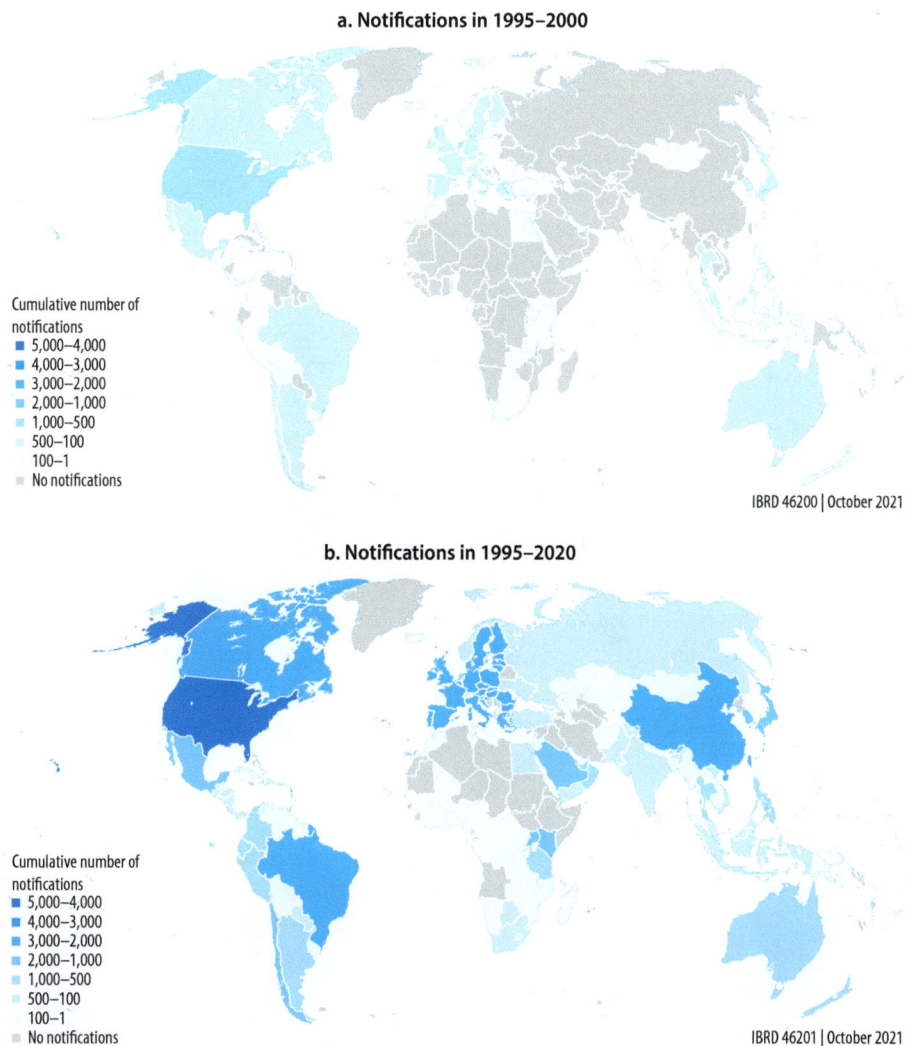

a. Notifications in 1995–2000

Cumulative number of notifications
- 5,000–4,000
- 4,000–3,000
- 3,000–2,000
- 2,000–1,000
- 1,000–500
- 500–100
- 100–1
- No notifications

IBRD 46200 | October 2021

b. Notifications in 1995–2020

Cumulative number of notifications
- 5,000–4,000
- 4,000–3,000
- 3,000–2,000
- 2,000–1,000
- 1,000–500
- 500–100
- 100–1
- No notifications

IBRD 46201 | October 2021

Source: World Trade Organization (WTO) official notifications of sanitary and phytosanitary (SPS) and technical barrier to trade (TBT) measures. © World Bank. Further permission required for reuse.

ANNEX 4C SPS AND TBT PROVISIONS IN PTAs

The measures of sanitary and phytosanitary (SPS) and technical barriers to trade (TBT) provisions in the World Bank's Deep Trade Agreements database (Mattoo, Rocha, and Ruta 2020) are based on the SPS chapters covered in 269 preferential trade agreements (PTAs) and TBT chapters covered in 263 PTAs signed between 1960 and 2017. The other policy areas covered in PTAs are subsidies, investment, export taxes, antidumping, labor markets, rules of origin, competition policy, trade facilitation, environmental laws, migration (visa and asylum), movement of capital, countervailing (CV) duties, intellectual property rights (IPR), public procurement, services, and state-owned enterprises.

Espitia et al. (2020) and Stone and Casilini (2020) provide details on mapping the content of TBT and SPS provisions in PTAs. Complete lists of SPS and TBT provisions in PTAs, as well as essential provisions, are provided in Fernandes, Lefebvre, and Rocha (2021).

Normalization of numbers of SPS and TBT provisions

To ease interpretation of estimated coefficients from gravity regressions, the main variables of interest were normalized by capturing numbers of SPS and TBT provisions (as well as number of other provisions to capture depth) between 0 and 1 based on the formula below. The formula is given for the example of essential SPS provisions:

$$SPS_{Normalized}^{Essential} = \frac{\left(SPS^{Essential} - MIN\left(SPS^{Essential}\right)\right)}{MAX\left(SPS^{Essential}\right) - MIN\left(SPS^{Essential}\right)}.$$

The maximum and minimum of essential provisions used in the formula above are computed based on the information in the Deep Trade Agreements database for all countries. For SPS and TBT provisions, the minimum across all countries is 0. This normalization captures the impact of increasing the number of SPS provisions (relative to the minimum of 0) as a fraction of the maximum number of SPS provisions. In a gravity equation Poisson pseudo maximum likelihood (PPML) estimation, a coefficient of 0.5 on the normalized numbers of essential SPS provisions indicates that an increase from 0 to the maximum number of essential SPS provisions (of 24) would increase trade values by 65 percent on average ($\exp(0.5) - 1 = 0.65$), with all else equal. In contrast to an alternative that would take the logarithm of the number of SPS provisions in each PTA, the normalization allows for an accounting of bilateral pairs of countries enforcing no SPS provisions.

ANNEX 4D AGGREGATE IMPACTS ON BILATERAL TRADE OF SPS AND TBT PROVISIONS IN PTAs

Table 4D.1   Impact of SPS or TBT provisions on bilateral exports from Latin America and the Caribbean versus the rest of the world

Provisions	Exports of agricultural products		Exports of all products	
	All SPS	**Essential SPS**	**All TBT**	**Essential TBT**
$\ln(1 + \tau)$	−0.505***	−0.521***	−0.751***	−0.771***
	(0.101)	(0.100)	(0.124)	(0.124)
LAC (exporter) × Depth	−0.165**	−0.117**	0.0247	0.117***
	(0.0707)	(0.0494)	(0.0723)	(0.0430)
LAC (exporter) × Prov	0.320***	0.353***	0.168*	0.149
	(0.103)	(0.0901)	(0.0921)	(0.184)

Continued

Table 4D.1 Impact of SPS or TBT provisions on bilateral exports from Latin America and the Caribbean versus the rest of the world *(continued)*

Provisions	Exports of agricultural products		Exports of all products	
	All SPS	**Essential SPS**	**All TBT**	**Essential TBT**
RoW (exporter) × Depth	0.127*** (0.0385)	0.0789*** (0.0292)	0.0533* (0.0276)	0.0540** (0.0217)
RoW (exporter) × Prov	−0.132** (0.0595)	−0.0783 (0.0592)	0.0346 (0.0246)	0.125*** (0.0221)
Fixed effects	it jt ij	it jt ij	it jt ij	it jt ij
Standard error	robust	robust	robust	robust
N	581,415	581,415	679,544	679,544

Source: World Bank calculations.

Note: Poisson pseudo maximum likelihood (PPML) estimation is used. Standard errors clustered by origin-destination presented in parentheses. Depth and provision measures are normalized between 0 and 1. Coefficients in bold are statistically different for Latin America and the Caribbean (LAC) (exporter) relative to rest of the world (RoW) (exporter). "Essential" provisions are those that require specific liberalization and integration commitments and obligations; relate to procedures, transparency, and enforcement; or relate to achievement of SPS and TBT integration. SPS = sanitary and phytosanitary; TBT = technical barrier to trade.

Significance level: * = 10 percent, ** = 5 percent, *** = 1 percent.

Table 4D.2 Impact of mutual recognition, harmonization, and transparency SPS or TBT provisions on bilateral exports from Latin America and the Caribbean versus the rest of the world

Provisions	Exports of agricultural products			Exports of all products		
	MR SPS	**Harmonization SPS**	**Transparency SPS**	**MR TBT**	**Harmonization TBT**	**Transparency TBT**
$\ln(1 + \tau)$	−0.537*** (0.0989)	−0.650*** (0.101)	−0.545*** (0.0992)	−0.782*** (0.124)	−0.764*** (0.124)	−0.741*** (0.123)
LAC (exporter) × Depth	−0.0527 (0.0446)	0.0159 (0.0393)	0.0359 (0.0492)	0.147*** (0.0364)	0.145*** (0.0360)	0.0900 (0.0608)
LAC (exporter) × Prov	**0.139*** (0.0444)	**0.0306** (0.0447)	**0.0309** (0.104)		**−0.106** (0.153)	**0.0553** (0.0638)
RoW (exporter) × Depth	0.0851*** (0.0271)	0.0353 (0.0227)	0.107*** (0.0296)	0.0627*** (0.0204)	0.0649*** (0.0203)	0.0465* (0.0259)
RoW (exporter) × Prov	−0.0639** (0.0268)	0.100*** (0.0142)	−0.168*** (0.0630)	0.0940*** (0.0136)	0.0869*** (0.0144)	0.0452** (0.0205)
Fixed effects	it jt ij	it jt ij	it jt ij	it jt ij	it jt ij	it jt ij
Standard error	robust	robust	robust	robust	robust	robust
N	581,415	581,415	581,415	679,544	679,544	679,544

Source: World Bank calculations.

Note: Poisson pseudo maximum likelihood (PPML) estimation is used. Standard errors clustered by origin-destination presented in parentheses. Depth and provision measures are normalized between 0 and 1. Coefficients in bold are statistically different for Latin America and the Caribbean (LAC) (exporter) relative to rest of the world (RoW) (exporter). MR = mutual recognition; SPS = sanitary and phytosanitary; TBT = technical barrier to trade.

Significance level: * = 10 percent, ** = 5 percent, *** = 1 percent.

Table 4D.3 Impact of TBT provisions on bilateral imports of intermediate inputs for Latin America and the Caribbean versus the rest of the world

	Imports of intermediates			
	All TBT	**Essential TBT**	**Harmonization TBT**	**Transparency TBT**
$ln(1 + \tau)$	−0.678***	−0.750***	−0.729***	−0.701***
	(0.161)	(0.161)	(0.160)	(0.159)
LAC (importer) × Depth	−0.259***	0.0181	0.149***	0.0737
	(0.0685)	(0.0415)	(0.0394)	(0.0633)
LAC (importer) × Prov	**0.594***	**0.986***	**−0.617***	**0.0833**
	(0.0977)	(0.206)	(0.0931)	(0.0594)
RoW (importer) × Depth	0.0755**	0.0648**	0.0706***	0.0563*
	(0.0326)	(0.0259)	(0.0242)	(0.0299)
RoW (importer) × Prov	0.00376	0.0707***	0.0484***	0.0327
	(0.0271)	(0.0250)	(0.0161)	(0.0241)
Fixed effects	it jt ij	it jt ij	it jt ij	it jt ij
N	651,702	651,702	651,702	651,702

Source: World Bank calculations.

Note: Poisson pseudo maximum likelihood (PPML) estimation is used. Standard errors clustered by destination-origin presented in parentheses. Depth and provision measures are normalized between 0 and 1. Coefficients in bold are statistically different for Latin America and the Caribbean (importer) relative to rest of the world (RoW) (importer). Estimation of LAC (importer) × Prov parameter for harmonization of technical barrier of trade (TBT) relies on one single agreement: European Free Trade Agreement (EFTA)–Peru (2011). "Essential" provisions are those that require specific liberalization and integration commitments and obligations; relate to procedures, transparency, and enforcement; or relate to achievement of SPS and TBT integration.

Significance level: * = 10 percent, ** = 5 percent, *** = 1 percent.

ANNEX 4E IMPACTS OF SPS AND TBT PROVISIONS IN PTAs ON FIRM-LEVEL BILATERAL EXPORTS

The firm-level results (tables 4E.1 and 4E.2) draw on Fernandes, Lefebvre, and Rocha (2021), and a brief description of the estimation approach is given below. The impact of the inclusion of sanitary and phytosanitary (SPS) and technical barriers to trade (TBT) provisions in PTAs on firm-level bilateral exports is estimated using a gravity equation framework given by

$$y_{fjkt} = exp(\alpha_{fjk} + \alpha_{fkt} + \gamma_1 * ln(1 + \tau_{ijkt}) + \gamma_2 * ln(GDP_{jt})$$
$$+ \gamma_3 * Depth_{ijt} + \gamma_4 * Prov_{ijt} * Tercile_{fjk}) + \varepsilon_{fjkt}, \qquad (4E.1)$$

where f is a firm (in origin country i); j is a destination market; k is an HS 6-digit product; t is a year; y_{fjkt} is bilateral exports; $Prov_{ijt}$ is, for SPS and for TBT separately, either

(a) the number of total, essential, or transparency provisions in a PTA (normalized as described in annex 4C), or (b) a dummy variable for harmonization or mutual recognition; and $Depth_{ijt}$ is the number of provisions in all non-SPS non-TBT chapters (normalized as described in annex 4B).

Equation (4E.1) includes firm-destination HS 6-digit fixed effects (α_{fjk}) that account for unobserved heterogeneity at a highly disaggregated level and allow for identifying the coefficients based on within-firm destination HS 6-digit changes in export values as PTAs with SPS and TBT provisions enter into force over the sample period. Equation (4E.1) also controls for stringent firm HS 6-digit product-year fixed effects (α_{fkt}) that capture both productivity differences and any supply shocks or demand shocks experienced by firms. Equation (4E.1) also includes the destination gross domestic product (GDP_{jt}) to account for time-varying demand and other macroeconomic factors affecting trade and for tariffs imposed by each importing country on a given exporting country—averaged across all HS 6-digit products (t_{ijt}) (Teti 2020).

The crucial aspect of equation (4E.1)—which allows for capturing the heterogeneity in the impacts of SPS and TBT provisions in PTAs on firms of different sizes—is the interaction between the variable $Prov_{ijt}$ and the variable $Tercile_{fjk}$. $Tercile_{fjk}$ is a set of three dummy variables that split the sample into three mutually exclusive size categories defined by the market share that each firm has in a destination HS 6-digit market in its initial year in the sample. We assume that most SPS and TBT measures are applicable to very narrowly defined HS 6-digit products, and thus the elimination or harmonization of the measures through provisions in the PTA could benefit small firms differently.

In line with the trade literature, the dataset used for the estimation of equation (4E.1) is the firm-level customs dataset, expanded so that each firm-destination HS 6-digit has an observation (a row) in all of that exporting country's sample years, with a 0 export value in a year when exports by the firm-destination HS 6-digit do not take place. Equation (4E.1) is estimated using PPML estimation introduced by Santos Silva and Tenreyro (2006) with the recent approach by Correia, Guimarães, and Zylkin (2019).

For all essential and transparency provisions, their estimated export impacts by firm size category are based on the following thought experiment: What would happen to a firm's bilateral exports if the firm's country signed a PTA with the maximum number of SPS or TBT provisions (the Chile–Peru PTA of 2009) in contrast to a PTA with a small number of SPS or TBT provisions (the EFTA–Mexico PTA of 2001)? For harmonization or mutual recognition, the estimated trade impacts are based on the comparison between PTAs that include such provisions relative to those that do not.

Table 4E.1 Impact of SPS or TBT provisions in PTAs on firms' exports across firm-size categories

	Export value of agricultural products				Total export value			
	All SPS	Essential SPS	All SPS	Essential SPS	All TBT	Essential TBT	All TBT	Essential TBT
$\ln(1 + \tau)$	-1.622***	-1.616***	-1.630***	-1.620***	-1.814***	-1.823***	-1.818***	-1.834***
	(0.412)	(0.412)	(0.411)	(0.412)	(0.420)	(0.420)	(0.422)	(0.422)
$\ln(GDP)$	1.332***	1.346***	1.315***	1.329***	2.170***	2.164***	2.163***	2.159***
	(0.191)	(0.192)	(0.189)	(0.190)	(0.177)	(0.177)	(0.177)	(0.175)
Depth	-0.363***	-0.262*	-0.382***	-0.279*	0.163	0.133	0.166	0.159
	(0.133)	(0.147)	(0.134)	(0.147)	(0.231)	(0.262)	(0.234)	(0.265)
Prov	0.0932	0.203**			0.145	0.278		
	(0.0596)	(0.0945)			(0.133)	(0.423)		
1st tercile × Prov			0.370***	0.657***			0.387***	0.842*
			(0.0779)	(0.122)			(0.150)	(0.443)
2nd tercile × Prov			-0.0123	0.0461			0.131	0.397
			(0.0698)	(0.104)			(0.176)	(0.512)
3rd tercile × Prov			0.0488	0.146			0.0871	0.0250
			(0.126)	(0.177)			(0.176)	(0.504)
Fixed effects	fkj fkt	fkj fkt	fkj fkt	fkj fkt	fkj fkt	fkj fkt	fkj fkt	fkj fkt
Cluster	ij	ij	ij	ij	ij	ij	ij	ij
N	1,532,134	1,532,134	1,532,134	1,532,134	6,283,454	6,283,454	6,283,454	6,283,454

Source: World Bank calculations.

Note: Poisson pseudo maximum likelihood (PPML) estimation is used. Robust standard errors clustered by origin–destination are presented in parentheses. Depth and Prov measures are normalized between 0 and 1. In the fixed effects, f is a firm in origin country i, j is a destination market, k is a Harmonized System (HS) 6-digit product, and t is a year. "Essential" provisions are those that require specific liberalization and integration commitments and obligations; relate to procedures, transparency, and enforcement; or relate to achievement of SPS and TBT integration. The 1st, 2nd, and 3rd tercile variables split the sample into three mutually exclusive firm-size categories defined by the market share that each firm has in a destination HS 6-digit market in its initial year in the sample. PTA = preferential trade agreement; SPS = sanitary and phytosanitary; TBT = technical barrier to trade.

Significance level: * = 10 percent, ** = 5 percent, *** = 1 percent.

Table 4E.2 Impact of mutual recognition, harmonization, and transparency SPS or TBT provisions in PTAs on firms' exports across firm-size categories

	Export value of agricultural products			Total export value	
	Mutual Recognition Agreements MRA SPS	Harmonization SPS	Transparency SPS	Harmonization TBT	Transparency TBT
$\ln(1 + \tau)$	−1.602*** (0.408)	−1.624*** (0.412)	−1.621*** (0.411)	−1.780*** (0.415)	−1.808*** (0.421)
$\ln(GDP)$	1.350*** (0.196)	1.287*** (0.195)	1.304*** (0.191)	2.159*** (0.182)	2.160*** (0.182)
Depth	−0.298** (0.133)	-0.110 (0.186)	−0.351*** (0.134)	0.0559 (0.222)	0.124 (0.210)
1st tercile × Prov	0.352*** (0.0658)	0.444*** (0.115)	0.616*** (0.169)	−0.585 (1.166)	0.212** (0.0908)
2nd tercile × Prov	0.00527 (0.0527)	0.0905 (0.0943)	−0.0690 (0.140)	1.001** (0.486)	0.0389 (0.110)
3rd tercile × Prov	0.143 (0.111)	0.203* (0.119)	−0.148 (0.281)	1.060*** (0.248)	0.164 (0.130)
Fixed effects	*fkj fkt*	*fkj fkt*	*fkj fkt*	*fkj fkt*	*fkj fkt*
Cluster	*ij*	*ij*	*ij*	*ij*	*ij*
N	1,532,134	1,532,134	1,532,134	6,283,454	6,283,454

Source: World Bank calculations.

Note: Poisson pseudo maximum likelihood (PPML) estimation is used. Robust standard errors clustered by origin–destination are presented in parentheses. Depth and Prov measures are normalized between 0 and 1. In the fixed effects, *f* is a firm in origin country *i*, *j* is a destination market, *k* is a Harmonized System (HS) 6-digit product, and *t* is a year. The 1st, 2nd, and 3rd tercile variables split the sample into three mutually exclusive firm-size categories defined by the market share that each firm has in a destination HS 6-digit market in its initial year in the sample. MRA = mutual recognition agreement; PTA = preferential trade agreement; SPS = sanitary and phytosanitary; TBT = technical barrier to trade.

Significance level: * = 10 percent, ** = 5 percent, *** = 1 percent.

NOTES

1. Macedoni and Weinberger (2020) rationalize regulatory heterogeneity across countries through a tolerance of higher levels of fixed costs rather than protectionist motives. Because they can tolerate higher fixed costs, larger countries and countries with more efficient production technologies optimally choose to set more restrictive regulations and standards.

2. Although the WTO's SPS and TBT agreements play a role in supporting international regulatory cooperation, they do not address the elimination or reduction of measures that are unnecessarily costly or duplicative, which drives deeper regulatory cooperation as in the context of preferential trade agreements (Goldberg 2019).

3. The regulatory divergence across countries in their SPS and TBT measures is often related to differences in countries' risk perceptions, preferences, and interpretations of scientific evidence. But regulatory divergence can also have protectionist motives.

4. Under mutual recognition, a PTA member recognizes the standards and regulations of its PTA partners as equivalent to its own, even if those standards and regulations are different. Mutual recognition can be particularly relevant for procedural regulations related to conformity and risk assessments whose complexity may require procedural regulations to remain country specific.

5. The European Union (EU) harmonizes product legislation in a few areas (such as vehicles, chemicals, medical devices, and protective equipment) but relies on mutual recognition in other areas, whereby products legally marketed in one EU member state can be sold in another EU member state, even if the products do not meet all the technical specifications of the EU member state in which the goods are sold (Goldberg 2019; Piermartini and Budetta 2009).

6. See Baldwin (2000) and Costinot (2008) for conceptual discussions on the contrast between harmonization and mutual recognition of standards for trade. WTO (2012, 150) also provides a detailed theoretical discussion.

7. Studies that estimate AVEs (such as Hoekman and Nicita 2011; Kee, Nicita, and Olarreaga 2009; and WTO 2012) show that NTMs almost double the level of trade restrictiveness imposed by tariffs and that the average AVE for agricultural products is much higher than for manufactured goods. Other studies estimate the impact of NTMs on trade using a price-gap method (WTO 2012).

8. This inventory-based examination uses NTM data collected from official sources by the United Nations Conference on International Trade and Development (UNCTAD) and the World Bank and is based on the *International Classification of Non-Tariff Measures* (UN 2019). For details, see annex 4A.

9. For the averages of those measures of trade restrictiveness across regions, see annex 4A, figure 4A.1.

10. WTO (2012) discusses the details of SPS and TBT notifications. These notification requirements are quite diverse and differ regarding the frequency with which they are required. The notifications providing information on the measures are either ad hoc, annual, or semiannual. When notification requirements cover NTMs that apply to specific products, members are required to indicate which products are covered. The notifications cover most of the categories in the *International Classification of Non-Tariff Measures* (UN 2019).

11. Data on notifications of SPS and TBT measures are from the WTO official notifications database.

12. For details on the content of SPS and TBT provisions in PTAs, see Espitia et al. (2020) and Stone and Casilini (2020).

13. The identification of essential provisions is based on expert knowledge and is thus subjective.

14. The total numbers of essential SPS and essential TBT provisions are, respectively, 24 and 19. The deepest PTAs in these policy areas include 13 essential SPS provisions and 9 essential TBT provisions.

15. Note that the maximum number of transparency provisions for TBT is only three. So any PTA with one such provision has more than 25 percent of the transparency provisions.

16. The estimation approach used to obtain the results in this section is described in box 4.2 for aggregate trade and in annex 4E for firm trade. SPS provisions are allowed to affect bilateral exports only of agricultural products and processed food and beverages (HS chapters 01–24). For bilateral imports of intermediate inputs—mostly manufacturing products—only impacts of TBT provisions are considered.

17. The impacts of mutual recognition and harmonization provisions for TBT do not appear in figures 4.9, 4.10, and 4.12 because none of the Latin American and Caribbean PTAs include those provisions.

18. The export impacts shown graphically are based on the same thought experiment as that used for the aggregate bilateral impacts in figure 4.9. For details on the firm–product gravity regressions and the tables with all estimated coefficients, see annex 4E.

19. The impacts of mutual recognition and harmonization provisions for TBT do not appear in figure 4.12 because none of the PTAs signed by Chile, Colombia, or Peru include these provisions.

20. This section draws heavily on the more detailed background policy note of González (2020).

21. Since 2005, imports of meat, dairy, and other agricultural products by Panama were subject to the certification by its health and agricultural officials of each individual plant or shipment (USTR 2007). Moreover, to delay imports, Panama claimed a lack of resources to complete inspections (*Inside U.S. Trade* 2006).

22. Information on AUPSA and other details of Panamanian implementation of the US–Panama PTA are from the Global Agricultural Information Network (GAIN) database of the US Department of Agriculture's Foreign Agricultural Service: https://gain.fas.usda.gov/#/.

23. This process is supported by the Inter-American Development Bank with the participation of regulatory authorities.

24. When harmonized regional import requirements already exist, products originating in the EU should comply with those requirements (and with registration where needed) in the Central American country of first import. Thereafter, free circulation in Central America is possible.

25. Vested interests in Panama opposed the implementation of this agreement, but the United States had several levers to induce compliance, including conclusion, implementation, and adoption of the free trade agreement itself.

REFERENCES

Baldwin, R. 2000. "Regulatory Protectionism, Developing Nations, and a Two-Tier World Trade System." Discussion Paper 2574, Centre for Economic Policy Research, London.

Chen, M., and A. Mattoo. 2008. "Regionalism in Standards: Good or Bad for Trade?" *Canadian Journal of Economics/Revue Canadienne d'économique* 41 (3): 838–63.

Correia, S., P. Guimarães, and T. Zylkin. 2019. "PPMLHDFE: Fast Poisson Estimation with High-Dimensional Fixed-Effects." *The Stata Journal: Promoting Communications on Statistics and Stata* 20 (1): 95–115.

Costinot, A. 2008. "A Comparative Institutional Analysis of Agreements on Product Standards." *Journal of International Economics* 75 (1): 197–213.

Disdier, A.-C., L. Fontagné, and O. Cadot. 2015. "North-South Standards Harmonization and International Trade." *The World Bank Economic Review* 29 (2): 327–52.

Dorantes, J. 2020. "Former Director General of International Trade Rules, Secretary of Economy, Mexico." Interview with the author, November 30.

Economist. 2020. "Wine Whinge: The Costs of Colombia's Closed Economy." *Economist*, February 8.

Ederington, J., and M. Ruta. 2016. "Nontariff Measures and the World Trading System." In *Handbook of Commercial Policy*, Vol. 1, Part B, edited by K. Bagwell and R. W. Staiger, 211–77. Amsterdam: North-Holland.

Espitia, A., S. Pardo, R. Piermartini, and N. Rocha. 2020. "Technical Barriers to Trade." In *Handbook of Deep Trade Agreements*, edited by A. Mattoo, N. Rocha, and M. Ruta, 343–65. Washington, DC: World Bank.

Fatat Romero, A. 2020. "Vice Minister of Trade, Colombia." Interview with Anabel Gonzalez, December 2.

Fernandes, A., E. Ferro, and J. Wilson. 2019. "Product Standards and Firms' Export Decisions." *The World Bank Economic Review* 33 (2): 353–74.

Fernandes, A. M., K. Lefebvre, and N. Rocha. 2021. "Heterogeneous Impacts of SPS and TBT Regulations: Firm-Level Evidence from Deep Trade Agreements." Policy Research Working Paper 9700, World Bank, Washington, DC.

Fontagné, L., G. Orefice, R. Piermartini, and N. Rocha. 2015. "Product Standards and Margins of Trade: Firm-Level Evidence." *Journal of International Economics* 97 (1): 29–44.

Gaulier, G., and S. Zignago. 2010. "BACI: International Trade Database at the Product-Level: The 1994–2007 Version." Working Paper 2010-23, Centre d'Études Prospectives et d'Informations Internationales (CEPII), Paris.

Goldberg, E. 2019. "Regulatory Cooperation: A Reality Check." M-RCBG Associate Working Paper Series 115, Harvard Kennedy School, Cambridge, MA.

González, A. 2020. "Deep Preferential Trade Agreements as Mechanisms to Support TBT and SPS Regulatory Cooperation in Latin America." Unpublished working paper, World Bank, Washington, DC.

Hoekman, B. 2015. "Trade Agreements and International Regulatory Cooperation in a Supply Chain World." Working Paper RSCAS 2015/04, European University Institute, Fiesole, Italy.

Hoekman, B. 2018. "'Behind-the-Border' Regulatory Policies and Trade Agreements." *East Asian Economic Review* 22 (3): 243–73.

Hoekman, B., and A. Nicita. 2011. "Trade Policy, Trade Costs, and Developing Country Trade." *World Development* 39 (12): 2069–79.

Hornbeck, J. 2012. "The US–Panama Free Trade Agreement." Congressional Research Service, November 8.

Ing, L., O. Cadot, and J. Walz. 2017. "Transparency in Non-Tariff Measures: An International Comparison." *The World Economy* 41 (3): 884–912.

Inside U.S. Trade. 2006. "Dispute over Agriculture Inspections Holding Up U.S.–Panama FTA Talks." *Inside U.S. Trade*, January 27.

Kee, H. L. 2019. "Trade Policies in Latin America Region and the Trade Impact." Unpublished manuscript, World Bank, Washington, DC.

Kee, H. L., and A. Forero. 2020. "Non-Tariff Measures of Colombia." Unpublished working paper, World Bank, Washington, DC.

Kee, H. L., A. Nicita, and M. Olarreaga. 2009. "Estimating Trade Restrictiveness Indices." *Economic Journal* 119 (534): 172–99.

Lejárraga, I., and B. Shepherd. 2013. "Quantitative Evidence on Transparency in Regional Trade Agreements." Trade Policy Paper No. 153, Organisation for Economic Co-operation and Development, Paris.

Macedoni, L., and A. Weinberger. 2020. "Quality Heterogeneity and Misallocation: The Welfare Benefits of Raising your Standards." MPRA Paper, University Library of Munich, Germany.

Mattoo, A., N. Rocha, and M. Ruta, eds. 2020. *Handbook of Deep Trade Agreements.* Washington, DC: World Bank.

Molina, A., and V. Khoroshavina. 2015. "TBT Provisions in Regional Trade Agreements: To What Extent Do They Go beyond the WTO TBT Agreement?" Staff Working Paper ERSD-2015-09, World Trade Organization, Geneva.

Mowatt, R. 2017. "Trade Policy Issues in Latin America and the Caribbean: Views from Country Authorities and Current State of Play." Survey report, International Monetary Fund, Washington, DC.

OECD (Organisation for Economic Co-operation and Development). 2013. *International Regulatory Co-operation: Addressing Global Challenges.* Paris: OECD Publishing.

OECD (Organisation for Economic Co-operation and Development). 2017. *International Regulatory Co-operation and Trade: Understanding the Trade Costs of Regulatory Divergence and the Remedies.* Paris: OECD Publishing.

Piermartini, R., and M. Budetta. 2009. "A Mapping of Regional Rules on Technical Barriers to Trade." In *Regional Rules in the Global Trading System*, edited by A. Estevadeordal, R. Teh, and K. Suominen, 250–315. Cambridge: Cambridge University Press.

Piermartini, R., and Y. Yotov. 2016. "Estimating Trade Policy Effects with Structural Gravity." School of Economics Working Paper No. 2016-10, LeBow College of Business, Drexel University, Philadelphia.

Polanco, R., and P. Sauvé. 2018. "The Treatment of Regulatory Convergence in Preferential Trade Agreements." *World Trade Review* 17 (4): 575–607.

Reyes, J.-D. 2011. "International Harmonization of Product Standards and Firm Heterogeneity in International Trade." Policy Research Working Paper 5677, World Bank, Washington, DC.

Santos Silva, J., and S. Tenreyro. 2006. "The Log of Gravity." *Review of Economics and Statistics* 88 (4): 641–58.

Schmidt, J., and W. Steingress. 2019. "No Double Standards: Quantifying the Impact of Standard Harmonization on Trade." Staff Working Paper No. 2019-36, Bank of Canada, Ottawa.

Stone, S., and F. Casilini. 2020. "Sanitary and Phytosanitary Measures." In *Handbook of Deep Trade Agreements*, edited by A. Mattoo, N. Rocha, and M. Ruta, 367–90. Washington, DC: World Bank.

Stone, S., and I. Lejárraga. 2018. "Regulatory Coherence." White paper, Global Value Chain Policy Series, World Economic Forum, Geneva.

Teti, F. 2020. "30 Years of Trade Policy: Evidence from 5.7 Billion Tariffs." Working Paper No. 334, ifo Institute – Leibniz Institute for Economic Research, University of Munich.

UN (United Nations). 2019. *International Classifications of Non-Tariff Measures: 2019 Version.* New York: UN.

UNCTAD (United Nations Conference on International Trade and Development). 2017. "UNCTAD TRAINS: The Global Database on Non-Tariff Measures User Guide." Publication UNCTAD/DITC/TAB/2017/3, UNCTAD, Geneva.

USTR (US Trade Representative). 2007. "National Trade Estimate Report on Foreign Trade Barriers." Annual report series, USTR, Washington, DC.

USTR (US Trade Representative). 2011. *Agriculture in the US–Panama Trade Promotion Agreement.* Washington, DC: USTR.

Van Tongeren, F., V. Bastien, and M. von Lampe. 2015. "International Regulatory Cooperation, a Trade-Facilitating Mechanism." Paper for the E-15 Initiative, International Centre for Trade and Sustainable Development (ICTSD) and the World Economic Forum, Geneva.

World Bank. 2019. *Trade Integration as a Pathway to Development?* Semiannual Report of the Latin America and Caribbean Region (October). Washington, DC: World Bank.

WTO (World Trade Organization). 2005. "Committee on Sanitary and Phytosanitary Measures. Summary of the Meeting Held on 29–30 June 2005." Document G/SPS/R/37, August 11, WTO, Geneva.

WTO (World Trade Organization). 2012. *World Trade Report 2012 – Trade and Public Policies: A Closer Look at Non-Tariff Measures in the 21st Century.* Geneva: WTO.

WTO and OECD (World Trade Organization and Organisation for Economic Co-operation and Development). 2019. *Facilitating Trade through Regulatory Cooperation: The Case of the WTO's TBT/SPS Agreements and Committees.* Geneva: WTO; Paris: OECD Publishing.

5 Services Trade: Reducing Skill and Technology Constraints

Ben Shepherd, with input from Gabriel Duque, Roberto Echandi, and Rodrigo Polanco

KEY MESSAGES

- Significant liberalization of services trade is crucial for promoting trade through deep preferential trade agreements (PTAs) and for supporting production sharing and global value chain (GVC) integration.
- Latin American and Caribbean intraregional agreements are much less ambitious than the region's extraregional agreements for General Agreement on Trade in Services (GATS) supply modes 3 and 4, which regulate sales by foreign affiliates and temporary movement by service providers.
- Latin American and Caribbean PTAs would need to reduce trade costs substantially to change the relative composition of trade in favor of GVC links within the region.
- Comprehensive data are urgently needed on services trade and policy setting and implementation to provide evidence-based recommendations on how to leverage services trade integration through the region's PTAs.

INTRODUCTION

Although the service economy in Latin American and Caribbean countries is large, with trade in services somewhat lower than in other regions, the region's integration into services global value chains (GVCs) is low. Services account for 60 percent of economic activity in the region and services trade for 7.3 percent of gross domestic product (GDP)—less than in most other regions. In GVCs, services are increasingly important, especially as inputs into production in other sectors, including manufacturing.

Compared with other regions in the world, Latin America and the Caribbean is less integrated into services GVCs, especially for intraregional trade.

The content of the region's preferential trade agreements (PTAs) helps explain the scarcity of services trade, especially regional trade, in the region's GVCs. Latin America and the Caribbean's intraregional trade costs are higher than trade costs with North America. Its PTAs with external partners tend to be more ambitious in content than those with regional partners. This configuration contributes to services trade patterns in Latin America and the Caribbean, aligning with evidence that deeper services PTAs increase trade by 15–65 percent and lead to more service value added being sourced from PTA partners.

Latin American and Caribbean countries can use deep trade agreements to increasingly liberalize service sector policies, such as posing a horizontal standstill on discriminatory measures and quantitative restrictions. They should also consider liberalizing a broader range of modes of services trade—particularly foreign investment and movement of people, which are associated with higher value added in services exports. PTAs can foster trade by including provisions to improve the transparency of measures that restrict trade in services and by strengthening data collection on services trade and policy.

THE COMPLEXITY OF SERVICES TRADE AGREEMENTS

As services become more tradable, policy makers need to know what facilitates services trade, especially since the incorporation of the General Agreement on Trade in Services (GATS) into the World Trade Organization (WTO) framework in 1995. Unlike goods trade, where the obstacle of tariffs is obvious, identifying, quantifying, and cataloging restrictions in services trade usually requires delving deeply into countries' regulatory frameworks. Similarly, however, removing or rationalizing restrictions to services trade often requires technically complex regulatory reform.

Because PTAs increasingly deal with such regulatory issues, it is natural to ask what their role might be in facilitating regional services trade. Linked to that general issue is a specific question about the increasing importance of digital trade, especially in light of the COVID-19 pandemic. Modern PTAs, especially those with extraregional partners, tend to include provisions on digital trade that are specific applications of more general principles for the coverage of services and the regulatory reforms needed to lift restrictions.

GVCs in trade and production worldwide raise a related issue. Although GVCs are traditionally associated with goods sectors, such as electronics and apparel, a wealth of evidence now suggests that they are also active in services sectors. Examples include call centers that provide customer support for back-office functions for finance from distant locations—services in which India and the Philippines have excelled. Because this type of trade is grounded in intermediate services moving across borders, transactions take place between firms rather than between firms and consumers. Services moving across borders are also important in manufacturing and agriculture, where networked production requires service inputs from sectors such as finance, professional services, and transportation and logistics. Trade policy can do much to facilitate or restrict the growth of both services GVCs and the use of services in goods GVCs, particularly in manufacturing.

Under GATS, services can be traded internationally through four supply "modes":

- *Mode 1* is pure cross-border supply, where, for example, a law firm in Buenos Aires advises a client in Lima. Mode 1 therefore includes digital trade.
- *Mode 2* involves movement of the consumer, where the client travels from Lima to Buenos Aires to receive legal advice from the law firm.
- *Mode 3* is sales by foreign affiliates through "commercial presence," where the law firm establishes a local office in Lima and uses it to provide advice to the client there.
- *Mode 4* is temporary movement by the service provider, where the Buenos Aires law firm sends a lawyer for a short period to Lima to advise the client there, after which the lawyer returns to Buenos Aires.

From a policy perspective, assessing the facilitative role of PTAs in services is not as simple as looking at a PTA's services chapter and the annexed lists of specific commitments. The evidence suggests that countries undertake very little liberalization in services PTAs. Adlung and Miroudot (2012), reviewing the general evidence on PTA provisions relative to GATS, found that backsliding was prevalent. And Shepherd et al. (2019), in a provision-by-provision analysis of the schedules of commitments in the European Union (EU)–Canada Comprehensive Economic and Trade Agreement (CETA), showed that there was little effective liberalization at a detailed sectoral level by either party relative to most-favored-nation (MFN) policies.

Other aspects of PTAs might also affect service providers. In many sectors where mode 3 is a way of contesting in foreign markets, PTA provisions on investment are key. Similarly, given the increased importance of mode 1 services trade during the COVID-19 pandemic—when in-person interactions have been substantially more difficult—PTA provisions on technology and data protection are important. And rules and institutions, on which services rely more heavily than other kinds of trade, are also vital (Beverelli, Fiorini, and Hoekman 2017). Even when a PTA contains little practical liberalization in its schedules of commitments, the regulatory framework it creates can nonetheless facilitate trade.

Whether PTAs promote services trade—specifically services trade within GVC frameworks—is largely an open question. It cannot be answered categorically. Instead, each agreement's provisions in a range of areas determine the net result. So, the key question that motivates this chapter is whether the evidence supports the view that PTAs in Latin America and the Caribbean are indeed facilitating services trade for GVCs in the region.

SERVICES IN THE EVOLVING GLOBAL ECONOMY

The rise of the service economy is an important ongoing global dynamic (Helble and Shepherd 2019). Combined changes in technology and regulatory policies have made services more tradable across borders just as firms are more able to reorganize production. The result is that services are seeing two "unbundlings" at much the same time (Baldwin 2011): increasing geographical distance between production and consumption, and increasing dispersion of location in the production process. Hoekman and Shepherd (2021) argue that these dynamics are likely to intensify over the medium term as technological changes—such as automation and the rise of 3-D printing—combine with other trends to promote (a) an increasing shift of economic output toward services, and (b) an increase of trade in services. The increases in digital trade are a particular example of these more general trends.

Countries in Latin America and the Caribbean are by no means excluded from these dynamics (figure 5.1). As of 2017, services accounted for just over 60 percent of economic activity in the region, similar to the share in East Asia and the Pacific. Although Latin American and Caribbean services trade is substantial—equating to around 7.3 percent of GDP, like the share for North America—it is lower than the shares in other regions.

Figure 5.1 Services and services trade as a percentage of GDP, by region, 2017

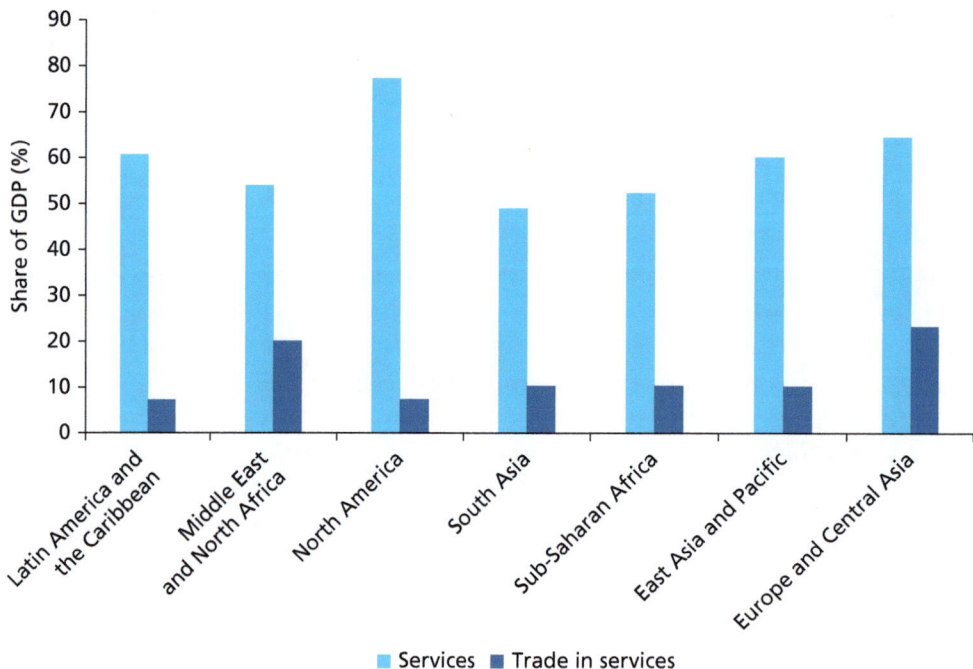

Source: World Development Indicators database.

Note: Regions are World Bank regions.

Data like those in figure 5.1 warrant an important caveat: they are based on services trade as reported in the balance of payments. But those statistics capture only a part of services trade as conceptualized under GATS—namely mode 1 and some elements of modes 2 and 4. Mode 3 (sales by foreign affiliates), though the most important, is absent. In some sectors, mode 3 is crucial to market entry, so including it to get a sense of its role in trade is important.

Services trade in the region, by mode and by sector

Recent work by the WTO provides a picture of trade in services through the experimental Trade in Services Data by Mode of Supply (TiSMoS) dataset. In 2017, the latest year of TiSMoS data, Latin American and Caribbean countries' total services exports—in the GATS sense—amounted to US$296.4 billion, compared with US$204.2 billion recorded in the balance of payments data reported in the World Development Indicators database. The discrepancy is nearly one-third of the TiSMoS total, so the potential to be misleading is high for an analysis that stops with the data in figure 5.1. TiSMoS shows that the Latin American and Caribbean region's services exports are almost all in mode 1 (35.6 percent), mode 3 (31.8 percent), and mode 2 (29.3 percent), with mode 4 playing a minor role.

Figures 5.2 and 5.3 break down the region's services trade by sector, summing all GATS modes of supply. On the export side (figure 5.2), the leading sectors

Figure 5.2 Latin American and Caribbean services exports, by sector, through all modes of supply, 2017

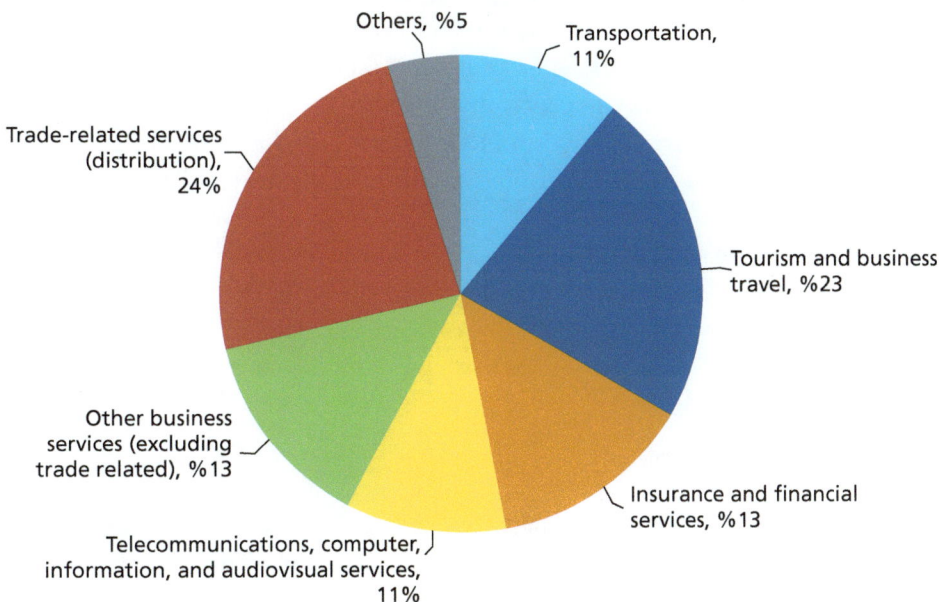

Source: Trade in Services data by Mode of Supply (TiSMoS) database, World Trade Organization.

Figure 5.3   Latin American and Caribbean services imports, by sector, through all modes of supply, 2017

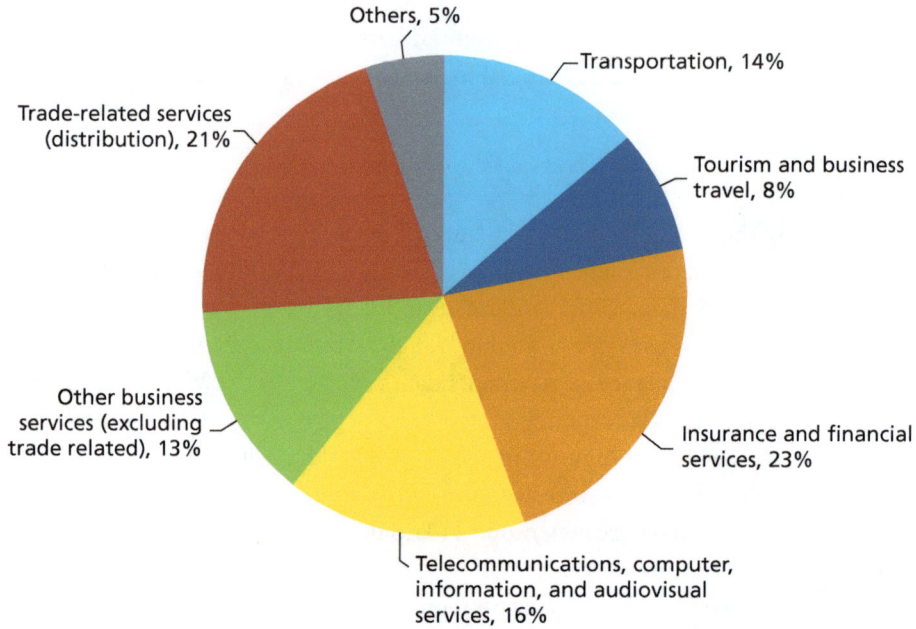

Source: Trade in Services data by Mode of Supply (TiSMoS) database, World Trade Organization.

are distribution (23.9 percent), tourism and travel (22.6 percent), insurance and finance (13.6 percent), other business services (13.6 percent), transportation (10.9 percent), and telecommunications (10.6 percent). For imports, the list is similar: insurance and finance (22.7 percent), distribution (21.0 percent), telecommunications (16.1 percent), transportation (13.6 percent), and other business services (13.2 percent). Trade in either direction is only minimally developed in the remaining sectors.

Although these data depict Latin American and Caribbean trade with the rest of the world, they are important indicators for the region's future economic integration since they highlight sectors where trade is both technologically feasible and commercially advantageous and thus should receive attention in PTA negotiations and implementation.

Impacts of the COVID-19 pandemic on services trade

The COVID-19 pandemic has posed particular challenges for the services sector. In the last global economic shock of comparable size, the 2007–08 Global Financial Crisis, services performed better than goods in that the value of trade in services declined less sharply and rebounded more quickly (Borchert and Mattoo 2010). But the situation has been reversed for the COVID-19 pandemic. Most services trade involves in-person interactions, which have become riskier and more difficult or impossible because of public health precautions around the world to manage the crisis. The United Nations Conference on Trade and Development (UNCTAD), for example, forecast a decline of 15.4 percent in global services trade in 2020 compared with 2019. For goods, the predicted decline was only 5.6 percent (UNCTAD 2020). These figures include the special case of digital trade, which increased through a substitution effect during the pandemic.

In the Latin American and Caribbean countries with data, services have been hard hit by the pandemic (figure 5.4). Only Honduras's export position was relatively unchanged in the third quarter of 2020 from the fourth quarter of 2019 (just before the pandemic). All other countries have seen large export declines—from 25 percent to nearly 80 percent by value.

All sectors have experienced declines, but the declines have varied considerably (figure 5.5). Exports in travel fell by 92 percent and in construction by 84 percent because both sectors require a personal presence (mode 2 for travel and typically mode 4 for construction). Telecommunications, other business services, and financial services declined by 45–65 percent, while the insurance and transportation sectors fell by around 30 percent. Clearly, the decline in the region's services exports has been major in all sectors, and it is likely a combination of the reduced scope for in-person transactions and of falling incomes in export markets that reduced demand even for exports that could be supplied online.

Figure 5.4   Change in the value of total services exports in Latin America and the Caribbean, selected countries, Q4 2019 to Q3 2020

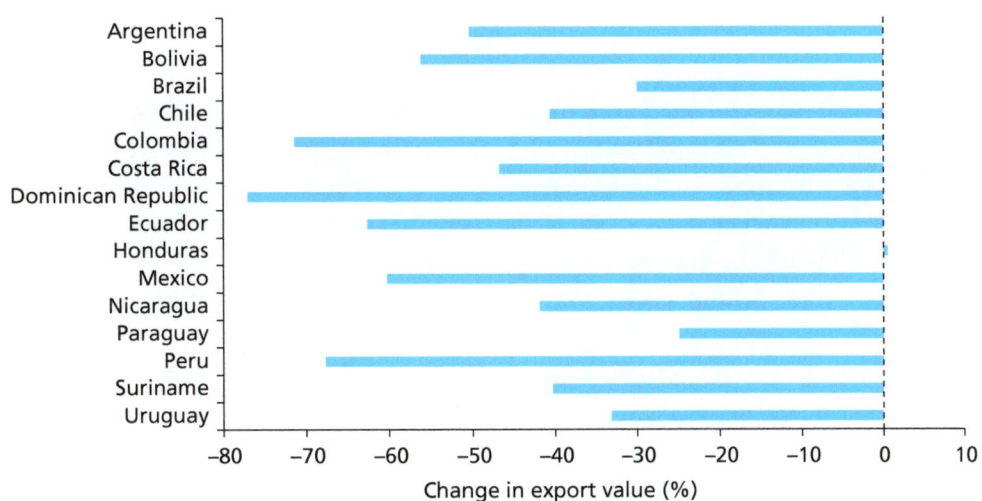

Source: Services trade data from the World Trade Organization's Stats portal, https://stats.wto.org/.

Note: The selected countries are those for which data were available for the specified periods. Q = quarter.

Figure 5.5   Changes in value of services exports in Latin America and the Caribbean, by sector, Q1 2018 to Q3 2020

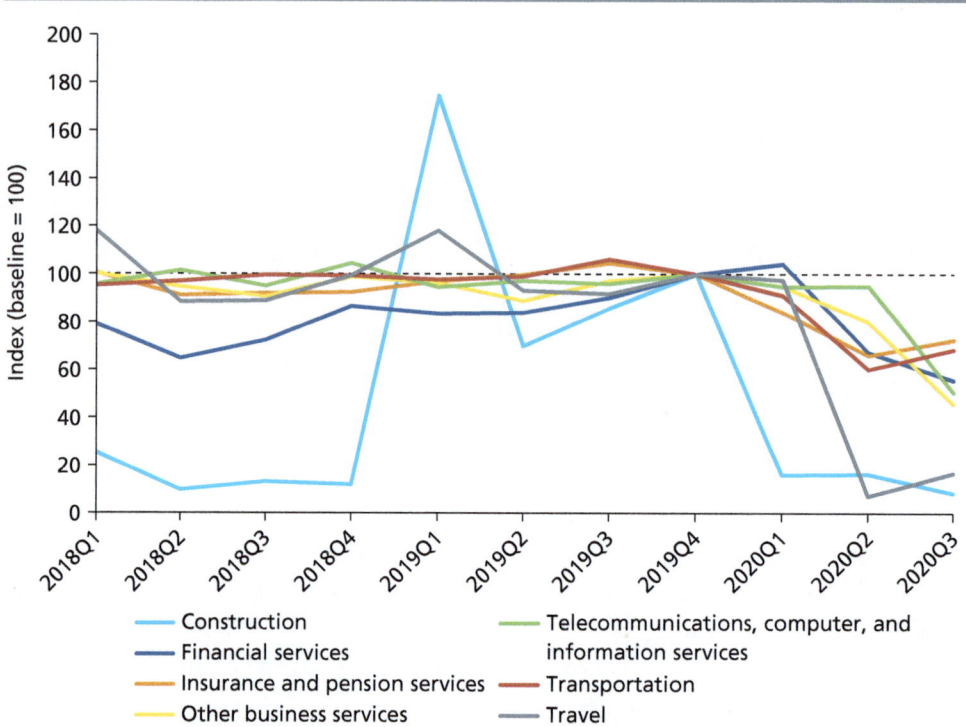

Source: Services trade data from the World Trade Organization's Stats portal, https://stats.wto.org/.

Note: The figure shows trade values based on Latin American and Caribbean countries that reported data to the World Trade Organization (WTO) for the third quarter of 2020. Trade values are indexed so that the immediate pre–COVID-19 period (2019Q4) is equal to 100. Q = quarter.

SERVICES IN LATIN AMERICAN AND CARIBBEAN GVCs

Conventional trade statistics, even those that account for the GATS modes of supply, are inadequate on their own for analyzing value chain integration. GVCs are characterized by intensive movements of intermediates—goods and services—during production, before the final product is sent to the consumer. But conventional trade statistics do not distinguish the end use of the traded good or service, and so analysts cannot disentangle trade within GVCs from more traditional point-to-point transactions between producers and consumers.

Borin and Mancini (2019), based on the Eora global supply chain database's multiregion input-output table, calculate backward and forward linkages at a disaggregated country-sector level for all countries in the database, including 31 from Latin America and the Caribbean. Input-output tables do not disaggregate services trade by mode of supply. Instead, they record services trade based on the balance of payments, which uses different statistical concepts, and can be seen as capturing primarily mode 1 (cross-border supply), but also some elements of mode 2 (consumption abroad) and mode 4 (movement of service provider). The data thus do not account for trade under GATS mode 3 (sales by foreign affiliates). Transactions are accounted for as domestic sales since input-output tables use a locational rather than an ownership principle. So, the tables attribute sales to companies based on their geographical location, not the geographical location of the owning entity.

General analysis of participation in services GVCs

In this general framework, in services markets, Latin America and the Caribbean is mostly an input supplier for GVCs: backward linkages—imports of intermediate inputs used in the production of the region's own services exports—are relatively small. Only in exports to North America and South Asia is the region's proportion of backward linkages in services exports higher than that of forward linkages—exports of inputs used in production of other countries' exports (figure 5.6).

Figure 5.6 Decomposition of Latin American and Caribbean services exports, by importing region and value-added component, 2015

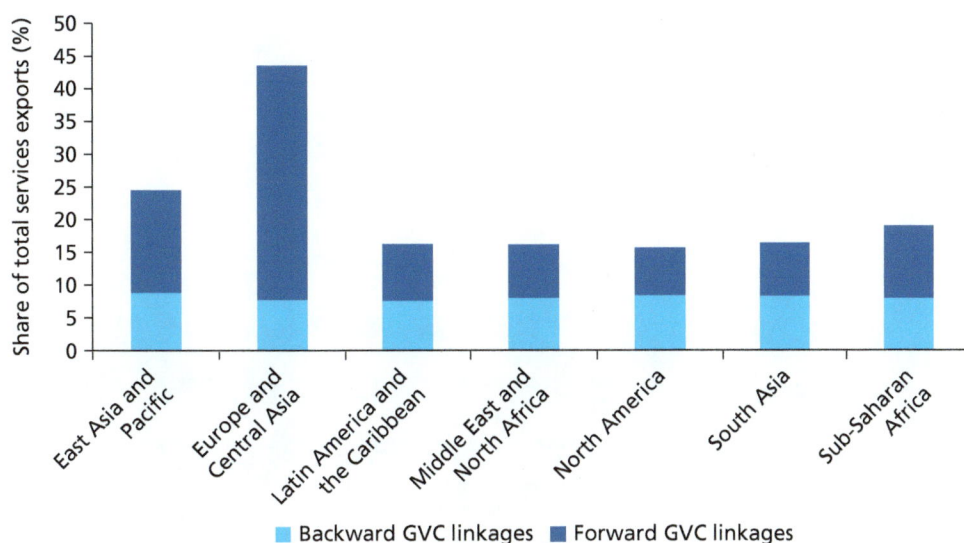

Source: Borin and Mancini 2019.

Note: The decomposition is based on data from the Eora global supply chain database's multiregion input-output table, which records services trade based on the balance of payments, capturing primarily General Agreement on Trade in Services (GATS) mode of supply 1 (cross-border supply) and some elements of mode 2 (consumption abroad) and mode 4 (movement of service provider) but not mode 3 (commercial presence of foreign affiliates). Because input-output tables use a locational rather than an ownership principle, they attribute sales to companies based on their geographical location, not the geographical location of the owning entity. "Backward global value chain (GVC) linkages" refer to imports of intermediate inputs used in the production of the Latin America and Caribbean region's own services exports. "Forward GVC linkages" refer to Latin American and Caribbean countries' exports of inputs used in other countries' export production.

Latin America and the Caribbean's intraregional exports have the third lowest level of GVC integration of any direction of Latin American and Caribbean trade (figure 5.6). Only exports to North America and the Middle East and North Africa have lower levels. In general, Latin American and Caribbean countries are more engaged in GVC services trade with extraregional partners than with intraregional ones.

A comparison of Latin American and Caribbean intraregional trade with East Asia and Pacific intraregional trade is instructive. The East Asia and Pacific region has backward and forward linkages totaling nearly 31 percent of gross intraregional services exports, compared with only 16 percent for the Latin American and Caribbean region. Of all world regions, only South Asia—which is subject to major political and policy impediments to trade—has a lower proportion of GVC linkages in gross services exports than Latin America and the Caribbean. The extent to which policy, particularly trade policy, may be a driver of these results is explored further below.

Intraregional variations

Aggregate results obscure variation across sectors, as does the balance between backward and forward linkages (figure 5.7). For example, the Latin American and Caribbean hotel

Figure 5.7 Decomposition of Latin American and Caribbean intraregional services exports, by sector and value-added component, 2015

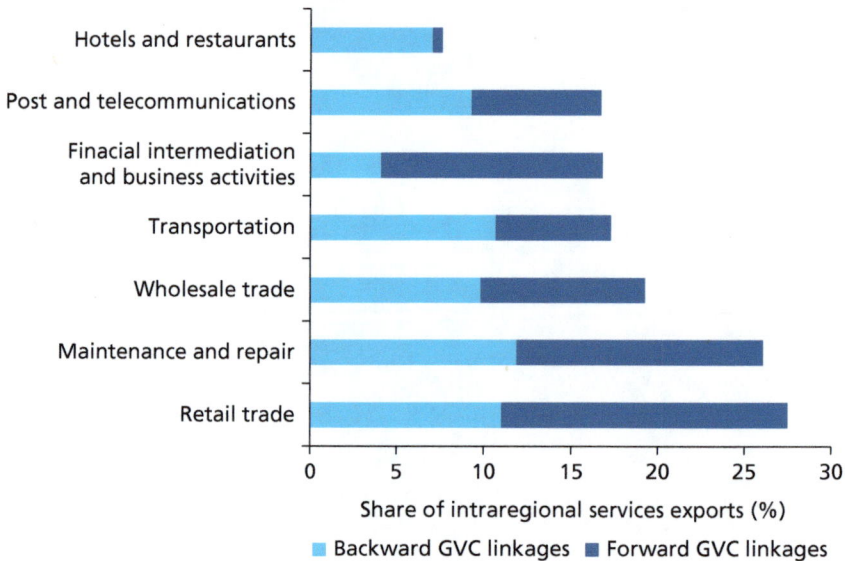

■ Backward GVC linkages   ■ Forward GVC linkages

Source: Borin and Mancini 2019.

Note: The decomposition is based on the Eora global supply chain database's multiregion input-output table, which records services trade based on the balance of payments, capturing primarily General Agreement on Trade in Services (GATS) mode of supply 1 (cross-border supply) and some elements of mode 2 (consumption abroad) and mode 4 (movement of service provider) but not mode 3 (commercial presence of foreign affiliates). Because input-output tables use a locational rather than an ownership principle, they attribute sales to companies based on their geographical location, not the geographical location of the owning entity. "Backward global value chain (GVC) linkages" refers to the share of imported inputs in a country's exports. "Forward GVC linkages" refers to the share of exports that are inputs for another country's export production.

and restaurant sector has a large proportion of backward linkages, but its overall GVC integration is the least of any sector. In other sectors, with the exception of transportation, forward linkages—supplying inputs for the production of partner country exports—tend to predominate. The most integrated sectors are wholesale and retail trade (distribution), as well as maintenance and repair. The next three sectors all have roughly average integration within the region, while hotels and restaurants have substantially less.

Similar variation is evident at the country level. Usually, smaller countries display more GVC integration (figure 5.8), though the balance of backward and

Figure 5.8 Decomposition of Latin American and Caribbean intraregional services exports, by exporting country and value-added component, 2015

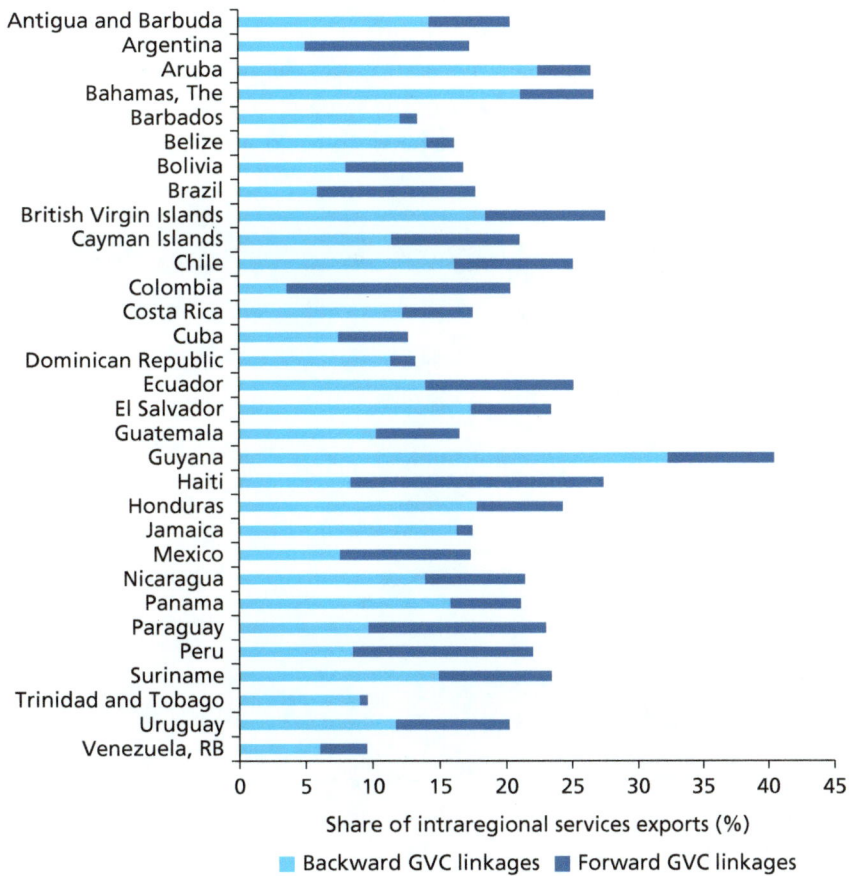

Share of intraregional services exports (%)

■ Backward GVC linkages ■ Forward GVC linkages

Source: Borin and Mancini 2019.

Note: The decomposition is based on the Eora global supply chain database's multiregion input-output table, which records services trade based on the balance of payments, capturing primarily General Agreement on Trade in Services (GATS) mode of supply 1 (cross-border supply) and some elements of mode 2 (consumption abroad) and mode 4 (movement of service provider) but not mode 3 (commercial presence of foreign affiliates). Because input-output tables use a locational rather than an ownership principle, they attribute sales to companies based on their geographical location, not the geographical location of the owning entity. "Backward global value chain (GVC) linkages" refers to the share of imported inputs in a country's exports. "Forward GVC linkages" refers to the share of exports that are inputs for another country's export production.

forward linkages tends to be reversed in smaller countries (where backward link-ages predominate) and larger countries (where forward linkages predominate). Keep in mind that some of the gross services export flows are very small, as are the economies in question. The high proportions for Guyana and Suriname are due to the transportation sector, where exports seem to be driven by external demand for the countries' minerals, such as gold. For other countries, the mix of sectors varies greatly, in some cases linked to goods trade but in others linked more to services-oriented trade. The British Virgin Islands, for example, shows substantial GVC integration in the financial sector but also in tourism—the two main pillars of the country's economy.

There is no evidence of rapid change in the level of GVC integration in Latin American and Caribbean intraregional trade (figure 5.9). There was a small overall decline between 2000 and 2015, but the picture is broadly static. Only in the Middle East and North Africa and Sub-Saharan Africa does the proportion of GVC trade in intraregional services exports decrease over the same period. The other regions gener-ally saw significant increases. The balance between backward and forward linkages in

Figure 5.9   Decomposition of Latin American and Caribbean intraregional services exports, by value-added component, 2000 and 2015

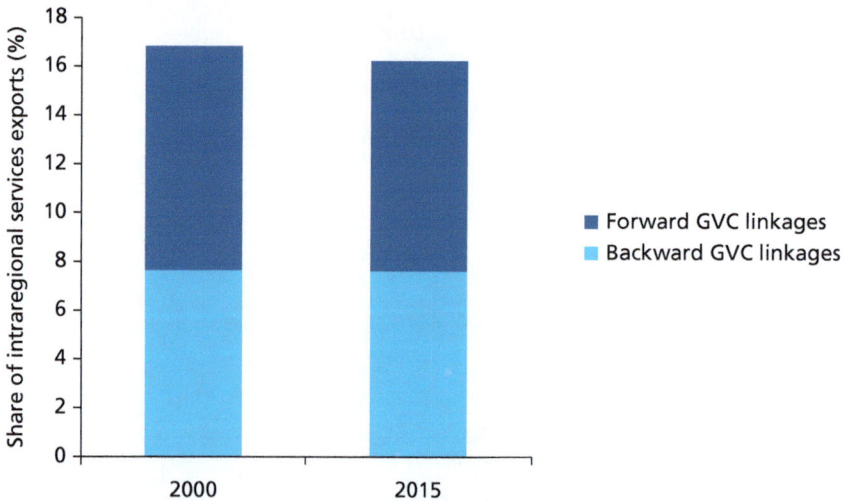

Source: Borin and Mancini 2019.

Note: The decomposition is based on the Eora global supply chain database's multiregion input-output table, which records services trade based on the balance of payments, capturing primarily General Agreement on Trade in Services (GATS) mode of supply 1 (cross-border supply) and some elements of mode 2 (consumption abroad) and mode 4 (movement of service provider) but not mode 3 (commercial presence of foreign affiliates). Because input-output tables use a locational rather than an ownership principle, they attribute sales to companies based on their geographical location, not the geographical location of the owning entity. "Backward global value chain (GVC) linkages" refer to imports of intermediate inputs used in the production of the Latin America and Caribbean region's own services exports. "Forward GVC linkages" refer to Latin American and Caribbean countries' exports of inputs used in production of other countries' exports.

Latin America and the Caribbean is stable over time, so there is no evidence that the region's countries on the whole are shifting their involvement in services GVCs in one direction or the other.

In sum, GVC integration in services markets is underdeveloped in the Latin American and Caribbean region compared with other parts of the developing world, particularly for intraregional trade. There is no clear evidence of increasing integration between 2000 and 2015; there is even a slight regression, contrary to the experience of most other regions. Although individual Latin American and Caribbean countries and sectors differ, the overall picture is consistent: GVC integration is important for services trade in the region, but it does not yet approach the levels seen in most other developing regions.

LATIN AMERICAN AND CARIBBEAN DEEP TRADE AGREEMENTS AND SERVICES IN GVCs

By their nature, PTAs affect trade costs and thus trade flows among partners as well as between partners and nonpartners. But can PTAs have impacts on the production-sharing model at the base of GVC trade? In services in particular, is there scope for lower trade costs linked to a PTA to translate into deeper GVC integration?

A thought experiment: Preferential versus most-favored-nation liberalization

Before moving to concrete issues in Latin American and Caribbean PTAs, a simple thought experiment using a quantitative trade model is useful. The model, described in full in Shepherd (2020), is based   closely on Aichele and Heiland (2018) and Caliendo and Parro (2015). It uses standard economic theory and explicitly incorporates production sharing across countries. As such, it makes it possible to simulate the impact of a change in trade costs—for example, as a result of signing a PTA—on intraregional and extraregional trade flows as well as on the level of backward and forward integration in those trade flows.[1]

In a trade costs measure that takes into account all the factors that drive a wedge between factory prices in the exporting country and consumer prices in the importing country (including geographical and historical factors as well as policy barriers), trade costs in services sectors are systematically higher than in goods sectors (Novy 2013), as shown in figure 5.10.[2] The difference is substantial: services trade costs are often 50 percent higher than goods trade costs, and even double in some cases.

For the Latin American and Caribbean region, somewhat unusually, trade costs are lowest when trading with North America, not when trading within the region. This result is in line with the GVC analysis presented above: intraregional GVC integration was low compared with other directions of trade, and high intraregional trade costs could be part of the reason. So, policy could have a role in further reducing services trade costs given the large cost gap relative to goods trade and the fact that the intraregional flows that travel the shortest distance do not have the lowest trade costs.

Figure 5.10   Simple average AVE trade costs in Latin America and the Caribbean, by sector and importing region, 2015

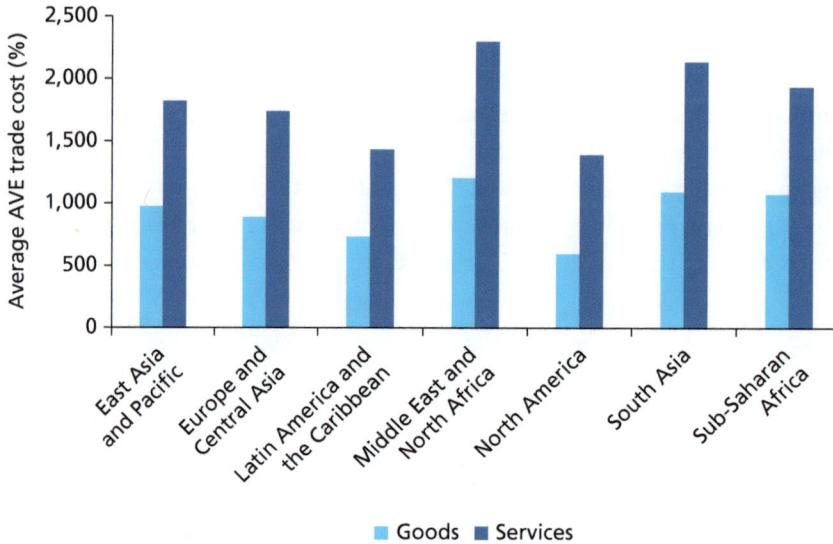

Source: Eora global supply chain database (https://worldmrio.com/), using methodology of Novy 2013.

Note: AVE = ad valorem equivalent.

What would GVC integration in the region look like if all Latin American and Caribbean countries reduced trade costs in services sectors by a proportion equal to the average observed effect of a services PTA (scenario 1)? Using a standard gravity model, Borchert and Di Ubaldo (2021) found that a two-year lagged impact of a services PTA was equal to a trade increase of 19.7 percent, on average. Both their model and the one used here have the same structural relationship between trade costs and trade flows, so mapping trade-flow impacts to trade-cost impacts is straightforward. Concretely, a 19.7 percent increase in the value of trade implies a decrease in trade costs of around 5 percent.[3]

Considering this change in a policy context shows the role of sectoral characteristics in determining the degree of liberalization. In maritime transportation, a 5 percent reduction in trade costs implies a reduction in a country's Organisation for Economic Co-operation and Development (OECD) Services Trade Restrictiveness Index (STRI) score of 0.04 points, relative to a sectoral baseline of 0.33 for Brazil, 0.20 for Chile, 0.27 for Costa Rica, and 0.27 for Mexico, based on estimates by Shepherd (2020). In telecommunications, by contrast, the same change would bring a much larger STRI reduction in relative terms—a reduction of 0.16 points, starting from a sectoral baseline of 0.28 in Brazil, 0.23 in Chile, 0.22 in Costa Rica, and 0.20 in Mexico. And in financial services, the needed reduction would be 0.04 points, starting from a sectoral baseline of 0.47 in Brazil, 0.21 in Chile, 0.21 in Costa Rica, and 0.37 in Mexico.

As these examples make clear, the thought experiment implies different levels of ambition in policy liberalization depending on country baselines and sectoral characteristics.

The above analysis does not take into account the difficulties inherent in making service policy changes preferential (Miroudot and Shepherd 2014). For comparison, a simulation of making the same policy change multilaterally—that is, through MFN liberalization applied to all trading partners, not just those in the region—uses the Asian Development Bank's multiregion input-output table, which incorporates data on 10 Latin American and Caribbean countries (scenario 2).

Headline simulation results from a 5 percent cut in intraregional services trade costs are exactly as would be expected. Latin American and Caribbean countries see increases in total exports of services, expressed as a 25.5 percent increase in intraregional trade but a –0.16 percent decrease in exports to extraregional partners. But the impact on GVC integration is relatively small (figure 5.11). For intraregional trade, where the overall increase in exports is very large, the sum of backward and forward GVC integration increases from 16.8 percent to 16.9 percent. With other countries, where exports fall overall, the sum of GVC integration goes from 23.55 percent to 23.58 percent.

Figure 5.11   GVC integration simulation results for services trade only between Latin America and the Caribbean and partners, by liberalization scenario

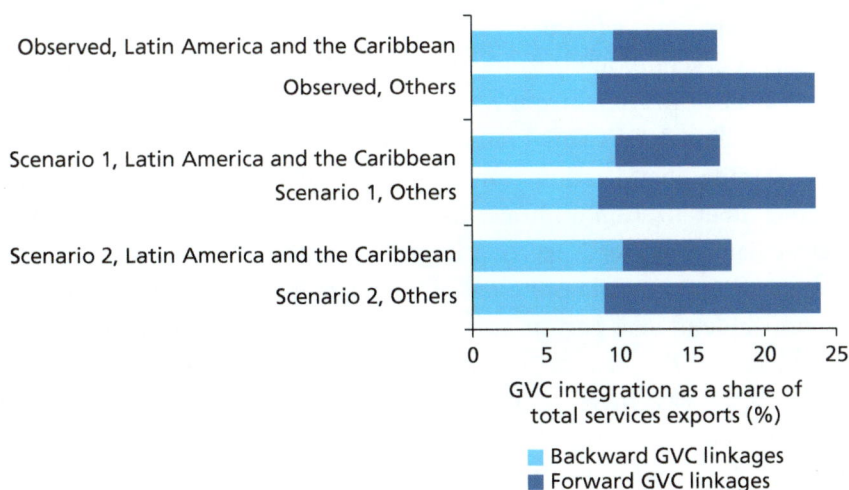

GVC integration as a share of total services exports (%)

■ Backward GVC linkages
■ Forward GVC linkages

Source: World Bank.

Note: In scenario 1, all Latin American and Caribbean countries reduce trade costs in services sectors by a proportion equal to the average observed effect of a preferential trade agreement (PTA) for services trade. In scenario 2, the same policy change is multilateral—that is, through most-favored-nation (MFN) liberalization applied to all trading partners, not just those in the Latin American and Caribbean region. "Backward global value chain (GVC) linkages" refers to the share of imported inputs in a country's exports. "Forward GVC linkages" refers to the share of exports that are inputs for another country's export production.

These changes are certainly small, though context is important. Latin American and Caribbean countries saw their total GVC integration fall from 18.7 percent of gross exports in 2007 to 17.5 percent in 2017, about 0.1 percentage point per year on average. So, the regional integration experiment would see Latin American and Caribbean countries increase intraregional GVC integration by the equivalent of around two years' worth of the previous decade's decline—a significant reversal. By contrast, GVC linkages with countries outside the region would increase by the equivalent of less than one year's worth of the previous decade's decline.

So, while the absolute impacts are not large, they demonstrate that regional integration that reduces trade costs can promote GVC deepening between regional partners. This could come at a small cost relative to GVC deepening with other partners. Even so, the simulation is highly stylized in that it applies the same change in trade costs to trade in final and intermediate services alike. If the policy shock applied to intermediate services only, the incentives facing producers would change more markedly, and a larger GVC effect would be expected. Nonetheless, the results as they are put a GVC spin on the standard "trade creation versus trade diversion" debate, suggesting limits to the effectiveness of common trade policies to directly promote greater GVC integration in services even when changes in overall trade patterns are large.

Comparing intraregional liberalization and MFN liberalization clarifies these points further (as shown in figure 5.11). Aggregate-level results are again predictable: exports within the Latin American and Caribbean region increase by less under MFN liberalization, but the gain is still significant (19.4 percent). There is also an export gain to extraregional partners equivalent to 3.2 percent of the baseline.

From a GVC standpoint, intraregional GVC integration increases more under intraregional liberalization (from 23.6 percent to 23.9 percent), and the same is true of extraregional GVC integration (from 16.8 percent to 17.7 percent). But multilateral trade liberalization would be expected to have a larger impact than intraregional liberalization on prices in Latin American and Caribbean countries. So, intermediate producers receive a larger competitiveness boost from multilateral liberalization than from preferential liberalization in the simulation, and they are therefore able to take part in more-distant sourcing arrangements than under either the baseline scenario or intraregional liberalization. Although preferential integration in this case increases intraregional GVC participation, multilateral liberalization increases it more.

This experiment is specific to Latin America and the Caribbean and does not consider policy changes in other regions, but the result would likely hold elsewhere in light of the mechanism just discussed. And the experiment is stylized in assuming that effectively liberalizing services preferentially is feasible as a matter of policy, even though there is evidence that many service policy reforms in PTAs are, in practice, MFN liberalizations. This point is examined further below, where particular provisions in PTAs are examined using new quantitative analysis.

Effects of service provisions in trade agreements

The extent to which PTAs can alter trade costs on the ground for participants (and nonparticipants) is not known. Borchert and Di Ubaldo (2021), using a gravity model, found that services PTAs can have a large effect on bilateral trade and that the effect is larger for bilateral than for multilateral agreements. Allowing for a two-year implementation lag, a bilateral PTA is associated with an increase in trade of 19.7 percent, compared with only 0.4 percent for a multilateral PTA. Those authors treated the EU differently since it has achieved a far greater integration of services markets than most other agreements. Country pairs in the EU tend to trade 26.0 percent more than other country pairs—substantially more than the bilateral PTA result and far more than the result for other multilateral agreements.

This information on the general trade-promoting effects of PTAs is important for policy. Further investigation into the structure and content of PTAs might identify particular factors that matter the most for lowering trade costs and boosting trade. Borchert and Di Ubaldo (2021) used the World Bank's Deep Trade Agreements database to examine this question. They found that bilateral and multilateral PTAs differ systematically in structure and provisions: bilateral agreements are more likely to use a negative list than a positive list approach to scheduling, are more likely to include a range of additional regulations, and are likely to have more chapters dealing with services. Such differences in structure and content could explain, at least in part, the difference in trade impacts discussed above.

Among agreements' specific provisions, a standstill clause (a provision locking in the current level of applied restrictions), provisions that provide for comprehensive dispute settlement (including both state-state and investor-state components), and provisions that use the US definition of market access (omitting foreign equity limitations as in US free trade agreements) are associated with trade increases about 10–16 percent higher than under agreements without these provisions (Borchert and Di Ubaldo 2021). Looking more broadly at different types of agreements based on the configuration of key provisions, the authors show that ambitious policy configurations, as they define them, increase trade by 15–65 percent. Their single sector gravity model is limited in its ability to identify changes in GVC participation. But their results on the links between PTA provisions and changes in trade costs can be used to influence the simulation reported above: if particular patterns of excluding provisions are associated with a given change in trade costs, the simulation then shows that change to be linked to changes in GVC participation once intersectoral links are accounted for.

Agreement structure and content therefore constitute important factors determining the extent to which trade costs are reduced and trade promoted. But an important aspect falling outside this analysis is the content of the schedules of commitments themselves—the policy ceilings in individual sectors that countries agree to beyond the structure and rules in the main text of the agreement.

Evidence is limited, but Shepherd et al. (2019), examining the EU–Canada CETA, found that it contains little effective liberalization of applied policies. To reconcile that finding with Borchert and Di Ubaldo's (2021) results requires a recognition that an agreement's structure can reduce trade costs by establishing rules and institutions surrounding trade in services. But an additional variable, which lies outside the Deep Trade Agreements database, is the extent to which countries adopt ambitious policy bindings—ceilings on restrictions rather than applied policies—in individual sectors.

Another possibility is that countries are more or less ambitious in implementing legislation than suggested by the bound policy ceilings they adopt in their PTA schedules of commitments. As yet, there is no systematic evidence comparing countries' STRI scores based on the policies they implement with the STRIs of their PTA partners. Only the OECD STRI provides evidence on a single set of PTA arrangements from the European Economic Area (EEA). Benz and Gonzales (2019) showed that applied policies are much more liberal than bound MFN policies. Although other PTAs do not go as far in liberalizing policies as the EEA, a systematic cataloging of applied treatments might disclose more substantial liberalization than is suggested by schedules of commitments, beyond the trade-promoting effects of shared rules and institutions.

Contents of Latin American and Caribbean services trade agreements

Given the evidence on the types of PTA provisions that are important for services trade, it makes sense to ask about their presence or absence in Latin American and Caribbean agreements, building on the analysis of Borchert and Di Ubaldo (2021). To what extent do the Latin American and Caribbean agreements have the provisions Borchert and Di Ubaldo empirically showed to have the strongest trade-promoting effects—specifically the following:

- Comprehensive dispute settlement provisions, both state-state and investor-state components
- A ratchet provision implying that unilateral liberalization is bound
- A standstill provision locking in the current level of applied restrictions
- US market access obligation, as defined in US free trade agreements—that is, omitting foreign equity limitations.

Borchert and Di Ubaldo (2021) addressed the associations between these provisions and trade flows, but their approach did not make clear the underlying economic mechanisms. From a conceptual standpoint, their argument distinguished between provisions—rules and institutions—and effective policy liberalization provisions at the sectoral level.

Dispute settlement is clearly a rules issue. Comprehensive dispute settlement provisions could increase certainty and facilitate both trade transactions and the investment relationships that support them. The other three provisions relate to effective policy liberalization A standstill means that the agreement locks in each party's current level of policy restrictiveness and thereby keeps a close relationship between applied and bound policies. GATS does not contain such a provision, so most countries have policy bindings that do not even reflect their effective degree of liberalization in 1995, when GATS came into force, let alone 25 years later. A ratchet provision creates a similar obligation. If a country unilaterally liberalizes, a ratchet provision locks in that new degree of policy liberalization as binding, thereby limiting the gap between applied and bound provisions. The market access regime relates to the types of restrictions identified in the agreement as being generally prohibited. GATS uses a six-category system:

- Limitations on the number of service providers
- Limitations on the value of service transactions
- Limitations on the number of service transactions
- Limitations on numbers of natural persons involved in services trade
- Measures that require particular legal entities for market entry
- Limitations on foreign equity participation.

Although the United States approach incorporates only the first five of these elements, Borchert and Di Ubaldo (2021) found that it promotes trade more strongly than the GATS approach.

The World Bank's Deep Trade Agreements database identifies 27 Latin American and Caribbean intraregional PTAs that have a services chapter or a relevant set of service provisions (table 5.1). Three intraregional agreements representing 11 percent of the total—the Andean Community, the Caribbean Community and Common Market (CARICOM), and the Southern Common Market (MERCOSUR)—do not contain any of these provisions. Borchert and Di Ubaldo's (2021) analysis suggests that they therefore do not have any trade-promoting effects as a result of these provisions. At the other extreme, 10 agreements (37 percent) have all the provisions, which combine to increase trade among members by 41 percent.[4] The remainder lie between these two points, with a trade increase of 10.6–25.0 percent. On average, Latin American and Caribbean intraregional agreements boost trade by 27.7 percent based on whether they include the four provisions described above: dispute settlement, ratchet, standstill, and the US market access.

The agreements with the strongest trade-promoting effects tend to be outside the southern part of the region, except Chile. Several countries—such as Chile, Colombia, Mexico, and Peru—are in more than one agreement that contain all the identified provisions. There is likely a kind of general ratchet effect in signing PTAs: once a provision has been locked in with an important trading partner, it is more likely that it will be included in subsequent agreements because its political economy "cost" has effectively been sunk.

A similar analysis can address the Latin American and Caribbean extraregional agreements in the database—those that have at least one Latin American and Caribbean

Table 5.1   Key services trade provisions in Latin American and Caribbean intraregional PTAs

PTA	US market access	Standstill	Ratchet	Dispute settlement	Trade increase (%)
Central American Common Market (CACM)	0	0	1	1	24.97
Caribbean Community and Common Market (CARICOM)	0	0	0	0	0.00
Andean Community (CAN)	0	0	0	0	0.00
Southern Common Market (MERCOSUR)	0	0	0	0	0.00
Chile–Mexico	0	1	1	1	24.97
Chile–Costa Rica (Chile–Central America)	0	1	1	1	24.97
Chile–El Salvador (Chile–Central America)	0	1	1	1	24.97
Panama–El Salvador (Panama–Central America)	0	1	1	1	24.97
Dominican Republic–Central America–USFTA (CAFTA–DR)	1	1	1	1	41.31
Panama–Costa Rica (Panama–Central America)	0	1	1	1	24.97
Chile–Colombia	1	1	1	1	41.31
Panama–Honduras (Panama–Central America)	0	1	1	1	24.97
Chile–Honduras (Chile–Central America)	0	1	1	1	24.97
Peru–Chile	1	1	1	1	41.31
Dominican Republic–Central America	0	1	1	0	10.63
Peru–Mexico	1	1	1	1	41.31
Chile–Guatemala (Chile–Central America)	0	1	1	1	24.97
Panama–Peru	1	1	1	1	41.31
Colombia–Northern Triangle (El Salvador, Guatemala, Honduras)	1	1	1	1	41.31
Panama–Guatemala (Panama–Central America)	0	1	1	1	24.97
Costa Rica–Peru	1	1	1	1	41.31
Chile–Nicaragua (Chile–Central America)	0	1	1	1	24.97

Continued

Table 5.1 Key services trade provisions in Latin American and Caribbean intraregional PTAs *(continued)*

PTA	US market access	Standstill	Ratchet	Dispute settlement	Trade increase (%)
Mexico–Uruguay	0	1	1	1	24.97
Mexico–Central America	1	1	1	1	41.31
Mexico–Panama	1	1	1	1	41.31
Costa Rica–Colombia	1	1	1	1	41.31
Pacific Alliance	0	1	1	1	24.97

Source: World Bank's Deep Trade Agreements database.

Note: The first four columns show the presence of each type of provision in each agreement, with 1 indicating that the agreement has the indicated provision. The final column calculates the trade increase associated with a country pair both being members of the agreement, using the estimates contained in Borchert and Di Ubaldo (2021). EFTA = European Free Trade Agreement; PTA = preferential trade agreement; USFTA = US Free Trade Agreement.

partner and at least one extraregional partner. The database includes 38 agreements in this category that have a services chapter or equivalent service coverage (table 5.2). Of the 38 agreements, 13 (34 percent) do not have any of the identified provisions and therefore do not have any trade-increasing effect from them.[5] The agreements without the four provisions are all with the EU, EFTA, or China as partners. So the choice of extraregional partner, as well as the age of the agreement, seems to influence the types of provisions included. At the other extreme, 14 agreements (37 percent) have all four provisions.[6] Again, except for Chile, it is countries in the northern parts of the Latin American and Caribbean region that tend to have more trade-promoting PTAs with external partners. Other agreements lie between these two extremes, with trade increases of 14–25 percent.

On average, Latin American and Caribbean agreements with partners outside the region have a trade-increasing effect of 21.5 percent. That is less than the comparable figure for intraregional agreements, which is surprising given the evidence presented earlier that trade costs tend to be lower and GVC participation higher with extraregional partners. An important nuance is that the EU and EFTA agreements have none of the four provisions, bringing down the average. If those agreements are excluded, the average is 29.2 percent, which is higher than for intraregional agreements. So, agreements with European partners typically lack the provisions that Borchert and Di Ubaldo (2021) found to have strong trade-increasing effects. But since these countries are relatively distant from the Latin American and Caribbean region, their possibly higher trade costs would weigh less in overall figures.

Another important nuance relates to other provisions in services PTAs. Each agreement, of course, has far more than four provisions. Borchert and Di Ubaldo (2021) suggest that such other areas could be important, particularly for trade in value added and GVC participation. But the analysis of these other areas is not as detailed as that of

Table 5.2   Key services trade provisions in Latin American and Caribbean extraregional PTAs

PTA	US market access	Standstill	Ratchet	Dispute settlement	Trade increase (%)
North American Free Trade Agreement (NAFTA)	1	1	1	1	41.31
Canada–Chile	0	1	1	1	24.97
EU–Mexico	0	0	0	0	0.00
EFTA–Mexico	0	0	0	0	0.00
Canada–Costa Rica	0	0	0	1	14.34
US–Chile	1	1	1	1	41.31
EU–Chile	0	0	0	0	0.00
Korea, Rep.–Chile	0	1	1	1	24.97
EFTA–Chile	0	0	0	0	0.00
Japan–Mexico	0	1	1	1	24.97
Chile–China	0	0	0	0	0.00
Chile–Japan	0	1	1	1	24.97
Panama–Chile	0	1	1	1	24.97
EU–CARIFORUM EPA	0	0	0	0	0.00
Australia–Chile	1	1	1	1	41.31
Peru–Singapore	1	1	1	1	41.31
Canada–Peru	1	1	1	1	41.31
Peru–China	0	0	0	1	14.34
El Salvador–Honduras–Taiwan, China	1	1	1	1	41.31
Colombia–Mexico	0	1	1	0	10.63
EFTA–Peru	0	0	0	0	0.00
Guatemala–Taiwan, China	0	1	1	1	24.97
Peru–Korea, Rep.	0	1	1	1	24.97
EFTA–Colombia	0	0	0	0	0.00
Canada–Colombia	1	1	1	1	41.31
Japan–Peru	1	1	1	1	41.31
China–Costa Rica	0	0	0	0	0.00
US–Colombia	1	1	1	1	41.31
US–Panama	1	1	1	1	41.31
EU–Colombia and Peru	0	0	0	0	0.00

Continued

Table 5.2 Key services trade provisions in Latin American and Caribbean extraregional PTAs *(continued)*

PTA	US market access	Standstill	Ratchet	Dispute settlement	Trade increase (%)
EU–Central America	0	0	0	0	0.00
Canada–Panama	1	1	1	1	41.31
Costa Rica–Singapore	0	1	1	1	24.97
Hong Kong SAR, China–Chile	0	0	0	0	0.00
EFTA–Central America (Costa Rica and Panama)	0	0	0	0	0.00
Canada–Honduras	1	1	1	1	41.31
Korea, Rep.–Colombia	1	1	1	1	41.31
CPTPP	1	1	1	1	41.31

Source: World Bank's Deep Trade Agreements database.

Note: The first four columns show the presence of each type of provision in each agreement, with 1 indicating that the agreement has the indicated provision. The final column calculates the trade increase associated with a country pair both being members of the agreement, using the estimates contained in Borchert and Di Ubaldo (2021). CARIFORUM = European Community-Caribbean Forum; CPTPP = Comprehensive and Progressive Agreement for Trans-Pacific Partnership; EFTA = European Free Trade Agreement; EPA = Economic Partnership Agreement; PTA = preferential trade agreement; SAR = Special Administrative Region.

the four provision just discussed. These issues are best examined from the perspective of reconciling the content of PTAs with the evidence presented above on trade costs.

More than half the Latin American and Caribbean region's PTAs have specific provisions that clarify the scope of presence of natural persons in the context of services trade (figure 5.12). The prevalence of these provisions is comparable between intraregional and extraregional agreements. However, the nature of specific provisions governing mode 4 trade (movement of natural persons) can be quite different between intraregional and extraregional agreements. More than twice the proportion of extraregional agreements contain provisions on licensing and standards, and nearly three times the proportion of extraregional agreements contain provisions on mutual recognition—both important ways of facilitating mode 4 trade. And although necessity tests (provisions that licensing requirements and technical standards are "necessary") are relatively uncommon in Latin American and Caribbean agreements, they are more common in intraregional agreements than extraregional ones. The general picture that emerges for mode 4 trade is that, although the basic framework is in place in both intraregional and extraregional agreements, the latter tend to go further in including detailed provisions that can substantially contribute to liberalization.

Another cluster of provisions identified by Borchert and Di Ubaldo (2021) relates to GATS mode 3 trade—sales by foreign affiliates. The main issue relates to investment (figure 5.13). The data show that Latin American and Caribbean intraregional

Figure 5.12   Inclusion of selected mode 4 service provisions in Latin American and Caribbean PTAs, by trade partner location, 2017

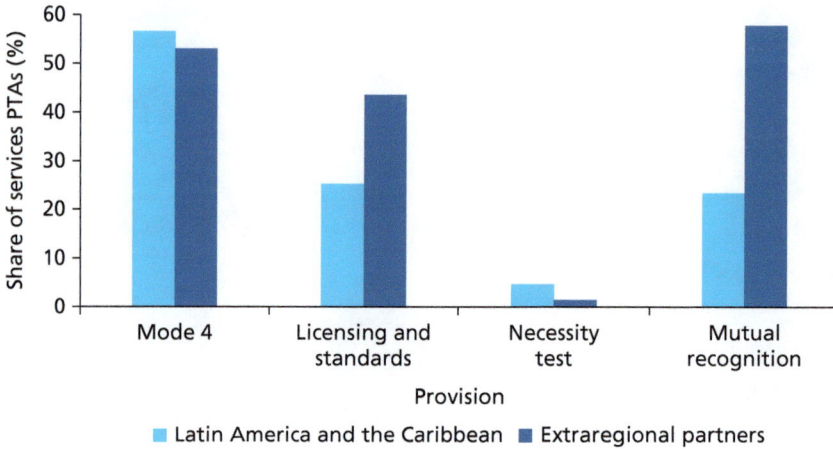

Source: World Bank's Deep Trade Agreements database.

Note: The figure shows the percentage of country pairs in preferential trade agreements (PTAs) whose agreement covers each of the four provisions shown. Under the General Agreement on Trade in Services (GATS) modes of supply, mode 4 is "movement of natural persons." Here, the "Mode 4" provision captures the existence of specific provisions covering the movement of service providers. "Licensing and standards" are aspects of domestic regulation that affect the ability of natural persons to provide services internationally. The "necessity test" in an agreement says whether licensing requirements and technical standards are "necessary." "Mutual recognition" occurs when the partner countries recognize each other's certification of service providers' qualifications—an important issue for natural persons providing services internationally.

Figure 5.13   Inclusion of selected investment provisions in Latin American and Caribbean PTAs, by trade partner location, 2017

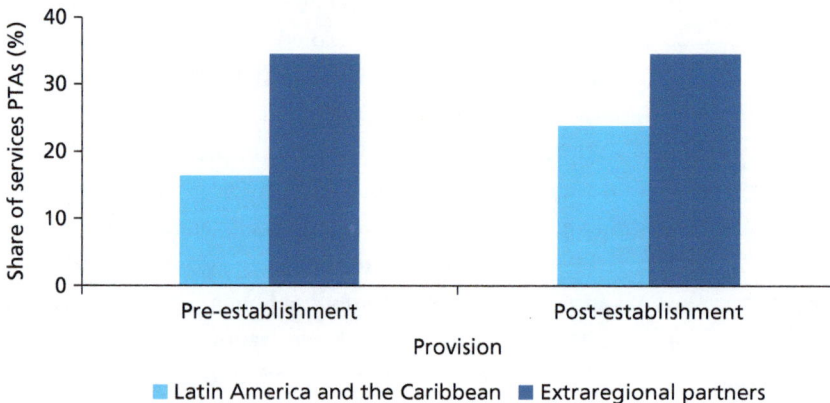

Source: World Bank's Deep Trade Agreements database.

Note: The figure shows the percentage of country pairs in preferential trade agreements (PTAs) whose agreement includes liberalizing provisions concerning investment, such as most-favored-nation treatment, either before or after establishment.

agreements are less likely to contain liberalizing measures on investment—such as MFN treatment both pre- and post-establishment—than are extraregional agreements. The difference is substantial—twice as high as for pre-establishment rules. As was the case for mode 4 trade, the evidence for mode 3 trade suggests that intraregional PTAs may not go as far as extraregional agreements in promoting provisions that can effectively liberalize services trade.

Taking this evidence together suggests that once the perspective is broadened to include a wider range of potentially relevant provisions, intraregional agreements are seen, on average, as less ambitious in scope and coverage for services than extraregional agreements.

So, although GATS mode 1 (cross-border supply) should not be neglected, particularly in light of the rise of digital trade, effective liberalization of trade in modes 3 and 4 is still a prerequisite for PTAs to significantly affect the pattern of production sharing and value-added trade typical of the GVC trading environment (box 5.1).

Box 5.1   Digital services in PTAs

The impact of the COVID-19 pandemic has varied substantially across sectors. A key determinant of that impact is the ability of service providers to work digitally. Services that require in-person contact have been hard-hit, but those that have moved online have generally done better.

The inclusion of provisions in preferential trade agreements (PTAs) that refer explicitly to e-commerce or digital trade has evolved significantly in recent years, according to the Trade Agreements Provisions on Electronic-commerce and Data (TAPED) dataset, a universe of 191 PTAs concluded in the past 20 years.[a] Currently, 116 PTAs include e-commerce or digital trade provisions, and 86 have dedicated chapters on these topics (figure B5.1.1). PTAs are highly heterogeneous. They address issues ranging from customs duties and nondiscriminatory

Figure B5.1.1   Number of PTAs with e-commerce or digital trade provisions, 2000–20

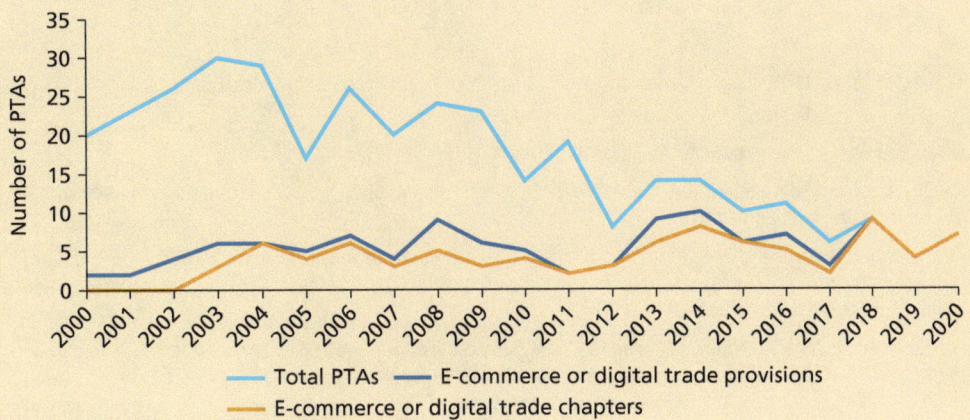

Source: Trade Agreements Provisions on Electronic-commerce and Data (TAPED) dataset.

Note: PTA = preferential trade agreement.

Continued

Box 5.1   Digital services in PTAs (*continued*)

treatment of digital products to electronic signatures; paperless trading; unsolicited electronic messages (spam); consumer protection; and data protection, flows, and localization.

Around 53 percent of the PTAs in Latin American and Caribbean countries have e-commerce or digital trade provisions (62 agreements, 47 chapters) (figure B5.1.2). Twenty-nine of these agreements have been concluded with developed countries and 33 with other developing countries, most in the Latin American and Caribbean region (26 agreements).[b]

These statistics reflect the overall trend that PTAs with e-commerce and digital trade provisions involve both developed and developing countries.[c] Around 49 percent of the PTAs were negotiated between developed and developing countries and 47 percent between developing countries.

Figure B5.1.2   Incidence of Latin American and Caribbean PTAs with e-commerce and digital trade provisions, by partner country type, as of 2020

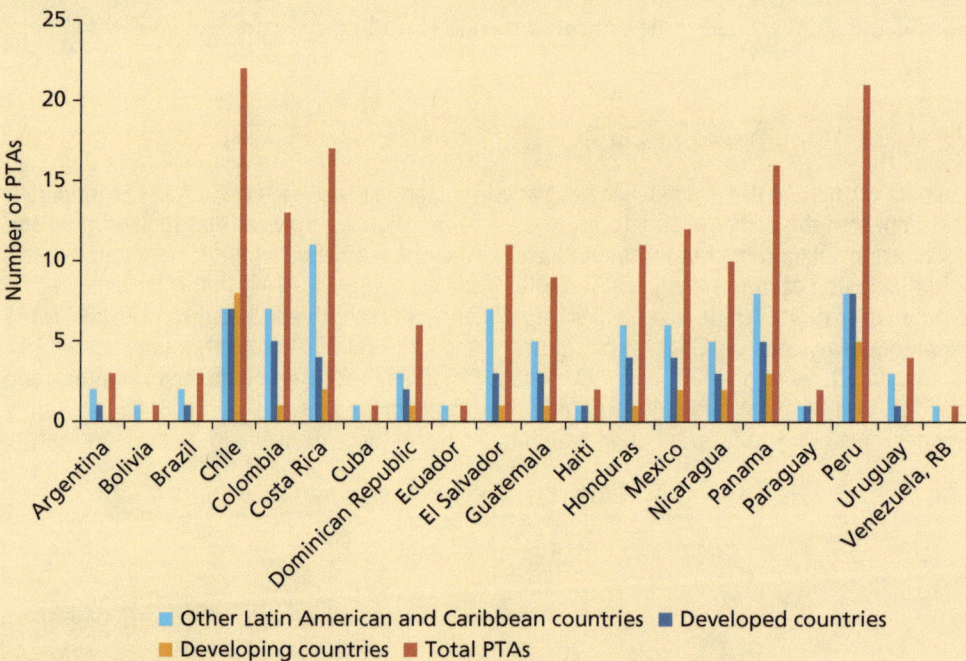

Legend: ■ Other Latin American and Caribbean countries   ■ Developed countries   ■ Developing countries   ■ Total PTAs

Source: Trade Agreements Provisions on Electronic-commerce and Data (TAPED) dataset.

Note: The data for "developed" or "developing" countries are according to United Nations classifications. PTA = preferential trade agreement.

a. All the data cited in this box come from the TAPED dataset, which includes detailed mapping and coding of PTAs—chapters, provisions, annexes, and side documents that directly or indirectly regulate e-commerce and data flows (Burri and Polanco 2020).

b. The earliest Latin American and Caribbean PTA with these provisions is the 2002 Canada–Costa Rica Free Trade Agreement (FTA), which included a Joint Statement on Global Electronic Commerce. In 2003, the Chile–European Union Association Agreement included e-commerce provisions in the text of the treaty. The first Latin American PTA having a dedicated e-commerce chapter is the 2004 Chile–United States FTA. In 2008, the Nicaragua–Taiwan, China FTA began the inclusion of provisions on data flows as part of its cooperation commitments.

c. Country classification as "developed" or "developing" is according to United Nations definitions.

Continued

Box 5.1   Digital services in PTAs (*continued*)

Overall, PTAs with e-commerce or digital trade provisions are mainly interregional. Yet the TAPED data show that around one-third of them have at least one Latin American and Caribbean country as a contracting party (34 treaties). The level of detail in the agreements has also increased over the years.

In Latin American and Caribbean PTAs, e-commerce and digital provisions are found mostly in dedicated chapters or sections or in the intellectual property chapter. They can also be found in annexes, joint statements, and side letters. When available, data flow provisions are also found in e-commerce or digital trade chapters or sections, but they are most commonly in chapters on specific services, notably telecommunication and financial services.

Source: Polanco 2021.

Borchert and Di Ubaldo (2021), again using an econometric model, provide some preliminary evidence. Their results need to be interpreted cautiously, as the determinants of value-added trade are not recognized as settled in the literature in the same ways as determinants of gross trade. They find that ambitious approaches are significantly associated with exports of service value added.

Figure 5.14 confirms this finding using a simple correlation. The x-axis shows the number of service provisions for each country pair, based on a count of all service provisions in the Deep Trade Agreements database. Panel a shows the percentage of backward GVC linkages in total services exports, and panel b shows the percentage of forward linkages. In both cases, the line of best fit slopes upward, meaning that broader service coverage in PTAs is associated with increased GVC links.

There is thus some preliminary evidence that deep PTAs can increase GVC integration in services, likely through a mechanism related to lower trade costs (as shown by simulation evidence here) but dependent on specific PTA provisions. The data suggest that Latin American and Caribbean countries tend to be fairly selective in the types of service-related provisions they include in their agreements. The data also suggest that the choice might be motivated in part by partner demands: broad-based coverage is more typical in extraregional agreements than in intraregional ones. This finding concurs with the initial empirical results, discussed above, that Latin American and Caribbean GVC integration in services tends to be stronger with extraregional partners than with intraregional ones.

Implementation of services trade agreements

Most PTAs are negotiated in terms of bindings—that is, ceilings on restrictiveness, rather than applied policies. But the question remains open as to how much countries go beyond bindings to effectively liberalize market access. To analyze this question rigorously would require collecting data on applied service policies within a large number

Figure 5.14   Number of service provisions in PTAs in relation to bilateral backward and forward GVC linkages, 2015

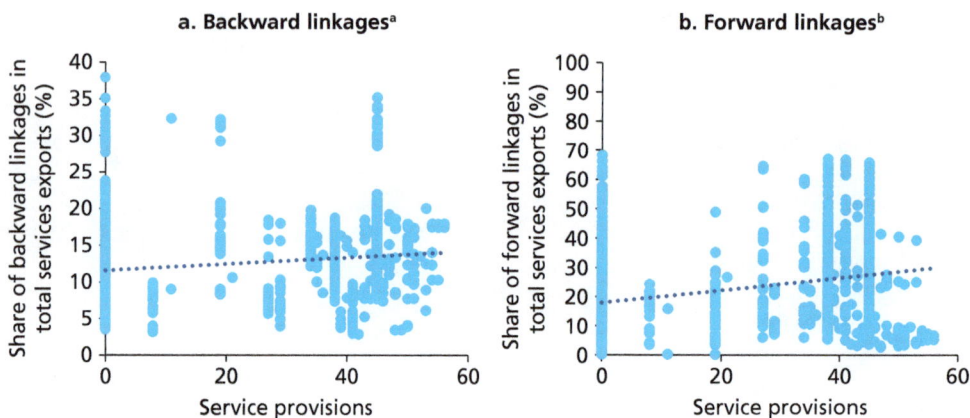

Source: World Bank's Deep Trade Agreements database; Mattoo, Rocha, and Ruta 2020.

Note: In both figure panels, the x-axis shows the number of service provisions for each country pair (blue dot) in a preferential trade agreement (PTA), based on a count of all service provisions in the Deep Trade Agreements database.

a. In panel a, the y-axis shows the percentage of backward global value chain (GVC) linkages—the share of imported inputs in total services exports.

b. In panel b, the y-axis shows the percentage of forward GVC linkages—the share of total services exports that are inputs for other countries' export production.

of PTAs, which has not been done by international organizations, except the coverage of the EEA countries by the OECD. Box 5.2 provides evidence from Brazil on specific commitments in services trade agreements and the gap between bindings and applied policies (called the "water").

This chapter has focused on legal provisions in agreements. But to what extent are provisions implemented in practice? Even highly ambitious trade agreements often lead to little practical liberalization, as in the case of the Canada–EU CETA (Shepherd et al. 2019). By contrast, the implementation of EEA service provisions has radically lowered the trade costs facing foreign suppliers (Benz and Gonzales 2019).

Implementation means incorporating commitments into legal frameworks. To do so, governments' procedures and actions vary since their requirements can be vastly different. For some countries, legal implementation implies just issuing government decrees. For others, it requires passing laws through the legislative branch or even revising, through the judicial branch, the compatibility of new commitments with constitutional law. Examples of these revisions include (a) commitments to ensure the neutrality of regulatory bodies (such as telecommunications regulators), whereby a legal separation is required between the regulator or supervisor and any public service provider; or (b) commitments that grant national treatment to foreign companies and so imply the derogation of discriminatory laws.

Box 5.2   Specific commitments and the "water": Evidence from Brazil

Echandi (2020), using an index methodology, analyzes specific commitments in Brazilian trade agreements relative to the maximum possible level of commitments.

There is a significant gap between (a) the level of concessions on market access and national treatment assumed by Brazil in its international agreements, and (b) the level that the country could actually implement, even assuming that Brazil would not undertake any commitment to reform any existing law or regulation.

This "water" between applied policies and international commitments is the lowest in the case of the Southern Common Market (MERCOSUR) Services Protocol, equivalent to 38 percent. For the 2018 Brazil–Chile Free Trade Agreement (FTA), it is 62 percent; for the 2019 MERCOSUR–EU FTA, it is 87 percent; and for GATS, it is as high as 95 percent.

Brazil's treaties tend not to include mechanisms (a) to ensure full transparency of nonliberalized barriers to services trade, or (b) to lock in unilateral openings that could occur in future ratchets. But Brazil could make its service treaties work better with domestic trade reforms through minor technical steps. These should not entail any political cost or reform of the regulatory status quo for services. With these technical steps, Brazil could quickly catch up with the commitments shown by Republic of Korea and the Pacific Alliance countries (Chile, Colombia, Mexico, and Peru). In other words, Brazil could quickly position itself among the international leaders of countries by undertaking service commitments in its trade agreements without a single reform to any national law or domestic regulation.

Brazil's evolution in the architecture of its trade in services chapters could be better leveraged to make these treaties more useful, thus complementing the government's current efforts to liberalize trade in services, attract investment, and foster policy coherence. Without undertaking political costs in eliminating additional restrictions to trade in services, agreements negotiated by Brazil could be adjusted to significantly improve the country's capacity to

- Lock in the existing opening for trade in services in Brazil;
- Increase the confidence of service providers by improving regulatory transparency and the predictability of remaining barriers to trade; and
- Lock in future domestic reforms, reducing services trade protectionism.

Source: Echandi 2020.

The legal implementation of commitments that change regulatory frameworks face several challenges. Depending on the internal procedures, specific stakeholders or interested groups might oppose the change in the status quo of certain provisions. Examples are the public sector monopolies in telecommunications and insurance in Costa Rica, adjustments to the television quota in Colombia, and the specific nationality of lawyers in Chile.

For administrative implementation, the functioning of government agencies and delegated authorities (for example, engineering boards) that intervene in the supply of a service must abide by specific provisions in agreements. This is the case for some transparency commitments. It usually implies developing particular functions (such as contact points) and procedures (such as providing information on application decisions). A specific challenge occurs when the obligations introduce criteria to evaluate government behavior, such as the objective and impartial administration of domestic regulation commitment measures.

The administrative implementation of commitments to make institutions operate under specific features and characteristics is also challenging. For some institutions, changes and adjustments might be easy. For others, owing to resource limitations or institutional deficiencies, they could be difficult. For example, some telecommunications obligations call for stronger supervisors to investigate and impose exemplary sanctions where doing so would require the structural reform of the agencies.

Additional challenges arise when commitments regarding measures adopted or maintained by one party—at all levels of government (central, regional, or local) or by nongovernmental institutions with delegated powers—affect the supply of services by agents in another country. Coordination and monitoring in these two dimensions represent clear challenges. This is especially challenging when multiple licenses are required to provide services, as is generally the case in the health, financial, and telecommunications sectors.

Types of commitments

Commitments in PTAs can be categorized into two broad types:

- Obligations "to do" that refer to specific guarantees to access a market
- Obligations "to abstain" that limit some government actions.

In most cases, these commitments do not require any change. Most countries can easily commit *not* to change a legal or administrative regime, according to the agreed-upon regulations (that is, nondiscrimination for specific service providers). Other commitments require either legal or administrative changes. An additional type of commitment refers to future changes that might imply the maintenance of certain treatment conditions (standstill) or a commitment, once treatment is changed to make it less restrictive, not to regress (ratchet).

Another variation among regulations in PTAs is that they could be mandatory, voluntary, subject to reservations and limitations, or requiring best efforts. The treatment varies based on the type of regulation. For example, regulations relating to such characteristics as market access, local presence, national treatment, MFN, performance requirements, or the nationality of directors are generally mandatory. Still, they normally allow for sectoral or specific reservations.

Treatment also varies with acceptability to the negotiating parties, usually given the development of the legal and regulatory framework and related institutions. Regulations evolve and, in some cases, they go from best practices and soft law to hard law. When regulations are voluntary or call for best efforts, challenges arise over the willingness of national agents to incorporate them into their own regulation and practices, even though they contribute to the framework of service provision and anticipate deeper provisions in future agreements.

Additional challenges are associated with the constant monitoring of legal or regulatory changes, ensuring they do not go against or contradict commitments. And this can be complicated by the multiple and varied institutions regulating and intervening in the heterogeneous world of services.

Timing of implementation

The time for implementing commitments presents another relevant question (ADB 2008). Identifying preparedness to assume specific obligations starts before negotiations, but sometimes these challenges appear during negotiations when governments are facing the implications of accepting new commitments. This is particularly relevant for services trade negotiations since they tend to consolidate only the status quo for obligations such as market access, nondiscrimination, and other protection commitments.

As members of the WTO, Latin American and Caribbean countries have internalized the types of commitments associated with GATS. After 1995, they received the support of the WTO Secretariat in this process. The process is usually reflected in the commitments' broad application, beyond any limited consolidation in the schedules. The risk of noncompliance is reduced by the constant monitoring of all parties by the WTO.

In most cases, the implementation of commitments is associated with the entry into force of PTAs. But some agreements establish specific times for the implementation and enforcement of particular regulations. And agreements can incorporate time frames for revising specific commitments, including the eventual negotiations.

The development of trade after an agreement's entry into force entails constant monitoring, consultation, and the administration of disputes. Because access to international markets depends on effective implementation of other parties' commitments, enforceability is essential. This aspect of implementation is highlighted in high-income countries (EU 2018; Luff 2011). Trade diplomacy ensures that the guarantees offered by agreements are correctly implemented. And the support of export promotion agencies should not be underrated, since their market intelligence activities monitor the real access and conditions that countries provide to foreign services and service suppliers.

Ultimately, implementing commitments depends on leadership and the availability of resources, normally those of the ministries in charge of trade. Leadership often requires coordinating different entities and working with the legislative branch and with regulatory agencies. It also requires interacting and regularly consulting with other stakeholders, including private sector agents and civil society associations.

CONCLUSION AND POLICY IMPLICATIONS

Evidence shows that Latin American and Caribbean countries' integration into GVCs through services is greater with extraregional partners than with intraregional ones. This result is somewhat unusual, since GVCs typically have a strong regional focus because trade costs determine the location of economic activity (ITC 2017).

Where Latin America and the Caribbean has its strongest GVC linkages in services, forward linkages rather than backward ones are prevalent—that is, supplying inputs for the production of partner country exports rather than the sourcing of intermediate services for Latin American and Caribbean firms' own production of exports. For intraregional trade, by contrast, backward linkages play a stronger role. So, the intraregional services trade is somewhat unusual, both because of the relatively underdeveloped nature of the region's GVC linkages in services and because its pattern of integration is different from its extraregional interactions.

A quantitative trade model suggests that, to the extent that PTAs reduce trade costs, they both boost aggregate trade flows and also shift the character of that trade modestly toward increased GVC linkages. Although trade diversion is weak in Latin America and the Caribbean, it has potential, both in the traditional sense of shifting supply from globally efficient producers to regional partners and in the sense of disrupting extraregional GVCs while deepening regional GVC linkages. But PTAs would have to make significant reductions in trade costs, with consequent large changes in recorded trade, before a substantial change occurred in the relative composition of trade in favor of GVC linkages.

Recent research shows that the agreement structure and, particularly, the ambition to increase GATS modes 3 and 4 trade are crucial for ensuring trade promotion through deep PTAs and for supporting production sharing and GVC integration. Although Latin American and Caribbean intraregional agreements have nondiscrimination rules basically like those in agreements with external partners, the available data suggest that the intraregional agreements are much less ambitious on modes 3 and 4 than the agreements with other regions. Even for mode 1 trade, using the specific example of digital trade, coverage tends to be more ambitious in extraregional than in intraregional agreements. This may be holding back the development of regional value chains in services.

This result is surprising given the prevalence of more ambitious provisions for mode 3 and mode 4 trade, as well as for digital trade, in the agreements Latin American and Caribbean countries have signed with external partners. The provisions indicate that, in the presence of partner demands, the region's countries are open to bindings in those terms. Given that Latin American and Caribbean countries have already signaled their willingness to abide by such provisions in PTAs with external partners, there is a clear case for revisiting intraregional agreements and importing, if not improving on, such provisions. More empirical evidence is required, but there are suggestions in the data that moving forward in these areas can boost GVC integration in services. Why intraregional agreements tend to be less ambitious is unclear, but a likely possibility is the absence of a large economy pressing Latin American and Caribbean partners on issues such as modes 3 and 4 or digital trade.

How far are agreements put into practice on the ground, and how far does practical liberalization go, even when legal policy bindings may be similar to existing WTO bindings? Further research is needed. Comprehensive data on applied service policies within PTAs are urgently needed. The OECD has shown that the standard STRI approach can easily be adapted to measure preferential, rather than MFN, policies. But a major effort is required to collect and process the necessary data in a timely way, since the OECD's work in this area is limited to the EEA (Benz and Gonzales 2019). Building on the OECD's work to catalog applied preferential service policies in the Latin American and Caribbean region and elsewhere is a clear research priority.

The structure of Latin American and Caribbean PTAs in services suggests that countries can go further in developing GVC linkages in services trade. Given the importance of services—not only as outputs in their own right but also as inputs into production in other sectors—governments should prioritize reinforcing existing regional integration structures by, at a minimum, importing the more-ambitious provisions that have proved politically feasible in agreements with extraregional partners. In addition, addressing possible gaps between the content of agreements and reality on the ground should be on the agenda, though systematic data collection is required to facilitate that process.

NOTES

1. Measurement of backward and forward linkages in the model is related to, but different from, the Borin and Mancini (2019) approach used above. It relies on the more common decomposition of Wang, Wei, and Zhu (2013).

2. For similar findings, see Miroudot, Sauvage, and Shepherd (2013) and WTO (2019).

3. From structural gravity: $\frac{t'}{t} = \exp\left(\frac{b_{rta}}{-\theta}\right)$ where t is trade costs, b is the gravity model coefficient on a trade agreement dummy, and θ is the trade elasticity, which is set equal to 3.68 (the average value for services reported by Egger et al. [2018]).

4. The 10 agreements containing all the provisions are Chile–Colombia, Colombia–Northern Triangle, Costa Rica–Colombia, Costa Rica–Peru, Dominican Republic–Central America, Mexico–Central America, Mexico–Panama, Panama–Peru, Peru–Chile, and Peru–Mexico.

5. Examples of agreements with none of the identified trade-promoting provisions include the EU and EFTA agreements with Mexico, EU–Chile, Chile–China, EU–CARIFORUM, EFTA–Peru, EFTA–Colombia, China–Costa Rica, EU–Colombia and Peru, and EU–Central America.

6. Agreements with all four provisions include those with the United States, as well as Australia–Chile; Peru–Singapore; Canada–Peru; El Salvador/Honduras–Taiwan, China; Canada–Colombia; Japan–Peru; Canada–Panama; Canada–Honduras; Republic of Korea–Colombia; and the Comprehensive and Progressive Agreement for Trans-Pacific Partnership (CPTPP).

REFERENCES

ADB (Asian Development Bank). 2008. *How to Design, Negotiate and Implement a Free Trade Agreement in Asia*. Manila: ADB.

Adlung, R., and S. Miroudot. 2012. "Poison in the Wine? Tracing GATS-Minus Commitments in Regional Trade Agreements." Staff Working Paper ERSD-2012-04, World Trade Organization, Geneva.

Aichele, R., and I. Heiland. 2018. "Where Is the Value Added? Trade Liberalization and Production Networks." *Journal of International Economics* 115: 130–44.

Baldwin, R. 2011. "Trade and Industrialization after Globalization's Second Unbundling: How Building and Joining a Supply Chain Are Different and Why It Matters." Working Paper 17716, National Bureau of Economic Research, Cambridge, MA.

Benz, S., and F. Gonzales. 2019. "Intra-EEA STRI Database: Methodology and Results." Trade Policy Paper No. 223, Organisation for Economic Co-operation and Development, Paris.

Beverelli, C., M. Fiorini, and B. Hoekman. 2017. "Services Trade Policy and Manufacturing Productivity: The Role of Institutions." *Journal of International Economics* 104: 166–82.

Borchert, I., and M. Di Ubaldo. 2021. "Deep Services Trade Agreements and Their Effect on Trade and Value Added." Policy Research Working Paper 9608, World Bank, Washington, DC.

Borchert, I., and A. Mattoo. 2010. "The Crisis Resilience of Services Trade." *Services Industries Journal* 30 (13): 2115–36.

Borin, A., and M. Mancini. 2019. "Measuring What Matters in Global Value Chains and Value Added Trade." Policy Research Working Paper 8804, World Bank, Washington, DC.

Burri, M., and R. Polanco. 2020. "Digital Trade Provisions in Preferential Trade Agreements: Introducing a New Dataset." *Journal of International Economic Law* 23 (1): 187–220.

Caliendo, L., and F. Parro. 2015. "Estimates of the Trade and Welfare Effects of NAFTA." *Review of Economic Studies* 82 (1): 1–44.

Echandi, R. 2020. "To What Extent Do International Trade Agreements on Services Contribute to Government's Efforts to Foster Progressive Liberalization? The Case of Brazil." Unpublished working paper, World Bank, Washington, DC.

Egger, P., M. Larch, S. Nigai, and Y. Yotov. 2018. "Trade Costs in the Global Economy: Measurement, Aggregation, and Decomposition." Staff Working Paper ERSD-2021-2, World Trade Organization, Geneva.

EU (European Union). 2018. *Report on Implementation of EU Free Trade Agreements: 1 January 2017 – 31 December 2017*. Luxembourg: EU.

Helble, M., and B. Shepherd, eds. 2019. *Leveraging Services for Development: Prospects and Policies*. Manila: Asian Development Bank Institute.

Hoekman, B., and B. Shepherd. 2021. "The Future of Global Trade." In *World Economic Situation and Prospects 2021*, 39–70. New York: United Nations.

ITC (International Trade Centre). 2017. *SME Competitiveness Outlook 2017 — The Region: A Door to Global Trade*. Geneva: ITC.

Luff, D. 2011. "Addressing the Implementation of Preferential Trade Agreements: The Law and Practice of the European Union." Policy Brief No. IDB-PB-126, Inter-American Development Bank, Washington, DC.

Mattoo, A., N. Rocha, and M. Ruta, eds. 2020. *Handbook of Deep Trade Agreements*. Washington, DC: World Bank.

Miroudot, S., J. Sauvage, and B. Shepherd. 2013. "Measuring the Cost of International Trade in Services." *World Trade Review* 12 (4): 719–35.

Miroudot, S., and B. Shepherd. 2014. "The Paradox of Preferences: Regional Trade Agreements and Trade Costs in Services." *World Economy* 37 (12): 1751–72.

Novy, D. 2013. "Gravity Redux: Measuring International Trade Costs with Panel Data." *Economic Inquiry* 51 (1): 101–21.

Polanco, R. 2021. "Digital Trade Provisions in Latin American Trade Agreements." Unpublished working paper, World Bank, Washington, DC.

Shepherd, B. 2020. "Structural Gravity, Panel Data, and Policy Effects: Evidence from Trade in Services." Working Paper DTC-2020-4, Developing Trade Consultants, New York.

Shepherd, B., M. Decosterd, C. Castillo Comabella, and D. Stivas. 2019. "EU Exit and Impacts on Northern Ireland's Services Trade." Report prepared for the Department for the Economy, Northern Ireland.

UNCTAD (United Nations Conference on International Trade and Development). 2020. "COVID-19 Drives Large International Trade Declines in 2020." News release, December 9.

Wang, Z., S.-J. Wei, and K. Zhu. 2013. "Quantifying International Production Sharing at the Bilateral and Sector Levels." Working Paper 19677 (revised 2018), National Bureau of Economic Research, Cambridge, MA.

WTO (World Trade Organization). 2019. *World Trade Report 2019: The Future of Services Trade.* Geneva: WTO.

6 State Support: Improving Economic Governance

Bernard Hoekman

KEY MESSAGES

- Preferential trade agreements (PTAs) can improve economic outcomes by enhancing the transparency of state support policies and by serving as a commitment device to bolster the state's adoption of rules against competition-distorting subsidies.
- Most PTAs include provisions on domestic policies, including subsidies. Such provisions usually constrain the government's ability to undo trade policy commitments through domestic measures that discriminate against foreign products.
- Latin American and Caribbean PTA regulations on subsidies and state-owned enterprises (SOEs) are below the world average in their coverage of possible provisions—much shallower than those in the European Union.
- In particular, the region's PTAs do little to subject participating countries to commonly agreed-upon rules of the game for subsidies and SOEs. They also do little to address the need for up-to-date information on subsidies and SOEs.
- PTAs do little to incentivize government engagement with companies that operate or rely on value chains. But the value of PTAs to the business community can grow if mechanisms are built to bring together key actors in regional value chains to identify policy gaps and frictions.

INTRODUCTION

Latin American and Caribbean countries use subsidies and state-owned enterprises (SOEs) intensively. Subsidies are often substantial, in the range of 4 percent of gross domestic product (GDP) for countries reporting data, in contrast to 1.4 percent in

European Union (EU) countries. And SOEs play a large role in many Latin American and Caribbean countries, potentially affecting market competition as well as having potentially large fiscal implications.

Deep trade agreements (DTAs) can help overcome political economy constraints to policy reforms by providing an external anchor for frameworks of state support. Including provisions or commitments that regulate state support to enterprises in trade agreements can reduce national support policies' harm to market competition and reduce adverse cross-border spillover effects. Agreements could include commitments to adopt a competitive neutrality framework in national legislation; adopt a regulation on competition, subsidies, and SOEs; require SOEs to operate on a commercial and nondiscriminatory basis; and expand the mandate of competition authorities to govern subsidies and SOEs.

DTAs can also improve the quality of institutions by requiring greater policy transparency, promoting evidence-based assessment of policy impact, and creating frameworks for public-private partnerships. Trade agreements can enhance policy transparency on subsidies and SOEs, which is currently limited and so constrains the analysis of the economic effects of subsidies and SOEs on trade and on participation in regional and global value chains. Using trade agreements as a commitment device to improve the availability of data on state support and the analysis of its effects on value-chain-based investment incentives can also increase the appeal of trade agreements to the private sector and to communities with a stake in economic upgrading.

UNDERSTANDING THE IMPACT OF STATE SUPPORT

State support instruments can affect competition in markets and thus can upset competition policies and the activities of national competition agencies. Subsidies, SOEs, and competition law regulate different but often overlapping aspects of government intervention in the economy. All three can create cross-border spillovers, so trade agreements may include rules that regulate their use. In recent decades, preferential trade agreements (PTAs) have tended to become "deeper"—to include more provisions—in part to attenuate potential competitive distortions and reduce the trade and transaction costs associated with domestic behind-the-border policies.

Including regulations in PTAs on state support to enterprises can help manage possible interference in market competition stemming from the use of subsidies or SOEs. Rules in these policy areas can help governments ensure competitive neutrality. Trade agreements thus offer a mechanism for states to reform subsidy and SOE policies to reduce adverse cross-border spillover effects (Brou and Ruta 2013). The use of subsidies and SOEs in some Latin American and Caribbean countries suggests that PTAs could have considerable importance.

Trade agreements can spur transparency even if they are not used to guide domestic competition policy. Information on subsidies and SOEs in Latin America and the Caribbean is limited, though it is needed to analyze their effects and effectiveness—whether they aim to address market failures, spur innovation, realize industrial policy goals, or improve social outcomes. Accurate and up-to-date information is also needed to discover where policies cause significant spillovers that can be addressed through international cooperation—that is, through regulations in PTAs. At present, though, policy monitoring and analysis are not core features of most Latin American and Caribbean PTAs, limiting the agreements' usefulness in improving domestic policy and attenuating cross-border competitive spillovers.

Improving the transparency of policies and the understanding of their impacts can also make PTAs more effective in supporting economic upgrading and expanded participation in global value chains (GVCs). Both subsidies and SOEs can influence investment incentives and the location or design of value chains. Their effects might be positive for some market participants but negative for others—notably for firms that see opportunities to expand along the extensive or intensive margin (to expand investment in new areas or in areas of ongoing interest, respectively) but refrain from doing so because subsidy policies or SOE activities distort the competitive environment.

Conversely, in some situations, subsidies could be better directed to address weak links in supply chains and so promote the expansion of internationally competitive activities (Hoekman 2016). The *World Development Report 2020* emphasized the role of institutional quality and competition to support growth in higher-value-added activities and to foster innovation (World Bank 2020). Sabel (2012) points to institutional mechanisms that encourage expansion along the extensive margin by identifying gaps in policy frameworks and factors discouraging investment in potentially profitable innovations.

PTAs can provide a framework supporting the identification of policy gaps and weaknesses and the generation of information on the action needed to promote economic upgrading. The constraints on upgrading can often be characterized as coordination or information problems, so subsidies or SOEs may be inappropriate or ineffective (Sabel 2012). PTAs can then go beyond acting as a commitment mechanism to regulate the use of subsidies and SOEs. They can also provide an institutional framework for making data more available on applied policies and can support analysis and informed deliberation on the effects and effectiveness of economic policy. Using PTAs in this way can be focused on supporting value-chain-based investment and economic activity, thereby increasing PTAs' relevance to the private sector and to stakeholders' pursuit of economic upgrading.

SUBSIDIES, SOEs, AND COMPETITION IN LATIN AMERICA AND THE CARIBBEAN

The trade impacts of subsidies

Before the COVID-19 pandemic, subsidies accounted for more than half of all trade-related measures implemented globally in 2009–19.[1] During 2020, in response to the pandemic, the share rose above 70 percent as subsidy programs increased significantly, depending on a country's available fiscal space.[2] By the end of 2020, more than 20,000 trade-related measures were included in the Global Trade Alert (GTA) database. Of these, three-fourths were trade distorting.

By far the largest share of trade-distorting measures was for subsidies to production or measures to support exports (figure 6.1). The GTA distinguishes several subsidy categories, among them state aid or production support and export support measures (including tax rebates and concessions). The most frequently observed firm-specific state aid measures were public sector loans or loan guarantees and tax or social insurance relief.

In Latin America and the Caribbean specifically, the share of subsidies in trade-related measures also increased, reaching 50 percent by 2019, up from about 20 percent in 2009–10 (figure 6.2). The share for the region's countries rose to 59 percent during the COVID-19 epidemic in 2020. Latin America and the Caribbean is like the rest of the world in using potentially trade- or competition-distorting measures, but it is unlike the rest of the world in how rarely it removes such measures (figure 6.3).

The share of subsidies in GDP or the government budget varies greatly across Latin American and Caribbean countries (figure 6.4). Subsidy levels are often substantial, in the range of 4 percent of GDP, for the countries reporting data.[3] In comparison, total state aid in the EU in 2018 equaled 1.44 percent of GDP (€230 billion), of which 0.37 percent (€59 billion) was allocated to agricultural activity and 0.31 percent to railways (€50 billion).

Figure 6.1 Subsidies as a share of all trade policy instruments globally, by effect on trade, 2009–20

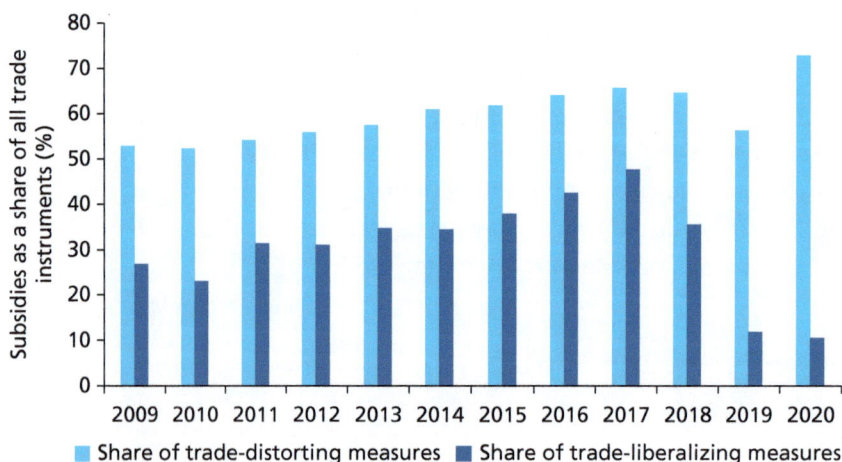

Source: Global Trade Alert database: http://www.globaltradealert.org/.

Note: "Trade-distorting" measures include subsidies supporting production or exports (such as including tax rebates and concessions) and state aid (such as public sector loans or loan guarantees and tax or social insurance relief). Liberalizing measures include reduction of removal of any kind of corporate subsidies.

Figure 6.2   Numbers of trade-related measures and subsidies in Latin America and the Caribbean, 2009–20

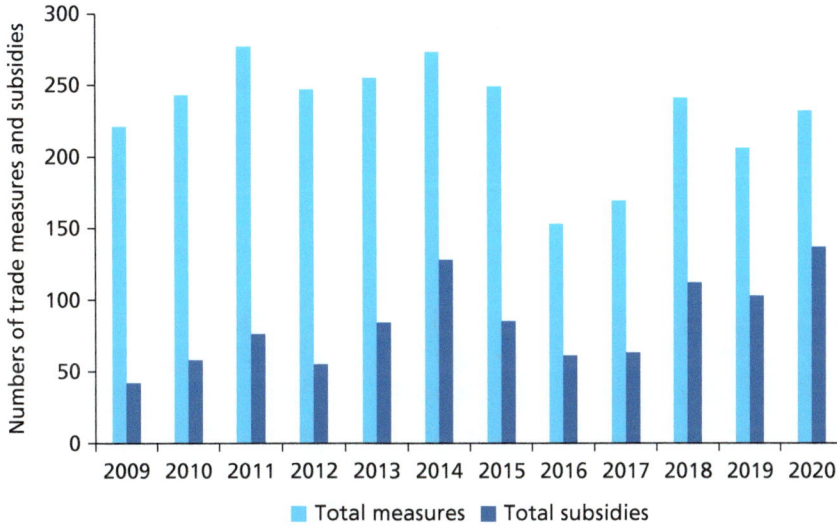

Source: Global Trade Alert database: http://www.globaltradealert.org/.

Figure 6.3   Share of subsidies in all trade measures in Latin America and the Caribbean compared with the rest of the world, by effect on trade, 2009–20

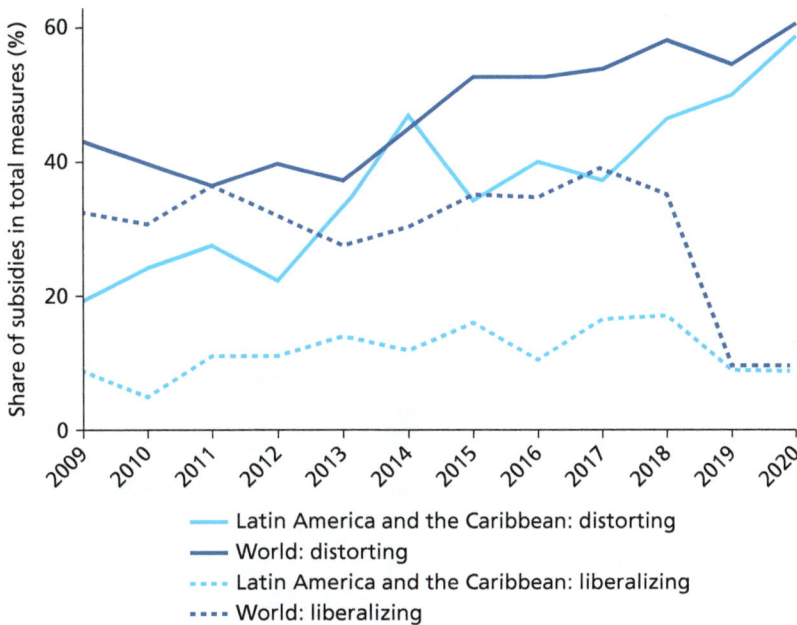

Source: Global Trade Alert database: http://www.globaltradealert.org/.

Note: "Trade-distorting" measures include subsidies supporting production or exports (such as including tax rebates and concessions) and state aid (such as public sector loans or loan guarantees and tax or social insurance relief). Liberalizing measures include reduction of removal of any kind of corporate subsidies.

Figure 6.4   Subsidies to public and private enterprises as a share of GDP in selected Latin American and Caribbean countries, 2010–19

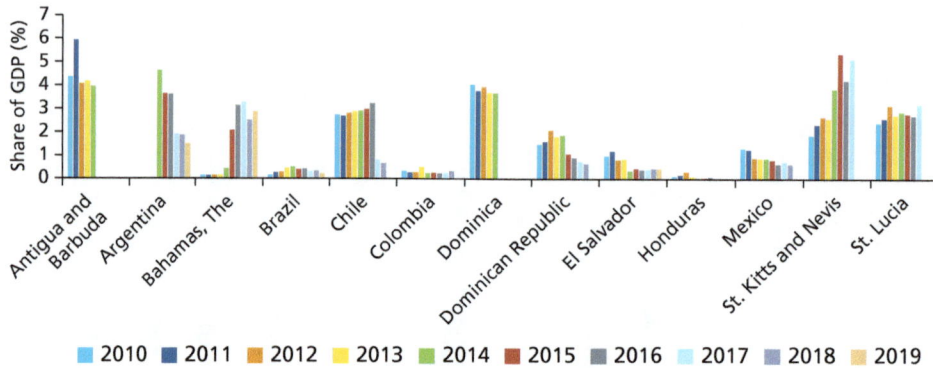

Source: International Monetary Fund Government Finance Statistics database.

Note: Missing bars indicate a lack of data for a given country in a given year. GDP = gross domestic product.

The role of state-owned enterprises

SOEs' role in many Latin American and Caribbean countries might distort market competition and, because of soft budget constraints, could have large fiscal implications in cases of weak SOE performance (Musacchio and Pineda Ayerbe 2019). Many Latin American and Caribbean countries have many SOEs, and, more important, some have many large SOEs (with assets greater than US$1 billion). Central America and Caribbean countries have more SOEs, but South American countries have more large SOEs.

Large SOEs averaged an estimated US$7.5 billion a year in revenue during 2010–16 in Latin American and the Caribbean (Musacchio and Pineda Ayerbe 2019), as shown in figure 6.5. Fewer of the region's SOEs are multinational than in other regions, suggesting that they focus mostly on local markets (figure 6.6).

Comparable cross-country information is limited on the extent of subsidy programs and on the prevalence and operations of SOEs in Latin America and the Caribbean. The information scarcity impedes any assessment of their impact on their countries' economic performance and their potential cross-border spillover effects. But spillover effects will be the focus of PTA commitments on subsidies and SOEs. PTAs' substantive provisions on subsidies and SOEs may also include commitments pertaining to (joint) collection and reporting of data on applied policies and proposed changes in policies to permit monitoring by signatories.

In practice, Latin American and Caribbean PTAs do little to subject participating countries to the rules of the game for subsidies and SOEs. They also do little to address the need for up-to-date information on subsidies and SOEs that is needed to assess cross-border spillover effects and, more important from a domestic perspective, to evaluate their effectiveness.

Figure 6.5   Average number and revenue of SOEs in Latin America and the Caribbean, by subregion, 2010–16

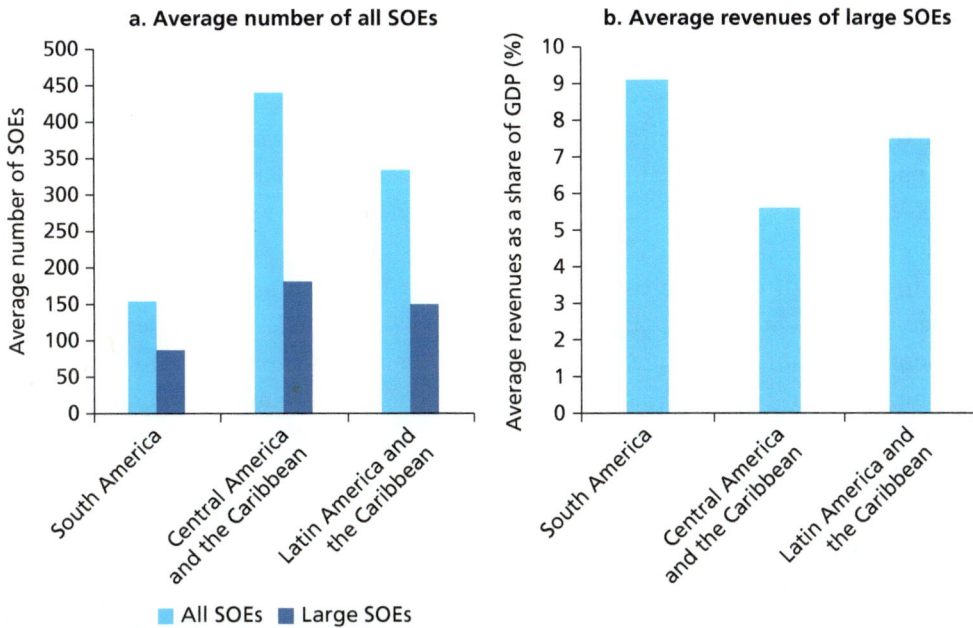

a. Average number of all SOEs

b. Average revenues of large SOEs

■ All SOEs ■ Large SOEs

Source: Musacchio and Pineda Ayerbe 2019.

Note: Large state-owned enterprises (SOEs) are defined as those with assets greater than US$1 billion. GDP = gross domestic product.

Figure 6.6   Number of multinational SOEs, by region, 2019

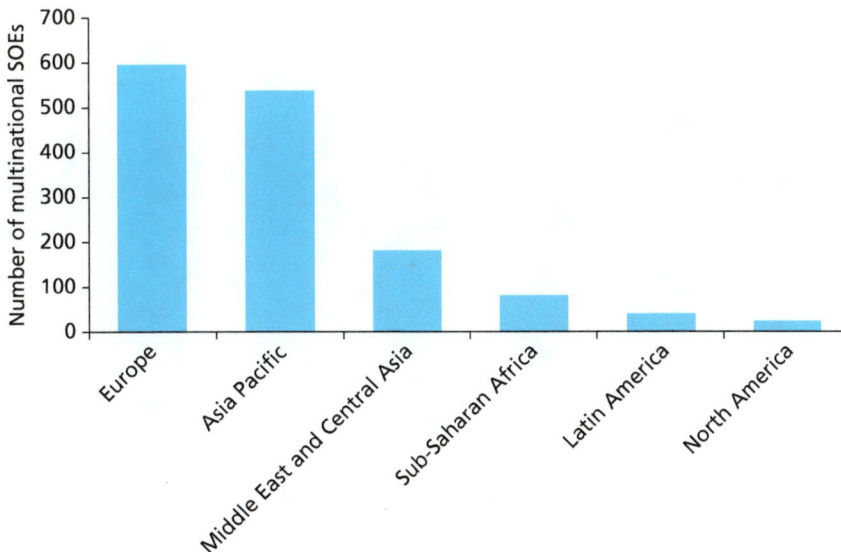

Source: International Monetary Fund (IMF) *Fiscal Monitor,* April 2020.

Note: Regions are defined according to IMF classifications. SOE = state-owned enterprise.

Indicators of domestic competition

Investigations of competition in Latin American and Caribbean countries tend to focus on cartels and the abuse of dominant positions (Bradford et al. 2019). Countries actively using competition policy in the region include Brazil, Chile, Colombia, Mexico, Panama, and Peru. They accounted for 10 percent (22 of a total of 220) of the cartel investigations resulting in fines that are included in the Organisation for Economic Co-operation and Development (OECD) International Cartels Database during 2012–19.[4] Other Latin American and Caribbean nations do not pursue competition policy as much.

Indicators of domestic competition in Latin American and Caribbean markets suggest that competition policy could be important in many countries. A World Economic Forum composite measure of the intensity of domestic competition in national markets indicates that Latin American and Caribbean performance is below average (Schwab 2019), reflecting the prevalence of competition-distorting tax subsidies, the dominance of a small number of firms in the domestic market, and the degree of competition in services markets (figure 6.7). These data are based on a global survey of executives and thus reflect perceptions rather than objective analysis, but they are suggestive nonetheless.

Figure 6.7   Domestic competition index, by region, 2019

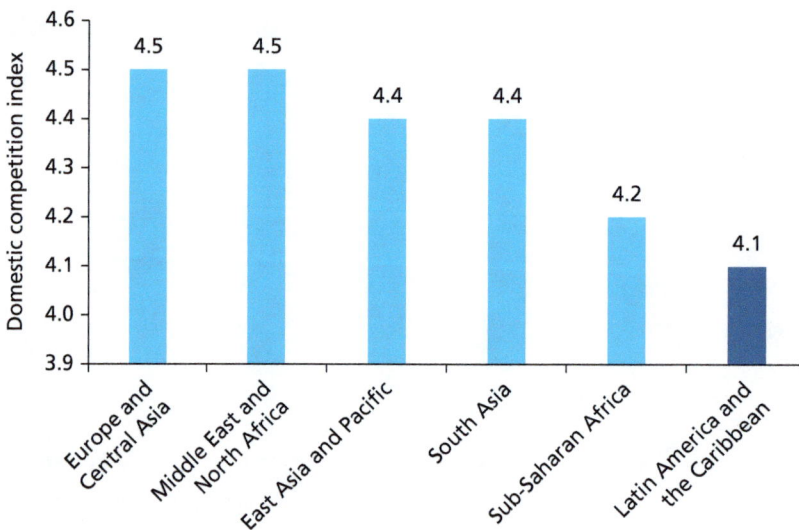

Source: Schwab 2019.

Note: The World Economic Forum's domestic competition index ranges from a maximum of 7 (best) to a minimum of 1. It is an average of three indicators: the distortive effect of taxes and subsidies on competition; the extent of market dominance; and the degree of competition in services.

SUBSIDY, SOE, AND COMPETITION POLICY REGULATIONS IN TRADE AGREEMENTS

As noted earlier, PTAs can act as commitment devices—mechanisms providing a government with the means to tie its own hands in dealing with domestic agents that lobby for state support. The incentive for governments is that even if SOEs and subsidies generate short-run rents for the actors involved (including the government), their sustained use will distort the allocation of resources as investors overinvest in the sectors expected to benefit from state support. Because the government will not benefit from that distortion, it has an incentive to commit to limits on its ability to back subsidies and SOEs (Maggi 2014).

Subsidy provisions in PTAs

Provisions on subsidies in most PTAs, whether among Latin American and Caribbean countries or elsewhere, build on the provisions established in the World Trade Organization (WTO) Agreement on Subsidies and Countervailing Measures (ASCM). The ASCM has a twofold objective: (a) to keep members from using subsidies to circumvent negotiated market access (tariff) concessions, and (b) to regulate the use of measures to countervail (offset) the adverse effects of foreign subsidies of goods on domestic producers.[5]

The WTO, though prohibiting export subsidies, does not regulate domestic subsidies as such. Governments may use subsidies other than export subsidies, but countervailing import duties can be imposed in destination markets, or challenges can be raised through dispute settlement procedures over adverse effects in third markets. The adverse trade effects, not the purposes of a subsidy, are what matters.

Exceptions are found in the so-called Green Box subsidy measures in the WTO's Agreement on Agriculture, which permits subsidies deemed not to distort trade significantly. The Green Box subsidies include environmental protection, regional development programs, and farmers' direct income support, decoupled from production levels or prices. A similar approach to nonagricultural subsidies became defunct in 1999, after failure to obtain the consensus required to extend the relevant provision (ASCM, article 8) beyond the initial five years negotiated in the Uruguay Round of multilateral trade negotiations.

PTA provisions on subsidies tend to mirror those found in the WTO (see Rubini 2020). Only a quarter of PTAs covered in the World Bank's Deep Trade Agreements database go beyond the ASCM with provisions specifying types of subsidies not considered trade distorting. The EU is a signatory to most of those PTAs. The permissible subsidies generally pertain to public services, regional aid, or environmental protection. If they are deemed to have detrimental spillover effects, the PTAs call for consultations rather than legal action. EU PTAs also regulate state guarantees and support to insolvent or ailing companies. Recent PTAs also have such provisions, as in the

Comprehensive and Progressive Agreement for Trans-Pacific Partnership (CPTPP), which prohibits state support on noncommercial terms for SOEs' commercial activities. Both EU PTAs and the CPTPP subsidy restrictions exclude activities providing governmental (public) services in domestic markets.

Virtually all Latin American and Caribbean PTAs (80 of 82) include language on subsidies, but most do not require partners to report to each other on subsidies, and only a handful include provisions for partners to discuss control or review of them. Most emulate the WTO in permitting subsidies allocated to the services sector (figure 6.8).

SOE provisions in PTAs

Provisions for SOEs follow a similar pattern. Latin American and Caribbean PTAs tend to replicate WTO rules on state trading enterprises, banning discrimination and requiring that they operate on a commercial basis.

Figure 6.8   Number of Latin American and Caribbean PTAs with selected provisions on subsidies and SOEs, 2017

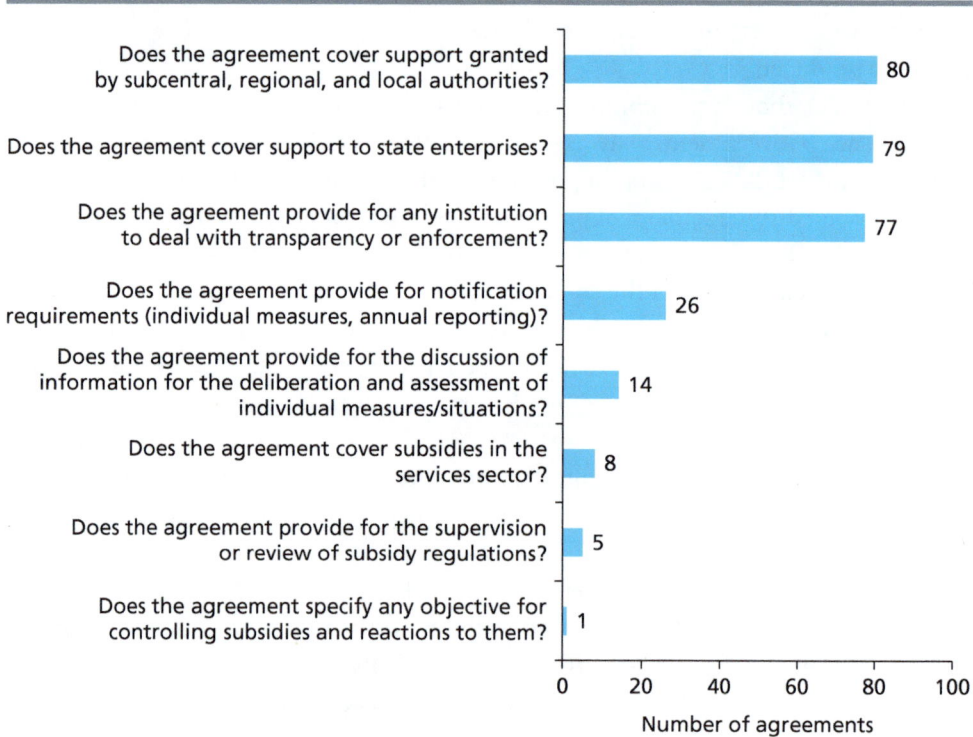

Source: World Bank's Deep Trade Agreements database.

Note: Data cover a total of 82 Latin American and Caribbean preferential trade agreements (PTAs). SOE = state-owned enterprise.

Recent EU PTAs, PTAs in East Asia and Pacific (including the CPTPP), and the US–Mexico–Canada Agreement (effective in 2020) require SOEs to operate on a commercial basis, ban them from providing subsidized inputs to producers in member countries, require them to operate on a nondiscriminatory basis, and prohibit anticompetitive practices. The CPTPP requires SOEs and designated monopolies to compete on quality and price rather than benefit from discriminatory regulation and distortive subsidies. More specifically, CPTPP signatories must avoid discrimination, apply commercial considerations to SOEs, limit the scope for designated monopolies to engage in anticompetitive practices, refrain from granting noncommercial assistance that might injure or adversely affect the interests of another party, and establish an impartial regulatory and institutional framework for SOEs (Licetti, Miralles, and Teh 2020).

Recent DTAs specifically require SOEs to operate on a nondiscriminatory and commercial basis. Two-thirds of the 283 DTAs assessed by Rubini and Wang (2020) included language requiring SOEs to behave in accordance with commercial considerations, and 70 percent of those included subsidy restrictions for SOEs. Consequently, signatories could act against subsidies to SOEs, whether direct fiscal transfers or indirect supports. One-third of the PTAs that included provisions on SOEs had notification requirements. For instance, the CPTPP requires signatories to publish data on extant SOEs and the measures that support them. Although a significant minority of DTAs included policy transparency provisions, only 10 of the 283 went further to cover generation of information on SOE operations (Rubini and Wang 2020).

Fewer Latin American and Caribbean PTAs have at least one provision on SOEs (63) than have at least one on subsidies (82). Only one-third of the region's PTAs call for SOEs to operate on a commercial basis, compared with two-thirds of PTAs in the World Bank database. Only two Latin American and Caribbean PTAs include provisions regulating state support in the economy through SOEs, and none includes a mechanism to increase the transparency of state intervention in the economy (figure 6.9).

Competition policy provisions in PTAs

Competition policy-related provisions in Latin American and Caribbean PTAs lead to similar conclusions. More than four-fifths (84 percent) of all the agreements in the World Bank's Deep Trade Agreements database have competition-policy related provisions (Licetti, Miralles, and Teh 2020). Latin American and Caribbean PTAs are similar: 80 percent (66 of 82) have provisions on competition policy. Of the 66, 43 are extraregional, meaning that agreements between Latin American and Caribbean countries are less likely to include competition policy provisions than are the region's agreements with extraregional partners. Most Latin American and Caribbean PTAs do not use the PTAs to foster coordination and collaboration

Figure 6.9 Number of Latin American and Caribbean PTAs with selected provisions on SOEs, 2017

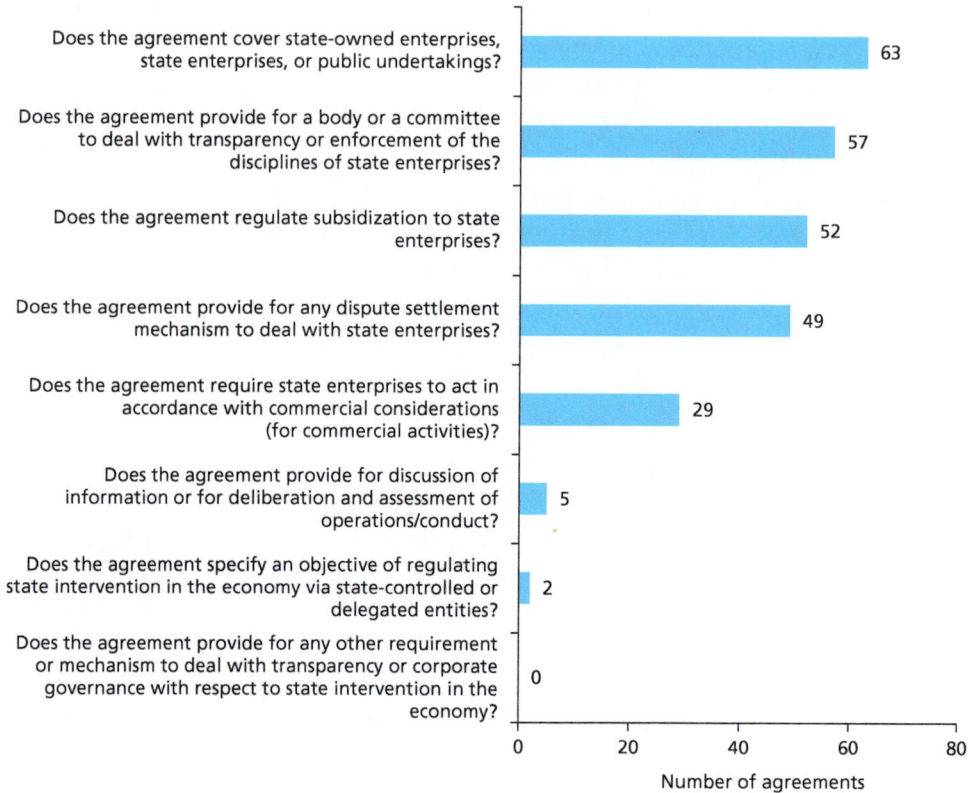

Source: World Bank's Deep Trade Agreements database.

Note: Data cover a total of 82 Latin American and Caribbean preferential trade agreements (PTAs). SOE = state-owned enterprise.

between competition agencies, nor do their competition policy chapters include provisions to regulate SOEs or state aid (figure 6.10).

Subsidy, SOE, and competition provisions relative to middle-income countries globally

In many of their provisions for SOEs, subsidies, and competition policy, PTAs in Latin America and the Caribbean are similar to those signed by middle-income countries (MICs) in other parts of the world (annex 6A, figures 6A.1–6A.3). On average, the coverage of subsidy provisions in the region's PTAs is like that found elsewhere, but a slightly greater share of Latin American and Caribbean PTAs (94 percent) include provisions on transparency and dispute settlement than do PTAs of MICs elsewhere (83 percent). Notification requirements and annual reporting for subsidies show a larger difference: fewer than one-third of Latin American and

Figure 6.10 Number of Latin American and Caribbean PTAs with competition policy provisions, 2017

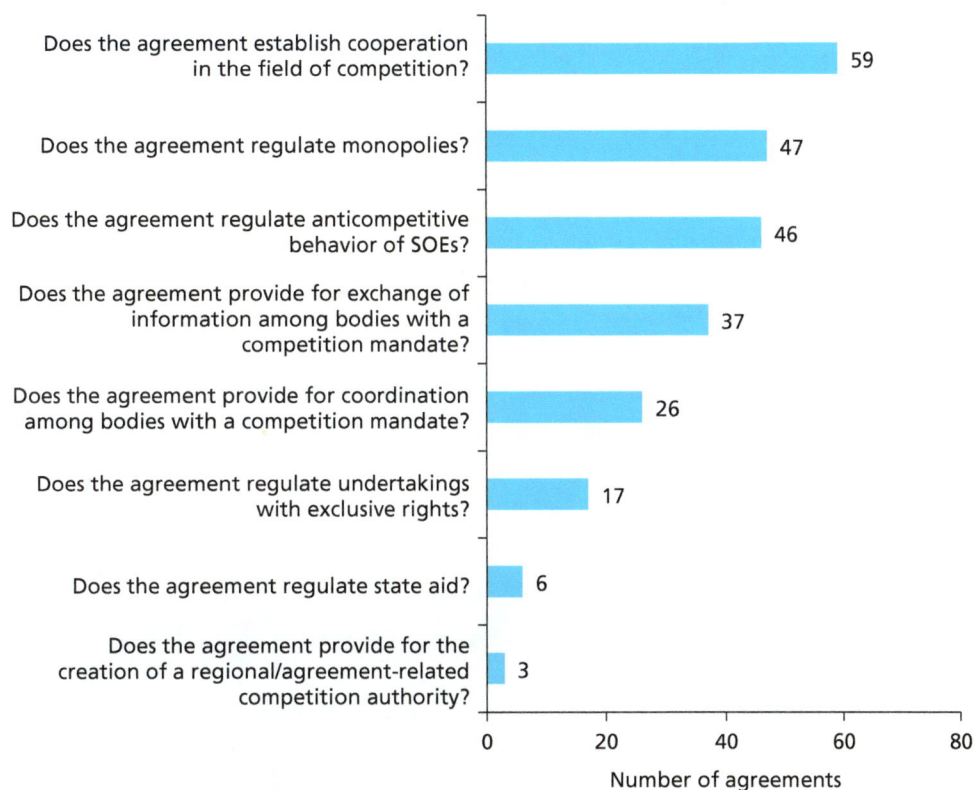

Question	Number of agreements
Does the agreement establish cooperation in the field of competition?	59
Does the agreement regulate monopolies?	47
Does the agreement regulate anticompetitive behavior of SOEs?	46
Does the agreement provide for exchange of information among bodies with a competition mandate?	37
Does the agreement provide for coordination among bodies with a competition mandate?	26
Does the agreement regulate undertakings with exclusive rights?	17
Does the agreement regulate state aid?	6
Does the agreement provide for the creation of a regional/agreement-related competition authority?	3

Source: World Bank's Deep Trade Agreements database.

Note: Data cover a total of 82 Latin American and Caribbean preferential trade agreements (PTAs). SOEs = state-owned enterprises.

Caribbean PTAs (31.7 percent) include such provisions, compared with half of other MICs' PTAs (51.6 percent) (annex 2A, figure 6A.1).

Latin American and Caribbean PTAs also generally differ from the PTAs of MICs elsewhere by placing provisions on subsidies for SOEs in SOE chapters rather than in chapters on subsidies or competition policy. More than 60 percent of the region's PTAs have such provisions in SOE chapters, compared with 2.5 percent of PTAs in MICs the rest of the world. Only 35 percent of the region's PTAs require SOEs to operate on a commercial basis, compared with 49 percent of other MICs' PTAs. And only 2.4 percent of Latin American and Caribbean PTAs include provisions treating the regulation of SOEs as an objective, compared with 16 percent of PTAs in other MICs.

Similarly, 21 percent of the chapters on competition policy in Latin American and Caribbean PTAs include provisions regulating undertakings with exclusive rights— that is, SOEs—in contrast to an average of 35 percent of such chapters in MICs'

PTAs elsewhere. The region's PTA chapters on competition also address subsidies much less frequently than do other MICs' PTA chapters on competition: 7 percent versus 44 percent. Conversely, the competition chapters of the region's PTAs more frequently include provisions dealing with anticompetitive behavior by SOEs.

Latin American and Caribbean governments thus recognize that PTAs should address subsidies and SOEs. But on average, they do less than other countries to use PTAs as commitment devices, as reflected in the infrequency of PTA provisions regulating subsidies for SOEs or requiring SOEs to operate on a commercial basis as well as the few references to subsidies in PTA competition chapters. Compared with the EU approach discussed below—where competition policy is the framework to regulate the use of subsidies and the behavior of all undertakings, both private and state owned—Latin American and Caribbean PTAs do much less to regulate either policy area. On average, the region's PTAs also have fewer provisions than the EU's and other MICs' PTAs requiring notification of subsidies (annex 6A, figure 6A.1), and so they do less to foster policy transparency.

LEVERAGING PTAs TO IMPROVE POLICY TRANSPARENCY

Most legal and economic analysis of PTAs focuses on the extent and substance of their coverage of different policy areas, whether provisions are binding, and whether binding provisions are enforceable. The status of commitments depends on whether they will be implemented, which is indirectly indicated by the ability to invoke dispute settlement proceedings.[6] This focus on legal norms—and whether they can, in principle, be enforced—depends on whether governments know whether provisions are being implemented, which in turn depends on whether market participants recognize instances of partner governments acting inconsistently with the provisions of the PTA.

The focus on enforceability is arguably too narrow, in part because many provisions in trade agreements call for undertaking good regulatory practice and relying on "soft law" focal points for dialogue and cooperation. From an economic perspective, soft law can be more important than hard law commitments. Trade agreements can be useful to economic policy makers—and to voters, citizens, and taxpayers—as instruments to support collecting and reporting information on policies that affect competition. They can also provide a vehicle for analytically informed deliberation between trade partners to assess domestic policies and their effects on trading partners.

Notification obligations feature in many trade agreements but often do not work well. For example, few WTO members live up to the notification obligations embodied in various WTO agreements (Hoekman 2012; Wolfe 2018). The implementation of PTA notification requirements has received less attention. In practice, the committees and councils tasked with overseeing PTA implementation provide the forums and focal points for dialogue and monitoring. PTAs provide stronger incentives than WTO agreements for governments to invest in monitoring implementation since they aim to remove substantially all trade barriers between signatories.

Whether PTAs lead to better monitoring is an empirical question about which little is known. Some Latin American and Caribbean PTAs include transparency obligations for all measures relating to trade. Mexico is a partner in many: examples include Mexico–Costa Rica and Mexico–Uruguay for trade in goods; Mexico–Japan for trade in services; and measures addressing specific sectors such as automobiles (Mexico–Colombia), financial services (Mexico–Peru), and telecommunications (Mexico–Nicaragua) (Kaufmann and Saffirio 2021).

The number of provisions in Latin American and Caribbean PTAs aimed at enhancing transparency has grown (figure 6.11). And when it comes to transparency, the region's PTAs on average do fairly well compared with PTAs in other regions, such as East Asia and Pacific and North America (figure 6.12).

Even so, Latin American and Caribbean PTAs do not generally appear to be used by signatories to cooperate in collecting and jointly analyzing policies covered by their PTAs.[7] The EU is the pacesetter for this practice, partly reflecting the depth of the integration being pursued by EU member states.

EU regulations on "state aids" belong to a broader framework of competition policy and pertain to both governments and firms. A key focus of EU state-aids regulation is safeguarding the European single market. Four criteria apply for state aid to be illegal: (1) state resources lead to (2) a selective advantage for a firm or activity that (3) distorts competition and (4) affects trade between member states. These criteria also apply to undertakings to which member states have granted special or exclusive rights—SOEs, among others. A competitive neutrality framework subjects undertakings "entrusted

Figure 6.11 Average coverage ratio of transparency provisions in Latin American and Caribbean PTAs, by period, pre-1995 to 2010–17

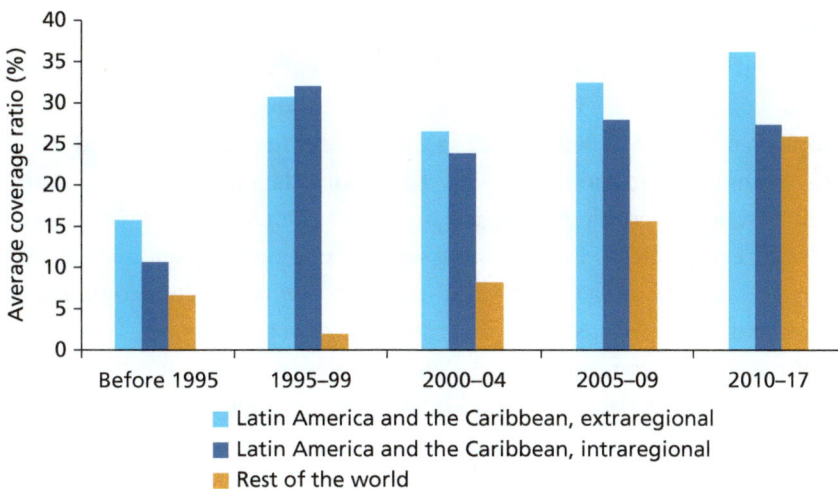

Source: World Bank's Deep Trade Agreements database.

Note: The coverage ratio is the share of provisions in an agreement relative to the maximum number of possible provisions. PTA = preferential trade agreement.

Figure 6.12   Average coverage ratio of transparency provisions in PTAs, by region, 2017

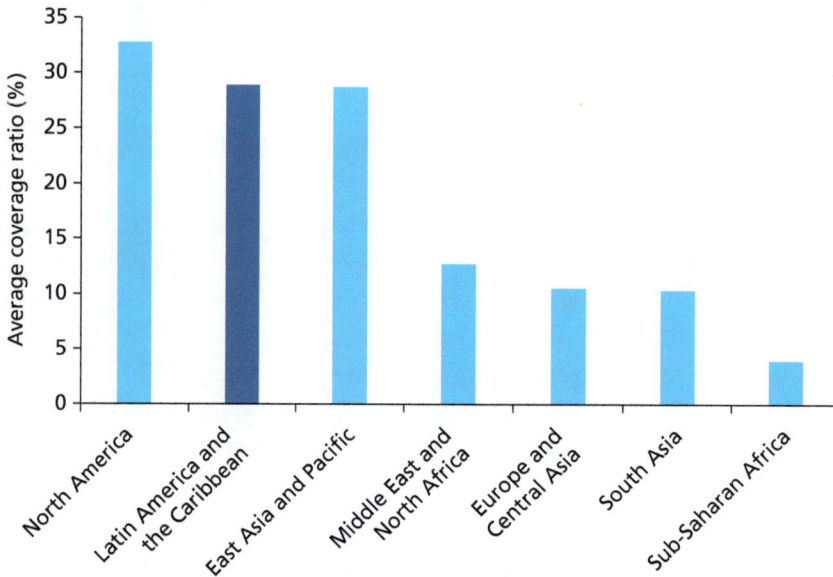

Source: World Bank's Deep Trade Agreements database.

Note: The coverage ratio is the share of provisions in an agreement relative to the maximum number of possible provisions. PTA = preferential trade agreement.

with the operation of services of general economic interest or having the character of a revenue-producing monopoly" to the general competition rules unless the rules obstruct the performance of undertakings' public tasks.[8]

Although the depth of EU integration is much greater than that of Latin American and Caribbean PTAs, elements of the EU's transparency policy for subsidies are relevant. EU member states are required to notify the European Commission of state aid allocations exceeding €500,000, including the name of the beneficiary and the amount granted. An annual State Aid Scoreboard that reports data on subsidy expenditures by EU member states covers all existing aid measures to industries, services, agriculture, and fisheries, except aid to railways and services of general economic interest.[9] The data, intended to foster transparency and facilitate monitoring, are complemented by impact evaluations of selected large or innovative state aid schemes to guide possible improvements in program design and state aid rules. A similar mechanism could be conceived for Latin American and Caribbean PTAs, perhaps offering significant economies given the number of PTAs signed by the region's countries with an interest in improving policy transparency.

The incentives for such an effort are determined in part by the regulations that countries agree to. In the case of the EU, notifications are encouraged by a General Block

Exemption Regulation (GBER) applied to subsidies deemed to raise few or no competition concerns, such as regional aid (including for ports and airports), assistance to small and medium enterprises, and support for sports and culture; employment and training; broadband infrastructure; natural disaster relief; energy and the environment; and research, development, and innovation.[10] Agreeing to subsidies unlikely to cause concern focuses attention on subsidies more likely to have harmful trade spillover effects.

Cooperation to improve transparency over subsidies and the operation of SOEs need not occur under the umbrella of a PTA. For example, the Global Forum on Steel Excess Capacity (GFSEC), established at the 2016 Group of Twenty (G-20) summit, produces and shares reliable statistics on production capacity and measures of excess capacity across major steel producers and identifies ways to reduce global production. The forum provides a platform for exchanging data on steel capacity and information on steel policies, including support measures—improving the information base and increasing the transparency of policies implemented by major steel-producing countries. The forum includes governments and industry (a key source of information on production and investment trends). It was supported by the OECD Secretariat.

Although the GFSEC was not linked to a trade agreement, PTAs would provide ready-made institutional frameworks for the types of activities it undertakes. An important feature of the GFSEC was its support by a trusted intermediary clearing-house organization: the OECD Secretariat. Delegating measurement and analysis to a neutral and technically capable body that acts as an agent for the principals (governments) is common practice in the EU and OECD—and also in the WTO, whose Secretariat has been mandated by the WTO membership to undertake trade policy reviews that document trade policy in member countries. The OECD has played such a role for decades, producing data on support policies in a range of sectors (including agriculture, fisheries, biofuels, and fossil fuels) and analyses of subsidies in specific sectors (such as aluminum and semiconductors) that explicitly incorporate value chains (OECD 2019a, 2019b, 2019c). Both the OECD and WTO experiences illustrate transparency as going beyond documenting policies to measuring the magnitude of interventions using well-defined indicators of the support the policies entail.[11]

Although Latin American and Caribbean PTAs include provisions to ensure transparency in applied trade policies, these provisions do not entail comprehensive and regular monitoring of applied policy or commitment implementation. Transparency-related provisions for subsidies and SOEs are limited, as noted earlier. Many government agencies participate in designing and implementing subsidy policies, and PTA forums bring these actors together. They include national finance ministries, competition agencies, and international organizations—notably the World Bank, International Monetary Fund, Inter-American Development Bank, and regional United Nations agencies. A focal mechanism is needed to map what data these entities already collect, identify gaps, and foster information sharing, building on the existing institutions and networks that have an interest and requisite expertise. For example, the International Competition Network (ICN), an informal grouping of competition agencies, is already active.[12]

The design of an institutional mechanism to create a comprehensive and up-to-date baseline for applied subsidy programs and operation of SOEs is beyond the scope of this chapter. It will require deliberation among PTA signatories and consultation with international organizations that might be asked to contribute to the effort. Any such mechanism can build on initiatives already being pursued under recent PTAs aimed at improving regulatory practices and supporting regulatory cooperation.

COOPERATION ON BEHIND-THE-BORDER REGULATION IN PTAs

The need for transparency and analysis (assessment) of policies extends beyond subsidies and SOEs. As tariffs have fallen, policy-induced market access frictions and trade costs are increasingly apparent in regulations—helping to explain why PTAs have become deeper. The associated cooperation agenda is driven by business community concerns regarding the trade-impeding and cost-raising effects of differences in domestic health, safety, privacy, and data security standards; prudential and licensing requirements; and certification and conformity assessment procedures for products and production processes.

Like nontariff measures, state support measures challenge international cooperative efforts to identify approaches to reducing competitive distortions without a political commitment to fully integrate markets and without supranational institutions tasked with reducing national policies' market-segmenting effects. National regulators frequently have mechanisms for interacting internationally. Governments at different levels (central, subcentral, and municipal), regulators, and international businesses are all engaged in mechanisms for cooperating with counterparts across jurisdictions. In the private sector, leading firms that set standards for health, safety, and quality for both products and processes in their supply chains may cooperate in private standard-setting activities that pursue interoperability and minimum standards across supply chains. They may work in cooperation with nongovernmental organizations (NGOs) and governments to do so.

Reducing the trade cost effects of regulatory differences is hindered by concerns about compromising countries' regulatory objectives and impeding the execution of regulatory agencies' legal mandates and obligations. Regulation is technical and dynamic, involving many actors with different degrees of autonomy and decentralization. And regulators must consider differences in local circumstances and priorities.

PTAs have a role in ensuring that regulations' trade effects are considered. National regulators and international standard-setting bodies often do not consider the international implications of their activities, the trade impacts of their requirements, or alternative approaches that might have fewer negative effects while still realizing regulatory objectives. Their authorizing environment does not require them to do so, and they may not recognize the economic costs to firms and consumers in other jurisdictions associated with implementing their regimes.

PTAs can have a similar role for state support measures. A simple yet powerful change that PTA partners could seek is to agree that regulatory processes include an assessment of trade effects—perhaps as part of a broader regulatory impact assessment, generally considered a good practice. To increase the chance of trade impact being assessed, regulatory agencies should be provided financial resources so that the effort would not threaten to crowd out other activities. Incorporating language in trade agreements regarding trade effects assessment can entitle regulatory agencies to claim additional resources from the government.

Several recent Latin American and Caribbean PTAs incorporate provisions calling for consultations on new horizontal regulations,[13] the use of regulatory impact analysis and evaluation, and language on pursuit of regulatory coherence across levels of government and on cooperation between national regulators (Kaufmann and Saffirio 2021). Examples include the not-yet-ratified Brazil–Chile trade agreement, the Chile–Uruguay PTA, the CPTPP, and the Pacific Alliance. Most of these establish a standing body to oversee the implementation of agreed-upon good regulatory practices and support regulatory cooperation. The standing body is also responsible for a review of the operation and lessons learned—to occur five years after implementation in the case of CPTPP and Chile–Uruguay PTA, and three years after implementation in the case of the Pacific Alliance.[14] The associated provisions are not subject to dispute settlement procedures; instead, the PTAs foresee periodic review of the respective provisions over domestic regulation. The Chile–Uruguay agreement, the CPTPP, and the Pacific Alliance call for signatories to consider creating a domestic coordinating body to support regulatory coherence by facilitating interagency coordination and regulatory oversight (Kaufmann and Saffirio 2021).

That cooperative approach can also be applied to state support measures. Deliberation among PTA partners on how to do so can be undertaken if governments are interested in using PTAs as commitment devices to enhance transparency and cooperative assessment of the economic impacts of state support measures—both subsidies and SOEs.

PRIVATE SECTOR ENGAGEMENT: GVC PARTNERSHIPS AS INPUTS AND COMPLEMENTS TO PTA REGULATIONS

Private sector involvement can bolster the collection of up-to-date information on applied policies as well as cooperation to reduce the drawbacks of state support policies and the trade costs of regulatory variation. Engaging the business community not only can generate political support to deepen cooperation on subsidies and SOEs but also can identify coordination problems that constrain economic upgrading and value chain expansion. PTAs do little to incentivize government engagement with companies that operate or rely on value chains. But the value of PTAs to the business community can grow if mechanisms are built to bring together key actors operating regional value chains to identify policy gaps and frictions, boosting progress toward national objectives.

Many multistakeholder initiatives focus on private governance in value chains to promote dialogue between value chain participants. They address certification of producers, voluntary production standards, monitoring implementation, and corporate social responsibility. Such value chain partnerships have mostly concentrated on forestry and agricultural products, but they have also been applied to textile and apparel and electronics value chains (Bitzer and Glasbergen 2015).[15] They can be designed to facilitate deliberation and cooperation between the government agencies that regulate value chain activities, the actors that operate them and are affected by policies, and the research community that assesses policy effects (Findlay and Hoekman 2020).

A value chain approach differs from the kind of industry- or product-specific focus that typically influences regulators, governments, and civil society considering trade agreements. Using value chains to frame analysis and argument—covering the clusters of firms in very different industries that depend on exporting and importing—might build greater support for deepening PTAs.

Value chains cut across sectors, spanning a variety of activities in international production networks. Value chain platforms can gather the knowledge of buyer firms, supplier firms, and other stakeholders to enhance understanding of value chains and possible investments and upgrades to improve them. Such platforms can identify and analyze coordination problems to boost innovation. Modern approaches to industrial policy—a major driver of subsidy programs and SOE operations in many Latin American and Caribbean countries—stress the need for public-private dialogue institutions to identify and resolve coordination problems (Devlin and Pietrobelli 2019; Ross-Schneider 2015; Sabel 2012). Such institutions aim to foster communication between stakeholders in an economic activity—in this case, upgrading value chains and expanding along the extensive margin to address constraints and market failures deterring new activity. The firms involved and local authorities and stakeholders, not the central government, typically have information on weak links and missing complementary inputs. Their communication—supporting assessment of the type of intervention needed to address specific gaps and constraints—might require tax or subsidy instruments but often does not.

The elements of value chain partnerships include regulators and government agency representatives responsible for policy (figure 6.13, bottom left) as well as producers, buyers, consumers, and other stakeholders such as workers and community representatives (figure 6.13, bottom right). Producers (figure 6.13, top left) can best identify the impediments to realizing value at different parts of the chain—including in different countries. Analysts (figure 6.13, top right) provide research capacity to assess impacts and facilitate discussion of transactions and operating costs, and they can also monitor progress in implementing measures to reduce costs.

Although no PTAs have created value chain partnerships, other initiatives offer examples that address some dimensions of what such bodies might do. Many countries have trade and investment promotion bodies to increase and diversify exports (moving along the extensive margin and upgrading participation in GVCs).

Figure 6.13 A framework for a value chain partnership

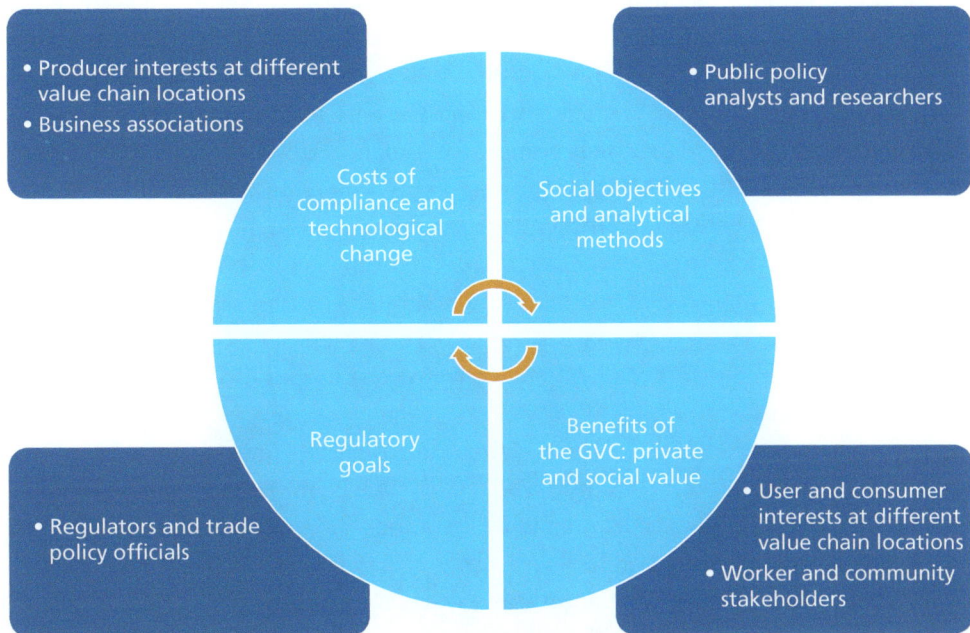

- Producer interests at different value chain locations
- Business associations

Costs of compliance and technological change

Social objectives and analytical methods

- Public policy analysts and researchers

Regulatory goals

Benefits of the GVC: private and social value

- Regulators and trade policy officials

- User and consumer interests at different value chain locations
- Worker and community stakeholders

Source: Findlay and Hoekman 2020.

Note: GVC = global value chain.

Many countries also have mechanisms to facilitate imports by reducing the transaction costs of moving goods across borders and along transportation and transit corridors. Although such mechanisms are multisectoral—including both public and private actors—they generally do not come to grips with the value chain arrangements of international production. Nor do they encompass noneconomic issues as a multistakeholder value chain sustainability partnership would (Soundararajan, Brown, and Wicks 2019).

Commitments to setting goals and monitoring performance would be critical. Possible indicators of value chain performance could relate to inventory management, the speed of movement of goods, and indexes of risk. To develop methods of mapping trade costs within value chains to such indicators and to regulatory policies requires research and analysis. Business can contribute by sharing data and experience.[16]

Elements of the needed public-private engagement are already found in some Latin American and Caribbean PTAs. In the Pacific Alliance, for example, national leaders agree on areas for joint action, which the ministers of foreign affairs and foreign trade of the member states then elaborate. A business council has a formal role in suggesting how to address frictions and regulatory differences that increase trade costs. It has proposed harmonizing technical standards in such sectors as cosmetics, pharmaceuticals, and processed food and making national single windows for trade interoperable to reduce the time and costs (WEF 2014). A high-level group is charged with monitoring the progress of the technical working groups implementing the action agenda that the ministers have defined. High-level monitoring based on performance and outcome measurement ensures accountability and thus boosts the prospects of success.

National committees on trade facilitation offer a path for operationalizing value chain partnerships in PTAs. Such committees, mandated under the WTO Trade Facilitation Agreement (TFA), exist in most Latin American and Caribbean countries.[17] They bring together government agencies that implement regulations applied at the border and include private sector representation, usually business associations or chambers of commerce. PTA signatories could expand the committees' mandate by asking the business representatives to go beyond the issues covered in the TFA and add considerations of policy impact on value chain operations and investment incentives.[18]

Value chain partnerships will entail fairly limited costs—time for consulting with participating firms on policy-induced sources of value chain friction, compiling performance indicators, and participating in deliberations. The return on that investment, which should be assessed periodically, is likely to greatly exceed the cost. The costs to government officials are just the time and travel for participating. Anchoring such activity to a trade agreement will facilitate the allocation of any needed budgetary resources. Civil society groups will have to fund their own participation, and for them as for business, the proof of the pudding is in the eating. The existence of a plethora of multistakeholder sustainability initiatives suggests that financing is unlikely to create an undue burden. The research and analysis needed to inform deliberation creates a cost to be shared by the core of the partnership—business and government—but requirements should not be great, especially if businesses are willing to work with analysts to identify and compile data on value chain frictions.

CONCLUSION

PTAs focus primarily on policies and the associated administrative procedures applied at the border. They can improve economic outcomes by enhancing the transparency of state support policies and by serving as a commitment device to support the state adopting rules restricting competition-distorting subsidies. Beyond that, they can enhance participation in cross-border value chains and the creation of an investment climate that supports economic upgrading. Transparency in state support and analysis of support programs' effects strengthen value chain participation and operations by increasing the understanding of possible subsidy and SOE disincentive effects and revealing how well-targeted support programs can address coordination failures and weak supply chain links.

Most PTAs include provisions on domestic policies, including subsidies, but they tend to be narrow in scope. In most cases, their regulations aim to constrain the governments' ability to undo trade policy commitments through domestic measures that discriminate against foreign products. This is one purpose of national treatment and nondiscrimination principles as sometimes applied to SOEs in PTAs.

Latin American and Caribbean PTA regulations on subsidies and SOEs are below the world average in their coverage of possible provisions and much shallower than those in the EU, which has the deepest extant integration agreement. Given the prevalence of subsidies and SOEs in many Latin American and Caribbean countries, PTAs offer a tool for governments that desire to take policy stances more consistent with competitive neutrality. PTAs can do so by expanding their regulation of subsidies—using PTAs as a commitment device—or by using the PTA institutional framework to increase policy makers' attention to the competitive spillovers of national subsidy policies and SOE operations (Brou and Ruta 2013).

There is little evidence about the economic effects of using PTAs as a commitment device to regulate states' use of subsidy policies (in contrast to a growing literature on the benefits of making commitments on using border barriers to reduce uncertainty). Subsidies are frequently the subject of disputes in the WTO, often focused on countervailing measures taken by a country against subsidized imports and on the adverse effects of subsidies in third markets. Neither the WTO nor most PTAs define "good" subsidies or those that should be subject to countervailing measures. A major exception is the EU. Because of the depth of the desired integration of national markets, it has extensive rules and delegates enforcement to a supranational body that considers both subsidies and the behavior of SOEs through the lens of competition policy.

Although Latin American and Caribbean countries could do more to use PTAs to discipline state support measures, that will only be possible if governments desire deeper market integration—which may not be the case. But PTAs are not solely devices for making binding commitments on economic policies. They can also make policies more transparent and foster domestic and international deliberations on the effects and effectiveness of policies affecting competition. That information generation role is underemphasized in the economic literature on trade agreements, which views information and transparency primarily in terms of enforcing commitments.

More and better information is needed on applied subsidy policies and the operation of SOEs in Latin America and the Caribbean. PTAs provide a framework for joint action among partners to enhance the transparency of policies and to assess their effects. The region's PTAs have above-average coverage of transparency provisions. Some recent agreements foster dialogue, regulatory cooperation, and engagement with the private sector, providing a basis to build on. Doing so requires creating an institution to collect the requisite data and pursuing government action to support the analysis of policy impacts and effectiveness. A lesson from the OECD, the EU, and the WTO is that a trusted intermediary is likely to be needed to collect that information. That lesson applies as much to governments eager to deepen commitments on subsidies and SOEs to lower competitive spillovers as to governments desiring to retain discretion but interested in using PTAs to support dialogue on good policy based on joint assessments of the effects of support policies.

PTAs have tended to support shallow integration, not focused on helping governments define good policies, though there is a strong presumption among economists that lowering border barriers constitutes good policy by supporting the efficient allocation of scarce resources. Recent PTAs are turning in that direction—for example, by including provisions supporting the adoption of good regulatory practices and international regulatory cooperation.

Governments can build on that change in direction by doing the same for subsidies and SOEs. A first step would be to use PTAs more as a framework for enhancing transparency and assessing the effects of subsidies and the operation of SOEs. That step could be complemented by improving understanding of how policies affect value chain investment and operations. Research on industrial policy has noted many cases of success associated with resolving a coordination or information problem (Sabel 2012). A focus on documenting and analyzing subsidies and SOEs can thus be combined with one on determining whether those instruments are appropriate or effective at attaining industrial diversification objectives through firms and stakeholders participating in value chains. Such research can identify areas where cooperation can both improve domestic policy outcomes and attenuate potential competitive spillovers.

ANNEX 6A SUPPLEMENTARY FIGURES

Figure 6A.1   Selected subsidy-related provisions in Latin American and Caribbean PTAs versus those of the rest of the world and other middle-income countries, 2017

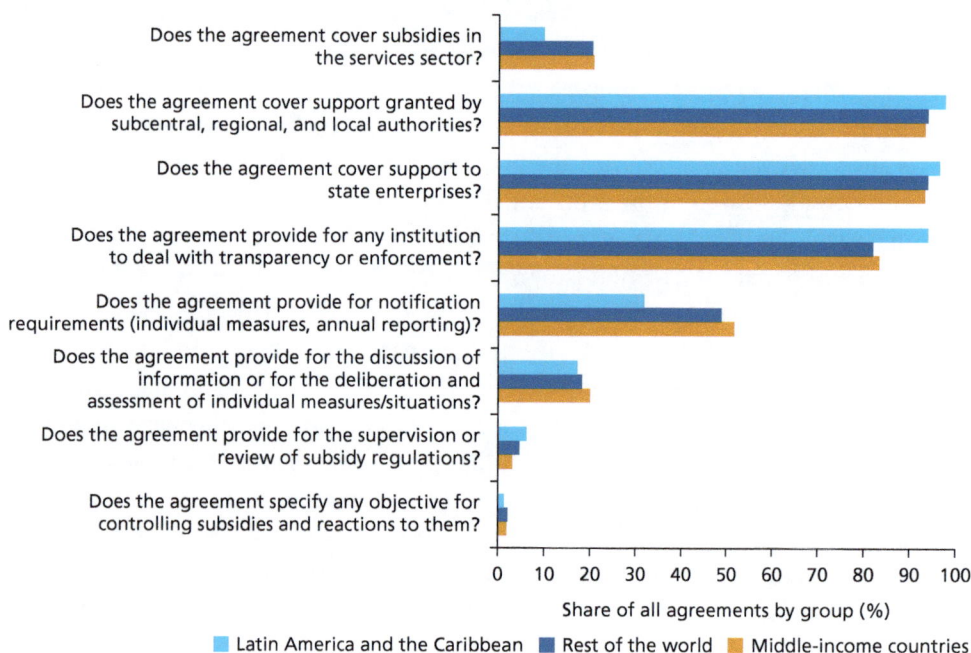

Source: World Bank's Deep Trade Agreements database.

Note: "Middle-income countries" are defined according to World Bank income classifications. PTA = preferential trade agreement.

Figure 6A.2   Selected SOE provisions in Latin American and Caribbean PTAs versus those of the rest of the world and other middle-income countries, 2017

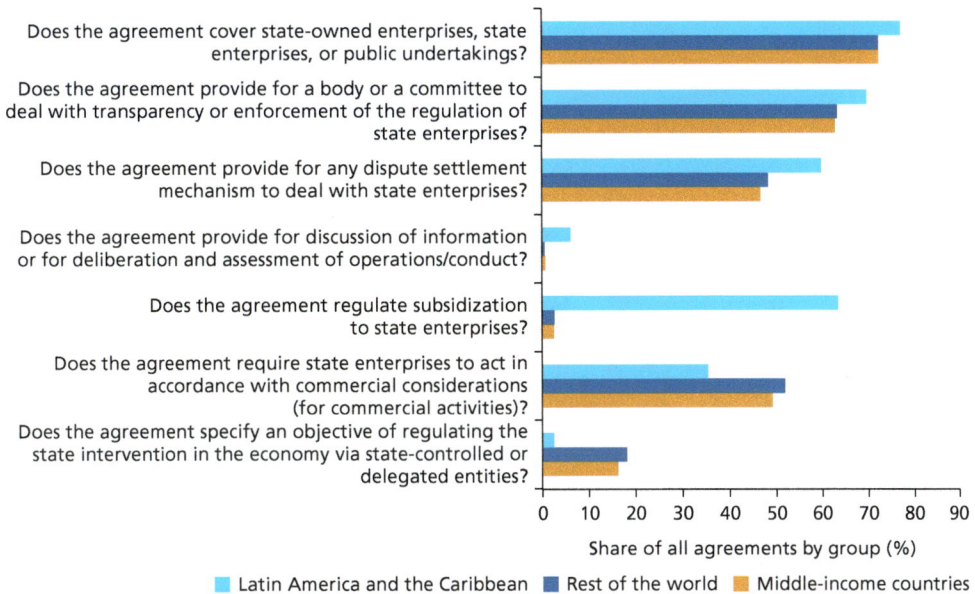

Source: World Bank Deep Trade Agreements database.

Note: "Middle-income countries" are defined according to World Bank income classifications. PTA = preferential trade agreement; SOE = state-owned enterprise.

Figure 6A.3   Selected competition-related provisions in Latin American and Caribbean PTAs versus those of the rest of the world and other middle-income countries, 2017

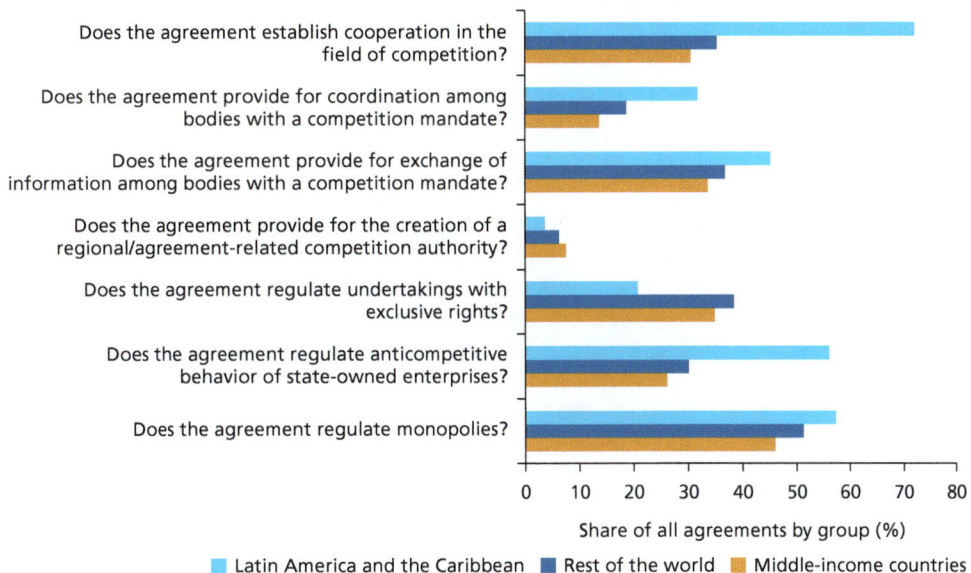

Source: World Bank Deep Trade Agreements database.

Note: "Middle-income countries" are defined according to World Bank income classifications. PTA = preferential trade agreement.

NOTES

1. Trade subsidy data are from Global Trade Alert: https://www.globaltradealert.org/.

2. The metric here is a simple count of measures, not the value of the support implied by a measure or its effects. Given that state aid and subsidies often are large in value, the implied share of subsidies versus other trade-impacting policies may be a downward-biased measure of the economic significance of such instruments.

3. Data on the share of subsidies in GDP or government budgets are from the International Monetary Fund (IMF) Government Finance Statistics (GFS) database. These statistics report IMF data on subsidies to enterprises—private and public—of the types the GTA monitors as potentially competition distorting. The GFS country coverage is limited, and such data are not reported for all Latin American and Caribbean economies.

4. The OECD International Cartels Database provides information on cartel investigations and fines imposed by six Latin American and Caribbean countries. See https://qdd.oecd.org/subject .aspx?Subject=OECD_HIC.

5. Adverse effects include injury to a domestic industry, nullification or impairment of tariff concessions, or serious prejudice to the country's interests. Serious prejudice is defined to exist if the total ad valorem subsidization of a product exceeds 5 percent, subsidies are used to cover operating losses of a firm or industry, or debt relief is granted for government-held liabilities. Serious prejudice may arise if the subsidy reduces exports of a foreign country, results in significant price undercutting, or increases the world market share of the subsidizing country in a primary product. WTO regulations in cases of prejudice focus on the amount of the assistance given, not on the extent to which a subsidy affects trade.

6. Most analyses of PTAs are limited to a focus on the legal text and assume that provisions dealing with policy areas such as subsidies, regulation, and SOEs are implemented, reflecting that little is known about whether and to what extent PTAs result in changes in the domestic policies of interest after signature or ratification. The analyses presume that if provisions are not implemented, dispute settlement proceedings would be pursued because trade agreements are self-enforcing for binding commitments (in contrast to "soft law" best endeavor promises).

7. As discussed later, a partial exception in several recent Latin American and Caribbean PTAs pertains to regulatory cooperation.

8. Article 106, Treaty on the Functioning of the European Union (TFEU). Article 107(3) lists measures considered compatible with the internal market, including (a) aid to promote the economic development of areas where the standard of living is abnormally low or there is serious underemployment, (b) aid to remedy a serious disturbance in the economy of a member state, and (c) aid to facilitate the development of certain economic activities or of certain economic areas, as long as it does not adversely affect trading conditions.

9. For the EU State Aid Scoreboard, see https://ec.europa.eu/competition-policy/state-aid /scoreboard_en.

10. Following a 2012 reform, EU member states are no longer required to notify state aid in advance to the EU Commission if the measures fall under the General Block Exemption Regulation.

11. Wolfe (2021) discusses the factors that allowed the OECD to calculate and report producer support estimates for agriculture in the 1980s, noting that a key factor was demand by finance ministers seeking to control agricultural support levels. There is a possible parallel today in the recourse to subsidy programs in response to the COVID-19 pandemic in many countries.

12. The ICN was formed in 2001 by national competition agencies in part because of the effort to launch negotiations on competition policy in the WTO in the early 2000s. See Hollman and Kovacic (2011).

13. Horizontal regulations are distinct from product-specific regulation—the technical standards and food and plant safety standards that are covered by separate chapters that generally parallel extant WTO disciplines.

14. As in all these cases, the PTAs are recent; there is no experience yet of how they (will) operate.

15. Bakker, Rasche, and Ponte (2019) review the literature on multistakeholder initiatives from a multidisciplinary perspective.

16. The amount of data available is likely to rise with the digitization of value chains (Schniederjans, Curado, and Khalajhedayati 2020).

17. For more about the national trade facilitation committees, as mandated under the WTO TFA, see the United Nations Conference on Trade and Development (UNCTAD) Database for National Trade Facilitation Committees: https://unctad.org/topic/transport-and-trade-logistics/trade -facilitation/committees-around-world.

18. Belastegui (2020) and Widdowson et al. (2018) further discuss national trade facilitation committees under the TFA.

REFERENCES

Bakker, F., A. Rasche, and S. Ponte. 2019. "Multi-Stakeholder Initiatives on Sustainability: A Cross-Disciplinary Review and Research Agenda." *Business Ethics Quarterly* 29 (3): 343–83.

Belastegui, A. 2020. "National Trade Facilitation Committees as Coordinators of Trade Facilitation." Transport and Trade Facilitation Series No. 14, United Nations Conference on Trade and Development, Geneva.

Bitzer, V., and P. Glasbergen. 2015. "Business–NGO Partnerships in Global Value Chains: Part of the Solution or Part of the Problem of Sustainable Change?" *Current Opinion in Environmental Sustainability* 12: 35–40.

Bradford, A., A. Chilton, C. Megaw, and N. Sokol. 2019. "Competition Law Gone Global: Introducing the Comparative Competition Law and Enforcement Datasets." *Journal of Empirical Legal Studies* 16 (2): 411–43.

Brou, D., and M. Ruta. 2013. "A Commitment Theory of Subsidy Agreements." *B.E. Journal of Economic Analysis and Policy* 13 (1): 239–70.

Devlin, R., and C. Pietrobelli. 2019. "Modern Industrial Policy and Public-Private Councils at the Subnational Level: Mexico's Experience." *Rivista di Economia e Politica Industriale* 4: 761–91.

Findlay, C., and B. Hoekman. 2020. "Value Chain Approaches to Reducing Policy Spillovers on International Business." *Journal of International Business Policy* 4: 390–409. doi:10.1057 /s42214-020-00083-5.

Hoekman, B. 2012. "Proposals for WTO Reform: A Synthesis and Assessment." In *The Oxford Handbook on the World Trade Organization*, edited by A. Narlikar, M. Daunton, and R. M. Stern, 743–75. Oxford: Oxford University Press.

Hoekman, B. 2016. "Subsidies, Spillovers and WTO Rules in a Value Chain World." *Global Policy* 7 (3): 351–59.

Hollman, H. M., and W. E. Kovacic. 2011. "The International Competition Network: Its Past, Current, and Future Role." *Minnesota Journal of International Law* 20: 274–323.

Kaufmann, C., and C. Saffirio. 2021. "Good Regulatory Practices and Co-operation in Trade Agreements." Regulatory Policy Working Papers 14, Organisation for Economic Co-operation and Development, Paris.

Licetti, M., G. Miralles, and R. Teh. 2020. "Competition Policy." In *Handbook of Deep Trade Agreements*, edited by A. Mattoo, N. Rocha, and M. Ruta, 505–52. Washington, DC: World Bank.

Maggi, G. 2014. "International Trade Agreements." In *Handbook of International Economics*, Vol. 4, edited by A. Gopinath, E. Helpman, and K. Rogoff, 317–90. Amsterdam: Elsevier.

Musacchio, A., and E. I. Pineda Ayerbe, eds. 2019. *Fixing State-Owned Enterprises: New Policy Solutions to Old Problems*. Washington, DC: Inter-American Development Bank.

OECD (Organisation for Economic Co-operation and Development). 2019a. "Levelling the Playing Field: Measuring and Addressing Trade-distorting Government Support." Summary record of the OECD Global Forum on Trade 2019, Paris, October 23–24. Document TAD/TC/GF/M(2019)1, OECD Secretariat, Paris.

OECD (Organisation for Economic Co-operation and Development). 2019b. "Measuring Distortions in International Markets: The Aluminium Value Chain." Trade Policy Papers, No. 218, OECD Publishing, Paris.

OECD (Organisation for Economic Co-operation and Development). 2019c. "Measuring Distortions in International Markets: The Semiconductor Value Chain." Trade Policy Papers, No. 234, OECD Publishing, Paris.

Ross-Schneider, B. 2015. *Designing Industrial Policy in Latin America: Business State Relations and the New Developmentalism*. New York: Palgrave Macmillan.

Rubini, L. 2020. "Subsidies." In *Handbook of Deep Trade Agreements*, edited by A. Mattoo, N. Rocha, and M. Ruta. Washington, DC: World Bank.

Rubini, L., and T. Wang. 2020. "State-Owned Enterprises." In *Handbook of Deep Trade Agreements*, edited by A. Mattoo, N. Rocha, and M. Ruta, 427–61. Washington, DC: World Bank.

Sabel, C. 2012. "Self-Discovery as a Coordination Problem." In *Export Pioneers in Latin America*, edited by C. Sabel, E. Fernández-Arias, R. Hausmann, A. Rodríguez-Clare, and E. Stein, 1–45. Washington, DC: Inter-American Development Bank.

Schniederjans, D., C. Curado, and M. Khalajhedayati. 2020. "Supply Chain Digitisation Trends: An Integration of Knowledge Management." *International Journal of Production Economics* 220: 107349.

Schwab, K., ed. 2019. *The Global Competitiveness Report 2019*. Geneva: World Economic Forum.

Soundararajan, V., J. Brown, and A. Wicks. 2019. "Can Multi-Stakeholder Initiatives Improve Global Supply Chains?" *Business Ethics Quarterly* 29 (3): 385–412.

WEF (World Economic Forum). 2014. "Enabling Trade: Enabling Trade in the Pacific Alliance." Report produced in collaboration with Inter-American Development Bank and Bain & Company, WEF, Geneva.

Widdowson, D., G. Short, B. Blegen, and M. Kashubsky. 2018. "National Committees on Trade Facilitation." *World Customs Journal* 12 (1): 27–48.

Wolfe, R. 2018. "Is World Trade Organization Information Good Enough? How a Systematic Reflection by Members on Transparency Could Promote Institutional Learning." Working Paper, Bertelsmann Stiftung, Gütersloh, Germany.

Wolfe, R. 2021. "Yours Is Bigger than Mine! Could an Index Like the Producer Subsidy Equivalent Help in Understanding the Comparative Incidence of Industrial Subsidies?" *The World Economy* 44 (2): 328–45.

World Bank. 2020. *World Development Report 2020: Trading for Development in the Age of Global Value Chains*. Washington, DC: World Bank.

7 Leveraging Deep Trade Agreements to Promote GVC Integration

Nadia Rocha and Michele Ruta

INTRODUCTION

Countries in Latin America and the Caribbean can exploit their considerable potential for integrating into global value chains (GVCs). In part, the gaps between actual and potential GVC integration are the result of economic fundamentals. Relative to other regions, Latin America and the Caribbean faces disadvantages due to its geographical distance from major trading partners, low average domestic market size, low-skilled labor and capital endowments, and less-efficient institutions.

This report shows that deep trade agreements can do much to overcome some of these disadvantages and shape the region's GVC participation: trade facilitation reforms can reduce the region's remoteness. Improving regulatory cooperation can help these countries achieve larger market size. More-open services sectors can remedy scarcity in factor endowments constraining Latin American and Caribbean countries. And regulating state support and competition can improve the quality of institutions in the region.

AN AGENDA OF PRIORITIES FOR REFORM

Although country circumstances differ, each of these policy areas has a key set of priority reforms that Latin American and Caribbean countries can adopt in the context of their deep trade agreements (table 7.1). Broadly speaking, proposed reforms fall into three categories of actions and rules:

- Those aiming at undertaking deeper policy commitments
- Those improving policy transparency and monitoring
- Those creating governance and enforcement structures for a more effective implementation of the agreements' provisions.

Some of these reforms may require only a little negotiation and can be introduced in the short term. For others, the process may entail legislative reforms in multiple countries or even setting up new common institutions, which would inevitably take longer. Clearly, table 7.1 provides only a sketch of these recommendations, which the chapters have discussed in greater detail.

Table 7.1   Key policy reforms to get the most from deep trade agreements

Objective	Proposed reforms	Time horizon
Trade facilitation		
Enhance the transparency of customs processes	≥ Publish and disseminate customs requirements and other information in a nondiscriminatory and easily accessible manner, including through electronic publication ≥ Institute monitoring and follow-up mechanisms in preferential trade agreements (PTAs), with transparency and accountability built in, based on objective measures of trade facilitation reforms and outcomes	Short term
Reduce border inspections and transaction and logistics costs	Promote an integrated risk management and postclearance audit process by (among others) ≥ Coordinating inspections on high-risk consignments; ≥ Implementing nonintrusive inspections of imports where inspection is required; ≥ Implementing complementary controls beyond the borders, such as postclearance audits, inspections, and inventory controls; ≥ Promoting prearrival processing and separating customs release from final clearance; ≥ Allowing presubmission of import documents and a declaration to initiate the clearance process; and ≥ Allowing the conduct of risk assessments before the arrival of goods, and immediately releasing them on arrival	Short term
Improve efficiency of import and export processes	≥ Promote development and interoperability of national trade single windows ≥ Establish the governance requirements for the automatic exchange of information; the redesign, automation, and digitization of business process and procedures; and the interoperability of trade single windows ≥ Promote cooperation between border agencies of neighboring countries, including mutual recognition of compliance controls by — Standardizing measures and actions among member countries, especially those related to opening hours of all public and private entities necessary for the management of import/export and international transit; — Reducing compliance costs for authorized economic operators (AEOs)—such as having them pass through green channels or not requiring physical documents; and — Promoting reductions of formalities and documents and increasing security using information and communication technologies	Medium to long term

Continued

Table 7.1   Key policy reforms to get the most from deep trade agreements (*continued*)

Objective	Proposed reforms	Time horizon
Increase coordination for implementation of, and regulatory cooperation on, trade facilitation provisions	≥ Promote the establishment of governance structures such as customs or trade facilitation committees to address any discrepancies in interpretation, further align understanding of provisions, and provide monitoring and accountability of reforms ≥ Establish public-private mechanisms to assess the effects of trade facilitation measures on trade and value chains	Medium term
Nontariff measures: Technical barriers to trade (TBT) and sanitary and phytosanitary (SPS) measures		
Increase transparency	≥ Publish and disseminate TBT and SPS measures and other relevant information in a nondiscriminatory and easily accessible manner, including through electronic publication ≥ Exchange information on the use of standards in connection with technical regulations	Short term
Eliminate sanitary and technical obstacles to trade	≥ Take the necessary steps to harmonize the definition of the sector under consideration ≥ Establish a "market surveillance system," based on international good regulatory practices, eliminating the need for prior sanitary authorization or replacing it by an automatic notification ≥ Harmonize labeling requirements for specific products, based on international standards, with a view to having one sole labeling format for consumer protection ≥ Harmonize the requisites and application of good manufacturing practices, based on international standards ≥ Follow up on legislative activity enacting new laws and regulations that may be incompatible with international commitments and regulatory standards, and leverage PTAs to resist such attempts ≥ Leverage regulatory audits to foster public-private dialogue on the logic and convenience of maintaining regulatory standards and regulations that may be trade restrictive	Medium term
Advance regulatory cooperation	≥ Define clear mandates at the political level to empower and guide regulators ≥ Aim to achieve concrete and binding outcomes at the measure, product, or sector level ≥ Align levels of ambition with starting conditions in the parties (such as institutional and administrative capacities—and previous experience in cooperation) ≥ Focus cooperation on moving toward international standards to support global trade integration and maximize welfare ≥ Embed continuous regulatory cooperation in effective institutional setups, with oversight from high-level trade officials and appropriate resources ≥ Establish regular work programs to provide structure and time frames for the discussions ≥ Put in place consultative mechanisms with the private sector and other stakeholders to prioritize sectoral cooperation, collect inputs, and guard against regulatory capture ≥ Formalize cooperation among regulators and provide opportunities for deliberation, learning, and trust building ≥ Institute monitoring and follow-up mechanisms in PTAs, with transparency and accountability built in ≥ Define a methodology to determine the economic impact of regulatory cooperation at the measure, product, or sector level to inform and support collaboration efforts	Medium to long term

Continued

Table 7.1 Key policy reforms to get the most from deep trade agreements (*continued*)

Objective	Proposed reforms	Time horizon
Services trade measures		
Foster transparency of measures restricting trade in services in all sectors and all modes of supply	≥ Regardless of whether a PTA has a negative or positive list with respect to commitments, prepare a single regulatory audit that lists all measures nonconforming with main obligations of services and investment chapters (national treatment, most-favored-nation, market access, local presence, performance requirements) ≥ In countries with federal systems of government, undertake such exercises at the subnational (state) level ≥ Update regulatory audits periodically (at least every couple of years) to unveil potential liberalization changes	Short to medium term
Improve data collection on services trade and policy	≥ Work with regional partners to collect bilaterally disaggregated trade-in-services statistics and to develop multiregion input-output tables that include services for as many economies as possible in the region ≥ Work with the World Trade Organization and regional partners to improve data on services trade by mode of supply, particularly sales by foreign affiliates (mode 3) ≥ Collect and disseminate data on services trade restrictiveness and digital trade restrictiveness, using established methodologies	Medium term
Decrease "water" between applied policies and regulations and international commitments	≥ Regardless of whether PTAs have a negative or positive list of liberalization commitments, promote the inclusion of a horizontal standstill for discriminatory measures and quantitative restrictions ≥ Promote the inclusion of a "ratchet" clause in PTAs, which will have the effect of delegating to national parliaments the pace of any potential gradual liberalization and automatically incorporating any progress in the agreement ≥ Follow up on legislative activity enacting new domestic laws and regulations that may be incompatible with international commitments, and leverage PTAs to promote the regulatory reforms needed to comply with international commitments ≥ Leverage regulatory audits to foster public-private dialogue on the logic and convenience of maintaining particular trade restrictions within specific laws and regulations	Medium term
Promote modes 3 and 4 of services supply	≥ Include investment chapters in trade agreements, with comprehensive dispute settlement provisions ≥ Include provisions on mutual recognition of professional qualifications in trade agreements ≥ Promote broad coverage of all modes of supply, and beware of different types of treaties addressing trade in services in mode 3 (sales by foreign affiliates) and mode 4 (movement of persons) and promote coherence among them	Medium term

Continued

Table 7.1 Key policy reforms to get the most from deep trade agreements (*continued*)

Objective	Proposed reforms	Time horizon
State support		
Increase policy transparency and data on state support	≥ Establish a notification or reporting requirement for central and local government bodies on subsidy programs for undertakings, private and public ≥ Create a central open-access database on subsidies to enterprises and state-owned enterprises (SOEs) ≥ Require an annual report on subsidy programs and activities of SOEs above a size threshold	Short to medium term
Improve the competitive environment	Use trade agreements to support domestic reform through commitments aimed to ≥ Adopt a competitive neutrality framework in national legislation and regulation on competition, subsidies, and SOEs; ≥ Require SOEs to operate on a commercial and nondiscriminatory basis; and ≥ Expand the mandate of competition authorities to encompass SOEs and subsidies	Medium to long term
Reduce adverse cross-border spillovers of national state support measures	≥ Apply provisions on state support measures and SOEs found in trade agreements of recent vintage (such as the Comprehensive and Progressive Agreement for Trans-Pacific Partnership [CPTPP]) on a nondiscriminatory basis ≥ Undertake analysis of state support measures implemented by trading partner ≥ Use PTA dialogue mechanisms to discuss spillover effects	Medium term
Improve value chain investment incentives and economic upgrading	≥ Establish public-private mechanisms to assess the effects of policies, including state support and competition measures, on value chains ≥ Use trade agreements to bring together stakeholders in international value chains to consider joint action to promote expansion and upgrading	Medium term

Source: World Bank.